Journal of the Society of

Christian
Ethics

VOLUME 27, No. 2 • FALL/WINTER 2007

T0204840

Editors

Mary Jo Iozzio, Barry University

Patricia Beattie Jung, Loyola University Chicago

Editorial Board

Mark Allman, Mount Union College

Elizabeth Bounds, Emory University

Andrew Flescher, California State University, Chico

Linda Hogan, Irish School of Ecumenics, Trinity College Dublin

James Nash, Boston University School of Theology

Dov Nelkin, Solomon Schecter High School of New York

Brian Stiltner, Sacred Heart University

Laura Stivers, Pfeiffer University

Christopher Vogt, Saint John's University, New York

Traci West, Drew Theological School

Sondra Wheeler, Wesley Theological Seminary

Tobias Winwright, Saint Louis University

Editorial Offices

Department of Theology

Loyola University Chicago

Chicago, IL 60626

Department of Theology and Philosophy

Barry University

Miami Shores, FL 33161-6695

Book Review Editor

Lois Malcolm

Luther Seminary

2481 Como Avenue

Saint Paul, MN 55108

Publisher

The Society of Christian Ethics

c/o Stewart W. Herman

Concordia College-Moorehead

901 8th Street South

Moorehead, MN 56562

Distributor

Georgetown University Press

c/o Hopkins Fulfillment Center

P.O. Box 50370

Baltimore, MD 21211-4370

www.press.georgetown.edu

Contents

Preface

This issue heralds a new phase in the *Journal*'s accountability to the members of the Society of Christian Ethics (SCE) and to its readers. As those of you who submitted papers to the *Journal* for publication review know, the authors of the essays that arose from the SCE's annual meeting in Dallas in January 2007 and the meeting of its Pacific Section shortly thereafter were requested to complete a brief demographic questionnaire. This questionnaire was devised to elicit information regarding our authors, their tenure in the SCE, degree and professional rank, gender, race, and primary field(s) of inquiry. In general, such data collection will enable the *Journal* to address the evolving needs of our scholarly field in accord with the initiatives endorsed by the Report of the Committee for the Twenty-First Century. This year's survey in particular will help us establish the baseline that will be necessary to assess our progress with regard to these initiatives. We thank all who completed this questionnaire; subsequent to this first round of data collection, the questionnaire was computerized and requested earlier in the review process of all those who submit proposals to the Program Committee for the 2008 annual meeting. You can expect to see the tabulated results of this data collection published in future issues of the *Journal*.

This issue opens with questions of justice. Christopher Marshall challenges standard accounts of justice in Christian ethics with his consideration of the Parable of the Prodigal Son (or is it prodigal father?), and the restoration required in response to harm done as illustrated in the experience of the Maori people of New Zealand. Julie Hanlon Rubio and the other members of the SCE's Women's Caucus held a preconference session at the SCE's annual meeting in which a panel of women ethicists explored the success, pitfalls, and obstacles to professional life that women experience in academic settings; in their essay, they propose that institutions consider family-friendly policies, which could begin to redress practices that currently penalize women who choose family and home over career security and/or advancement.

Moving from the considerations of justice in particular contexts to the virtues more broadly defined, you will find a series of essays that engage the multiple facets of virtue ethics. William Werpehowski places the work of Aquinas and his contemporary interlocutors in dialogue with Dietrich Bonhoeffer to advance the theological underpinnings of repentance, renewal, and perseverance in the moral life. Elizabeth Agnew Cochran grounds her consideration of the work of Jonathan Edwards in the virtues in both his Christology and his understanding of the humility requisite for the proper relation between creatures and God. William McDonough brings the work on infused virtue of Eberhard Schockenhoff, which remains largely unavailable to English-only readers, forward as a key to establishing common ground for interreligious dialogue as well as a key for understanding the distinctiveness of Christian ethics qua Christian ethics. Margaret Pfeil considers environmental and energy conservation as a call for liturgical asceticism, humility, and an understanding of sacramentality that extends beyond ritual to encompass the eschatological horizon of the fullness of life in God. Finally, from the Pacific Section meeting of the SCE, Lisa Fullam complements these discussions of virtue with an appreciation of sex and the virtues attendant to the ends or purposes of sex—which, she reckons, include a feel for the Incarnation, intimacy, and insight.

The final five essays cover both familiar and new territory. Gerald Schlabach retrieves the historical context of the Mennonite "Goshen School" of thought in the first and second thirds of the twentieth century school to situate the dissent inherent to Anabaptist discipleship and, in particular, to contextualize the work of John Howard Yoder, whose corpus when so situated is quite distinct from that of Stanley Hauerwas. In another essay from the Pacific Section, John Crossley moves the discussion of the theology and politics of dissent to an examination of the Weberian "elective affinity" recognizable not only in Protestant ascetic practices and capitalism but also in liberal theology and liberal politics. John Perry likewise takes the influence of a historical figure, John Locke, to expose the ideological roots of the critique of democratic liberalism, especially as it has unfolded in the exchanges between Jeffrey Stout and those whom Stout identifies as Christian Traditionalists. David Clough and Brian Stiltner retrieve the historical development of the "just war" tradition in comparison with recent preemptive war thinking to argue against speculative threats. Todd Whitmore presents a case for fieldwork as one of the principal locations of a different kind of "lived" text, expressive perhaps alongside of the written text of ethical values and virtues that may be at stake in a particular community at a particular time in its history.

Selected Essays

Offending, Restoration, and the Law-Abiding Community: Restorative Justice in the New Testament and in the New Zealand Experience

Christopher D. Marshall

DURING THE PAST THIRTY YEARS, A GROWING CONVERSATION ABOUT THE "restorative" dimensions of justice in contrast to its "retributive" dimensions in addressing crime, wrongdoing, and cultural conflict has emerged around the world. In New Zealand, an initiative known as Family Group Conferencing has virtually replaced the conventional juvenile justice that preceded it. This initiative has inspired many people around the world to adapt that restorative approach in many different settings.

I am honored to have been invited to contribute this essay to the *JSCE*, especially because I am not a professional ethicist by training or vocation. The invitation was extended on the basis of my published work in the area of restorative justice, and in particular my 2001 book *Beyond Retribution: A New Testament Vision for Justice, Crime and Punishment*. In that book, I seek to explore New Testament teaching on crime and punishment in light of restorative justice theory. My goal is partly to allow restorative justice insights to cast new light on early Christian texts on justice and punishment, and partly to furnish a biblical and theological basis for Christian involvement in criminal justice reform in a restorative direction.

The extent to which I read restorative justice conceptions *into* the biblical text, or draw *out* of the text what was already there, is hard to say (in biblical studies, it is nearly always a mixture of both). But I have found that bringing a restorative justice lens to the task of New Testament interpretation has been enormously productive. It has afforded me, for example, a fresh way of thinking about the great Pauline doctrine of justification by faith, the logic of which, I think, makes far more sense when conceptualized within a restorative rather than a retributive justice frame of reference.

The topic of this essay is restorative justice in the New Testament and in the New Zealand experience. I was asked to investigate the possibility of a senior Maori figure from New Zealand accompanying me to the Society of Christian

Journal of the Society of Christian Ethics, 27, 2 (2007): 3–30

Ethics conference where this essay was first presented so that he or she could speak on restorative justice from an indigenous perspective. Despite my best efforts, that was not possible—which is a shame, really, because the New Testament text on which I here reflect includes features that I suspect indigenous readers are far better equipped to appreciate than are Western biblical scholars, who instinctively bring with them a set of individualistic assumptions that are often ill suited to the cultural horizons of the text itself.

What, then, is "restorative justice"? What place does it occupy in the New Zealand justice system? And what has the New Testament got to do with it?

The Character of Restorative Justice

Restorative justice is known by a variety of names and takes many different forms. Some call it "transformative justice," others call it "relational justice," and still others prefer "community justice," "collaborative justice," "reparative justice," or simply "real justice." Whatever it is called, advocates of restorative justice insist that it is not simply a minor variation on the current justice system, a way of helping the existing system to become more effective or more humane. It is, rather, an alternative way of doing justice, a "third way" between the retributive and rehabilitative models that have dominated penal philosophy for a very long time, a distinctive way of thinking about crime and punishment, a different "paradigm," to use Howard Zehr's term, to conceptualize justice and its demands, even if this new paradigm shares many features with existing paradigms.[1]

For some, the distinctiveness of the restorative paradigm lies in its *processes or practices*. Restorative justice is understood as a particular process in which all those affected by an incident of wrongdoing—victims, offenders, and their supporters—come together, in a safe and controlled environment, with trained facilitators, to name the wrong done, to describe how they have been personally affected by it, to speak about the material and emotional needs it has created, and to resolve together how best to repair the harm and to prevent recurrence. On this understanding, the heart and genius of restorative justice lie in its use of face-to-face meetings between affected parties, and its concern to empower those present, and especially victims, to deal with the harm in a way that best addresses their needs.

For others, the distinctiveness of restorative justice lies in its *core values or its moral commitments*. Restorative justice here is distinguished by the priority it gives to the values of healing and respect, democratic participation, accountability, truth telling, empathy, mutual care, reconciliation, and peacemaking. Guided by such values, restorative justice seeks to deal with the full moral, spiritual, relational and emotional consequences of offending, not simply its legal description and punitive implications.

Happily, there is no need to set these "process" and "values" conceptions against each other. Both must be held together to appreciate the special character of restorative justice, for it is the values that determine the process, and the process that makes visible the values.[2] If restorative justice privileges the values of respect and truth, for example, it is crucially important that the practices followed in a restorative justice setting exhibit equal respect for all parties and give ample opportunity for everyone present to speak their truth freely. Conversely, as long as these values are honored, there is room for a diversity of processes, a flexibility of practice, and a variety of cultural expressions.

Thus, restorative justice is *both* a distinctive process *and* a distinctive set of values, with each requiring the other. Having said that, what is most important, I believe, to the success and the future of restorative justice—especially as it becomes more professionalized and institutionalized—is that restorative *values* are nurtured and affirmed by its practitioners.[3] Of course, as every ethicist knows, values do not exist in a vacuum; they are held by flesh-and-blood people who belong to particular historical communities. If it is to flourish, then, restorative justice must be anchored in alternative "communities of value," that is, in communities of people who accord the highest importance to the values of mutual care and moral accountability, honesty and compassion, confession, forgiveness, and reconciliation.

One such community in which this ought to be the case is the church. After all, Christians boast a religion that centers on repentance, forgiveness, and new life—convictions that also lie at the heart of restorative justice. One would therefore expect Christians to be vigorous supporters of judicial and penal reform in a restorative direction. Sadly, this has not been the case historically (with some notable exceptions), and it is not always the case today (again with exceptions). Perhaps, part of the mission of the restorative justice movement, which is itself now hugely diverse and extensive, is to remind the church of what it supposedly believes and ought to practice more consistently.[4]

Restorative Justice in New Zealand

Restorative justice in New Zealand arose in the 1980s out of dissatisfaction in the Maori community with the way its young people were being treated by the criminal justice system. The basic social unit in Maori society is the *whanau* or extended family, and Maori had become increasingly troubled at the way the justice system functioned to remove young offenders from any positive influence from their *whanau* by dumping them into prisons or other punitive facilities. After a lengthy consultation process, the government undertook to overhaul the entire juvenile justice system.

At the center of the new system that emerged lay the concept of a "Family Group Conference," which all first-time young offenders are required to attend.

Such conferences bring together the offender with his family and friends, police officers, youth justice workers, and, if in agreement, the victims of the offense to discuss what happened and why, and to determine appropriate sanctions and reparation plans.[5] This new mechanism quickly led to a massive reduction in custodial sentences for juvenile offenders: Some 55 percent of those attending Family Group Conferences did not reoffend in the future.[6]

Despite such positive outcomes, little interest was shown by the government in extending similar provisions into the adult system, even though many community-based groups had already developed models for doing so and were actively employing them. But after a ground swell of popular agitation, in 2001 the government commissioned a four-year-long restorative justice pilot scheme for serious adult offenders in four district courts in the land, with a view to evaluating its potential. But by now a head of steam had built up, and even before the evaluation process had been completed, four major pieces of legislation had been passed by Parliament, which served, inter alia, to embed restorative practices permanently into the New Zealand adult justice system. The Sentencing Act 2002, the Parole Act 2002, the Victims' Rights Act 2002, and the Corrections Act 2004 all make explicit provision for restorative justice and impose a duty on all members of the judicial system to encourage meetings between offenders and their victims, although always at the victim's discretion.

In some respects, then, New Zealand has made a progressive and principled commitment to the integration of restorative justice options into its national justice system. But do not be too impressed. For there is still a dark side to the country's corrections system, which has witnessed, for example, an enormous increase in rates of imprisonment during the past ten years and a continuing pattern of racial and socioeconomic bias that sees 60 percent of the prison muster drawn from the 20 percent of the population with brown skins. Yet, arguably, it is this overrepresentation of indigenous peoples in criminal justice statistics that underscores the importance of continuing to cultivate restorative justice alternatives. For, as many researchers have observed, restorative processes resemble the traditional mechanisms used in many indigenous societies for dealing with wrongdoing and restoring well-being.

One recurring feature of such traditional mechanisms is the overt place they give to the realm of the spirit and spirituality. Among indigenous peoples, there seems to be an instinctive recognition that doing justice in the face of harm is a deeply *spiritual* undertaking.[7] It is not simply a matter of assessing facts, determining blame, and allocating penalties. It is also about addressing the loss of what Maori call *mana* or spiritual dignity caused by the offense, of lifting the shame inflicted on the victim and incurred by the offender and shared by their wider kinship groups, of repairing the rupture done to the fabric of the community, and restoring order and balance to the spiritual domain, which interconnects all things.

Behind this approach lies a realization, I believe, that justice is fundamentally to do with persons and with relationships, and with the right ordering of relationships, both in community and on a broader spiritual plane. For that reason, justice can never be wholly reduced to abstract notions of just deserts or the application of legal rulings but must also attend to the moral, emotional, and relational integrity of the persons affected, and it is this that gives to justice an irreducibly spiritual quality.

Such an understanding of justice, it seems to me, is similar to what we find in the Bible. There, too, justice has to do with the right ordering of the universe, with things being as God intends them to be, and with the restoring of harmony or shalom when things go wrong. In my book, I trace how this integrated understanding of justice emerges in the New Testament, particularly in Paul's extensive reflections on the saving justice of God disclosed in the life, death, and resurrection of Christ. It is this larger biblical apprehension of God's redeeming justice at work in the world, I argue, that furnished the horizons for early Christian thinking about how justice should operate within the human community. Human justice making ought to be a response to divine justice making.

This is not to suggest that we can look to the New Testament for a ready-made set of criminal justice policies that can be transposed directly into our societies. That's *not* what the New Testament offers us. What it does offer, however, is a vision of what human life and human relationships ought to be like—and *can* be like—in consequence of the revelation of God's redeeming justice in Christ to set the world aright, and it invites us to imagine forms of social policy that bear witness, however imperfectly, to that reality. The New Testament does not prescribe a set of criminal justice norms, but it does point us in a direction. And that direction, I submit, is a decidedly restorative direction.

Consider this extended illustration. Recently, I have been pondering what is perhaps the best known and most-loved of all of Jesus' parables, the parable of the Prodigal Son (Luke 15:11–32).[8] I make no mention of this parable whatsoever in my book—which now seems a major oversight, for in many ways this parable perfectly captures both the restorative impulse of God's justice and what it might mean for us to enact this kind of justice in the world. I offer here a few reflections on this parable, as a kind of case study of restorative justice in action or at least of certain aspects of restorative justice, because not everything important about restorative justice can be located in any one biblical story.

A New Testament Illustration: Prodigious Justice

The parable of the Prodigal Son is the story of a young man who demands his share of the family inheritance in advance, squanders it in wild living in a distant land, and then comes to his senses and returns home deeply chastened, where he is joyfully reconciled with his father and profoundly resented by his churlish older brother. The impact of this parable on Christian thought and practice, and on Western cultural formation in general, has been incalculable. It is the parable most frequently represented in European art, and it has furnished the subject matter for numerous works of music, choreography, drama, literature, and philosophy.[9]

At over 390 words in the Greek text, it is also the longest and the most elaborate of Jesus' extant parables. It has substantial dramatis personae, including three well-developed individual characters, and it is full of vivid background detail, features that have invited extensive allegorization at the hands of Christian interpreters through the centuries.[10] Classical allegory is now rightly repudiated as an interpretive procedure for expounding Jesus' parables.[11] Yet so richly evocative is the texture of this parable that it invites legitimate interpretation at multiple levels and from many different perspectives. As one who has spent the best part of his academic career pondering this parable, Kenneth Bailey observes, "Nearly everyone who wrestles seriously with this pericope ends up with a sense of awe at its inexhaustible content."[12]

The reasons why this exquisite parable has exercised such a powerful influence on the Western imagination are not hard to find. In purely literary terms, it is a masterpiece of storytelling, lauded by one literary critic as "an absolutely flawless piece of work."[13] It employs a wide range of narrative devices and rhetorical techniques, including extensive use of direct speech to underscore key concerns. The characters are all true to life, utterly believable at one level, yet shockingly unconventional at another. The plot is realistic and straightforward, moving in a simple linear direction through a sequence of brief scenes, yet involving ironical reversals and concluding on a strikingly open-ended note. Hearers are left dangling in suspense, not knowing whether the angry elder son relented of his indignation and joined the family festivities or whether he stood his ground on a self-evident matter of principle. The resolution of the affair is purposefully unstated, requiring listeners to finish the story for themselves and to ponder deeply where their own sympathies in the whole affair lie.

Another reason why the parable has been so highly prized is for its penetrating insights into human psychology. The story deals with universal human themes of freedom and responsibility, of leaving and returning, of offending and forgiveness, of estrangement and reconciliation, of shame and honor, of generosity and ingratitude, of justice, jealousy, and joy. In particular, it explores the anatomy of moral change: what spawns it, what it requires in practice, what it achieves, and how it may sometimes be greeted with sullen resistance on the part of more respectable onlookers.

But beyond its literary qualities and its psychological acuity, the parable has been cherished most of all for its theological value. It is unsurpassed in the biblical tradition in its depiction of the love and forgiveness of God. It has frequently been dubbed an *evangelium in evangelio*, a gospel within the Gospel. Some balk at this label because the parable contains little Christology and no atonement theology, no indication of the objective basis on which sins are forgiven and sinners restored.[14] Yet there is an important sense in which the parable goes beyond or behind any external mechanics of atonement to accentuate the fundamental driving force behind the good news of salvation proclaimed by Jesus in the Gospel tradition: the yearning love and renewing power of the Reign of God.

For these three reasons, then, the Parable of the Prodigal Son has lodged itself so deeply in the Western mind: its superb literary qualities, its emotional intensity and psychological insight, and its theological depth. The parable has not only furnished the subject matter of great literature, art, music, poetry drama, and theological reflection through the generations, it has also surfaced in discussions of moral and ethical issues, including, from time to time, discussions of crime and punishment. It is mentioned briefly, for example, in the November 2000 statement by U.S. Council of Catholic Bishops on criminal justice, where it is used to encourage the acceptance of offenders who are contrite and change their way of life.[15] In a more radical vein, Thomas Shaffer uses the parable to commend what he calls a "jurisprudence of forgiveness," which inevitably opposes and subverts "the legal order that serves the politics of coercive power."[16]

Yet there is still more blessing to be wrested from this parable, if we read it from a restorative justice point of view. There are two reasons why I think this is a legitimate thing to do. The first is that the main characters in the story occupy the roles of the three main parties to every incident of criminal wrongdoing: those of offender, victim, and the wider law-abiding community. The younger son is portrayed as a serious and serial offender. The father is the primary victim of his offending, as well as being a cipher for the divine judge of human sin, while the older brother is expressly depicted as a diligent and law-abiding member of the wider household community who is outraged at the judicial leniency extended to his offending sibling.[17]

This leads to the second reason why it is profitable to read the parable from a criminal justice angle: the older brother's reaction centers directly on the contestable *justice* of his father's actions: "Listen! For all these years I have been working like a slave for you, and I have never disobeyed your command; yet you have never given me even a young goat so that I might celebrate with my friends. But when this son of yours came back, who has devoured your property with prostitutes, you killed the fatted calf for him!" (Luke 15:29–30).

The actual terminology of justice is not used here, but without question it is the *idea* of justice that drives this final scene of the narrative, just as the ideas of repentance, love, forgiveness, and mercy drive earlier scenes in the story without the actual terminology being employed. The parable reaches its climax, then, in a dispute about whether the father, in restoring his offending son to the community, has acted justly or unjustly.

For these two reasons, then, it is appropriate to read the parable in a jurisprudential light. This is not to suggest, of course, that the parable provides normative guidelines for how we should go about constructing a Christian ethics of justice. It is, after all, just a parable, not a moral or legal treatise. But it is precisely *as* a parable that it is relevant to Christian reflection on justice issues—for the leading purpose of Jesus' parables is to break open existing frames of reference, to challenge or overturn taken-for-granted ways of understanding the world and its notions of justice, and to offer a different way of conceiving reality, a way that is conditioned by the inbreaking of God's eschatological Kingdom of justice and peace. Surely if there is anything that makes Christian ethics distinctively "Christian," it is its attempt to formulate ethical truth in a way that is informed not just by the downward drag of normal human behavior but also by the radical possibilities for human transformation opened up by the manifestation of God's saving power in Jesus Christ.

What insights, then, does this parable offer that may be germane to Christian reflection on criminal justice? Perhaps the first thing it offers is an emphasis on the *relational impact of human offending*. It underscores the restorative justice principle that what makes criminal behavior so harmful is that it violates human relationships, those relationships that bind us together in community and that constitute our very humanity.[18]

Offending as Relational Rupture

The parable involves three main characters. Interpreters have long debated which of the three is the intended focus of attention. The parable's traditional title suggests that the story is principally about the prodigal son, and there are still scholars who defend this view.[19] More commonly, however, the father is viewed as the main character, because he is mentioned in most scenes of the story and his actions and values are most critical to its meaning.[20] Yet a case has also been made for seeing the elder son as the focal point of the narrative, especially because it is his sullen response to his father's forgiveness of his brother that gives the parable its sharply polemical edge (cf. Luke 15:1–3).[21]

But to insist on one central protagonist is surely to miss the important narrative clue given at the very outset in the story. The parable's pointed introduction, "a certain man had two sons" (v. 11), functions to direct attention away from any one individual performer and on to the *relational* bonds between them. The parable is all about interpersonal relationships. Even in the description of the prodigal's degraded lifestyle in the second scene of the story (vv. 13–19), fully half the text is occupied by a soliloquy in which the estranged boy reflects on his relationship with "my father" (vv. 17–19). The older son, too, is detached from his father, though in a different way, and he speaks contemptuously of his brother as "this so-called son of yours" (v. 30). It is the dysfunctional, triangular relationship between family members that is the real subject matter of the story, with the spotlight falling on what is needed to bring about reconciliation and renewal.

This relational focus of the story is not simply a narrative deduction; it is also a cultural prerequisite for a tale that "was originally a Mediterranean story, told by a Mediterranean storyteller, for a Mediterranean audience."[22] Personal identity in ancient Mediterranean peasant society was an inherently relational rather than an individualistic construct. That is to say, people's sense of selfhood—of who they were and where they belonged in the world—stemmed first from their place in the family unit, and second from their participation in the village community. At the center of peasant psychology lay not the Western modernist ideal of an autonomous, self-sufficient ego but what anthropologists term a "dyadic" or group-oriented personality. This is where self-understanding and self-worth involve internalizing and satisfying the expectations of others, especially those within one's immediate kin group.[23]

Conforming to these expectations is the sine qua non for maintaining social cohesion, as well as for preserving individual emotional and mental well-being. Considered within such a cultural setting, it is simply impossible to appreciate the significance of the actions of any individual character in the Parable of the Prodigal Son without taking into account the ties of loyalty and identity that bound them together as a family unit and as interdependent members of community networks.

The first part of the parable is devoted to the offending of the younger son (who is probably around seventeen years of age, because he is old enough to leave home but is not yet married).[24] It is ironic that whereas the boy himself comes to interpret his behavior in the gravest possible terms as a case of "sinning against heaven and against his father" (vv. 18, 21), modern readers often struggle to see wherein his sin actually lay. True, he was a spendthrift who squandered his possessions in an intemperate lifestyle.[25] That was certainly a foolish thing to do, but to modern sensibilities it scarcely counts as dreadfully *sinful* (except perhaps to tight-fisted capitalists!), and it is not clear why the boy's wastefulness of his own possessions constituted a grievous sin against his father. In any event, living like there's no tomorrow is fairly typical teenage behavior, and at least this lad ends up getting a job to support himself, which actually makes him quite a good role model for contemporary kids!

Later in the story, his older brother accuses him of having spent his money on prostitutes (v. 30). This does perhaps up the sin stakes a little further. But the narrative description of the prodigal's behavior does *not* include him visiting brothels, and the accusation that he did so could simply be prurient speculation on the part of his uptight brother.[26] As for his initial act of asking for his slice of the inheritance in advance, several commentators can see no objection whatsoever in this request. Some even consider it a commendable sign of industriousness on the part of an ambitious young entrepreneur.[27]

But what appears to modern Western readers to be relatively innocent teenage behavior would have surely struck Jesus' first-century Palestinian audience and many indigenous hearers today as utterly repugnant and wholly blameworthy. They would have been appalled at the younger son's actions, which breached prevailing social and legal custom in a succession of ways, so that his offending behavior actually compounds as the story advances. His behavior is not merely irregular; it is offensive to such a severe degree that he almost certainly stood in breach of the Fifth Commandment to honor one's parents,[28] and he could well have been viewed as a candidate for the category of the "stubborn and rebellious son" in Deuteronomy 21:21 who is adjudged worthy of execution.[29]

His rebellion comprised a thoroughgoing rejection of his relational connection with, and responsibilities toward, his father, his brother, and his local community. He exhibited profound disrespect for his father in demanding a share of his estate in advance of his death. He then proceeded to act as though his father were *already* dead, and with no further moral or legal or emotional claims upon him, by cashing up his inheritance and emigrating, leaving no provision behind him for the support of his father in his declining years. He also abandoned his brother and spurned his village community, which would have been horrified at how glibly he discarded his family patrimony (v. 13). Once resident in foreign territory, he shows total disdain for the value of what he had received, scattering it to the four winds in hedonistic excess.

But then he experiences what F. W. Farrer terms "retributive anguish," as the intrinsic consequences of his choices come home to roost.[30] He is reduced to rags. But instead of returning home at this point or seeking help from fellow Jews in the Diaspora, he "glues himself" (ἐκολλήθη, v. 15) to a Gentile patron, being prepared even to wallow among unclean animals, and to accept the religious compromises and ritual pollution that came from doing so.[31] He is portrayed, in other words, as a serious and repeat offender, one who has so thoroughly covered himself in sin and shame that no place remained for him in regular society. He is utterly unclean, in every sense of the word.

But then, at the point of utter degradation, something shifts in him, and his long journey back to right standing in society commences. This brings us to a second lesson the parable teaches about the nature of justice: *the obligation it confers on offenders.*

The Obligation of Offenders

According to restorative justice thinking, the first crucial step in restoration is for an offender to accept responsibility for his or her actions and freely undertake to make amends. The theological word for this is "repentance," and in both Jewish and Christian understandings repentance is neither cheap nor painless. It requires contrition, confession, correction of life, and atonement.[32] Although the terminology of repentance is never used in the parable of the Prodigal Son, and some interpreters believe there is an enduring ambiguity throughout the narrative about the lad's true motivations, almost all the standard Jewish elements of repentance are present in the description of the prodigal's transformation in the middle section of the parable (Luke 15:17–21).[33] Certainly Luke's editorial placement of the story after the parables of the good shepherd and the good woman (15:3–10) indicates that he considered the boy's response to be emblematic of the "sinner who repents" and ignites joy in heaven, and there is no good reason to suspect that Luke got it wrong.

On the edge of starvation, the boy's downward spiral finally bottoms out. In a lengthy soliloquy, he compares his own destitution with the circumstances of his father's hired hands, who not only have bread to eat in place of pigswill but have it in abundance (v. 17). He therefore hatches a plan to return home and throw himself on his father's mercy. His decision could be construed merely as an act of self-centered expediency, but there are several textual clues that genuine contrition is being signaled.

To begin with, the entire soliloquy is predicated on the boy having "come to himself" (v. 17), an idiom found in several languages to denote a thoroughgoing change of heart.[34] Though this change of heart is triggered by hunger pangs, what the boy *actually* laments is the forfeited relationship with his father. It is the recollection of his father and of his father's generosity, as much as his own physical need, that evokes remorse. Twice in the monologue he uses the phrase "my father" (v. 17), and later he addresses him with the vocative "father." The verbal confession he rehearses in his head also centers on his father: on the wrong he has done to him and on his unworthiness to be called his son (v. 19).

When the boy finally puts his plan into action, embarking on the return journey (itself a biblical metaphor for repentance), the parable touchingly says that "he went to his father"—not to his house or to his village but to "his very *own* father" (πρὸς τὸν πατέρα ἑαυτοῦ).[35] It is significant that the offender comes to himself (ἐις ἑαυτὸν δὲ ἐλθὼν, v. 17) as a result of remembering that he was deeply connected to another human being, his father, and that it was with his father where he really belonged. As Miroslav Volf wisely observes, "There is no coming to oneself without the memory of belonging. The self is constructed in relation to others, and it can come to itself only through relationship to others. The first link with the other in a distant country of broken relationships is memory."[36] The boy's contrition, then, was evinced by his recollection of the bonds of belonging that grounded him in relationship and by his realization of the relational damage his behavior had caused, things that restorative justice also seeks to place center stage in its response to crime.

Contrition, if it is genuine, will lead to confession and apology, which, as restorative justice strongly emphasizes, plays an important role in vindicating the victim and promoting healing. What is remarkable about the boy's confession or apology in the parable is how it crystallizes so succinctly what it means for an offender to assume moral responsibility.

The first thing moral responsibility requires is an *acceptance of moral blame:* "Father," the boy admits, "I have sinned." He offers no plea of mitigation. He makes no attempt to minimize his offending as a mistake or as a lapse of judgment. Nor does he try to shift the blame on to anyone else, least of all on to the one he has injured. He makes no reference to what he has personally suffered or lost in the sad course of events. We know from earlier in the story that the offending boy has himself also been a victim, both of natural calamity (the famine, v. 14) and of human exploitation (the miserly citizen, vv. 15, 17), but he makes no mention of it here. All his attention is focused on the transgression he has committed, and he assumes full responsibility for it. Without him doing so, no basis would exist for relational repair.

The prodigal also accepts, second, that *his actions have injured others:* "Father, I have sinned against heaven and against you." The phrase "against heaven" underscores the fact that when a wrong is committed against another human being, a spiritual as well as a material harm is done—a sin is committed against God.[37] This is not just because God's law is broken (in this case the Fifth Commandment) but also because, in the biblical tradition, God so deeply identifies with innocent victims that when they are abused, God is also personally offended. To injure another person *is* to sin against God; they are not two separate offenses.

A third element in the boy's confession is the recognition that his wrongful actions have *changed the nature of his relationship to his victim.* Once he stood in a relation of filial duty and respect. But things have changed. By his actions the boy has chosen, in effect, to "un-son himself" and "de-father" his father. He has betrayed his father's trust and abused his love, and so now he concedes, "I am no longer worthy to be called your son; treat me like one of your hired hands." By these words, he renounces any immutable right to receive the forgiveness or protection or affection of his father in return for his confession. He must instead adopt the place of a distant acquaintance, one whose connection with his father is that of an expendable day laborer (μισθίως). If this distance is ever to be lessened, if he is ever to be restored to a more intimate relationship with his father, if he is ever to be remade as a son, the initiative must come from his father. Relational renewal in the aftermath of victimization, if it is to occur at all, can only ever come as a *gift* from victim to offender; it is not a commodity that can be unilaterally purchased by confession.[38]

Interestingly, a number of scholars detect in this request to become a hired hand an intention by the boy to earn sufficient income from his labors to pay restitution to his father, something prescribed in biblical law and strongly affirmed in restorative justice theory. Knowing that his father is a generous employer (v. 17), the boy hopes to get vocational training as a skilled craftsman so that he can save money and repay the losses inflicted on his father.[39] Such a suggestion cannot be wholly discounted, given the importance of restitution in the Jewish concept of repentance. But at most it is a possible inference from the text, not the main point at issue. Day laborers were the lowest of the three main classes of workers, and they were not considered part of the extended household.[40] In asking to be ranked among them, the prodigal was expressing his readiness to accept the most menial role available to again be near to his father and to render him service. His request was not just a means to some nobler end, as Kenneth Bailey proposes, for the boy does not ask to be made a hired servant but to be made "*as* a hired servant" (v. 19), that is, to be *treated* as someone of equivalent status and value as a hired worker.[41] It is also worth noting that day laborers usually lived at a mere subsistence level, because casual work was not always available. It is hard to believe that the prodigal, who himself had wasted away as a laborer on a pig farm (v. 16), imagined that by becoming a μισθίως of his father's he could generate enough surplus income to repay all his debts. If restitution is in view, it is a restitution of service more than a restitution of money.

Therefore, as much as I would like to believe otherwise in light of restorative justice commitments, I doubt that the penitent boy is thinking of monetary restitution at this point. Rather, he is openly acknowledging that his offending has destroyed the relationship of mutuality and trust he once enjoyed with his victim, and he has no right to imagine otherwise. Simple justice dictates that he relinquish his status as a son and adopt a more formal, distant relationship. The most he can hope for is that enough mercy will prevail that he is not banished forever from contact with his father but can find a place on his estate as a humble day laborer.

But what the boy now encounters transcends all recognizable notions of justice or mercy. He experiences the *justice of grace*, a justice in which his father restores him fully to the position of sonship he had so casually renounced.

The Challenge to Forgiveness

The father's role in the parable of the Prodigal Son is double-sided: at the story level he represents the human victim of wrongdoing, whereas at the discourse level he signifies the divine judge to whom sinners are accountable. But at both levels, the father's response to his returning son is nothing short of breathtaking. It is so out of character for a wronged Palestinian paterfamilias to act as he does, and so unjustified by the particular circumstances of the offense, that he will later be accused of behaving unjustly (Luke 15:29–30). But according to the father's scale of values, no injustice is entailed by allowing new life to trump former death, or recovery of the lost to cancel out their alienation and separation (v. 32, cf. v. 24). To favor restorative forgiveness over punitive exclusion permits a *better* justice to emerge, a justice that is satisfied not by punitive retribution but by the reconciliation of aggrieved parties and the reintegration of the offender into healthy community.

Several features of the father's behavior are hugely instructive in this connection, such as the culturally exceptional respect he shows for his son's moral agency and autonomy; the way he refuses, over many years, to give up hope for his son's ultimate return; and the profound empathy he feels for the boy's derelict condition, as he is "filled with compassion" at the mere sight of him.[42] But what is most striking is the father's utter self-abnegation in the interests of reconciliation. He does not stand on ceremony, which would dictate that he wait at a dignified distance until his son approached and bowed before him. Instead, the parable says, "he ran and put his arms around him and kissed him" (v. 20).

There is an interesting parallel in the apocryphal book of Tobit, in which Tobias's mother is waiting for her son's return, looking intently down the road on which he would travel. When she sees him, she tells her blind husband of the boy's approach then runs to embrace him with tears of joy (Tob. 11:5–15). In our story, it is the *father* who runs down the road to greet the traveler. As commentators invariably point out, it was extremely undignified for a great man or the head of the household to hike up his robes, expose his legs, and run in public. No ordinary Oriental father would humiliate himself in this way. But the father of the prodigal sprints toward his lost boy and falls on his neck, kissing him repeatedly (v. 20).[43]

Yet for all his eagerness to welcome him, and thereby also to protect him from any ill treatment at the hands of other villagers, he still makes space for moral accountability, as the boy confesses his wrongdoing and his unworthiness to be counted as a son (v. 21).[44] The father receives the confession without protest. He does not challenge the accuracy of his son's account, nor does he play down the impact of what has happened. According to restorative justice thinking, confession is an important prerequisite for restoration because it serves to clarify where the moral culpability for the incident truly lies. This enables victims to overcome the self-blame and self-loathing to which they are so often inclined. But confession is equally important for offenders, for it is in confessing their wrongdoing that they begin to recalibrate their moral compass, to refocus their moral desires on what is good and true, and in so doing to promote their own healing and rehabilitation.[45]

Yet no sooner is the confession out than the father quickly (Ταχύ, v. 22) sets about restoring the sinner to a place of honor and dignity in the local community.[46] He orders the slaves to fetch clothing and dress the boy, just as they would the master of the house, an action that would serve to reestablish an appropriate relationship between the servants and the restored son, as well as to draw attention to the moral transformation in the boy that had made this restoration possible (being clothed in new garments is a common biblical metaphor for a change of moral character).

In the ancient world, clothing was a crucial indicator of social standing. The impoverished majority of the population wore short, unbleached tunics of poor quality, and slaves about went about barefooted. Those of higher rank wore richly colored garments, with the length, fullness, quality of fabric, and degree of ornamentation being visible markers of social location.[47] The prodigal expected to be relegated to the class of a manual laborer. Instead he is clothed in his father's finest robe, his calloused feet are shod with sandals, and a signet ring of authority is placed on his finger. It is impossible to miss the message conveyed by these actions: The father does not merely supply the boy's bare physical necessities, he does him an extraordinary honor. He confers upon him the full dignity and esteem of sonship, notwithstanding his past offenses.

This emphasis on the bestowing of honor on the penitent son makes sense when seen in the context of a Mediterranean social order in which honor and shame were pivotal values in public life. In such a cultural setting, to offend against social and legal convention, in the way the prodigal had done, incurred shame as well as moral guilt, and forgiveness was as much about restoring honor as assuaging guilt.[48] Though honor and shame play a less significant public role in contemporary Western society, the impact of being humiliated or honored in the eyes of others still carries immense, almost primal, psychological potency. Intriguingly, the criminologist Howard Zehr has argued that much criminal offending is rooted in the offender's sense of shame and in their drive to remove or transform that shame by projecting it on to others. Here we might speculate that the prodigal's downward spiral in the faraway land was a case of him "acting out" the shame he knew he had incurred through his disgraceful treatment of his father. Certainly his verbal confession drips with intense feelings of unworthiness (οὐκέτι εἰμὶ ἄξιος, vv. 19, 21), which is the essence of all shame, and he attributes this shame to having sinned against his father. Therefore when his father reaffirms his worthiness by symbolically attiring him as a son-to-be-proud-of, it would function to release him from the crippling shame he felt, as well as to rehabilitate him in the eyes of others. By contrast, in our criminal justice system, as Zehr points out, prosecution and punishment usually serve to exacerbate rather than to alleviate the offender's sense of shame: "If it is true . . . that shame and the desire to remove it motivates much crime, then our prescription for crime is bizarre: we impose more shame, stigmatising offenders in ways that begin to define their identities and encourages them to join other 'outsiders' in delinquent subcultures. Guilt and shame become a self-perpetuating cycle, feeding one another. In fact, psychiatrist [James] Gilligan argues that punishment decreases the sense of guilt while at the same time accentuating shame, the very motor which drives offending behaviour."[49]

It is noteworthy in the parable that the person who was instrumental in lifting the boy's shame was the victim of his offending, the one who had himself been publicly shamed by what he had happened to him. At a profound level, the father's restorative gestures effected a remarkable interchange of honor and shame between victim and offender. Just as the boy's admission of wrongdoing served to restore honor to his humiliated father, so the father's open-hearted acknowledgement of his son's repentance and his reinstatement as a son ended his humiliation and restored his pride. Punishment, let it be clear, plays no role whatsoever in this interchange. Punishment may serve other valuable ends in social life, but it is not empowered to exorcise shame. Replacing shame and humiliation with honor and respect requires something far more potent than punishment; it requires confession, compassion, and forgiveness, and these in turn require a personal transaction between offender and victim. Perhaps the profoundest insight of restorative justice theory is its recognition that offenders and victims are on parallel journeys of dealing with the debilitating impact of shame—whether the shame of having done wrong or the shame of having been wronged—and that each party therefore, paradoxically, holds the key to the other's healing.

Although the *feeling* of shame is an interior reality, the *condition* of shame is also a social reality, a reproach in the eyes of others that needs to be publicly removed. Perhaps for this reason, the father caps off his restorative gestures by going public and throwing a lavish party. Feasts were not a common occurrence in village life, and few could afford to eat meat. So when the father assembles musicians and dancers (Luke 15:25) and orders the slaughtering of the fatted calf (vv. 23, 27, 30), he is announcing to the whole village society the great esteem his son now enjoyed. The young lad had disowned his father by selling up and leaving forever. But the father had not disowned his son. For all the son's spiteful actions, when he came back his father embraced him as "this son of mine" (v. 24, cf. 30). He refused to exclude him from belonging and would not let others exclude him either (v.32). He ensured that the entire community, which would have felt deep antagonism toward the treacherous teen, knew that he was home again and reinstalled as an honored member of the household, absolved of his previous wrongdoing. "Let us eat and celebrate," he demands (v. 23), and "they began to celebrate" (v. 24). Their celebration symbolizes "the joy, interdependence and mutual enrichment of healthy human community."[50]

All this stands in stark contrast to what usually prevails with ex-offenders today. A former prison inmate in New Zealand recently made this comment: "In the eyes of society, I am condemned forever to the underclass, to subcitizenship. I will carry the stigma of a convicted career criminal for the rest of my life—never to be accepted by society as a person worthy of any meaningful degree of respect or dignity. The weight of shame and guilt is too great a burden to carry with me forever. Slowly the depth of my punishment became clear to me and I realized that certain elements of my punishment and stigmatisation will follow me back into society and remain in place as long as I live. There will be no forgiveness."[51]

Not so with the prodigal son, who is forgiven. Of course, the sheer magnanimity of the father's response to him in the parable is intended to depict the nature of God—a God who, as Psalm 103 observes, is also "filled with compassion" at the distressed state of his children and delights to heal, forgive, and restore them.[52] But it is clear from the placement of the parable in Luke 15 that Jesus is doing more than speaking about God in the abstract. He is using God as a viable model for how his hearers are to treat those who victimize them, and those whom the community judges to be treacherous offenders worthy only of exclusion or even execution. They are to emulate the restoring love of God for them, which means inviting their repentance, receiving their confession without objection, and restoring them to full participation in community. To do this is to imitate the love of God; but it is equally to imitate the *justice* of God, for, in the final scene of the parable, the father must defend himself from the harsh accusations of having perpetrated an injustice.

The Challenge to the Law-Abiding Community

The response of the older brother brings a note of stark realism to the incident. He is portrayed as a hard-working and law-abiding individual who recoils in disgust at the sheer unfairness of showing grace to a serious and repeat offender. "All these years I have slaved for you," he complains to his father, "and I have never disobeyed your command [οὐδέποτε ἐντολήν σου παρῆλθον]. Yet you have never given me even a young goat so that I might celebrate with my friends" (Luke 15:29). As one commentator observes, the older boy is clearly "jealous, and regards his father as utterly weak in his treatment of the prodigal; but what specially moves him is the *injustice* of it all. His own unflagging service and propriety have never been recognised in any way, while the spendthrift has only to show himself in order to receive a handsome recognition."[53]

It is not hard to feel sympathy for the older son. On the face of it, he has a valid complaint. But the instant rage (ὠργίσθη, v. 28) he experiences at news of his father's actions suggests that behind the facade of a conscientious, law-abiding individual who wants simple justice to prevail lies a range of attitudes and attributes that blind him to the justness of his father's actions. These attitudes and attributes are present in all of us to some degree. But they are magnified out of all proportion in the psyche of collective society, which so often greets efforts to rehabilitate or reintegrate offenders with indignation and disgust.

One such attribute in the older son is his tendency toward haughty judgmentalism. The parable makes it clear that he was "in the field" when his brother returned and had no idea why music and dancing were emanating from the house (v. 25). When told by a servant of his brother's return and his father's joy, he explodes in anger. He does not inquire into his brother's moral condition or attitude; he does not contemplate the possibility of him having changed. He simply recalls his past identity as someone who had defrauded his father and consorted with prostitutes, someone completely beyond the pale who ought to be excluded from communal gatherings, not fed the fatted calf!

There is a telling parallelism between the three-part narrative description of the prodigal's actions in verse 13 and his brother's cynical summation of his behavior in verse 30:[54]

v. 13	"... he squandered	his property	in dissolute living"
	διεσκόρπισεν	τὴν οὐσίαν αὐτοῦ	ζῶν ἀσώτως
v. 30	"... he devoured	your property	with prostitutes"
	Ὁ καταφαγών	σου τὸν βίον	μετὰ πορνῶν

Obviously, the older brother puts the worst possible construction on his sibling's conduct. The youth's careless wastefulness is construed as greedy consumption, his disregard for his own property is rendered as a despoiling of his father's livelihood, and his loose living is given explicitly sexual overtones. The mention of prostitutes is particularly scurrilous. Given that there is no reference to prostitutes in the earlier part of the story, the older son was presumably making this lurid deduction on the basis of what he considered to be his brother's inherent character. It is a classic example of "deviance labeling"—a commonplace in the criminal justice domain—where attaching an abnormal label to someone functions to stigmatize him or her in the eyes of the public, and even to prescribe for them the kind of behaviors that will match their deviant identity.[55] "If he can make the promiscuous label stick," Richard Rohrbaugh comments, "he can destroy the younger brother's place in the family and probably in the village as well. The fear would be that down the road 'sons' of the prodigal might show up claiming family and village rights and chaos would ensue. If the older son's label sticks, therefore, the younger son would have to leave the village for good and no progeny of his could ever return."[56]

Clearly, then, the law-abiding brother views his returned brother in the darkest of terms. He makes no allowance for the possibility that, as a result of bitter experience, he might have changed. His persona as transgressor is fixed forever, and it eclipses all else in his character. He is simply "a bad apple" who ought to be banished forever from respectable society.

Such exclusionary judgmentalism is paired, second, with an exaggerated sense of his own virtue. "For all these years I have slaved for you, and I have never disobeyed your command" (Luke 15:29). There are two tragic ironies here. The first is that he views himself as a slave when in fact he is the first-born son. His work on the estate is performed from a cold sense of duty, not out of loving devotion to his father. His virtue runs only skin deep, an exterior conformity to rules and regulations rather than an inner fidelity to what is true. He has no conception of what it really means to be a devoted son. Although his father addresses him affectionately as a "dear son" (Τέκνον, v. 31), the son never once calls him "father." Although his father delights in his son's companionship as one who is "always with me" (v. 31), the boy's emotional ties lie elsewhere, for what he wants is to "celebrate with my friends," not with his father (v. 29). What the father has shown by his manner of response to the prodigal son that he wanted most from his offspring—a warm, loving relationship—the non-prodigal son has not given him either. This older son treats his father as a master to be unquestioningly obeyed, not as a father to be loved and respected, and he sees this as a positive virtue.

The second irony is that at the very point of appealing to his unstinting obedience to his father, the older son is actually standing in defiance of him. Custom required that he should be present at family banquets, where he would serve as joint host with the master. Yet despite his father's repeated pleading (v. 28), he refuses to join the feast, launching instead a bitter and deeply insulting tirade against his father's integrity. So culturally deplorable is his refusal to heed his father's plea to share in the communal meal that there can be little doubt that he is deliberately seeking to humiliate his father.

It is because the older son exaggerates his own virtue and magnifies his brother's vice that he fails to see their common kinship. He considers himself more virtuous than his brother, but in fact he resembles him in so many ways. Both boys are fully prepared to dishonor their father for personal ends—one by selling off his livelihood, the other by refusing to join him as village host. Both are preoccupied with money and pleasure. The younger son asks for his inheritance so that he can live the high life now; the older son complains that his father has never given him anything so he can party with his friends. Both are disloyal to their father, and both injure him deeply. The lawbreaker injures him by his selfish actions; the lawkeeper injures him by his angry words and cold-hearted attitude. Both sons are equally lost to their father. But whereas the prodigal comes to acknowledge his sin and confess his unworthiness, his older brother cannot see beyond his own meticulous morality.

Structures of exclusion and stigmatization, of which the fantastically misnamed "Corrections System" is the most hideous and violent example, are invariably sustained by such refusal on the part of the "righteous" to admit their common, flawed humanity with those they deem to be intractable sinners and criminals. Because "we" are not like "them," we allow them to be treated in ways that we would never consider appropriate for ourselves.

A third attribute that precludes the law-abiding son from accepting his father's actions is his acute sense of victimhood. On the one hand, he encourages his father to dwell on his personal victimization at the hands of his villainous off-spring, who "devoured *your* property with prostitutes" (Luke 15:30). On the other hand, he casts himself as a victim of his father's callous neglect in the past ("You did not even give me a goat") and blatant favoritism in the present ("but for this son of yours you kill the fatted calf!") (vv. 29–30). His sense of victimhood runs so deep that he assumes the celebration thrown for his brother somehow detracts from his own superior virtue or devalues his standing in his father's eyes.

This entrenched sense of personal victimhood explains yet another attribute observable in the older brother and all too familiar in collective society: an instinctive distrust of judicial leniency. He is angered by his father's apparent indulgence of his brother's wrongdoing, and he contests the justice of throwing a party for someone so undeserving. The father repudiates this charge of injustice in two ways. First, he rejects the implication that love is a limited commodity, that love shown to the delinquent son must first be deducted from the love available for his other son. "Dear child," the father says with great tenderness, "you are always with me, and all that is mine is yours" (v. 31). He loses nothing from the love displayed to his brother; his standing is in no way diminished. If anything it is enhanced, for the offender's return to right relationship only serves to vindicate his brother's choice to remain always with his father. True virtue ought need no other reward than to see vice freely relinquished by the penitent.

The second defense the father offers is more significant. The older son assumed that the banquet in full swing was simply a celebration of his brother's homecoming, for all he had been told by a passing servant was that "your brother has come" (Luke 15:27). Such merriment he judged to be an indulgence, even a condoning of, the prodigal's wrongdoing, and hence without any moral justification. For the father, however, the banquet was a celebration not just of his son's return home but of his *transformation*. "We *had* [ἔδει] to celebrate and rejoice," he explains, "*because* [ὅτι] this brother of yours was dead and has come to life; he was lost and has been found" (v. 32, cf. v. 24). Here the father underscores the *changed* standing of his wayward son, as one who had moved from death to life and from separation to reconciliation, as the grounds for the celebration, and he deems such celebration to be nothing less than a divine necessity [ἔδει].[57] As David Holgate observes: "The father's words express a recognition that the son has gone through a life-changing experience. What is celebrated is not the son's restoration to his former state (which was one of moral death leading to physical death, v.17c), but a celebration of his new state, which is one of moral life. There is also the implication that part of this recovery of life is a recovery of relationship."[58] That is why no injustice has occurred. What made the feast entirely just and equitable was that it marked the prodigal's renewed commitment to right living, in parallel with his brother's alleged commitment.

Behind the differing responses of the father and the law-abiding son lie two different conceptions of justice. The older son works with a morality-based notion of justice that gives priority to just deserts (vv. 29–30). For him justice is a matter of arithmetical fairness, so that his father's largesse toward the prodigal rather than toward him necessarily constitutes an injustice. The son prefers the simplicity of punitive ostracism to the complexity of wrestling with the ambiguities and shared liabilities that always surround situations of human offending, victimization, and restoration. The father, by contrast, works with a *relational* conception of justice, as is shown by he way he interprets the situation in entirely relational or familial categories ("dear son . . . all that is mine is yours . . . this brother of yours . . . this son of mine," vv. 31–32). It is not that the father considers the rules of natural justice to which his older son appeals are somehow flawed. Quite the contrary, by anyone's standards, hard work deserves greater reward than profligacy, and obedience to the law warrants more respect than disobedience. The father obviously believes that the rules tying deed to consequence should be observed in the household community; after all, he pays his workers well for their labors (v. 17) and expects his slaves to fulfill their duties (vv. 22–23). It is not the rules themselves that are the problem but his son's obsession with enforcing the rules of just desert as the only way to ensure that true justice prevails.

According to the relational justice of the father, moral rules and legal codes should not have the final say in human affairs. Relationships should. Upholding the law and observing the dictates of natural justice remains crucially important for the household community to operate wholesomely, and moral earnestness is required in the face of wrongdoing (cf. v. 18). But the community itself, and the very humanity of those within the community, is constituted by something far deeper than, and ontologically prior to, any set of rules. It is constituted by relationships, which impose obligations that are inescapable ("this brother of yours," v. 32) and the success of which depends ultimately on humility, compassion, grace, and forgiveness. Moral performance *affects* the quality of our relationships, but it does not *create* those relationships, and it never discharges us from the responsibility of working to repair broken relationships when confession and repentance are present.

The essential "justice" of restorative justice, in other words, depends on factoring in repentance. Genuine repentance induces a transformation of identity, so that the contrite sinner becomes, in a real sense, a different person than he was before and therefore a candidate not merely for an amnesty but also for a new beginning. No injustice transpires when the lost are recovered, when the dead are restored to life, when sinners are forgiven. Justice is vindicated in such transformations, for things are returned to how they ought to be, and righteousness prevails once more.

Conclusion

In the parable of the Prodigal Son, the father's final words to his older son contain a double challenge. Would he recognize the forgiven offender as "this brother of yours," someone to whom he owed fraternal love as flesh of his flesh, as a fellow, flawed human being, or would he continue to despise him as an outcast? And would he join in the celebration of his restoration and eat his share of the fatted calf, or would he keep his distance on the strict principle of retributive justice?

One last point needs making, though it is rarely noticed. For the older son to relinquish his objections and join in the feast of forgiveness would be costly for him, for it could require of him a willingness to share his goods with his penniless brother. The prodigal had lost everything through his reckless living, and though his father could confer on him the symbols of forgiveness and familial esteem, he could not give him any more land, for what remained had already been given as a gift to his other son (vv. 12, 31). The prodigal's inheritance had gone for good, *unless* his upright brother would graciously choose to give him a stake in what he possessed.

This, then, is the final challenge of this parable of restorative justice to the law-abiding community: a challenge to contemplate not only the restoration and reintegration of offenders, as an outworking of the Christian discipline of forgiveness, but also to display toward them an openhanded hospitality, a readiness to share with them what the parable calls our "living" (*bios*) and "substance" (*ousia*), so that they may again participate as equals in the social and economic life of society. Nothing less than this qualifies, finally, as restorative justice. Nothing less accords with the graciousness of God, who "makes his sun to rise on the evil and on the good, and sends rain on the righteous and on the unrighteous" (Matt. 5:45). If all this leaves us shaking our heads and thinking "it couldn't possibly work in our society," then perhaps we have begun to "hear" this parable in all its offensive glory.

Notes

1. Howard Zehr, *Changing Lenses: A New Focus for Crime and Justice* (Scottdale, Pa.: Herald Press, 1990). See also his *The Little Book of Restorative Justice* (Intercourse, Pa.: Good Books, 2002).

2. Heather Strang and John Braithwaite rightly insist that a combination of values and process conceptions should be seen as a "normative ideal" for restorative justice, *Restorative Justice and Civil Society* (Cambridge: Cambridge University Press, 2001), 13.

3. On this, see Jim Boyack, Helen Bowen, and Christopher Marshall, "How Does Restorative Justice Ensure Good Practice? A Values-Based Approach," in *Critical Issues in Restorative*

Justice, ed. Howard Zehr and Barb Toews (Palisades, N.Y.: Criminal Justice Press, 2004), 265–76.

4. For a superb, up-to-date review of restorative justice theory and practice, see Jerry G. Johnstone and Dan van Ness, *Handbook of Restorative Justice* (Cullompton, U.K.: Wilan, 2007).

5. Cf. Howard Zehr and Alan Macrae, *The Little Book on Family Group Conferences, New Zealand-Style* (Intercourse, Pa.: Good Books, 2003).

6. Some 15,000 family group conferences were held in New Zealand in 2005. Research shows that 55 percent of those who attend Family Group Conferences do not go on to reoffend. See further the comments of the Principal Youth Court judge, Andrew Beacroft, "Towards a Restorative Society," www.vuw.ac.nz/ips/completed-activities/Becroft.Paper/percent20 Octoberpercent202005.pdf (file has been corrupted and is no longer available; however, see http://ips.ac.nz/events/completed-activities/restorative.html).

7. On the indigenous contribution to restorative justice, see briefly Jim Consedine, *Restorative Justice: Healing the Effects of Crime* (Lyttelton, U.K.: Ploughshares Publications, 1995), e.g., 81–89. More extensively, see Wanda D. McCaslin, ed., *Justice as Healing: Indigenous Ways* (Saint Paul: Living Justice Press, 2005). See also Church Council on Justice and Corrections, *Satisfying Justice: A Compendium on Initiatives, Programs and Legislative Measures* (Ottawa: Church Council on Justice and Corrections, 1996).

8. That the parable goes back to Jesus himself is now almost universally accepted in New Testament scholarship, despite the fact that it shows signs of Lukan redaction and coheres with characteristically Lukan themes, such as inclusion of outcasts. As Luke Timothy Johnson observes, the parable combines "the distinctive note of originality we associate with Jesus, and the distinctive literary sensibility of Luke. It is however impossible entirely to disentangle tradition from redaction, precisely because Luke covers the traces of his sources so thoroughly." *The Gospel of Luke*, Sacra Pagina 3 (Collegeville, Minn.: Michael Glazier, 1991), 239; cf. Charles E. Carlston, "Reminiscence and Redaction in Luke 15:11–32," *Journal of Biblical Literature* 94 (1975): 368–90. For a convenient listing of the evidence for authenticity, see Greg Forbes, "Repentance and Conflict in the Parable of the Lost Son (Luke 15:11–32)," *Journal of the Evangelical Theological Society* 42/2 (1999): 211–29; and T. W. Manson, *The Sayings of Jesus* (London: SCM Press, 1957), 285–86. Luise Schotroff, who once ascribed the parable to Luke's authorship, now ascribes it to "a vital orality" in which there is no single author, *The Parables of Jesus*, trans. Linda M. Maloney (Minneapolis: Fortress Press, 2006), 243 n. 20. But for an important critique of the whole notion of anonymous orality in the gospel tradition, see Richard Bauckham, *Jesus and the Eyewitnesses: The Gospels as Eye Witness Testimony* (Grand Rapids: William B. Eerdmans, 2006).

9. See Manfried Siebald and Leland Ryken, "Prodigal Son," in *A Dictionary of Biblical Tradition in English Literature*, ed. David Lyle Jeffrey (Grand Rapids: William B. Eerdmans, 1992), 640–44. More briefly, see Joseph A. Fitzmyer, *The Gospel According to Luke*, 2 vols. (Garden City, N.Y.: Doubleday, 1985), vol 2, 1083. For a comprehensive discussion of Greco-Roman parallels, see David A. Holgate, *Prodigality, Liberality and Meanness: The Prodigal Son in Greco-Roman Perspective* (Sheffield, U.K.: Sheffield Academic Press, 1999). For a contemporary rabbinic parallel, see Roger David Aus, "Luke 15:11–32 and R. Eliezer Ben Hyrcanus's Rise to Fame," *Journal of Biblical Literature* 104, no. 3 (1985): 443–69.

10. See Y. Tissot, "Patristic Allegories of the Lukan Parable of the Two Sons," in *Exegesis: Problems of Method and Exercises in Reading*, ed. F. Bovon and G. Rouiller and trans. D. G. Miller (Pittsburgh: Pickwick Press, 1978), 362–409.

11. Cf. Klyne Snodgrass, "From Allegorizing to Allegorizing: A History of the Interpretation of the Parables of Jesus," in *The Challenge of Jesus' Parables*, ed. Richard N. Longenecker (Grand Rapids: William B. Eerdmans, 2000), 3–29; and Klyne Snodgrass, "Modern

Approaches to the Parables," in *The Face of New Testament Studies: A Survey of Recent Research*, ed. Scot McKnight and Grant R. Osborne (Grand Rapids: Baker Academic, 2004), 177–90.

12. Kenneth E. Bailey, *Poet and Peasant and Through Peasant Eyes: A Literary-Cultural Approach to the Parables in Luke* (Grand Rapids: William B. Eerdmans, 1983), 158. For a helpful analysis of how and why the parables are polyvalent or plurisignificant, see Susan Wittig, "A Theory of Multiple Meanings," *Semeia* 9 (1977): 75–103.

13. Robert Bridges, quoted by A. M. Hunter, *Interpreting the Parables* (London: SCM Press, 1964), 61.

14. Kenneth E. Bailey captures the problem succinctly: "The parable of the prodigal son appears to have no savior. . . . The story appears to have no incarnation, no 'word that becomes flesh,' no cross, no crown, no suffering, no death, no resurrection and no mediator between God and human beings. How can this be a 'gospel within the gospel' when the gospel, as known throughout the New Testament, is apparently missing?" *Jacob and the Prodigal: How Jesus Retold Israel's Story* (Downers Grove, Ill.; InterVarsity Press, 2003), 16.

15. "Responsibility, Rehabilitation, and Restoration: A Catholic Perspective on Crime and Criminal Justice," Statement of the Catholic Bishops of the United States, November 15, 2000, www.usccb.org/sdwp/criminal.htm, 9.

16. Thomas L. Shaffer, "The Radical Reformation and the Jurisprudence of Forgiveness," in *Christian Perspectives on Legal Thought*, ed. Michael W. McConnell, Robert F. Chochran Jr., and Angela C. Carmella (New Haven, Conn.: Yale University Press, 2001), 321–40 (the quotation is on 324). For a critique of Shaffer, see Jeffrie Murphy, "Christianity and Criminal Punishment," *Punishment and Society* 5, no. 3 (2003): 261–77.

17. In an extraordinary reversal of narrative logic, Mary Ann Beavis takes the younger son to be a victim of incest and his father to be the perpetrator of homosexual abuse! Beavis is clear that her interpretation "does not purport to uncover the 'true' or 'original' meaning of the parable, the meaning intended by Jesus, or the meaning intended by Luke. Rather, informed by the skills of a professional biblical scholar, it attempts to read the parable from the perspective of an implied reader with the life experience of one of the runaways described above" (103, cf. 120–21). Reading against the grain in this way is all very well for "professional biblical scholars" who assume that their profession gives them license to massage textual meaning for their own ends. But one wonders what controls, textual or ethical, such a mode of interpretation is subject to. If the teller and recorder of the parable intended the father to serve as a positive role model in the story, even as a metaphor for God, by what right does a professional biblical scholar reverse the intended referent for ideological reasons? The very fact that parables functioned to blow open existing worldviews and afford new ways of perceiving reality presupposes that they possessed some "givenness" of meaning that could effectively subvert conventional wisdom. The parables lose any subversive power if their meaning is viewed as entirely the product of essentially arbitrary reading strategies.

18. See my discussion on the relational nature of the *imago Dei* in *Crowned with Glory and Honor: Human Rights in the Biblical Tradition* (Telford, Pa.: Cascadia Press, 2001), esp. 54–63.

19. Cf. Adolf Jülicher, *Die Gleichnisreden Jesu: Zweiter Teil—Auslegung der Gleichnisreden der drei ersten Evanelien* (Freiburg i. B., Leipzig, Tübingen, 1899), 420; Dan Otto Via, *The Parables: Their Literary and Existential Dimension* (Philadelphia: Fortress Press, 1967), 164, 167; Joel B. Green, *The Gospel of Luke*, New International Commentary on the New Testament Series (Grand Rapids: William B. Eerdmans, 1997), 578.

20. Joachim Jeremias, *The Parables of Jesus*, rev. ed. (London: SCM Press, 1972), 128; John R. Donahue, *The Gospel in Parable: Metaphor, Narrative and Theology in the Synoptic Gospels* (Philadelphia: Fortress Press, 1988), 160 (cf. 152–53); Fitzmyer, *Luke*, 1084; Holgate, *Prodigality*, 53–54, 67.

21. Cf. Francois Bovon, "The Parable of the Prodigal Son, Luke 15:11–32, First Reading," in *Exegesis*, ed. Bovon and Rouiller, 43–74 (on 49, citing D. Buzy). Several exegetes think both brothers share the limelight equally, each serving as a foil for the other.

22. Richard L. Rohrbaugh, "A Dysfunctional Family and Its Neighbours," in *Jesus and His Parables: Interpreting the Parables of Jesus Today*, ed. V. George Shillington (Edinburgh: T. & T. Clark, 1997), 141–64 (the quotation is on 143).

23. On this, see Bruce J. Malina, *The New Testament World: Insights from Cultural Anthropology* (Louisville: Westminster / John Knox Press, 1993 rev. ed.), 63–89. Of course, it is important not to exaggerate collective identity in antiquity to the extent that it excludes the possibility of individual personality and moral agency (cf. Bauckham, *Eyewitnesses*, 172–74), both of which are evident in the parable.

24. So Jeremias, *Parables*, 129; I. Also see Howard Marshall, *The Gospel of Luke: A Commentary on the Greek Text* (Exeter, U.K.: Paternoster, 1978), 607.

25. On the moral seriousness of profligacy in the ancient world, nonetheless, see Holgate, *Prodigality*, 90–130.

26. As G. B. Caird observes, the older son "had no more evidence for the harlots than his imagination and bad temper could supply"; *Saint Luke* (Hammondsworth, U.K.: Penguin Books, 1963), 183. So, too, Johnson: *Luke*, 238, who notes the similarity with accusations against Jesus for keeping bad company (Luke 7:34, 39); cf. Holgate, *Prodigality*, 144 n. 49. The decadence of his lifestyle is conveyed by the adverb ἀσώτως (literally "unsaving" or "nonsalutary") in v. 13, which suggests wildness and wastefulness, but not necessarily sexual license; see W. Foerster, *Theological Dictionary of the New Testament* I: 506–7; Alfred Plummer, *The Gospel According to St Luke*, International Critical Commentary Series (Edinburgh: T. & T. Clark, 1901), 373; and Manson, *Sayings*, 287. Bailey stresses that neither the Greek text nor the various oriental versions indicate that the boy was guilty of sexual immorality (Bailey, *Poet and Peasant*, 170), although Holgate notes the common link between covetousness and immorality in Jewish, Greco-Roman, and early Christian literature (Holgate, *Prodigality*, 142–48).

27. So, e.g., A. E. Harvey, *The New English Bible Companion to the New Testament* (Cambridge and Oxford; Cambridge University Press and Oxford University Press, 1970), 266; Eta Linnemann, *Parables of Jesus: Introduction and Exposition* (London: SPCK, 1966), 75; Joachim Gnilka, *Jesus of Nazareth: Message and History*, Trans. by Siegfried S. Schatzmann (Peabody, Mass.: Hendrickson, 1997), 99; Via, *Parables*, 170.

28. Exod. 20:12; Lev. 19:3; Deut. 6:13; Prov. 3:9. The biblical command to honor one's parents was not merely an ethical rule but an economic responsibility as well. This responsibility was in no way diminished by any discourtesy, unfairness, or favoritism on the part of the parent. See J. Duncan M. Derrett, *Law in the New Testament* (London: Darton, Longman & Todd, 1970), 109–11.

29. Space does not permit a discussion of the technical legal realities presupposed in the parable, for which see the standard commentaries and the other works cited elsewhere in the notes.

30. F. W. Farrer, *The Gospel According to St Luke* (Cambridge: Cambridge University Press, 1905), 257. Early pagan, Jewish, and Christian moralists differed on whether famines could be attributed to providence as a form of divine punishment, or were simply an inescapable part of life (cf. Holgate, *Prodigality*, 148–53). Here the retribution is not the famine, but the boy's inability to cope with it due to his wrongful choices.

31. The radical dependency implied here is illustrated by the way the same verb (κολλάω) is sometimes used to depict exclusive religious devotion to God (e.g., Deut. 6:13; 10:20; 2 Kings 18:6; Ps 63:8; 119:31; 1 Cor 6:17), and to portray sexual intimacy (e.g., 1 Kings 11:2; 1 Esdr. 4:20; Sir. 19:2; Matt. 19:5; 1 Cor. 6:16). Beavis is one of the few interpreters to note

the sexual overtones of the verb, though instead of seeing this use of the term as an analogy for the close dependency created between the boy and his patron, she takes it as evidence that the runaway boy had "initial sexual contact, followed by rejection and degradation" with the Gentile pig farmer, "Making Up Stories," 112. For the legal institution possibly evoked by the verb here, see J. Albert Harrill, "The Indentured Labor of the Prodigal Son (Luke 15:15)," *Journal of Biblical Literature* 115, no. 4 (1996): 714–17.

32. In rabbinic Judaism, "Repentance entails confession of the sin before God and formulation of a resolve not to commit the same sin again. In the case of a sin against another person, repentance is possible only after full restitution or correction of the wrong deed has been made and a pardon from the other person has been obtained. In Scripture's system, repentance is followed by an expiatory offering. After the destruction of the temple and the cessation of the sacrificial cult, the rabbis found a replacement for this offering in charitable deeds. Rabbinic authorities viewed repentance and charity together as a person's greatest advocates before God (*B. Shabbat* 32a)," Jacob Neusner and William Scott Green, eds., *Dictionary of Judaism in the Biblical Period: 450 B.C.E. to 600 C.E.* (Peabody, Mass.: Hendrickson, 1996), 524. See also George Foot Moore, *Judaism in the First Centuries of the Christian Era: The Age of the Tannaim* (Peabody, Mass.: Hendrickson, 1960; orig. pub. 1927), vol. 2, 507–45.

33. Cf. George W. Ramsey, "Plots, Gaps, Repetitions, and Ambiguity in Luke 15," *Perspectives in Religious Studies* 17, no. 1 (1990): 37–42.

34. Both Jeremias, *Parables*, 130, and Marshall, *Luke*, 609, deem it to be a Semitic phrase for repentance, and Manson, *Sayings*, 288, notes that the same construction is found in the Greek, Latin, and Hebrew languages. Holgate reviews its usage in the Greco-Roman philosophical tradition and concludes that Luke's readers would have understood it here to designate either a sudden or a gradual conversion resulting from some form of moral self-analysis stimulated by adverse circumstances; Holgate, *Prodigality*, 198–206. By contrast, Bailey thinks it merely signals a "face saving plan" on the part of the boy, not real repentance. Bailey, *Poet and Peasant*, 173–74; Bailey, *Jacob the Prodigal*, 103–17; Bailey, *Finding the Lost Cultural Keys to Luke 15* (Saint Louis: Concordia, 1992), 129–42; Bailey, *The Cross and the Prodigal: Luke 15 through the Eyes of Middle Eastern Peasants*, rev. ed. (Downers Grove, Ill.: InverVarsity Press, 2005; orig. pub. 1973), 52–62.

35. Plummer rightly takes ἑαυτοῦ to be emphatic ("his own father"), in *Luke*, 375, although not all exegetes do so. In any event, Bailey is wrong to surmise that the boy plans "to go back to his village but not to his home. Planning to work as a servant and live in the village, he intends to save himself" (Bailey, *Poet and Peasant*, 205–6), since the text quite clearly has him returning specifically to his father.

36. Miroslav Volf, *Exclusion and Embrace: A Theological Exploration of Identity, Otherness, and Reconciliation* (Nashville: Abingdon Press, 1996), 158.

37. Cf. Num. 5:6–7; Lev. 6:1–7; Exod. 10:16; Ps. 32:5; 51:4.

38. See my extended analysis of forgiveness in *Beyond Retribution*, 72–77, 263–84.

39. So Bailey, *Poet and Peasant*, 177–80; Brad H. Young, *Jesus the Jewish Theologian* (Peabody, Mass.: Hendrickson, 1995), 150; and Derrett, *Law*, 110–16. Cf. Forbes, "Repentance," 219; and Holgate, *Prodigality*, 193–97.

40. Darrell L. Bock, *Luke* Baker Exegetical Commentary of the New Testament (Grand Rapids: Baker, 1997), vol. 2, 1313.

41. Nigel Turner notes that ὡς in biblical Greek may serve, as here, to soften a statement, meaning "as it were," "approximately," "perhaps" N.A. Turner, *A Grammar of New Testament Greek* (Edinburgh: T. & T. Clark, 1965), vol. 3, 320.

42. We are not told how long the younger son had been gone from home, but the older brother's complaint about having worked as a slave for "all these years" (v. 29) probably

refers to the period since the division of the inheritance in v. 12, as this would underscore his virtuousness of continuing to work like a slave even though he was now the legal proprietor of the estate (v. 31). The prodigal clearly saw his own departure as permanent. His selling up lock, stock and barrel indicated that he had no intention of ever returning, so that for all intents and purposes his father considered him as good as dead (vv. 24, 32).

43. One older commentator who points this out is A. B. Bruce, "The Synoptic Gospels," in *The Expositor's Greek Testament* (London: Hodder & Stoughton, 1903), 581. Virtually all modern exegetes do likewise.

44. So Bailey, *Poet and Peasant*, 181–82; Bailey, *Jacob the Prodigal*, 168; and Rohrbaugh, "Dysfunctional," 156–57.

45. See the wonderfully insightful essay by Aristotle Papanikolaou, in which he traces the moral, emotional, and therapeutic power of the act of confession, in addition to its juridical significance; "Liberating Eros: Confession and Desire," *Journal of the Society of Christian Ethics* 26, no. 1 (2006): 115–36.

46. The boy's actual confession in v. 21 is an abbreviation of the one he rehearses ahead of time in v. 18, and most commentators suggest that the father interrupted his son's apology before he had tome to complete it, so eager was he to forgive. Some commentators think the boy revised his confession once he experienced his father's reception, realizing that his intended offer to serve as a hired hand was superfluous and would do nothing to heal the broken relationship; Bailey, *Poet and Peasant*, 183–84; Forbes, "Repentance," 220; Via, *Parables*, 173–74. In either case, the truncated confession should not be taken to minimize the importance of the act of confession itself. Several good manuscripts repeat the confession of v. 18 in full in v. 21, and although current critical editions of the New Testament prefer the shorter reading, the longer reading might well be original.

47. See James L. Resseguie, *Spiritual Landscape: Images of the Spiritual Life in the Gospel of Luke* (Peabody, Mass.: Hendrickson, 2004), 89–100.

48. On the meaning of these categories, see Malina, *New Testament World*, 28–62; Halvor Moxnes, "Honor and Shame," in *The Social Sciences and New Testament Interpretation*, ed. Richard Rohrbaugh (Peabody, Mass.: Hendrickson, 1996), 19–40.

49. Howard Zehr, "Journey to Belonging," in *Restorative Justice: Theoretical Foundations*, ed. Elmar Weitekamp and Hans-Jürgen Kerner (Cullompton, U.K.: Wilan, 2002), 21–31; the quotation is on 27. The seminal book on the role of shame in criminal justice is John Braithwaite, *Crime, Shame and Reintegration* (Cambridge: Cambridge University Press, 1989).

50. Holgate, *Prodigality*, 218.

51. Dan Cahill, "Victimisation," *Movement for Alternatives to Prison* 98 (October 2006): 2.

52. Not that the father is portrayed as a divine figure in any direct sense; he is an earthly father who is clearly differentiated from God within the plot itself (vv. 18, 21). But he is an earthly father whose feelings and actions are so consistent with those of God that, as Jeremias puts it, "in his love he is an image of God." The parable describes with "touching simplicity what God is like, his goodness, his grace, his boundless mercy, his abounding love," *Parables*, 128, 131; so also Fitzmyer, *Luke*, 1085; Green, *Luke*, 579; Bailey, *Poet and Peasant*, 159. From a feminist perspective, Schotroff flatly denies that the actions of the father should be seen as an illustration of the love of God. "The father is a patriarch and is to be distinguished from God," *Parables*, 149. Cf. Beavis, "Making up Stories," 98–122. More helpful is Bailey's suggestion that Jesus does not use a standard Oriental patriarch as a model for God, but only this father insofar as he breaks "all the bounds of Middle Eastern patriarchy, . . . Jesus elevates the figure of father beyond its human limitations as he reshapes it into his primary metaphor for God." Bailey, *Jacob the Prodigal*, 101, 138–47; so, too, Donahue, *Gospel in Parable*, 160–62.

53. Plummer, *Luke*, 378 (emphasis added); also Holgate, *Prodigality*, 185.

54. I am indebted to Ramsey for noting this parallel, in "Plots, Gaps," 36–37.

55. Interestingly deviance labeling seems to be less common in small-scale social units than in large scale, complex societies. The interdependence and relative equality of people in smaller settings evidently inhibits the labeling and exclusion of individuals as deviants, unless their behavior threatens the very integrity of the community, as might be the situation in the parable. It also encourages a readiness to de-label people after they conform. See Douglas Raybeck, "Anthropology and Labeling Theory: A Constructive Critique," *Ethos* 16, no. 4 (1988): 371–97.

56. Rohrbaugh, "Dysfunctional," 161. The extent to which the labeling of criminals encourages further offending is debated in the literature, cf. Charles Wellford "Labelling Theory and Criminology: An Assessment," *Social Problems* 22, no. 3 (1975): 332–45.

57. Use of the verb δεῖ, "it is necessary," is one of Luke's favorite ways of speaking of God's will, e.g., 2:49; 4:43; 9:22; 11:42; 15:7, 10.

58. Holgate, *Prodigality*, 167. Mary Anne Tolbert is therefore quite wrong when she asserts that "neither son has been presented as having fundamentally changed his nature." Mary Anne Tolbert, "The Prodigal Son: An Essay in Literary Criticism from a Psychoanalytic Perspective," *Semeia* 9 (1977): 1–20; the quotation is on 16.

Women Scholars in Christian Ethics: The Impact and Value of Family Care

Julie Hanlon Rubio, Barbara Hilkert Andolsen, Rebecca Todd Peters, and Cheryl Kirk-Duggan

THE CREATION OF FAMILY-FRIENDLY DEPARTMENTS IS A JUSTICE ISSUE affecting primary caregivers and their dependents as well as the academic profession as a whole. This essay asks: "How do conflicts between work and family care affect the profession, the Society of Christian Ethics, and ultimately scholarship in ethics?"

Currently, women occupy a more significant space in the Society of Christian Ethics (SCE) than they have ever occupied. A glance at the 2007 program for the annual meeting reveals that women are active participants in the intellectual work of the society. Though the SCE's current president and executive director are male, the editors of the *Journal of the Society of Christian Ethics*, the vice president, and two-thirds of the board members are female. Why, one might ask, would the Women's Caucus chose this year to sponsor a panel on scholars with dependents and raise questions about the lagging presence of women in the field of Christian Ethics?

In this essay, we offer a four-part response to this question. First, we present Julie Hanlon Rubio's demographic research on women's participation in the SCE over the last forty-eight years. Second, we contextualize these specific findings with Rebecca Todd Peters's analysis of how the demands of parenting affect women's success in academia and Barbara Hilkert Andolsen's' research on the similar demands of elder care. Having established the problem, we present Andolsen's argument that norms of justice and care obligate scholars to accommodate caregivers in the academy and Cheryl Kirk-Duggan's call for hospitality to transform academic culture. We conclude with proposed policy and cultural changes as well as some cautionary notes.

We argue in the essay that though the presence of women in the field of Christian Ethics has increased markedly from years past, the absence of women is striking and clearly linked to responsibility for their dependents. Thus, if the SCE truly desires more gender parity, it must press its home institutions to accommodate scholars who engage in family care.[1]

Women in the Society of Christian Ethics

In the SCE Archives, housed in the University of Syracuse library, old member-ship lists reveal both the SCE's male-dominated history and its gradual prog-ress toward parity. These lists show that in 1965, five years after the SCE was formed, only 4 of 218 members (2 percent) were women.[2] In 1975, 5 percent were women, and by 1985, women made up 11 percent of the SCE. After this time, membership lists were kept on computer and new members were simply added to the list, so the rosters indicative of each year's membership are un-available. However, the 2005 list of just over 1,000 members includes 25 per-cent women members. Progress is undeniable, yet membership totals of women and men are still far from the more desirable parity to which gender equity ef-forts may lead.

The situation for women in ethics is somewhat worse than the situation for women in academia as a whole. In 1975 women made up 22.5 percent of full-time faculty; in 2001 their presence had increased to 36 percent. Even today, women disproportionately hold lecturer, instructor, and other non-tenure-track positions. Only 26 percent of tenured professors are women, and only 19 percent of tenured professors at doctoral institutions are women.[3] It is not clear that this situation will improve over time, as in the field of theology and religion, while the number of women with PhDs has increased (to 38 per-cent in 1996), the number of women hired for tenure-track positions has actu-ally declined.[4]

This fall, Rubio completed a study of current women members of the SCE that adds flesh to these numbers. Over 200 short questionnaires were sent to all current women members and nearly 100 were returned. These surveys included a remarkable diversity of women, many of whom have elected not to follow the traditional path of the tenure track. Thirty percent hold adjunct, research, or other positions that allow them greater flexibility than the traditional full-time track. Though women make up nearly half of those pursuing doctorates in the field, a much lower percentage hold tenure-track positions and membership in academic societies. The situation in the SCE is thus typical of academia as a whole, in that women constitute a growing minority and are overrepresented in nontraditional career tracks.

Women's growing membership in the SCE has been accompanied by in-creasing participation at the annual meetings.[5] The sixth annual meeting of the SCE in 1965 included no presentations by women. By 1975, one woman (Mar-garet Farley) had made it onto the program. Like membership rosters, pro-grams of annual meetings from the 1980s and 1990s are absent from the ar-chives, so progress cannot be measured.[6] However, in 2005, the program had changed significantly. Of approximately one hundred presentations, one-third were given by women.[7]

Women's participation in the governance of the SCE has also increased over time. Several women have served the SCE as president, and many more have served on the board and journal. Still, the uniqueness of the current situation (a board and journal dominated by women) should be placed in the context of the history of the SCE, in which male domination has been the norm. The great increases in participation can be celebrated even as members recognize that forty-eight years after the founding of the SCE, women only constitute approximately one-fourth of the membership and one-third of active participants.

Scholarship is yet another measure of women's participation in the field of Christian ethics. Rubio studied the authors of articles published in the *Journal of the Society of Christian Ethics* (formerly the *Annual of the Society of Christian Ethics*) from 1975 to the present.[8] In the early years, counting the numbers of women authors was an easy task. In reviewing issues of the journal in the 1970s and 1980s, articles by women averaged about 15 percent of the total (one or two per issue). In the 1990s, this picture changed significantly, as women came to write 25 percent of the articles in the journal; and by the 2000s, this increased to about 33 percent. In comparison, the trajectory for the *Journal of Religious Ethics* is a little less progressive, as women wrote 18 percent of articles in the 1990s and 30 percent in the 2000s. These figures can be somewhat misleading; as for the *Journal of Religious Ethics*, particular themes may call forth more participation by women, yet it is still not unusual for an issue to contain one or two articles by women and eight or ten by men.[9] Also, 2004 seems to have been the high year for women authors in both journals, which published 47 percent of articles by women, but percentages have fallen since then to about 25 percent for both in 2006. It is not clear that the inclusion of women will continue to grow at the pace it did in the 1990s and early 2000s.

When one reviews the history of women's absence and women's presence in the SCE, questions inevitably arise about the reasons for progress and its limits. Though factors such as cultural expectations for women and sexism in academia contributed to the problem, we contend that family care is a key factor limiting women's involvement from the 1960s until the present.

In the 1960s and 1970s, women were just beginning to be admitted to the best colleges and graduate programs, second-wave feminism was just starting to affect women's choices about career paths, and churches were in the early stages of opening their doors to women's participation at various levels. It is not surprising that few women attended SCE meetings or published in academic journals. Those who did were clearly path blazers. A total of 46 percent of those in Rubio's study were born in the 1930s, 1940s, or 1950s. Richard McCormick commented in 1989 that the field had changed because it was then "common to see such fine scholars as "[Leslie] Griffin, [Lisa] Cahill, [Carol] Tauer, Anne Patrick, Sidney Callahan, Christine Gudorf, Margaret Farley, Judith Dwyer, Eileen Flynn, Diane Bader, Corrine Bayley, Barbara Andolsen, Elizabeth

McMillan—to mention but a few."[10] We would add Carol Robb and Beverly Harrison to McCormick's list. Clearly, their scholarship reshaped ethical discussions, in part because they were more aware of issues affecting women's lives.

However, it is important to note that about half these women (many more than in the general population) did not have children.[11] Although they certainly faced challenges related to gender, and may have engaged in more care of sick and elder relatives than their male colleagues, they did not have to contend with the demands of combining academia with childbearing and childrearing. The success of those who did choose to have children is all the more impressive because it occurred in an era when women who had children could count on far less support from their male partners or departments. Some had spouses who were unusually supportive for the times, while others carried the lion's share of housework and child care while contending with demands of institutions that assumed their employees were not primary caregivers. These women sacrificed much more of their personal lives than did most of their male colleagues to be both good scholars and good parents. Clearly, however, not many women were able to carry off such amazing balancing acts.

The next generation of women born in the 1960s and 1970s grew up knowing far fewer limits, believing they could have it all. They make up more than half of the women in the SCE. Still, about half the women in this group do not have children, although we can infer that a larger percentage will have children, because many are still of childbearing age. Among those who are mothers, the average number of children is a little higher than their professional peers of the earlier generation, suggesting that women are now somewhat freer to have the number of children they desire while working at an academic career. However, given the continuing gender disparity, we must ask why more women with children do not participate in the SCE in 2007.

Although women who chose not to have children will no doubt continue to make important contributions to the SCE, if the number of women in the field of Christian ethics is going to increase significantly, women who do want children (the majority of women) will have to enter the field and succeed in it. Moreover, because most of these women will have far more responsibility for home and children than most men in the field have ever had, the profession will need to abandon the paradigm of the ideal worker and reenvision the life of the professor.[12]

Women, Parenting, and Academia

Women's absence from the SCE is not simply a matter of choice. Although women themselves often use the language of choice to explain their decisions to put family above career, choice does not capture the whole reality of the situation. The legal scholar Joan Williams's trenchant analysis of women's so-called choices in the workplace is instructive. She argues that women choose to leave professions that do not accommodate them. This is not a choice against work but against work and home as currently structured to accommodate ideal workers and full-time caregivers. She writes:

> "It just wasn't working"—this formulation encodes as choice an economy with work schedules and career tracks that assume one adult in charge of caregiving and one ideal worker, men's felt entitlement to work "success," and a sense that children need close parental attention. It encodes a *habitus* structured by domesticity, with default modes that set up powerful force fields pulling women back toward traditional gender roles. Women's sense of relief when they give up trying to perform as ideal workers reflects the fact that they no longer have to fight the stiff headwinds from domesticity: they can go with the flow of domesticity's ideal worker/marginalized care-giver patterning.[13]

Women who leave academia or abandon its more rigorous tracks give up a seemingly losing battle, acknowledging that the ideal worker model for professors assumes unlimited availability and no spillover between work and home. Those who stay pay the price of straddling two worlds that are still not structured to account for their reality.

However, the old paradigms are beginning to shift. The expectations of many younger faculty members are changing. More female academics have or expect to have children *and* be productive teachers and scholars. Likewise, professional men and women are sharing household responsibilities more equally than before, including the responsibilities of child care. With an increase in childbearing among female faculty and in child care responsibilities among both female and male academics, a transformation of the structure of higher education that recognizes and allows for the complex needs of faculty in the twenty-first century is necessary.

Though many younger male faculty are more actively involved in parenting than were their older colleagues, significant gender bias still exists in higher education today. Despite a sharp rise in women's participation in graduate education nationwide and larger numbers of women faculty than ever before, the timing and presence of babies in the household remains a significant factor in the male/female achievement gap within the academy. A recent study found that twelve to fourteen years after receiving a terminal degree, 62 percent of tenured women in the humanities and social sciences did not have children compared with 39 percent of men in the academy[14] and 8.7 percent of women nationwide.[15] Even more significant were the tenure statistics. Women who have babies within five years of earning a PhD are nearly 30 percent less likely than women without babies to get a tenure-track job.[16] Of the women who did get tenure-track jobs, only 56 percent with early babies earned tenure within fourteen years of receiving the PhD; but of men who had early babies, 77 percent earned tenure—a higher percentage than the men who never had babies (71 percent).[17]

Another study examined the culture of colleges and universities in relation to faculty with families. They identified something they labeled "daddy privilege," which they defined as "circumstances wherein men are lauded for the intrusion of family on work commitments, while women would experience bias against caregiving for similar intrusions."[18] Even within the academy, women with children face more impediments toward success than their male or childless peers. For instance, in 1999, 52 percent of the spouses of married male full professors did not work full time, compared with 9 percent of the spouses of their female colleagues.[19] In a 2004 study, a large majority of academic women described themselves as primarily responsible for both child care and home care.[20] Women's more intensive family care duties can be correlated with their difficulty in achieving tenure, advancing to the rank of full professor, and holding powerful administrative positions.[21]

Although no one study yet details exactly why this is the case, there are a number of factors that women of childbearing years face that are unique to women. In considering the professorate in the twenty-first century and how it needs to be transformed, all of them are significant. The average age of receipt of the PhD is thirty-three years.[22] By this age, women are already nearing the end of their most healthy reproductive years; by age thirty-five, pregnant women are labeled by the medical establishment as AMA, Advanced Maternal Age. Many academic women delay childbearing until after graduate school or even until after they have achieved tenure.[23] At age thirty-five, the risk of infertility, fetal anomalies, and stillbirth all increase significantly. One can imagine the difficulties of trying to teach a normal course load, attend meetings, chair committees, and write articles while trying unsuccessfully to get pregnant, an experience that can last several years, or after finding out that an ultrasound has just revealed fetal anomalies. Moreover, 30 percent of women over thirty-five experience a miscarriage,[24] 8 percent of the population on the pill and 15 percent using condoms experience a failure of birth control and have to contend with an unplanned pregnancy,[25] and 50 percent of women who experience unplanned pregnancy decide to have an abortion.[26]

Each of these situations is stressful, emotionally difficult, and potentially traumatic for the women involved and must be lived out in a culture of high performance and excellence that is already tainted by negative stereotypes of women as overly emotional or as more interested in children than their careers. Sexually active heterosexual women of childbearing age face an array of potential hazards and challenges that are unique to their biological beings. Many adoptive parents face equally challenging situations as they wait expectantly for a telephone call that might require them to fly across country at a moment's notice to pick up a newborn baby. Likewise, dealing with miscarriages, stillbirths, birth defects, or serious illness in an infant in an atmosphere of publish or perish is extraordinarily difficult. Most institutions are not equipped to handle emergencies of these kinds.

A major problem with the tenure-track system for women who wish to have children is that graduate school and the pretenure years coincide with the peak reproductive and early childhood years. Some women who are very committed scholars and teachers may desire part-time or job-sharing tenure-track positions early in their career so that they can spend time with their children and still pursue an academic career. A recent article in the *Chronicle of Higher Education* promoted the idea of encouraging women to have children in graduate school rather than wait until they are on the tenure track.[27] However, studies of women in academic life show that women are more likely to drop out of graduate school, either because they are already in the midst of childbearing and cannot complete their work or because they see the compromises the future would require them to make and choose another field.[28] Among those who graduate, many are less competitive, because they have less time for research and conferences due to family responsibilities.[29] A large number end up as adjunct professors, with or without terminal degrees.[30] At the interview stage for tenure-track positions, colleges receive significantly fewer applications from females than males and subsequently hire more men than women.[31] This research begins to explain why there are fewer women in the higher echelons of academia. Caring for children makes women's progress toward tenure a difficult proposition.

Elder Care and the Professorate

Child care is only the beginning of issues concerning care of dependents that affect both women and men in academia. At any stage in one's academic career, one could find oneself responsible for primary caregiving for a disabled spouse or family member, such as an adult sibling or elder parent(s). Demographic information about North America indicates that in the near future—for the first time in human history—society will have more members over sixty-five years of age than under eighteen. The fastest-growing demographic group in both Canada and the United States is the "old-old," people who are eighty years of age and above.

We need to give special attention to issues of elder care, particularly because of the graying of the academic workforce. Especially since mandatory retirement policies became illegal in United States, a growing number of university professors chose to work past age sixty-five and even throughout their seventies.

Based upon 2003 data, more than one-third of all faculty teaching philosophy and religion in the United States are fifty-five or older. A total of 31.5 percent of women who are teaching philosophy and religion are fifty-five and older.[32]

When a large portion of those teaching religion and philosophy in universities and colleges are over age fifty-five, it is easy to predict that a significant number of faculty members will have major responsibilities for the care of frail elderly parents, other relatives, or spouses and life partners. In a survey for the Faculty of Arts and Sciences at the University of Toronto, for example, 6 percent of female faculty and 5 percent of male faculty reported caring for an adult dependent. In an average week, the women estimated spending an average of 9.6 hours in caring labor; and men estimated 2.9 hours.[33] A survey at Pennsylvania State University found that almost 14 percent of faculty were spending at least 3 hours a week assisting a disabled or elderly relative.[34] Both those surveys were snapshots indicating the percentage of faculty taking care of a dependent adult when the survey data were collected. However, over a somewhat longer period, a greater portion of workers between thirty-five and sixty-four, up to one in five of these employees, will be caring for a disabled or elderly relative.[35]

Much of the talk about policies that sustain caretaking by faculty members focuses on child care. Elder care responsibilities involve distinctive challenges. The onset of a need for elder care may be more unpredictable. Jim's wife has a heart attack or stroke. Mary's mother has to be hospitalized for a broken hip. She has been the chief caretaker for Mary's father, who is suffering from dementia, so his caretaking needs are suddenly disrupted as well. The caring needs for frail elders may be quite varied. In contrast, child care responsibilities may be more predictable in advance, unless the child has serious health problems or other disabling conditions. Like child care, for some caregivers, elder care is a long-term project. Caregiving responsibilities for an elderly person can extend for six years or more.

According to research done in 1999, women were two-thirds of the primary caregivers for the frail elderly. However, men were somewhat more likely to be primary caregivers than they had been in the past.[36] Some women who are doing substantial caregiving for another adult reduce their work hours to part time or quit altogether. Though these findings describe gender and elder caregiving generally, this social picture suggests that female colleagues may disappear from our institutions—and from our circle of scholars at annual meetings—because of the ongoing demands of elder care. Male colleagues who have substantial responsibilities for elderly spouses and partners or parents may face similar difficulties in remaining active in the profession.

General information about communities of color suggests that faculty members of color may face particularly heavy family burdens. A study by the Kaiser Foundation showed that a higher percentage of African Americans and Hispanics were helping their parents with medical and financial decisions when compared with white, non-Hispanic caregivers. African Americans and Hispanics also voiced more concern about the quality of services available to their elders, which makes caregiving more fraught with anxiety. The Kaiser study reported: "A greater share of African Americans (47 percent) and Latinos (57 percent) than whites (34 percent) are concerned about juggling caregiving with other responsibilities."[37] In other research, caregivers who were persons of color reported less support from their institutions for caregiving of their own family members. They were more likely to take a leave of absence from work for caregiving reasons.[38]

Elder care may be less discussed because we imagine incorrectly that only tenured faculty face elder care responsibilities. In response, these thought-provoking comments were offered by researchers from Pennsylvania State University:

> It might seem that the tenure system would make it easy for tenured faculty to take care of aging parents. The faculty member could simply come to work periodically to meet teaching and committee responsibilities but would otherwise concentrate on elder care. Even if this situation occurred, it is not ideal from the perspective of either the institution or the individual. For the individual, the entire brunt of elder care is born by reductions in research, a phenomenon with severe long-term consequences for academics (even if the loss of job security is not one). For the institution, a surreptitious reduction in workload is involved. Both parties could be better served by a policy motivating the faculty member to make such commitments explicit in order to better meet family needs and the needs of the institution.[39]

It should be noted that meeting the dependent care needs of faculty requires more than good policies. A 2005 study by the Center for the Education of Women at the University of Michigan indicates that the greatest array of formal, family-friendly policies are offered at better-funded, large, research institutions, but the research universities are less likely to hire women faculty in the first place.[40] Moreover, research universities may also be the types of institutions in which women may feel the strongest informal pressure not to make use of the policies that exist, lest they appear inadequately committed to their academic careers. Thus, the creation of an academic culture supportive of family-friendly polices remains a crucial aspect of the solution.

Professing an Ethic of Care and Justice

In the preceding sections, we have shown that gender parity has not yet been achieved in the SCE at least in part due to women's family care responsibilities, discussed the problems academic parents face, and sketched the difficulties of academics providing elder care. Clearly, some sort of restructuring of the profession is desirable, but given the resource limitations of most academic institutions, anyone advocating for an increase in family care policies requiring additional resources must make an ethical argument for the desirability of such policies. We contend here that family care policies should be supported by those committed to care and justice.

A key characteristic that differentiates professional work from other types of labor is that professionals have chosen a kind of work that promotes core values of society. Lawyers, as officers of the court, serve justice. Medical professionals promote community health. University professors share a dedication to truth and knowledge. Admittedly, we have very different epistemological understandings about the ways in which human beings have access to truth and about the degree of certainty that appropriately attaches to their knowledge claims. Nonetheless, we are making the assumption that scholars who profess to teach religious ethics struggle together with students to discover certain truths about the right and the good.

We here stress two virtues that reveal key aspects of the good and the right: care and justice. We assume that we professors of religious ethics agree upon the need for and goodness of caring behavior among human beings. By caring behavior, we mean other-regarding behavior that strives to advance the well-being of another motivated by an engaged concern for the good of the other. We recognize that caring work is essential for the survival and well-being of human beings as soon as we forthrightly acknowledge that dependency is an integral part of finite human existence. We come into existence as fragile babes, we are all always at risk of serious illness or disability, and most of us will become frail at some point during the aging and/or dying process. All of us will at some times during our lives need to be cared for. Thus caring labor is an indispensable feature of social life.

David Hollenbach once said that "the good of persons exists 'between' persons in the relations that make them who they are."[41] One crucial relationship that characterizes who we are as relational beings is the relationship of caring. Nel Noddings made an important point when she insisted that a taproot of our capacity to be moral and of our motivation to do the right thing is the memory of being cared for and a desire to remain in caring relationships. We experience being cared for as a fundamentally good state and realize that, to remain in caring relationships, we must offer care as well as receive it.[42] However, whenever we talk about care within intimate relationships, we should be cautious about a temptation to romanticize them. We need never to forget that some persons are brutalized and terrorized by those who are most responsible for their care. Nonetheless, we may appeal to what is good in experiences of loving care to envision communities that intentionally make ample room for caring, including the time, effort, and mindfulness it takes to do caring work.

If we ought to support caring because it is a significant contribution to the common good, we can also do so because caring functions to enrich our discipline, our departments, and our programs. Those involved in the experience of caring can infuse our field with critical perspectives and insights that have heretofore been excluded. For instance, parenting is a foundational social act of human society. Though not everyone will become a parent, the act of being parented—of being loved, socialized, and cared for (or not)—is our first experience of the interconnectedness and interdependence of life. It is this experience of parental love and affection as altruistic and selfless love that we use to teach children about the love of God. It is our first human connection, an utter dependence that can function to remind us all of our own indebtedness to those who have cared for us, taught us, and loved us into being. It is an ever-present reminder that we are never entirely self-made. Similarly, caring for elders evidences respect for those who came before us and places us in touch with our own mortality. Caring for those who are sick or disabled honors obligations of fidelity and allows us to be in contact with the frailty of the human condition. All caring work shapes those who do it in profound ways and has the potential to shape scholarship in the field of Christian ethics.[43]

This kind of caring work has always been done by families, yet providing it is becoming more problematic. As result of economic and social changes in North America over more than the past half century, society is plagued by the tensions created at the interface between pubic and private worlds. Individual workers are expected to give their entire attention and energy to the duties of their jobs in the public realm, while frail dependents require attentive, consistent care in the private realm. In the mid–twentieth century, many economically privileged families could manage by relying on the caring activities of full-time homemakers. Though this arrangement is no longer possible or desirable, Christine Firer Hinze, makes an often-voiced feminist critique when she describes "the contradiction involved in moving domestic caregivers into the ideal-worker arena without either reformulating the relations between household and public economy, or reinvesting energy and attention into the household economy through other means (such as greater presence and participation by men)."[44] Hinze deplores society's failure to recognize the need for major institutional change in order to sustain both satisfying public roles for adults and considerate caregiving for those dependents who need it.

Refusing to acknowledge the realities of caregiving contributes to the development of what the authors of a recent *Harvard Business Review* article call "extreme jobs." The article defines an extreme job as one where the professional or manager works sixty hours or more per week and faces high performance demands.[45] Gloria Albrecht has described time pressures, such as mandatory overtime, experienced by less well-paid workers, too.[46] The danger is that extreme jobs may become the new social norm, making it even harder for those with significant responsibilities for dependent care to be seen as good workers.

Refusing to restructure social institutions, including higher education, in a way that acknowledges and facilitates participants' caregiving responsibilities serves the interests of those who benefit from the present uneven distribution of the burdens associated with caring labor. As Joan Tronto says, "by not noticing how pervasive and central care is to human life," those who are relieved disproportionately of the burdens of caring work, but who benefit from care as a widespread activity, can continue to take unfair advantage of caregivers.[47] This benefit/burden is the point at which the virtue of justice becomes relevant. Justice prods us to examine our treatment of other human beings. Justice demands that we critically examine the distribution of social benefits and burdens, with a special concern for situations where heavy burdens continue to be borne by members of socially disadvantaged groups. Given the long history of the social subordination of women, justice leads us to repudiate present patterns of caregiving work that leave women disadvantaged in their ability to participate fully in economic and civic life.

Feminist ethical thought has certainly made plain over the past twenty-five or more years that a primary cause of injustice toward women is society's refusal to refashion those institutions that severely disadvantage women by assigning to women the responsibilities and burdens of caregiving while maintaining that the good worker, including the good faculty member, is responsible for devoting all of his or her attentions over a full work week to the demands of the job. Since 1977, the majority of adult women, including women with children under eighteen, have moved into the labor force.[48] However, in the United States, society has refused to engage in the social transformation necessary for gender parity. Instead, individuals and families are left coping as best they can amid the broken remnants of the old male breadwinner / female homemaker system.

As professional ethicists, our only chance to preserve both care and justice (understood as mandating gender equity) is to advocate for institutional policies and practices that make possible the humane integration of caregiving labor and productive professional work. Simultaneously, our profession must challenge its male members to assume an equitable share of caring labor, so that women will have truly equal opportunities to make their full contribution to the profession. Ultimately, enabling academics to engage in a wide variety of caring activities will benefit both society and the academy.

Hospitality in the Academy

Preserving justice and care will require a restructuring of the academic workplace. Though some change must be at the policy level, we have indicated throughout this essay that much of the needed change is cultural. Academics have to learn new ways to relate to each other. We suggest that this cultural change might be understood in terms of the practice of hospitality. Christian ethicists in academic institutions are called to practice hospitality toward colleagues with family care responsibilities. Lucien J. Richard defines hospitality as a scripturally based action, vital to civilization that characterizes how we relate to and meet with strangers.[49] Hospitality, a reality central to the mission and expansion of the early church, is a practice of life and love that builds community, creates social bonds, and produces unity. Table fellowship in the New Testament embodies hospitality; when Jesus embraced the marginalized, they experienced revelation, sacrament, and God's word. Reviewing the history of hospitality in the Christian tradition, Christine Pohl shows that the "distinctive quality of Christian hospitality is that it offers a generous welcome to the 'least,' without concern for advantage or benefit to the host. Such hospitality reflects God's greater hospitality that welcomes the undeserving, provides the lonely with a home, and sets a banquet table for the hungry."[50] Christians have traditionally practiced hospitality as imitation of God's welcome. The practice of hospitality ought to shape Christian rituals, worship, preaching, spirituality, ethics, and ways of caring. In short, hospitality—the engaged welcoming of another—is a crucial dimension of Christian life and thus of the lives of Christian academics.

Hospitality as engaged welcoming is first relational; we open ourselves to care for the neighbor in our midst. M. Shawn Copeland reminds us that educators help preserve, transmit, and transform the "cultural capital of civilization."[51] Healthy community building among faculty, staff, and students can create shared accountability and shared power. Too often, academics make significant contributions to charities overseas but do not know the birth date of their next-door colleague.[52] Relationality means that there is a commitment to live civilly, respecting differences and celebrating similarities. Though there is a hope that people are able to like one another, they can be in a relationship that is responsive and minimally caring without being best friends. Hospitality as engaged welcoming is inclusive and grace filled. We honor diversity, experience others as being made in the divine image, and work to enlarge the circle of participants. For academics, this means contributing to an environment where colleagues feel comfortable letting others know about domestic stresses, asking for help when necessary, and giving and receiving support without fear of compromising their reputation.

Engaged welcoming embodies mutuality. Mutuality invites empathy.[53] We appreciate and understand another's problems and feelings by remembering or imagining being in a similar situation. It also calls for introspection and observation beyond the self to find workable solutions. This is made difficult by the prevalence of work addiction in academia.[54] Some faculty may be so burned out that they are bitter and see a request for leave as a sign of weakness or an encumbrance to the institution meeting its goals. Those feeling threatened may feel the need to launch an attack to preserve the old ways or save face.

Instead, those with more power and privilege may need to think about extending some of that privilege to others. For example, if a colleague needs time to care for a new baby, her need for leave may take priority over the need of a full professor to finish a book project. Later, the woman who was helped may find herself able to take on extra work so that her senior colleague can care for an elderly parent. Engaged welcoming honors the need to be flexible. And part of being flexible is realizing that not everyone has the same requirements for healthy living and that circumstances may arise where we may need to adjust our expectations and assumptions. Sometimes that means we may have to extend ourselves for the well-being of others. At other times, the most hospitable act for the well-being of the community and the individual may be to say "No." Working out solutions that cut across the boundaries of seniority and privilege is key if academics are serious about wanting a more diverse faculty.

Hospitality that is engaged welcoming is also just, in that it gives to each what is due. "Just hospitality" honors the total person, is sensitive to his or her needs, and rallies to meet people where they are to support them in being where they need to be. Just hospitality names the differences and does not live at the intersection of denial and delusion. Just hospitality requires us to ask difficult questions: Are some jobs too demanding? Do certain jobs need to be reenvisioned? Are junior faculty mentored and supported? Is the accrued wisdom of senior faculty appreciated? Does the institution recognize faculty accomplishments as well as the seasons in the lives of its members? How can the department implement contingencies before the onset of a crisis or need for leave? What is the work ethos of the institution? How can it be made more hospitable?

Just hospitality knows that sometimes difficult decisions need to be made; it exposes oppressions and seeks balanced solutions to problems. Just hospitality emerges out of discernment and attempts to afford all faculty the resources for their own and their families' health and well-being. Hospitality that is just, mutual, and relational has the potential to shape an academic culture that is truly accepting of scholars engaged in family care.

Work/Life Balance Policies: Best Practices

The Women's Caucus of the SCE is proposing that this organization advocate policies, both for the SCE itself and for institutions of higher education where we work, that promote care and justice by making it easier for caregivers to combine caregiving responsibilities with their workplace obligations. In November 2001, the American Academy of University Professors adopted a "Statement of Principles on Family Responsibility" that encouraged institutions of higher education to use their principles and guidelines to construct appropriate policies and practices to support faculty with caregiving responsibilities.[55] The Women's Caucus brought its recommendations to the SCE Board in 2007, and the board voted to support the recommendations.[56] Like the caucus, we clearly hope that changes in policy and practice will make success in the field of ethics more of a possibility for women. However, we also seek family-friendly changes for the benefit of all faculty and staff. As we seek to promote good practices for achieving a work/life balance, we offer six recommendations and six cautions.

Recommendations for Family-Friendly Policies

The first recommendation: Paid family leave should be advocated. The Family and Medical Leave Act of 1993 (FMLA; Public Law 103-3, enacted February 5, 1993) states that *covered* employers, those involved with any industry or commerce activities who have in their employ fifty or more employees, for each day the business is open, during each of twenty or more workweeks in a given calendar year must provide eligible workers or employees,[57] "up to a total of 12 workweeks of unpaid leave during any 12-month period for one or more of the following reasons: the birth and care of the newborn child of the employee; for placement with the employee of a son or daughter for adoption or foster care; to care for an immediate family member (spouse, child, or parent) with a serious health condition; or to take medical leave when the employee is unable to work because of a serious health condition."[58]

Many of our institutions still do not offer adequate family leave.[59] The FMLA is part of a healthy work ethic that takes family life into consideration. The American Association of University Presses recommends that universities should offer adequate paid family leave to parents of new birth or adopted children.[60] In addition, faculty should be aware that the FMLA is now under scrutiny. Recently, the U.S. Department of Labor has been in conversation with companies about how the law has worked. Many human resource groups want the Department of Labor to limit the definitions of "serious health condition" and "intermittent leave." Labor statistics show that roughly 6.1 million workers took FMLA leave in 2005. Some argue that people are abusing the system. Advocates fear that the Department of Labor will go overboard in its attempts to deal with abuses of the law.[61] It is crucial for those who care about the participation of academics involved in family care to monitor these developments, advocate for FMLA at the federal level, and ensure that their own institutions offer adequate leave.[62]

The second recommendation: Flexibility in stopping the tenure clock should be allowed. Faculty who take advantage of family leave policies before reaching tenure should have the option of stopping the tenure clock for the leave period. If faculty members are able to continue with their research, they will not want to slow down the process of reaching possible tenure; but if their time is given to care, they should not be expected to progress in the usual way. Currently, most universities allow for this option, though many faculty still do not use it.[63] As we noted above, the employment climate needs to change at such institutions so that people are not discouraged in this way from taking advantage of this very useful option.

The third recommendation: Active service with modified duties should be considered. Some universities offer reduced teaching loads or service expectations for limited time periods for faculty with acute care responsibilities. Such policies recognize the difficulties of providing care for vulnerable family members and continuing to work full time.[64]

The fourth recommendation: High-quality care for children and elders should be sought. Though some institutions offer child care on campus, most do not and very few offer options for short-term child care or elder care.[65] The cost of full-time care is often exorbitant, and some universities offer subsidies to offset this. The diversity of institutions is such that a uniform recommendation is not possible, but universities should be aware of the problem and look to similar institutions for practices they can adopt.

The fifth recommendation: Flexible scheduling should be offered. The scheduling of meetings and classes can have a significant impact on the manageability of a faculty member's day-to-day routine. These issues are part of the larger problem of needing to develop institutional cultures that recognize that faculty members have obligations that extend beyond the institution. No institution can design policies that can accommodate each and every unforeseen circumstance relating to family care, but surely academic and professional norms that are biased against academics with heavy care responsibilities must be challenged.

The sixth recommendation: Allow reconsideration of standards for academic success. Though there is no set publishing quota for achieving tenure, traditional expectations for achieving success include a pretenure period of six to eight years, during which one is expected to publish critically valued work as evidenced by reviews, awards, prestigious publishing venues, and rising stature in the field; relocating to a more prestigious institution anywhere in the country if a fellowship or job becomes available; presenting academic work at national and international professional meetings; and contributing to one's department and institution (often meaning junior faculty members serve on multiple time-consuming committees before tenure out of fear of appearing uncollegial if they refuse). These requirements often mean that junior faculty members need to work sixty-, seventy-, and even eighty-hour weeks to achieve tenure.

Transforming the academy in ways that respond to the realities of women and men's lives may mean new and creative ways of supporting and assessing academic excellence. Research institutions may need to rethink research expectations and timelines for tenure to attract and retain excellent faculty who are interested in having both a distinguished career and a healthy family life. Non-research institutions may want to consider developing research professorships and other support systems for outstanding scholars who choose to teach in institutions that are more family friendly.

The point of transforming the academy is to recognize the patriarchal conditions of the eighteenth and nineteenth centuries, when many of current academic institutions were born. During these eras, social conditions and gender relations were quite different. Faculties were mostly male, and many of those who were married and/or had children did not expect to have the kind of relationships with partners, children, and elders that many professionals expect today. Challenging the academy to recognize, support, and reward academic excellence that is realized in a variety of ways will allow for the broader participation of women *and* men in a variety of life situations.

Concerns about Enacting Family-Friendly Policies

The first concern: Diverse contexts need to be acknowledged. The new policies that we promote should be written in a way that explicitly recognizes the plurality of settings and career stages in which caregiving demands arise. Policies should define eligible dependents broadly to include domestic partners, adult children or siblings who require assistance, and grandparents. Perhaps language can be found to cover what sociologists sometimes called fictive kin: persons who, though not blood relatives, have provided family support for the faculty member.

The second concern: Solidarity with other workers is imperative. Recognizing the dignity of all forms of work, we need to advocate for policies in solidarity with other workers at our home institutions, particularly less privileged workers, such as clerical workers or janitorial staff. Institutions should consider the needs of contingent faculty members for family-friendly accommodations. (According to the American Association of University Presses, in 2003, 11.7 percent of philosophy and religion faculty were not on the tenure track, and 43.3 percent were part time.)[66] Those concerned about solidarity, particularly with less advantaged fellow employees, would do well to heed the warning offered by Gloria Albrecht, who cautioned that low-income workers have a harder time taking advantage of family-friendly policies, particularly to the extent that these policies offer only time off but not financial resources.[67]

The third concern: Equitable accommodations for all should be the rule. Some institutions of higher education make allowances for faculty caregiving responsibilities on an ad hoc basis. A pattern of informal accommodations may be humane and may allow maximum flexibility in response to varying personal circumstances. However, administrators need to be very careful to avoid discrimination. Accommodations should be provided for all who need them, not just those who are well connected to informal administration and information networks. The best way to avoid discrimination is to enact formal policies.

The fourth concern: Significant secondary caregiving should be supported. Some institutions of higher education are restricting certain accommodations to faculty who confirm that they are providing a major portion of care or even that they will be the primary caregiver. This practice raises issues of fairness and may undermine secondary, but significant, caregiving activity, particularly male caregiving after childbirth.

The fifth concern: Faculty reluctance to request accommodation needs to be addressed. Several recent studies of work/life balance programs in higher education have shown that even when good policies exist, faculty are often reluctant to make use of them. Faculty members are afraid they will be perceived as not being dedicated professionals. White women and persons of color may fear, in addition, that an absence from the department while making use of these policies will further underline their "outsider" status. In one study, some faculty members were afraid that if they merely requested information about work/life balance policies, they would appear lacking in professional dedication and would suffer adverse career consequences. Women were more likely than men to report that they did not request family leave when the situation called for it.[68] To combat this problem, cultural change is crucial.

The sixth concern: It is essential that both men and women take advantage of family-friendly accommodations. An unintended consequence of the proliferation of family-friendly policies is that more women take substantial time away from the job while their children are young and never develop the range of career experiences necessary to be considered for promotion to senior positions. It is essential to create an atmosphere in which men, in proportions similar to those of women, make use of work/life balance programs. Unless and until we create gender equity, these programs may have the unintended consequence of undermining women's leadership in our profession.

Toward Gender Equity in the SCE

In conclusion, we believe that women's progress in the field of Christian ethics has been and continues to be limited by the unwillingness of some academic institutions to offer work-family balance policies that accommodate caregiving responsibilities. We have argued that all faculty members, but particularly ethicists concerned about care and justice, ought to support such policies and work toward the construction of an academic culture in which both men and women feel able to claim time for caregiving. Committing to good policy and a supportive culture will not only enable more women to succeed in the field of Christian ethics but will also make possible more balanced lives for all in our field.

Notes

1. We use "family care" in the broadest possible sense to include care for heterosexual and gay, lesbian, bisexual, and transgendered spouses or partners who are ill or disabled, birth and adopted children, and elder relatives.

2. Julie Rubio chose to use 1965, 1975, 1985, and 2005 as useful points of comparison. The SCE was formed in 1959 when a small group of male, Protestant theologians began meeting. Records are spotty for the earliest years, but begin to regularize in 1965.

3. American Academy of University Professors, "Statement of Principles on Family Responsibilities and Academic Work" (approved May 2001), www.aaup.org/statements/re01fa.

4. Margaret Miles, "From the Garden to the Academy: Blame, Battle, or a Better Way? Exploring Sex and Power in the Academy," *Journal of Feminist Studies in Religion* 17, no. 1 (Spring 2001): 103. Miles predicted women would earn about half of all PhDs in theology/religion by 2006.

5. Participation was defined as giving a single paper, a panel presentation, or a presidential address.

6. The upkeep of the archives has varied considerably over the history of the SCE. The current executive director and secretary are taking steps to regularize and maintain the contents.

7. The archives include very few proposals, so it is impossible to know if women submitted proposals in the earliest years or whether their proposals were accepted at lower rates at any point in the SCE's history. In 2007, record keeping with reference to race and gender will begin.

8. We counted single-author articles, multiple-author pieces, and longer book reviews.

9. This is also true for other journals in the field of theology, including *Horizons* and *Theological Studies*. In comparison, the *Journal of the Society of Christian Ethics* is somewhat more inclusive.

10. Richard A. McCormick, "Moral Theology 1940–1989: An Overview," in *The Historical Development of Fundamental Moral Theology in the United States*, by Charles E. Curran and Richard A. McCormick, SJ (New York: Paulist Press, 1999), 46–72.

11. The overwhelming majority of those who did have children had one or two. A recent study of 8,700 professors in the University of California system found that 38 percent of women faculty had fewer children than they desired. Reported in Robin Wilson, "How Babies Alter Careers for Academics," *Chronicle of Higher Education*, December 5, 2003, A1.

12. Our hope is that men and women will one day share the burdens and delights of family care. All recommendations for change are made in gender-neutral language. We seek to recognize and respond to the particular situation of women today while looking forward to a different future.

13. Joan Williams, *Unbending Gender: Why Family and Work Conflict and What to Do about It* (Oxford: Oxford University Press, 2000), 38.

14. Mary Ann Mason and Marc Goulden, "Do Babies Matter? The Effect of Family Formation on the Lifelong Careers of Academic Men and Women," *Academe* 88, no. 6 (November–December 2002): 4.

15. A. Chandra, G. M. Martinez, W. D. Mosher, J. C. Abma, and J. Jones, "Fertility, Family Planning, and Reproductive Health of U.S. Women: Data from the 2002 National Survey of Family Growth," *National Center for Health Statistics, Vital Health Stat* 23, no. 25 (2005): 7–8, www.cdc.gov/nchs/products/pubs/pubd/series/sr23/pre-1/sr23_25.htm.

16. Robin Wilson, "How Babies Alter Careers for Academics," *Chronicle of Higher Education*, December 5, 2003, A1.

17. Ibid.

18. Mason and Goulden, "Do Babies Matter?" 4.

19. Wilson, "How Babies Alter Careers."

20. Kelly Ward and Lisa Wolf-Wendel, "Academic Motherhood: Managing Complex Roles in Research Universities," *Review of Higher Education* 27, no. 2 (Winter 2004): 233–57.

21. See Susan Kolker Finkel and Steven G. Olswang, "Child Rearing as a Career Impediment to Women Assistant Professors," *Review of Higher Education* 19, no. 2 (Winter 1996): 123–39. In a survey of women professors at one university, 82 percent of women with children under six years of age and 59 percent of all women with children believed that the time required for childrearing was a serious impediment to their careers (p. 131). See also Florence Caffrey Bourg, "The Dual Vocation of Parenthood and Professional Theology," *Horizons* 32, no. 1 (Spring 2005): 26–52, which shows that 54 percent of parent-theologians say their research has been slowed due to children. Some studies show no direct relationship between marital status or number of children and publishing productivity. See Marcia L. Bellas and Robert K. Toutkoushian, "Faculty Time Allocations and Research Productivity: Gender, Race, and Family Effects," *Review of Higher Education* 22, no. 4 (Summer 1999): 367–90. These studies do not distinguish between men and women and fail to account for the impact on women of their lower levels of mobility and greater family responsibilities. See Laura W. Perna, "The Relationship between Family Responsibilities and Employment Status among College and University Faculty," *Journal of Higher Education* 72, no. 5 (September 2001): 582–608.

22. Wilson, "How Babies Alter Careers."

23. Nationwide, births among older women have doubled since 1970. Amy Varner, "The Consequences and Costs of Delaying Attempted Childbirth for Women Faculty," unpublished paper, http://lser.la.psu.edu/workfam/facultyfamilies.htm.

24. Ibid., 2.

25. Guttmacher Institute, "Get 'In the Know'": Questions about Pregnancy, Contraception, and Abortion," www.guttmacher.org/in-the-know/prevention.html.

26. Ibid.

27. Kathryn Lynch, "An Immodest Proposal: How to Have Children in Graduate School," *Chronicle of Higher Education*, June 7, 2002, B5.

28. According to Mason and Goulden, "Do Babies Matter?" 25, 59 percent of women with children indicated they were considering leaving academic life.

29. Ibid.

30. See Perna, "Relationship between Family Responsibilities and Employment Status," 603; Mason and Goulden, "Do Babies Matter?" 5.

31. Miles, "From the Garden to the Academy," 104. Miles cites a 1998–99 study by Richard Rosengarten for the Council of Graduate Studies in Religion, which found that institutions received about 70 percent of applications from men and 30 percent from women. Of those hired, 60 percent were male and 40 percent were female.

32. These figures were extracted from the 2004 National Study of Postsecondary Faculty—Institutional Survey Using DAS—Online Data Analysis System, http://nces.ed.gov/dasol/tables/index.asp.

33. University of Toronto, A&S Survey: Survey Results Part 2, www.artsci.utoronto.ca/main/faculty/faculty-survey/part2#FAMILY percent20CARE.

34. Robert Drago, Ann C. Crouter, Mark Wardell, and Billie S. Willits, "The Final Report to the Alfred P. Sloan Foundation for the Faculty and Families Project," Pennsylvania State University, March 14, 2001, 42; http://lsir.la.psu.edu/workfam/FFFinalReport.pdf.

35. Eliza K. Pavalko and Kathryn A. Henderson, "Combining Care Work and Paid Work: Do Workplace Policies Make a Difference?" *Research on Aging* 28 (May 2006): 360.

36. Jennifer L. Wolff and Judith D. Kasper, "Care Givers of Frail Elders: Updating a National Profile," *The Gerontologist* 46 (June 2006): 348.

37. The Family Circle / Kaiser Family Foundation, "National Survey on Health Care and Other Elder Care Issues: Summary of Findings and Chart Pack," September 2000, www.kff.org/kaiserpolls/upload/-i-Family-Circle-i-Kaiser-Family-Foundation-National-Survey-on-Health-Care-Other-Elder-Care-Issues-Summary-of-Findings.pdf.

38. Margaret B. Neal and Donna L. Wagner, "Working Caregivers: Issues, Challenges, and Opportunities for the Aging Network," www.aoa.gov/prof/aoaprog/caregiver/careprof/progguidance/background/program_issues/Fin-Neal-Wagner.pdf.

39. Drago et al., "Final Report to Sloan Foundation," 54.

40. Center for the Education of Women, *Family-Friendly Policies in Higher Education: Where Do We Stand?* (Ann Arbor, Mich.: Center for the Education of Women, 2005), 4–5; www.umich.edu/~cew/PDFs/pubs/wherestand.pdf.

41. David Hollenbach, "The Common Good Revisited," *Theological Studies* 50 (March 1989): 86.

42. Nel Noddings, *Caring: A Feminine Approach to Ethics and Moral Education* (Berkeley: University of California Press, 1984), 4–6; 79–84.

43. Examples of this work include Bonnie Miller McLemore, *Also a Mother: Work and Motherhood as Theological Dilemma* (Nashville: Abingdon, 1994); Marilyn Martone, "What Does Our Society Owe to Those Who Are Minimally Conscious?" *Journal of the Society of Christian Ethics* 26, no. 2 (Fall–Winter 2002): 201–17; and Christine E. Gudorf, "Parenting, Mutual Love, and Sacrifice," in *Women's Consciousness, Women's Conscience: A Reader in Feminist Ethics*, ed. Barbara Hilkert Andolsen, Christine E. Gudorf, and Mary D. Pellaur (Minneapolis: Winston Press, 1985).

44. Christine Firer Hinze, "U.S. Catholic Social Thought, Gender and Economic Livelihood," *Theological Studies* 66 (2005): 586.

45. Sylvia Ann Hewlett and Carolyn Buck Luce, "Extreme Jobs: The Dangerous Allure of the 70-Hour Workweek," *Harvard Business Review* 84 (December 2006): 49–59.

46. Gloria Albrecht, *Hitting Home: Feminist Ethics, Women's Work and the Betrayal of "Family Values"* (New York: Continuum International Publishing Group, 2002), 102–5.

47. Joan C. Tronto, *Moral Boundaries: A Political Argument for an Ethic of Care* (New York: Routledge, 1993), 111.

48. U.S. Bureau of Labor Statistics, *Women in the Labor Force: A Databook*, Report 985 (Washington, D.C.: U.S. Government Printing Office, 2005), table 7, 19.

49. Lucien J. Richard, "Hospitality," in *The New Westminster Dictionary of Christian Spirituality*, ed. Philip Sheldrake (Louisville: Westminster John Knox Press, 2005), 347–48.

50. Christine Pohl, *Making Room: Recovering Hospitality as a Christian Tradition* (Grand Rapids: William B. Eerdmans, 1999), 16.

51. M. Shawn Copeland, "Collegiality as a Moral and Ethical Practice," in *Practice What You Preach: Virtues, Ethics, and Power in the Lives of Pastoral Ministers and Their Congregations*, ed. James F. Keenan and Joseph Kotva Jr. (Franklin, Wis.: Sheed & Ward, 1999), 325.

52. Pohl notes that academics engage in abstract discussions of hospitality but avoid practicing it. She suggests that practice can challenge and transform in ways discussion cannot. Pohl, *Making Room*, 14.

53. Pohl speaks of the recognition and respect involved in hospitality, claiming it is based on God's image in the person, despite his or her wrongdoing or neediness. Ibid., 65.

54. Cheryl A. Kirk-Duggan, "Elegant Elitism: Professional Abuse in Higher Education as a Human Rights Issue," in *Promises to Keep: Prospects for Human Rights*, ed. Charles S. McKoy (Berkeley, Calif.: Center for Ethics and Social Policy, Graduate Theological Union, 2002), 108–22.

55. View the statement at www.aaup.org/statements/re01fam.

56. See "Enabling a Family-Friendly Institution: Creative Practices," available at www.sce.org.

57. An "eligible employee" is an employee of a covered employer who has been employed by the employer for at least twelve months, and has been employed for at least 1,250 hours of service during the twelve-month period immediately preceding the commencement of the leave, and is employed at a worksite where fifty or more employees are employed by the employer within seventy-five miles of that worksite. See Sec. 825.105(a) regarding employees who work outside the United States, www.dol.gov/esa/whd/fmla.

58. See ibid.

59. One-third of academic institutions have family-leave policies that violate federal law. See Joan C. Williams, "Are Your Parental-Leave Policies Legal?" *Chronicle of Higher Education*, February 11, 2005, C5. Julie Rubio completed a phone survey in 2003 that included seventy academic institutions. Of these, 19 percent offered one semester of paid leave, 35 percent offered a shorter period of paid leave (sometimes as little as two weeks), and 46 percent offered no paid leave. Religious and private universities where most religion faculty teach were less likely than large public institutions to offer good family leave packages.

60. See www.aaup.org/statements/re01fam.

61. Mike Drummond, "Family Leave and Minimum Wage Scrutinized," *News & Observer*, December 31, 2006.

62. Family leave is an inadequate solution on its own. Though Europeans typically have access to generous family leave, gender parity has proved elusive. In an internal study at one university in 2003, despite an allowance of twenty-six weeks of family leave, women represent only 5 percent of full professors, 14 percent of associate professors, 22 percent of senior lecturers, and 39 percent of assistant lecturers. Administrators receive far more applications from men for promotion to senior positions. This study was made available to us by a colleague who asked that the university would not be identified by name.

63. In Julie Rubio's 2003 study of seventy institutions, 94 percent offered this option. However, the problem of reluctance to use the option remains. See Cautions, 5.

64. See www.aaup.org/statements/re01fam. The University of California system is among the most generous.

65. The Foundation of the College and University Personnel Association and Families and Work Institute Study (1996) divided universities into leadership campuses (the top 25 percent) and nonleadership campuses. Among leadership campuses, 72 percent had child care centers and 16 percent had sick or evening child care. Among the others, 32 percent had child care centers and 4 percent had sick or evening child care. About half offered referrals for elder care. See Dana E. Friedman, Cathy Rimsky, and Arlene A. Johnson, *The College and University Reference Guide to Work-Family Programs* (Washington, D.C.: CUPA Foundation, 1996).

66. "Tenure Status of Instructional Faculty, by Principal Field of Teaching, Fall 2003," *Academe* 92 (November–December 2006): 46.

67. Albrecht, *Hitting Home*, 113–17.

68. Susan K. Finkel and Steven Olswang, "Childbirth, Tenure and Promotion for Women Faculty," *Review of Higher Education* 17 (1994): 259–70; Robert Drago, Carol Colbeck, Kai Dawn Stauffer, and Amy Piretti, "Bias against Caregiving," *Academe* 91 (September–October 2005): 22–25.

Practical Wisdom and the Integrity of Christian Life

William Werpehowski

THEOLOGICALLY CONSIDERED, THE VIRTUE OF PRUDENCE OR PRACTICAL wisdom disposes a moral agent to "reason rightly about things to be done" insofar as the acts of counsel, judgment, and command enable both the discernment and the embodiment of moral reality in the world created and redeemed by God in Jesus Christ. In that world, Christians live and act as both sinful and righteous, and they find their integrity and maturity in an ongoing practice of repentance, renewal, and perseverance.

Commending Dietrich Bonhoeffer's readiness "to see divine immanence in the world," Marilynne Robinson observes that this seeing "is an act of faith, not a matter to be interpreted in other than its own terms, if one grants the reasonableness of the perceiver. And Dietrich Bonhoeffer thought and believed his way to a surpassing reasonableness."[1] In this essay, I consider not so much Bonhoeffer but rather a version of what he is here taken to exemplify: the skills of moral perception, and for that matter judgment and action, as acts of Christian faith. My focus is the virtue of prudence or practical wisdom and the sort of "surpassing reasonableness" to which it disposes in the sanctified life of the justified sinner, reconciled with God in Jesus Christ. To see divine immanence in such a life, as Bonhoeffer did, is to apprehend in the world that claims us morally an unfolding of God's agency in liberating pardon, sovereign judgment, creaturely blessing, and faithful love over against the damage brought by sin, suffering, death, and hopelessness. In the course of my account and with a particular ecumenical interest, I address some traditional questions about the theological construal of human agency, "natural" and "revealed" morality, one's standing before God as at once sinful and made right, and about what on earth "growth in grace" can possibly mean.

My reflections intend to signal two projects that I think are important, among several others, for Christian ethical inquiry. The first concerns the critical theological description of the integrity or wholeness of the moral life, taken here to be a truthful self-understanding that is embodied in one's acts and relations in the

Journal of the Society of Christian Ethics, 27, 2 (2007): 55–72

world.[2] I think in this connection of H. Richard Niebuhr's battle against the polytheism and henotheism of modern existence; William Schweiker's related appeal to a more universal responsibility; Margaret Farley's suggestions about the way human commitments fragilely but really bind time; James Cone's career-long reflections on liberation, suffering, and African American Christian vision and struggle; and Stanley Hauerwas's charting connections between human actions, personal narrative unity, and the story of God made present in the practices of the church. The virtue of prudence may be invoked to account for a kind of unity, too, insofar as it is held to perfect creaturely inclinations in the realization of virtue, to direct agents substantively to the human good, and to integrate human powers and desires in accordance with moral truth.[3] Without wanting to deny the insights in each of these proposals, I imagine integrity to consist of a kind of self-renewing perseverance.

The second project is thorough and honest attention to the "prospects for rapprochement" between Christian communities in their ethics, and here, Protestant and Roman Catholic ethics in particular.[4] Nobody wants cheap grace, including the "grace" of a phony ecumenical unity. Nobody, either, should want a phony separation, fueled by stances that are patient, were we patient, of fitting revision or that confer an exclusively distinctive identity by way of oppositional definition. For my purposes the two projects are linked, as I present, experiment with, and improvise upon texts and themes in Catholic and Reformation theology and ethics with a view to examining moral integrity.

Following an examination of the fundamental features of the virtue of prudence, I address its location, as a perfection of moral agency, in the world that belongs to God in Jesus Christ. Next I consider how prudence figures in the life of one who stands before God as both justified and sinful. Finally, I offer an interpretation of Christian moral integrity and growth that highlights practices of repentance, renewal, and perseverance.

The Rudiments of Prudence

Following Thomas Aquinas, we can say that prudence or practical wisdom has to do with the right use of reason regarding things to be done.[5] As it is exercised for the sake of human actions in the pursuit of the good, it involves universal principles of practical reason but also and especially the "singulars" about which these actions are invariably concerned (*Summa theologiae* [hereafter *ST*], II-II, q. 47, a. 3). As a human virtue, prudence affords a certain rectitude to our powers of reason, but also to our appetites or desires, as these are specifically placed in their proper course in the deeds the prudent person performs. These deeds concern the ends of virtues pertaining to the will and sensible desire that are generally "appointed" by natural reason with reference to constitutively creaturely inclinations (*ST*, II-II, q. 47, a. 6).[6] Prudence "prepares the way" to these ends by "disposing the means" for attaining them, and prudence prepares the way by showing the way.

"It belongs to the ruling of prudence to decide in what manner and by what means man shall obtain the mean of reason in his deeds" (*ST*, II-II, q. 47, a. 7). An act that responds fittingly to a colleague who has aided you in your scholarship depends in part, according to the rule of justice, upon whether the benefit bespeaks a kind of professional quid pro quo, some sort of intellectual friendship, or a gift (cf. *ST*, II-II, q. 106, a. 5). Identifying the character and quality—the *manner*—of the collegial relation, insofar as one or many of these descriptions may be accurate, is a crucial feature of apprehending what the good, as a kind of justice generally considered, requires. A successful identification prompts a second reflection on the *means* to attaining that good in the particular case; and that reply as it is to be realized in action is a finding of the *mean*, which must be neither too little nor too much, neither ungrateful nor overweening toward our helpful colleague. Now it also seems that practical wisdom specifically orients or configures the ends of the moral virtues, insofar as prudence in its apprehension of what is to be done *attunes* the virtues, with these general ends, to their specific operation. Thus a scholar may come to see and desire that an earlier kind of expression of justice or gratitude to a mentor should now become less "formal" and more "friendly" with the passage of time. It appears right to say that the will and the passions may need to *appreciate* that gratitude and its point in this new and perhaps strange context.

The exercise of prudence requires a deliberative inquiry into the moral realities present in a particular situation, an asking of questions about the sorts of goods and evils to be discovered in it, and with which one as an agent is involved. Take a father's inquiry into what is going on with his teenaged son whose schoolwork is in decline. What good is the schoolwork anyway, and for whom? Is the poor performance due to boredom, a standing chronic illness, what parents cunningly call "rebellion," or intellectual capacity? How do these determinations bear on his flourishing as the young man he is? And what is at stake in dad's involvement? The work of "counsel" involves a discriminating and generous memory of relevant goods, persons, and relations; an ability to compare and contrast critically and without flights of fantasy (as with the situation of your son, "other" young people, and a father's own youth); and a welcoming desire to accept the viewpoints of others. Counsel goes wrong in stubborn refusals and premature conclusions that betray failures of insight and misplaced desire (*ST*, II-II, q. 47, a. 8; II-II, q. 49, a. 1-3; II-II, q. 53, a. 3).

The questions comprising reason's discovery of the realities *in* the situation anticipate and prepare for new questions about the about the moral truth *of* the situation. Ideally having brought "to bear upon a situation the greatest number of genuinely pertinent concerns and genuinely relevant considerations commensurate with the importance of the deliberative context," a prudent person *deliberates* for the sake of rendering a *judgment* about what is to be done to accomplish the good in the situation at hand.[7] Wise judgment intends an adequate appreciation of the order of goods and the morally salient characteristics that are present in the particular case. Hence we may speak of situational *discernment.*[8] In consideration of alternative "readings" of the situation, one comes to understand and clearly perceive how the highly general ends of the moral virtues contributing to human flourishing are specifically, substantively, and objectively embodied. One judges appropriately to act for those ends, accordingly. "Situational appreciation" takes a keen view to specific circumstances, and it includes a cautious estimate of the harm one may face in responding to them (*ST*, II-II, q. 49, a. 7-8). It includes reliance on moral rules that may have presumptive or even absolute normative force in securing human well-being and the character of a good human life; but for the prudent person moral experience seems more a matter of the world pressing in on the rules, *making the latter obey reality* through human action, rather than the other way around. Thus prudence disposes to judgments that adapt and refine those rules as they might better fit and reflect the impress of the world God has made and the goods afforded us, and this includes the "world" and the "good" of the agent oneself.[9]

Inquiry, deliberation, and judgment reach forward to affect what Aquinas calls "command," which has to do with decisively generating action (*ST*, II-II, q. 47, a. 8). It is also true to say that command reaches back to affect these other activities considered as an ongoing affair. The embodied, interdependent, and interacting life of the human agent includes engagement with the world in action that may be wise. We have here to do with singulars, and these become present to us by way of our own personal and sensual involvement. Bonhoeffer's interrogation at the hands of the Nazis may understandably be viewed as a source of the insight that there is a difference between the truthful word in the reality of the world that God has entered in Jesus Christ, and a cynical frankness that pretends to be executing the judgment of God.[10] James Gustafson's famous example of his colleague—a "moral virtuoso" capable of decisive and supple response on behalf of an impaired and exploited young soldier—also indicates the challenges of *discerning action within the situation* as distinct from the process and moment of deliberative and judging discernment about the moral truth *of* the situation.[11] In light of the lessons of enacted action, inquiries may be expanded, judgment may be enriched, and decision about what is to be done may become more surely watchful about what our actions *do* at the same time as our affections become better oriented to the reality in which human ends are pursued.

Prudence, in the act of command, reaches back to inform and to instruct our historical agency. In its "watchfulness" or "solicitousness," it also reaches forward in its attention to future contingencies, to what parties to a situation would be going through, and crafts acts in response to their implications and consequences. Now we ought also to say that wise action *reaches into* the heart of the human agent. It rightly *orders* the "singular" that is the human subject to its active self-disposal and self-relation in the world. Reason and desire are constituted rightly thereby to express an individual's embodied life history in its response to the truth of things. And in this self-expression a human subject would risk and venture to take part in that truth, and just so in the forms of divine love that are immanent in the world. Prudence includes "clear-sightedness" not just about the situation at hand but also and rather about oneself in the situation at hand, in which one's action is decisively one's own, in which "what is on offer is a true expression of who I am, a real continuation of the life-story which is myself." One finally discerns, decides, and acts for the good on one's own because *"nobody else is my body*, and it is only by my bodily presence that the concrete particularity of my action can be grasped and judged."[12]

The matter of how properly to describe and account for moral agency as the concrete self-expression of a human individual's embodied life history in its response to the truth of things has been a characteristic concern in Christian theological ethics.

Bonhoeffer's consideration that there can be no possibility of being a Christian outside the reality of the world that has been reconciled to God in Jesus Christ brought him to a suspicion of ideologies and evasions that separated the world into two spheres, one "holy" and the other "profane."[13] Karl Barth's criticisms of casuistical ethics, in contrast to the "practical casuistry" he commends, oppose that mistaking of the good by virtue of an upholding of norms that misdirect our seeking it for the sake of a security and certainty that misses what it is we ought to do.[14] Bernard Haring's theological ethics developed the category of responsibility, the graced power to make all of one's moral aspirations and decisions a self-giving response to the summons of God in Jesus Christ. Contrasting his vision with an isolated stress on moral norms, discrete acts, and a static view of conscience, Haring drew attention to the eschatological virtue of "vigilance," which in its alliance with prudence affords to conscience a delicate tact to appraise moral reality in light of the present history of salvation and redemption.[15]

More recent work in theological ethics aims to place agents truthfully in the contexts of their lives. Consider three distinct (if not necessarily exclusive) examples: (1) Moral actors are taken to be bearers of a tradition in a particular kind of community of character, which forms their lives in practices of prayer and worship that resist and indict political ideologies of liberalism and violence. (2) They are understood to be caught up in patriarchal traditions that deny through their ethics of self-sacrifice, disembodiment, and disinterestedness the reality and authenticity of women's experience within and for relations of mutual love that are just and empowering. (3) They are named by God to be agents of liberation through solidarity with the suffering, marginalized, oppressed, and otherwise disempowered.

These approaches intend to perceive what the world is and what is going on within it. They attend to who moral actors are and are meant to be and address the tasks of perception and self-expression in these terms, over against ideas, categories, relations, and forces that tempt them to missighting, presumption, escape, and falsehood. They show a devotion to the *discriminations* that make up and distinguish human actions. Though neither ignoring nor degrading the general and ruled sources of human decency, they should also concern themselves with the differences between a playful joke and a hostile affront, fitting self-protectiveness and chilly disregard, necessary concealment and damaging deception, disinterested inquiry and timid noninvolvement, honoring particular commitments and neglecting widespread suffering "outside of them," fair criticism and insidious bullying. Impediments accounting for failure in discrimination may be hasty judgment, the neglect of circumstance, the disordering or misordering of goods present in a situation due to the weakness of reason or appetite or both, a kind of self-blinding or sloth, an overreliance on conventional rules or the teachings of others as dictating action, an underreliance on the collective wisdom present in the traditions and practices of the Christian community, and so on.

The ability to act wisely and well as oneself before, in, and in response to the love of God occasions reflection on the meaning of moral integrity. So how may we go on to describe the work and lineaments of practical wisdom within the Christian life? Here I respond to this question with three theses that concern, respectively, the meaning and value of Christological concreteness, the character of Christian existence as both sinful and righteous, and the nature and measure of moral wholeness and "growth."

Concreteness

The first thesis is that acts of practical wisdom, as acts in keeping with the reality of things, are grounded in and communicate God's decisive action in Jesus Christ in his presence and power: "For God sent the Son into the world, not to condemn the world, but that the world might be saved through him. . . . And this is the judgment, that the light has come into the world, and men loved darkness rather than light, because their deeds were evil. . . . But he who does what is true comes to the light, that it may be clearly seen that his deeds have been wrought in God" (Jn. 3:17, 19, 21).

Christian moral action may be true or real insofar as it is *concrete*. One sense of "concreteness" in theological ethics refers to its basis in the revelation of God in Jesus Christ. Moral life is measured and directed by this revelation contained in the biblical narrative of God, Israel, and Jesus as it applies to the divine activities of creation, redemption, and consummation. It responds to and expresses the will of God because all these activities have God's faithful love in Christ at the center. Though the news of God's Word is heard in the form of address, it includes the promise that this love may be "clearly seen," insofar as moral actors "see clearly" and so truthfully with and for the light that has come into the world *apart from* us and, therefore, *freely for us* by God's gracious initiative. The appeal to concreteness stresses, in its implications for deliberation, judgment, and action, the free and therefore obedient understanding of that initiative in the one Word of God, in contrast to dark or shadowy sources of moral knowledge that claim our allegiance in flight from light, whether these be abstract appeals to rational duty, the general good, the happy life, or justice. Reasoning rightly about things to be done thus involves adherence to the sovereign graciousness that breaks in, that comes to us, and that as such we can never control.

Usually associated with the ethics of Barth, this case for concreteness rightly insists on the particularity and distinctiveness of theological ethics as a divine gift.[16] But the case in its reference to scripture, tradition, and worship, and relying on an "act of faith . . . not to be interpreted in other than its own terms," brings with it two challenges. First—and to avoid an abstract "positivism of revelation" that simply valorizes Christian particularity—moral judgment from a Christological center must *display* the "surpassing reasonableness" of "seeing divine immanence in the world" in and through human relations and the goods they may both attain and corrupt.[17] It is in these relations and practices—friendships, families, work, citizenships, and life in the church—that Christ is present preserving and reconciling the world to himself. Returning to Bonhoeffer's profound remarks about telling the truth, we note his appeal to an "attentive discernment" of the limits and possibilities of trust, loyalty, healing discretion, and fraternal correction within the bonds that make human life more fully human. Seeing those possibilities makes way for discriminations between cynicism and disarming candor, unjustly hurtful talk and just speech (even if hurtful), shamelessness and confession, fearful self-protectiveness and self-respect, "schoolmasterly" patronizing and considerate concern.[18] To this end, the best insights from other disciplines of inquiry—such as history, literature, and the sciences—are put in service toward a fuller understanding of real humanity.

The second challenge—for the sake of rejecting an abstract "positivism of the church" that simply valorizes Christian distinctiveness—is that one must resist yoking the revelation of God to communal identity in a way that tempts the faithful to understand themselves as an irreducibly closed society, with its own special god and destiny, away and separate from the "world."[19] On the contrary, the world has received the light that Christ has brought in coming to it. Discernment is wrongly solicitous if it is primarily about how that community and its members survive in self-defense.

The full position sketched above intends to oppose various forms of self-justification in moral action. It commends a fidelity to reality undistracted by an abstract foregrounding of moral norms, religious doctrine, or ecclesial need that, as such, resists the sovereignty and scope of divine grace. Now the truth of divine justification and its central place in Reformation ethics has led some of its adherents to what may be yet another distracting abstraction. A denial that human works in any way contribute to our salvation can remove from sight the Christian moral actor who is acting wisely; for to the extent that she is doing so, she has heeded and learned of the world claimed by God in the singular instance, has discerned something of its moral truth, and has committed herself to action as a faithful servant. She participates in a unilateral movement of grace and shares in the goodness and life of God the Father, in the Holy Spirit and through the Son, as an adopted child of God. As a creature, she moves toward her final end, the enjoyment of God in love, as a free and responsible agent. Along this line, we arrive at a notion of *merit* that for Aquinas names the fit between human agents and their end (*ST*, I-II, q. 114, a.1). "That grace brings us to this end we never merit; but grace will bring us to this end as ones who merit it."[20]

In the case at hand, moreover, for Thomas the virtue of (infused) prudence that accompanies the theological virtue of charity includes the gift of counsel whereby the soul is rendered amenable to the motion of the Holy Spirit and directed, as though counseled by God, in the discernment of singular and contingent things; for the "thoughts of mortal men are fearful, and our counsels uncertain" (*ST*, II-II, q. 52, a.1, ad.1). Counsel particularly directs the wise to works of *mercy* (*ST*, II-II, q. 52, a.4), and this direction appears to presuppose "in the merciful one and in the one to be shown mercy a common 'defect,' or at least vulnerability to defect," in the sense of affliction or neediness.[21] That such a view need not theologically or spiritually entail self-justification or reduce a sense of human neediness comes clear in John Donne's "Holy Sonnet":

> Thou hast made me, And shall thy worke decay?
> Repaire me now, for now mine end doth haste,
> I runne to death, and death meets me as fast,
> And all my pleasures are like yesterday;
> I dare not move my dimme eyes any way,
> Despaire behind, and death before doth cast
> Such terrour, and my feeble flesh doth waste
> By sinne in it, which it t'wards hell doth weigh;
> Onely thou art above, and when towards thee
> By thy leave I can looke, I rise againe;
> But our old subtle foe so tempteth me,

That not one houre my selfe I can sustaine;
Thy Grace may wing me to prevent his art,
And thou like Adamant draw mine iron heart.[22]

Christian practical wisdom is made concrete in one's responsibility to God revealed in Jesus Christ, as a member of the Christian community, in one's self-giving responsibility for the world. In their conformity to Christ present, in judgment and reconciliation, within the social bonds constitutive of human living, disciples may discover the way they are uniquely called to their lives as the singulars they bodily are. In thus coming themselves to light as God's adopted children, they bring God's love to light in worship and service. The task of virtue therefore both presupposes and anticipates a process of responding to a calling, a vocation, a *beckoning* that makes possible, if you will, *discerning ourselves discerned* "as a living sacrifice, holy and acceptable to God" (Rom. 12:1). With respect to the individual human subject, the virtues without vocation are blind, vocation without the virtues is empty, and prudence embraces both the self-integration of the virtues and the *ecstasis* of vocation in a mutuality of requirement. One lives before God by living outside that abstraction, "oneself," in answering God's call, oneself. Moral deliberation, judgment, and action are thus made more complex, communally and individually. For example, in "docility" one consults with the faithful and the communion of saints at the same time as one understands how one's own mission is a personal affair with a reference to God that is irreducible. Consider as well how the virtues of *synesis* and *gnome* (virtues that perfect our capacities to judge well in the general and unique instances, respectively) play an interrelating role in distinguishing expressions of vocation from idolatrous posturing or a refined dismissal of one's general obligations (cf. *ST*, II-II, q. 51, aa.3-4).

What I have said about theological concreteness, it is essential to add now, is not only fully compatible with but requires an affirmation of an objectively valid "natural morality" that may be attained, even in the weakness of sin, through some sort of "acquired virtue." The peril of "natural theology," and of natural morality as an instance of it, is that it establishes a foundation for attention to the good from which any Christological focus emerges merely as a reflection or projection. The problem emerges also in defenses of humanity's "natural" felicity that effectively render its eternal life in God external, obscure, and finally subsidiary. In addition, appeals to natural and acquired moral virtue may bring with them the trappings of self-justification. All these important corrections, however, readily turn to overcorrections, through one-sided employments of an ethic of divine command, critiques of natural law that reduce it without remainder to its ideological employments (in, e.g., "liberal society"), and sweeping accounts of the "transcendental" that risk collapsing nature into grace.

Above all, for my purposes here, worry over self-justification can overcorrect into a Christian refusal to countenance a properly *human* creaturely good in the announcement of the Gospel.

If Jesus Christ is the "image of the invisible God, the first-born of creation," in whom all things were created—if, indeed, "all things were created through him and for him" in whom "all things hold together," (Col. 1:15–17)—then the human creature's reality is in, through, and for Jesus Christ. A theological ethic of natural morality must generally but still concretely identify how the goods that human creatures seek as such are in their distinction grounded in, ordered to, and hold together with God's sovereign, reconciling, and redeeming love. "Natural" morality and virtue must itself be ordered to something like a creaturely end of just mutual relation, joyful fellow humanity, "just generosity," "dignity in solidarity," or "the penultimate," as each and all of these "prepare the way" for God's decisively gracious Word in whom fallen creatures may discover themselves at once both "dead and risen" *and* "at home."[23] When Christians honor *humanity* in these ways, they distinguish it from its sinful perversion and its radically new perfection, and they take upon themselves the work of making their message a word of hope to human beings in their honest yearning and woeful suffering. When they do not, they tend to make sin too massive or grace too sweeping, and thus they present to the world an image of itself that it finds either unrecognizable or utterly obvious; consequently, they may speak a dead letter word that is found to be, in this way or another, irrelevant.[24]

Barth, of all people—writing of the "downward connection" of Christian love, by way of humanity's cheerful freedom in fellow humanity, to the presence of such freedom even in the sinful flights of pagan *eros*—puts the point precisely: "What we have here is a relationship between the Church and world without which the Church cannot discharge its function to the world because without it it would not be the Church, the Church of Christian love."[25]

Sinner and Righteous

The second thesis is that in, from, and for the love of God, moral wisdom in Christian existence is gained by persons who are at once both sinners and justified. Because wisdom before God is marked by merciful attention, folly displays itself in covetous evasion: "Let no one deceive himself. If any one among you thinks that he is wise, let him become a fool that he may become wise. For the wisdom of the world is folly with God. For it is written, 'He catches the wise in their craftiness'" (1 Cor. 3:18–19).

One may understandably think that no theological dictum does more to stop the Christian moral life dead in its tracks than *simul justus et peccator*. If our complete justice before God is exclusively eschatological, and hence is here and now exclusively forensic, then our moral agency for the good—precisely in the sense that it can be *ours*—is made into an insurmountable problem. But an effort to "save" Christian ethics by rejecting the *simul* in favor of our responsible freedom from sin risks evacuating the Gospel of its meaning, that "God shows his love for us in that while we were yet sinners Christ died for us" (Rom. 5:8). Christian ethics does so by stalking a moralism that leads to self-serving scrupulosity or failure of heart or both.

The claim that we are both sinner and justified gains its meaning in the context of the love of God that is offered to us and in which we are invited to share. We come to know that love and its unconditional acceptance most pointedly in the cross, and there our sinfulness is also unmasked. "Whether we are sinners or not does not matter to God, his love comes to us anyway, but because we are sinners it begins in us the difficult and painful process of transforming us into saints."[26] It follows that the *simul* is only a "state" or a "status" insofar as it sets the terms for a *history* of relation with God. Our utterly unmerited justification names in its promise of forgiveness and new life the point of departure for worship and service. Our existence in its entirety apart from this promise has no future, and the ascription of our "simultaneous" sinfulness locates the point of departure for our comprehending how it is that that is always so—that is, how it is, in the evidences of our acts, omissions, motives, complicity, and conspiracies, that we continue to exhibit in the face of God's generous and gracious love a hopeless resistance and reservation.

In this history of relation, an increase in love is promised to us, and our sanctification is real; we may press on to make the righteousness from God that depends on grace and faith our own, because Christ has made us his own (Phil. 3:12).[27] So we are "sinners" in an analogous sense; what remains of the self's resistance to grace—its ignorance, fear, and self-loss in either encompassing absorption or denigrating disintegration—both is and is not sin. It renders us in one way or other always halting or reserved or otherwise shoddy lovers before and within the love that keeps us. However, in that the divine love keeps us in its circle, sin does not rule.[28] An implication of *simul justus et peccator* must be that Christian faith and hope may trust in God's "promise of pardon to the disobedient *in* their disobedience—a pardon that must sometimes be trusted in the face of considerable evidence to the contrary in our lives."[29]

Within the circle of divine love, the Christian life may be marked by mounting awareness of dependence on the transforming power of grace in all that one is, does, and seeks to do. This mark does not seem to be an accomplishment of progressive self-awareness, as if what one first of all seeks is some settled and empowered image of oneself, even as the bearer of the image of God. The awareness is instead of the love of God, some turning to God, and, with both, some healing and peace in the turning, as well as a sort of fearless vulnerability or vulnerable fearlessness.[30] There is also an increasing comprehension of the power of sin that grace opposes. One discovers that power personally in temptation and on the occasions one succumbs to it. One finds it socially in one's involvement in the world, which structures an arena of fearful desires and constricted loyalties. That involvement prompts the reminder of solidarity with others in the sin of the world, and with that the active perception that one may in service give a reminder of the possibility of peace to suffering humanity. All this indicates that we may live as selves outside ourselves and in Christ in response to the need of our neighbors, whose needs we share as the needy beings we are.[31] Such is the moral meaning of *simul justus et peccator.*

The freedom of God for humanity and humanity's freedom for God are encountered in a love that is known in the suffering Jesus Christ. The wise, guided by the counsel of the Holy Spirit, will know and act on behalf of their sisters and brothers whose wounds, suffering, and sin are joined with, enclosed in, and contained by the wounds of Christ. Their power for and insight into the good issue from that space of pardon and welcome; and so pardon and welcome in answer to need, in what Bonhoeffer calls "deputyship," may mark the judgments and actions of those fools who are wise.

A father will not transgress the limits of the bond that make his fatherhood possible and fitting. He may be friendly to his child but will not play the friend; nor for that matter will he presume upon the proper responsibilities of teachers, physicians, or confessors. Seeking his children's well-being, he will act for them, "working for them, caring for them, interceding, fighting, and suffering for them. Thus in a real sense he is their deputy. He is not an isolated individual, but combines in himself the selves of a number of human beings."[32] And he will act well by responding compassionately to a child's need out of self-giving readiness that presupposes his own dependence, weakness, failures, and need. It is exactly from this presupposition that his authority rather than his power may be properly exercised. Still, we are tempted away from a merciful attention that acknowledges our poverty and reliance on blessing, our fellowship in error, and our complicity in the sin of the world. Coveting for our own security preconceived images of our children (perfect or imperfect, innocent or guilty), of the "real world" and "what it takes" to "make it" there, and of the nature and importance of our own experience, we evade the reality of our children, of reality, of what is necessary, and of just how important (or not) are our experiences. Thus we ask for or demand too much or too little; we confuse adolescent moodiness with serious illness; we come close to making ourselves godlike to our children or making them godlike to us. In these failures of prudence—built, as Aquinas has it, out of an anxious covetousness that breeds failures in watchful and diligent attention to the good (*ST*, II-II, q. 55, a. 78)—we act on our children's behalf falsely, craftily, or cunningly, because they are not in fact who we see them to be.

So we may commend our children to God in prayer, in the hope of seeing them aright, for God is "the great iconoclast," whose shattering of our images of Him is "one of the marks of His presence." Just so "all reality is iconoclastic. The earthly beloved . . . incessantly triumphs over your mere idea of her," and the neighbor we are to love is not "the picture—almost the *précis*—we've made of him in our own minds."[33] The discriminating work of prudence includes understanding these illusions we build and harbor as well as the truth on which we rely. And so we move to my third thesis.

Repetition, Renewal, and Perseverance

The third thesis is that the integrity and growth in the moral life that Christian practical wisdom affords consist in an ongoing practice of repentance, renewal, and perseverance: "Ask, and it will be given you; seek, and you will find; knock, and it will be opened to you. For everyone who asks receives, and he who seeks finds, and to him who knocks it will be opened. Or what man of you, if his son asks him for bread, will give him a stone?" (Matt. 7:7–9).

It is not difficult to draw from my reflections the following description of moral integrity before God: Through a "spiral" in which will and desire direct practical intelligence and practical intelligence instructs will and desire, a personal subject achieves an integration of self that conforms to the truth of the good as it is given by God, and in charity participates in the divine love.[34] Instruction in the moral good includes learning the fundamental terms of a natural morality that is ordered to and perfected by the grace of Christ, and such instruction will of course include regard for the rules that set the limits of right conduct, and the sorts of paradigmatic acts to which moral virtue disposes. Moreover, the clarity of vision about the good that practical wisdom perfected by charity enables encompasses also clear-sightedness about oneself in one's specific vocation. Though the moral life forever involves sinful failures and struggles with temptation, it keeps its direction, by the guidance of the Holy Spirit, toward healing and holiness and therefore toward a growth in the virtues that renders us better able to delight in God and love our neighbors. In all, our moral deliberations may become more thorough and attentive; our judgments may turn more nuanced and thoughtful; and our decisions for action may be more insightful, sure, and prompt.

Although we should generally affirm this description, we also ought to inflect it toward some features of Christian vision that we lose at our peril. To that end, I am interested in defending this proposal of Barth: "The principle of necessary repetition and renewal, and not a law of stability, is the law of the spiritual growth and continuity of our life. It is when we observe this law that we practice perseverance in the biblical meaning of the term; a perseverance corresponding to the steadfastness of God Himself, which does not signify the suspension, but the continuing and indestructible possession of His freedom."[35]

The proposal is part of Barth's ethics of divine command. To several of his interpreters, it mortally assaults a theological ethics of the virtues with accounts of human and divine agency that are merely episodic and voluntarist.

The interpretation is too quick. This passage is part of a depiction of the "sincere humility" with which one "genuinely and indefatigably" asks: What ought we to do? It is a part of that humility to acknowledge that we do learn of God's will, that we are not tabula rasa, that we "always come from the school of the divine command," and not in vain. Nevertheless, we are not so complacent about the moral course we have taken as secretly to ask: "How can I progress further on the right path which I am, of course, already treading?" Instead, we repent of lapses and seek from the goodness of God, which as grace is "new every morning," instruction and guidance. Moral continuity and growth take place in the expansion of a readiness to ask and seek, from each experience of instruction and conversion, another opportunity for the same: "The continuity of a life which steadily affirms itself from one decision to another, developing from within itself, can only be the continuity of disobedience."[36] Now, I have suggested that a discerning openness to reality as God in Jesus Christ is present to and within it, and as guided by the Holy Spirit, includes a parallel moral stance—one that develops from one's own need and yet stands outside oneself in conformity with the truth of things, including, crucially, the needs of the neighbor. Whatever we might make of Barth's talk of divine commands, we can say, in alignment with his thinking, that the skills constituting practical wisdom, far from being possessions with which we defend ourselves, enable a fervent and humble inquiry into the moral good, a desire to be instructed concretely, and a disposition to see the world rightly that is precisely not a matter of disobedience, arrogant self-imposition, or self-dispersing neglect.

Growth and wholeness may be accomplished in a repetition and renewal of asking and seeking that do not erase but rather test our previous answers to the ethical question in terms of what is now present and incumbent. This sort of perseverance is a virtue that disposes one to "stand firm" in the good by resolutely and readily releasing a hold on whatever may hinder clear vision, judgment, and action. And clear vision confirms that "the individual is true to himself, and to the history of the act of God from which he derives, when he allows his baptism to be the sign which stands over every new day."[37]

I said above that moral insight includes an understanding of the illusions we are prone to keep, and that keep us in their grip, as well as of the truth on which we depend. To allow one's baptism to be the sign that stands over every new day is to allow for a dying and rising in which there may be both an unmasking of these false powers and our breaking with them in hope and for the sake of the Kingdom of God. It calls us to a struggle in which we "watch with unceasing vigilance," as Augustine put it, "lest a semblance of truth mislead us; lest cunning speech deceive us; lest some error plunge us into darkness; lest we believe good to be evil or evil good; . . . and lest in this struggle, filled as it is with hardship and peril, we either hope to win victory by our own strength, or attribute it when won to our own strength, and not to the grace" of God.[38] In that struggle, which yields in our merits no integrity of which we can boast, we may always be called in one way or another in perseverance to make a break with our identities as they are constituted by possessions, by worldly reputation, by structures of relation that foster disregard and domination, or by maintaining ourselves either violently over against our enemies or violently within the "inner ring" of this or that special bond of smaller or greater extent.[39] We attempt to break with the powers of sin in the world for the sake of the love of God, who redeems us from them in a history that we *live into*.[40]

Following scripture, Aquinas writes in connection with prudence of a kind of disordered solicitousness about the circumstances of time, "for every time has its own fitting proper solicitude" (*ST*, II-II, q. 55, a. 7). The time of our life, taken as a whole, does, too, and formally speaking perseverance, again referring to Aquinas, has to do with "standing firm against the difficulty arising from length of time" (*ST*, II-II, q. 137, a. 2, ad. 1). Living into life before God, this "standing firm" preserves against the temptation of prematurely closing for oneself one's self-understanding. It protects against that particular difficulty of length of time, anxiety, and then against securing and holding on to ourselves once and for all—"holding on" either by ourselves or by way of others. Perseverance in repetition and renewal formally makes for "growth" by making more possible a moral integrity that, consistent with an understanding of one's specific vocation, is given by God.

Substantively, perseverance contributes to an integrity into which we grow and live as well. Shattering illusions about our identity, making a break with what falsely claims to make it up, and acting in the world from our suffering and need for the sake of our needy and suffering neighbors, we may in some substantial way see the world, and take on a "look" that responds in moral action, whatever our specific place of responsibility, with regard for the spiritual and corporal works of mercy. These works of mercy are, as Dorothy Day put it, "a wonderful stimulus to our growth in faith as well as love. Our faith is taxed to the utmost and so grows through this strain put upon it. It is pruned again and again, and springs up bearing much fruit."[41] Thomas Merton suggested the connection with perseverance in a letter to Dorothy Day, when he reflected on God's great love for those "who are so beat and have so much nothing when they come to die that it is almost as if they had persevered in nothing but had gradually lost everything, piece by piece, until there was nothing left but God. Hence perseverance is not hanging on but letting go. That of course is terrible. But . . . it is a question of [God's] hanging on to us."[42]

To see, again and again, a healing justice in the world that permits admonishing the sinner; to discover a truth and a faithfulness through which the ignorant may be instructed and the doubtful counseled; to discern a source of solace and mercy by which the sad may be comforted and injuries may be forgiven; to locate a basis for hope through which wrongs may be borne with patience, and from which prayer may be said for the living and the dead; to find in the hungry, the thirsty, the homeless, the naked, the prisoner, the sick, and the dead a neediness and a poverty that we share, and the self-identification of Jesus Christ with them and with us—to see again and again is a way of understanding how moral vision, deliberation, judgment, and action may attain a surpassing reasonableness.

Notes

This essay is a revised version of a presidential address delivered at the annual meeting of the Society of Christian Ethics in Dallas on January 5, 2007. I have been exceedingly fortunate to have engaged Gilbert Meilaender for over thirty years on many of the issues in theological ethics that are raised in this study, and I am most grateful to him for his insight, criticism, and friendship. I am also indebted to James F. Keenan, SJ, and Jean Porter for providing in their person and work a variety of challenges and opportunities for reflection. The editors of the *Journal of the Society of Christian Ethics* and an anonymous reviewer have made a number of excellent critical suggestions regarding an earlier draft. Finally, I want to thank my colleagues at Villanova University—Mark Graham, Kevin Hughes, and Darlene Fozard Weaver—for their very helpful encouragement and assistance.

1. Marilynne Robinson, *The Death of Adam: Essays on Modern Thought* (New York: Picador, 1998), 120.

2. Darlene Fozard Weaver, *Self-Love and Christian Ethics* (Cambridge: Cambridge University Press, 2002), 91.

3. James F. Keenan, SJ, "The Virtue of Prudence," in *The Ethics of Aquinas*, ed. Stephen J. Pope (Washington, D.C: Georgetown University Press, 2002), 259–71.

4. See James M Gustafson, *Protestant and Roman Catholic Ethics: Prospects for Rapprochement* (Chicago: University of Chicago Press, 1978).

5. Thomas Aquinas, *Summa theologiae*, II-II, q. 47, a. 2 (Allen, Tex.: Christian Classics, 1981). Hereafter, references to the *Summa theologiae* appear in the text following this notation: *ST*, II-II, q. 47, a. 2.

6. See Keenan, "Virtue of Prudence," 259–62.

7. David Wiggins, "Deliberation and Practical Reason," in *Practical Reasoning*, ed. Joseph Raz (Oxford: Oxford University Press, 1978), 146–47.

8. See James M. Gustafson, "Moral Discernment in the Christian Life," in *Norm and Context in Christian Ethics*, ed. Gene H. Outka and Paul Ramsey (New York: Charles Scribner's Sons, 1968), 17–36.

9. See Jean Porter, *Nature as Reason: A Thomistic Theory of the Natural Law* (Grand Rapids: William B. Eerdmans, 2005), 309–24; and Josef Pieper, *The Four Cardinal Virtues* (Notre Dame, Ind.: University of Notre Dame Press, 1966), 3–40.

10. See Eberhard Bethge, *Dietrich Bonhoeffer* (New York: Harper & Row, 1970), 717; and Dietrich Bonhoeffer, *Ethics* (New York: Macmillan, 1955), 363–72.

11. James M. Gustafson, *Can Ethics Be Christian?* (Chicago: University of Chicago Press, 1975), 1–13.

12. Herbert McCabe, OP, *God Still Matters* (New York: Continuum, 2002), 196, 209–10; emphasis in original.

13. Bonhoeffer, *Ethics*, 196–207.

14. Karl Barth, *Church Dogmatics*, III/4 (Edinburgh: T. & T. Clark, 1961), 6–19. See also Pieper, *Four Cardinal Virtues*, 27–29.

15. Bernard Haring, *Free and Faithful in Christ, Volume 2: The Truth Will Set You Free* (New York: Crossroad, 1979), 254.

16. See, e.g., Karl Barth, *Church Dogmatics*, II/2 (Edinburgh: T. & T. Clark, 1957), 552–630.

17. Dietrich Bonhoeffer, *Letters and Papers from Prison* (New York: Macmillan, 1972), 280, 327–29. See also Andreas Pangritz, *Karl Barth in the Theology of Dietrich Bonhoeffer* (Grand Rapids: William B. Eerdmans, 2000); and Paul Lehmann, "The Concreteness of Theology: Reflections on the Conversation Between Barth and Bonhoeffer," in *Footnotes to a Theology: The Karl Barth Colloquium of 1972*, ed. Martin Rumscheidt (Waterloo, Ont.: Canadian Corporation for Studies in Religion, 1974), 53–76.

18. Bonhoeffer, *Ethics*, 363–72.

19. H. Richard Niebuhr, *Radical Monotheism and Western Culture* (New York: Harper & Row, 1960), 29. See also his *The Responsible Self* (New York: Harper & Row, 1963), 150–51; and "Reformation: Continuing Imperative, *Christian Century* 77 (March 1960): 248–51. This last essay seems also to raise questions allied with the first challenge. My appreciation of Niebuhr here does not extend to his apparent rejection of Christocentric concreteness as I develop it in this essay. On this theme, see Hans W. Frei, *Theology and Narrative*, ed. George Hunsinger and William C. Placher (Oxford: Oxford University Press, 1993), 213–33; and William Werpehowski, *American Protestant Ethics and the Legacy of H. Richard Niebuhr* (Washington, D.C.: Georgetown University Press, 2002), 214–17.

20. Michael Root, "Aquinas, Merit, and Reformation Theology after the *Joint Declaration on the Doctrine of Justification*," *Modern Theology* 20, no. 1 (January 2004): 14. Contrast George Hunsinger, "*Fides Christo Formata*: Luther, Barth, and the Joint Declaration," in *The Gospel of Justification in Christ: Where Does the Church Stand Today?* ed. Wayne C. Stumme (Grand Rapids: William B. Eerdmans, 2006), 69–84. I have profited considerably from exchanges with Root and Hunsinger on these and other issues over several years.

21. Amy Laura Hall, "Love: A Kinship of Affliction and Redemption," in *The Oxford Handbook of Theological Ethics*, ed. Gilbert Meilaender and William Werpehowski (Oxford: Oxford University Press, 2005), 312. With this passage, Hall is commenting specifically on *ST*, II-II, q. 30, a. 2.

22. John Donne, *Poetry and Prose*, ed. Frank J. Warnke (New York: Random House, 1967), 272. See also Root, "Aquinas, Merit, and Reformation Theology," 16–18.

23. See Bonhoeffer, *Ethics*, 125–43.

24. Karl Barth, *Church Dogmatics*, III/2 (Edinburgh: T. & T. Clark, 1960), 276–79.

25. Ibid., 285.

26. Herbert McCabe, O.P, *God Matters* (London: Geoffrey Chapman, 1987), 99.

27. Here and in what follows see Hans Urs von Balthasar, *The Theology of Karl Barth* (Garden City, N.Y.: Anchor Books, 1972), 254–60.

28. Michael Root, "Continuing the Conversation: Deeper Agreement on Justification as Criterion and on the Christian as *Simul Justus et Peccator*," in *Gospel of Justification in Christ*, ed. Stumme, 54–59. See also Gilbert Meilaender, *The Freedom of a Christian: Grace, Vocation, and the Meaning of our Humanity* (Grand Rapids: Brazos Press, 2006), 67–71.

29. Meilaender, *Freedom of a Christian*, 34.

30. See Gene Outka, "Theocentric Love and the Augustinian Legacy: Honoring Differences and Likenesses between God and Ourselves," *Journal of the Society of Christian Ethics* 22 (2002): 103.

31. Martin Luther, *The Freedom of a Christian*, in *Martin Luther: Selections From His Writings*, ed. John Dillenberger (Garden City, N.Y.: Anchor Books, 1961), 73–80.

32. Bonhoeffer, *Ethics*, 224. See also Gerald P. McKenny, "Responsibility," in *Oxford Handbook of Theological Ethics*, ed. Meilaender and Werpehowski, 248–51.

33. C. S. Lewis, *A Grief Observed* (New York: Bantam Books, 1876), 76–78.

34. Keenan, "Virtue of Prudence," 259.

35. Karl Barth, *Church Dogmatics*, II/2, 647. See also David Clough, *Ethics in Crisis: Interpreting Barth's Ethics* (Aldershot, U.K.: Ashgate, 2005).

36. Ibid., 646–47.

37. Ibid., 647.

38. Augustine, *The City of God against the Pagans*, ed R. W. Dyson (Cambridge: Cambridge University Press, 1998), XXII.23, 1158.

39. See Karl Barth, *Church Dogmatics*, IV/2 (Edinburgh: T. & T. Clark, 1958), 546 ff; C. S. Lewis, "The Inner Ring," in *The Weight of Glory* (Grand Rapids: William B. Eerdmans, 1949), 55–66.

40. See David H. Kelsey, *Imagining Redemption* (Louisville: Westminster John Knox Press, 2005), 38.

41. Dorothy Day, *Selected Writings*, ed. Robert Ellsberg (Maryknoll, N.Y.: Orbis, 1992), 99.

42. Thomas Merton, *The Hidden Ground of Love*, ed. William H. Shannon (New York: Harcourt Brace Jovanovich, 1993), 137.

Creaturely Virtues in Jonathan Edwards: The Significance of Christology for the Moral Life

Elizabeth Agnew Cochran

JONATHAN EDWARDS NAMES HIS CHRISTOLOGICAL ACCOUNT OF THE VIR-
tue of humility as an "excellency proper to creatures" rather than of God's divine
nature, which differentiates it from "true virtue" or benevolence. He presents the
incarnate Christ as the moral archetype for humility. This has two implications
for contemporary ethics. First, it suggests that we would have needed God's revelation in Christ to understand and pursue the virtues, even if the Fall had not occurred. Second, it indicates that there is a necessary relation between love and
humility in the Christian life.

M any contemporary theorists of virtue follow Aristotle in suggesting
that virtues are excellences of human nature and constitutive of the
human good, excellences that are proper to the end or purpose for
which humans were created. Yet twentieth-century readings of Jonathan Edwards's ethics recognize that Edwards decisively presents the virtues as fundamentally perfections of God, qualities proper to the divine nature.[1] In light of
this scholarly consensus, this essay considers the implications of this feature of
Edwards's account of virtue for how we can understand Edwards's view of "humility," a virtue that he himself acknowledges is *not* a perfection of God as God
but that is instead a "proper excellency only of a created nature."[2]

It might seem that Edwards's identification of humility as a virtue that the
divine nature does not possess would call into question the accepted interpretation of Edwardsean virtues as divine perfections, but I suggest that Edwards understands humility as a perfection of the human nature of the incarnate Jesus
Christ; and a comparison to Thomas Aquinas's account of humility underscores
the significance of this Edwardsean claim. Though Edwards views humility as a
creaturely excellence,[3] his account of the meaning of this virtue is decidedly
Christological and thereby tied to his doctrine of God. His account of humility
as an excellence of Christ reinforces humanity's need for the incarnation in order to aspire not only to Edwards's "true virtue" or Christian love but also to
those virtues that are proper to our natures.

Journal of the Society of Christian Ethics, 27, 2 (2007): 73–95

Recognizing the Christological character of Edwards's view of humility is significant both because it refines our understanding of Edwards and because it deepens our understanding of the meaning of Christian love. Christ embodies perfectly the divine excellence of love and the human excellence of humility and, in doing so, draws these two excellences into one. I argue, in the second section of this essay, that a unity between love and humility is revealed in Edwards's account of condescension, a divine virtue that functions as a counterpart to humility in humans. Though Edwards himself does not make this claim explicitly, I contend that this view of condescension, coupled with a recognition of his concern to emphasize the union of Christ's divine and human natures, demonstrates that Edwardsean humility can be understood as an image or type of divine mercy. In affirming Christ as a union of divine with human excellences, Edwards's ethic points to a union of love and humility that suggests that each virtue is partly constitutive of the other and that the two together are essential for a Christian understanding of the moral life.

Christological Exemplarity in Edwards's Virtue Ethic

In the incarnate Christ, both the true virtue that is the ultimate fulfillment of creatures and the virtues that Edwards describes as moral excellences of created natures are made manifest. Unlike love, which Edwards affirms as proper to God and particularly to the Holy Spirit,[4] Edwards's humility is a quality more proper to creatures than to God: "For though the divine nature be infinitely abhorrent to pride, yet humility is not properly predicable of God the Father, and the Holy Ghost, that exist only in the divine nature."[5] Yet because Christ is fully human as well as fully divine, he exhibits and practices divine love and creaturely humility. God as God cannot practice humility, but in Christ, divine virtue is joined to this created excellence. For Edwards, therefore, the incarnate Christ is a moral exemplar for both divine and human virtues. Understanding Edwards's depiction of Christ's exemplarity of these virtues provides a basis for understanding more closely the precise meaning of humility and its relation to the divine virtues that Christ possesses.

The Redemptive and Revelatory Quality of Christ's Virtues

A consideration of Edwards's understanding of redemption reveals his theological motives for presenting Christ as the embodiment of both divine and creaturely virtue. Redemption is an important part of Edwards's theology; George Marsden contends that it is central for understanding Edwards's view of God's design for the world,[6] and Stephen Holmes argues that the work of redemption is the framework through which all other aspects of Edwards's theology can best be understood.[7] In his posthumously published collection of sermons *A History of the Work of Redemption*, Edwards calls redemption God's greatest work,[8] and he suggests, at one point, that the world was created so that it could be the site in which the "glorious work" of redemption is accomplished.[9] Redemption, in turn, involves both a "satisfaction" for sin, achieved through Christ's atonement, and a "purchase" of salvation, achieved through Christ's righteousness or merit.[10] Edwards suggests that the entire incarnation, the events of the incarnate Christ's life on earth, have the purpose of purchasing our salvation,[11] a claim that stands in keeping with Calvin and the broader tradition of Reformed theology. Holmes observes that Edwards presents the entire life of Christ, rather than solely the atonement, as redemptive,[12] and *A History of the Work of Redemption* likewise makes it clear that salvation does not lie exclusively in the work of the atonement but also in the virtues and obedience that Christ displayed while incarnate. For Edwards, then, our salvation is partly achieved as Christ embodies righteousness and exhibits "merit" in the situations he encounters.

It is in the context of this theology of redemption and the purchase of salvation that Edwards discusses Christ's virtues. Christ's righteousness and perfect virtue are important means through which God accomplishes redemption; the redemptive "merit" of the incarnate Christ consists in Christ's obedience and Christ's virtue.[13] Edwards is careful to explain that Christ salvifically displays his righteousness *both* through actions of obeying laws ("all laws of God that ever have been given to mankind, both the law of nature and also all political commands that were ever given to man"[14]) *and* through the manifestation of virtues. Christ exercised "every possible virtue" in the course of "doing the work that he had to do here in the world for our redemption."[15] Edwards implies here that Christ's obedience to the law was important as a means of fulfilling the covenant humans had broken. But true "righteousness," such as that which Christ possessed, involves the perfect exercise of virtues as well as the obedience of laws,[16] and Edwards devotes an entire sermon in *A History of the Work of Redemption* to delineating the specific virtues Christ practiced. He reiterates this understanding of Christ's virtue as redemptive in his sermon "Like Rain upon Mown Grass"[17] and in his *Treatise on Original Sin*.[18] Christ's virtue is a cornerstone of Edwards's theology because it is a central means through which human salvation is achieved.[19]

In addition to its redemptive function, Christ's practice of virtue also reveals to us the very meaning of virtue;[20] through this affirmation, Edwards keeps his virtue ethic consistent with his view of original sin. He sees humans as not only unable to practice virtue independently of God but also as unable to know the meaning of a virtue such as humility apart from God's revelation. *Religious Affections* suggests that a proper understanding of these virtues, as well as an ability to practice them, requires God's grace. Edwards emphasizes the difficulty of pursuing a life of humility apart from the "Christian" disposition of the spiritual sense that we are given in conversion,[21] a disposition we require because original sin has changed our natures.[22] *Original Sin* likewise affirms humanity's need for an exemplar, suggesting that one of God's purposes in becoming incarnate was to reveal perfect virtue to humanity.[23] For Edwards, we are able to come to know what humility means not because of instincts that are natural to us but because the incarnate Christ reveals it to us through his actions and the Holy Spirit moves our senses to respond.[24] Our knowledge and pursuit of true virtue and the virtues proper to our natures therefore depend radically upon the incarnation.

Christ as the Moral Exemplar of Divine and Human Virtues

As I noted in the previous section, *A History of the Work of Redemption* affirms that the incarnate Christ exercised all virtues that do not presuppose sin,[25] including both divine and human excellences. Christ perfectly embodies God's true virtue, which Edwards characterizes as a benevolence directed toward God and toward the created universe as a whole.[26] Christ "manifested a wonderful love to God." Edwards affirms that the love to God that Christ exhibited surpasses that of the angels and saints, and that he displayed this love in part through his "labor of love" and his suffering for love's sake. He exercised a perfect love to God, a "holy fear and reverence toward God the Father," and although he was not subject to temptation, he withstood temptations to abandon the worship of God. Edwards underscores the noteworthiness of Christ's determination to continue in the worship of God by observing that even the angels that fell succumbed to this temptation, but that Christ, as God's son, was "infinitely more worthy and honorable than they."[27]

Not only does Christ's love exceed that of angels, but Edwards also affirms that Christ's demonstration of love surpasses that of all ordinary humans and even of saints: "The angels give great testimonies of their love to God in their constancy and activity in doing the will of God. And many saints have given great testimonies of their love, who from love to God have endured great labors and sufferings. But none ever gave such testimonies of love to God as Christ has done, none ever performed such a labor of love as he, or suffered so much from love to God as he."[28] Edwards concedes that "some of the saints," such as Paul and John, have manifested love remarkably, but he concludes that "the love to men that Christ showed when on earth as much exceeded the love of all other men as the ocean exceeds a small stream."[29] True virtue is exhibited perfectly in Christ, and Christ's virtue surpasses that of any creature.[30]

In the person of Christ, moreover, this divine virtue is conjoined to perfect manifestations of virtues that are most properly connected to creatures. Christ's human nature embodies these virtues perfectly. "The Sweet Harmony of Christ" affirms that Christ became human so "that he might be as they [his people] are." He assumed their human nature "in its weak, broken state to be like them" and thereby assumed a nature "subject to affliction and temptation" and to "those disadvantages that are the fruits of sin."[31] It is this complete humanity of Christ that gives him the capacity to practice creaturely virtues as well as divine virtue. In "The Excellency of Christ," Edwards explains that although Christ is equal with God, in Christ's perfect humanity he simultaneously feels and exhibits "the deepest reverence toward God."[32] Edwards's revival text *The Distinguishing Marks of a Work of the Spirit of God* reiterates the humility in Christ's character and practice: "The love that appeared in the Lamb of God was not only a love to friends, but to enemies, and attended with a meek and humble spirit."[33] In Christ, perfect humility coincides with the qualities of God's divine nature, including the perfect love in which divine virtue consists.

A History of the Work of Redemption likewise presents Christ's human nature as a moral exemplar for the virtue of humility. Edwards explains that because Christ's humanity was joined to a divine nature,[34] he had more reason to be proud than any other creature, and yet his humility surpasses that of all creatures: "Christ, though he was the most excellent and honorable of men, yet was the most humble. Yea, he was the most humble of all creatures. No angels nor men ever equaled him in humility though he was the highest of all creatures in dignity and honorableness. Christ would have been under the greatest temptation to pride if it had been possible that anything could have been a temptation to him . . . the man, Christ Jesus, [was not] at all lifted up with pride with all those wonderful works [such as] raising the dead."[35]

Though he is God as well as human, Christ models this human virtue more fully than creatures do. Indeed, Christ, as God and human, embodies these virtues "perfectly": "Every virtue in him was perfect."[36] Christ embodies and reveals the content not only of divine love but also of creaturely humility.

Toward a Definition of Edwards's Humility: An "Abhorrence of Pride"

Thus we see that although Edwards conceives humility as a creaturely excellence, it is the divine and human Christ who embodies this virtue perfectly. Christians exercise this virtue in the context of sanctification, as they are conformed to Christ by receiving his grace.[37] This point, in turn, suggests that the creaturely virtues of the elect are reflections of Christ's character.[38] Edwards's account of humility is distinctively Christological; looking to the incarnate Christ as a model of humility leads him to understand humility as involving both the avoidance of pride (in keeping with other thinkers in the Christian tradition, e.g., Augustine and Aquinas), and also a more active self-renunciation that images and participates in Christ's self-renunciation. This emphasis upon self-renunciation distinguishes Edwards's position from Aristotelian and Thomist perspectives that conceive magnanimity as a virtue (a distinction that is not surprising in light of his critiques of Aristotelian accounts of habit and moral formation).[39]

Edwards defines humility in multiple ways throughout his corpus, and one definition that he frequently offers is that humility is the opposite of pride.[40] He describes the pride that a humble moral agent should avoid in *Some Thoughts Concerning the Present Revival of Religion in New England*, a defense of the religious revivals that he wrote in 1742 and 1743. He likens this "spiritual pride" to a disease through which a moral agent perceives herself to be greater than she is.[41] Pride is the "first sin that ever entered into the universe" and a quality that "the best of us" have "in our hearts."[42] Edwards explains that pride prevents us from seeing ourselves as we are, and leads us to believe that we are not in need of external instruction.[43] Whereas a humble moral agent "easily receives instruction" and participates in careful self-examination of her moral qualities,[44] a person affected by spiritual pride is unable to see herself rightly and to subject herself to others where appropriate.[45]

At the same time, though Edwards strongly exhorts Christians to avoid pride, both his presentation of Christ as exemplar for this virtue and his claim that God does not practice humility suggest that Christ's humility cannot be defined solely in terms of the avoidance of pride. God is not subject to pride, and if humility were solely the avoidance or absence of pride, then this virtue could be attributed to God. Edwards develops an argument in *The End for Which God Created the World* that explains the incongruity of ascribing pride to God. For Edwards, God logically cannot be subject to pride because God is the being to whom glory is most properly given; God cannot esteem Godself higher than God is because God is the highest being. Consequently, in contrast to the self-love of creatures, in whom pride threatens to undermine the practice of virtue, the self-love of God is equivalent to God's virtue. For Edwards, God is the only being in whom virtue and self-love can be said to coincide.[46] In contrast to creatures, God may seek his own good and be assured that he is simultaneously seeking the general good of all creation.[47] It is fitting for God to receive glory, and it is therefore impossible that God's self-glorification could be considered excessive or inappropriate. Edwards thereby presents God as logically incapable of pride. God necessarily avoids pride because of his status as the greatest being, and it is therefore the case that if humility were simply the avoidance of pride, God *could* be said to exercise it.

As I noted above, however, Edwards affirms that humility cannot be attributed to the divine nature, except in the person of Christ. Humility, then, must be more than simply the absence of pride. A closer examination of Edwards's conception of humility demonstrates that he sees the humility that Christ modeled perfectly as involving a radical renunciation of his own righteousness and a disposition of self-abasement. Whereas Edwards's view of true virtue suggests that a virtuous life can bring about happiness, his view of humility requires an agent's willingness to suffer and even to suffer unjustly. Humility is not simply the avoidance of pride; it is instead a deeper act of self-renunciation.

Perfect Humility as the Renunciation of Self: The Distinctively Christological Character of Edwards's Humility

A study of Edwards's writings reveals that his account of Christ's actions leads him to understand humility as involving a denial of self and a willingness to submit oneself to suffering, particularly to suffering that is unjust. In *A History of the Work of Redemption*, Edwards argues that submitting to low circumstances, when appropriate, is a testimony to one's humility: "The proper trial and evidence of humility is stooping or complying with those acts of circumstances when called to it that are very low and contain great abasement." Christ manifests his humility by consenting to being made low. Speaking of the incarnate Christ's redemptive suffering, Edwards affirms, "Was this not a wonderful manifestation of humility when he cheerfully and most freely complied with this abasement?" Virtues, Edwards contends, are most striking in times of trial, and so Christ's humility and other virtues are most evident in his most extreme experiences of suffering.[48] In presenting a willingness to undergo suffering as evidence of perfect humility, then, Edwards indicates that true humility requires openness to self-abasement.

In drawing this connection between humility and self-abasement, Edwards underscores the excessive character of Christ's humility. Christ's extreme humility is made manifest in his failure to claim his just deserts. Christ avoids feelings of pride even though his status puts him in a situation in which a certain type of pride (the quality Aquinas calls magnanimity) might have been legitimate. Christ was "infinitely honorable" and knew it, but he humbly and willingly subjected himself to treatment unbefitting to his station and identity: "Though he knew he was the heir of God the Father's kingdom, yet such was his humility that he did not disdain to be abased and depressed down into lower and viler circumstances and sufferings than ever any other elect creature was; so that he became least and lowest of all."[49]

Christ's suffering was undeserved, and Edwards suggests that this undeserved quality increases its moral excellence. He affirms this point more generally in praising the virtuous meekness that Christ displayed in the atonement; this meekness, like humility, is demonstrated well in conditions of suffering. In praising Christ's meekness as an embodiment of this virtue in its perfect form, Edwards implies that the virtue is greater because the suffering is undeserved; it is, he says, "unreasonable."[50] Christ's willingness not to demand the praise he deserves is a sign of his humility. By elevating Christ as an example whose actions define the ideal forms of the virtues of humility and meekness, Edwards suggests that the most perfect forms of these virtues are made evident in actions consistent with a denial of one's own merits and desert.

This argument is echoed in Edwards's discussion of humility in the lives of Christians. In *Some Thoughts Concerning the Revival*, Edward draws a contrast between the behavior of a spiritually proud person and the behavior of a humble person; his account suggests that a mark of humility is the denial of such good as may be present in one's heart. Whereas pride makes us see ourselves as better than we are, humility requires not that we view ourselves as we truly are but that we view ourselves as *less* than we might be so that we strive to eradicate those things we would wish to change in ourselves. Edwards explains that a humble person will be disposed to view his or her own failings in the most negative light possible: "Pure Christian humility disposes a person to take notice of everything that is in any respect good in others, and to make the best of it, and to diminish their failings; but to have his eye chiefly on those things that are bad in himself, and to take much notice of everything that aggravates him." Seeing oneself as excessively low, and as lower than others, is a mark of humility, whether one is actually lower than others or not.[51]

Edwards reiterates this point in *Religious Affections*, arguing that the truly humble tend not to recognize their own humility, whereas the proud and the hypocrites falsely perceive themselves to have merit that they lack. Humility shares with pride the feature that an agent does not see herself as she truly is, and in the case of a humble agent, she esteems herself lower than she should.[52] These characteristics of humility are not strictly reflective of Christ's own humility, because Christ is not deceived about his own merits, whereas humans, who are subject to pride, may well be deceived. Nevertheless, from Edwards's depiction of Christ, we see that self-renunciation is central to humility; Christ renounces praise that he legitimately deserves, and humans renounce praise that we may erroneously think we deserve.

The Moral Legitimacy of Self-Renunciation: Edwards's Avoidance of Pusillanimity

Edwards's advocacy of what could be seen as excessive self-renunciation might surprise contemporary scholars who are familiar with Aquinas's view of humility. For Aquinas, virtuous humility involves the avoidance of pride but is compatible with the virtue of magnanimity, a rightly ordered acknowledgment of gifts and abilities that God has given to an agent. Aquinas's humility guards against a pride that is disproportionate to one's merits[53] but not against magnanimity, which an agent practices by recognizing the honors that she legitimately possesses and by offering them to God.[54] Humility and magnanimity, for Aquinas, are complements: "A twofold virtue is necessary with regard to the difficult good: one, to temper and restrain the mind, lest it tend to high things immoderately; and this belongs to the virtue of humility; and another to strengthen the mind against despair, and urge it on to the pursuit of great things according to right reason; and this is magnanimity."[55] Both humility and magnanimity encourage the mind to pursue the good in accordance with right reason and truth. Humility guards against excessive or unmerited pursuits of the mind, magnanimity against its inordinately low pursuits.

In light of Aquinas's emphasis upon the importance of magnanimity, Edwards's view of humility raises questions about whether an Edwardsean humble agent would be subject to what Aquinas calls the sin of pusillanimity. For Aquinas, any agent that is not magnanimous risks falling into pusillanimity.[56] Pusillanimity is the failure of a moral agent to act virtuously in keeping with his or her own abilities, either because she does not understand these abilities or because she is afraid to use them.[57] Yet I contend that although Edwards neglects to make a distinction between pride and magnanimity, his view of humility nevertheless effectively guards against a suggestion that Christ or his followers must neglect their gifts in order to be humble. Instead, Edwards is clear that the incarnate Christ shows us that the exercise of humility *is* the proper use of one's gifts.

Edwards makes this point most explicitly in his discussion of the creaturely virtue of meekness. Meekness is not identical to humility, but it is closely enough related that it is useful to consider meekness in relation to this question of pusillanimity. As with humility, Edwards deems meekness a virtue and a moral excellence of humans that Christ exhibits perfectly. He distinguishes the two in *A History of the Work of Redemption* by suggesting that humility and patience are virtues a moral agent cultivates respecting herself, and meekness is a virtue that an agent exercises toward others.[58] Yet he defines Christ's meekness partly in relation to the attribute of humility, suggesting some sort of close relationship between the two qualities: "Christ's meekness was his humble calmness of spirit under the provocations that he met with."[59]

Additionally, the signs Edwards describes as evidence of the two virtuous dispositions are similar; as with humility, Christ's patient resignation to suffering is evidence of his meekness.[60] *The Distinguishing Marks of a Work of the Spirit of God* draws an additional parallel between the two qualities by suggesting that meekness and humility are each dispositional attributes that describe the nature of the love that the incarnate Christ practiced: "The love that appeared in the Lamb of God was not only a love to friends, but to enemies, and attended with a meek and humble spirit."[61] These passages point to a relation between meekness and humility in Edwards's thought.

This similarity is important because it helps us to engage the question of pusillanimity. On one hand, it should be noted that Edwards's view of original sin logically prevents a human moral agent from being pusillanimous. Because of sin, the natural powers that we could be said to possess through creation are so distorted that it could be argued that we have no moral expectation to make use of our natural abilities; instead, we should cleave to God's righteousness. But Edwards addresses the issue of pusillanimity more directly (though without appealing to the term) in his discussion of meekness in *The Religious Affections*. After defending meekness as a virtue, he raises the question of whether upholding meekness requires that we reject a potentially meritorious form of boldness or self-assertion: "Here some may be ready to say, is there no such thing as Christian fortitude, and boldness for Christ, being good soldiers in the Christian warfare, and coming out bold against the enemies of Christ and his people? To which I answer, there doubtless is such a thing."[62] He argues that we must look to Christ to understand what true fortitude is and how we may properly assert our gifts for the sake of God's glory. The incarnate Christ shows us how to exercise fortitude effectively: "The directest and surest way in the world, to make a right judgment, what a holy fortitude is, in fighting with God's enemies, is to look to the captain of all God's hosts, and our great leader and example; and see wherein his fortitude and valor appeared, in his chief conflict, and in the time of the greatest battle that ever was . . . when he . . . exercised his fortitude in the highest degree that ever he did . . . even to Jesus Christ in the time of his last sufferings."[63]

Through Christ's example, we learn that true strength, and the proper use of the abilities we may possess, lies in meekness. Passionate or violent self-assertion is a sign of weakness,[64] but the exercise of humility and meekness is our strength: "But how did he [Christ] show his boldness and valor at that time? Not in the exercise of any fiery passions . . . but in not opening his mouth when afflicted and oppressed, in going as a lamb to the slaughter, and as a sheep before his shearers, is dumb . . . not shedding others' blood; but with all-conquering patience and love, shedding his own."[65]

Indeed, Edwards goes on to refer to the example of Christ's disciple who attempted to wield the sword before Christ's arrest and observes how Christ "meekly" rebukes this disciple. He concludes that Christ models for us the contours of a Christian warrior in this instance; Christ's meekness is not a passive submission but is instead the action of a true soldier. In rebuking the sword-handling disciple, Christ exhibits perfect virtue.[66] Through appealing to Christ's example, then, Edwards explains that meekness and humility are the strength we are to exercise. True virtuous boldness, or fortitude, lies in these Christian virtues that Christ embodied perfectly.

Edwards's defense of the boldness exercised in meekness is important because it shows that he is concerned to present humility as an active self-renunciation rather than a more passive and indifferent submission to fate,[67] a submission that could possibly be characterized as pusillanimous. Humble Christians choose to submit themselves to God and to resign themselves to suffering, and, in doing so, embody their affirmation of the proper order of the world and of their own affections. Virtue and goodness are central to the being of the Trinitarian God, and the task of creatures is to praise God, in part, by recognizing their own weakness in comparison with God and by clinging to the only being who is truly righteous. Edwards affirms that humans should actively and willfully pursue virtue, and this pursuit is the means through which humans use their natural inclinations and faculties properly.

Christological Humility and Divine Mercy

The priority that Edwards gives to Christology in developing this account of humility thus leads him to understand this virtue as involving acts of self-renunciation. Furthermore, his Christological emphasis has a second implication for our view of the moral life and the place of humility within it: Edwards's account of Christ as a moral exemplar for divine and human excellences points to a unity among these excellences, even as we recognize that some are proper to humans and others to God. Indeed, Edwards presents the divine excellence of love and the human excellence of humility as interconnected attributes. He affirms that "Christian love, or charity, is an humble love;"[68] humility is complementary to Christian love, moreover, in that it helps distinguish true virtue from false. In contrast to a nonvirtuous love, truly Christian love is practiced with a humble spirit, "with a renunciation of all our own excellency and righteousness."[69] *The Distinguishing Marks of a Work of the Spirit of God* likewise links love and humility, suggesting that they are together the "two things the most contrary to the spirit of the Devil, of anything in the world."[70] Christian love, for Edwards, is most perfectly exercised and expressed in humility, in a willingness to renounce oneself and to forgo even acts of self-assertion that could be justified.

This point is underscored through a careful consideration of Edwards's account of the union of the divine and human natures in Christ and in his account of Christ's virtue of "condescension," a disposition markedly similar to humility. These features of Edwards's thought provide a foundation for suggesting that Christian humility can be properly understood as an image or type of divine mercy. Though humility is a virtue proper to creatures and not to God, we can best recognize its meaning and pursue its practice through striving to emulate the merciful love and condescension of the incarnate God.

Unifying Two Diverse Excellences: Christ as a Unity of Divine and Human Virtue

I have argued that Edwards locates divine and human perfections radically in the person of Jesus Christ. This argument is important because it suggests that Edwards's understanding of the unity of Christ's divine and human natures logically indicates a unity in the divine and human virtues. He affirms such unity in his writings. "The Excellency of Christ" explains that in the divine and human natures of Christ, "two diverse excellencies" are unified: the infinite majesty characteristic of God and the "superlative humility" that exceeds that of creatures.[71] In Christ, God intentionally chooses to become flesh and to assume its potential weaknesses. "The Sweet Harmony of Christ" affirms that Christ became human so "that he might be as they [his people] are." He assumed their human nature "in its weak, broken state to be like them," and thereby assumed a nature "subject to affliction and temptation" and to "those disadvantages that are the fruits of sin."[72] At the same time, in becoming flesh Christ also develops the capacity to practice human excellences. Christ retains his divinity, but alongside this divinity he can embody the excellences proper to humanity. Though Christ is equal to God, he simultaneously feels and exhibits deep reverence for and love toward God, a reverence that is fitting to him "as he was one that had taken on him the human nature."[73] In Christ, divine excellences and creaturely excellences are brought together.

Edwards is forthright in cautioning that the congruence of divine and human excellences in Christ does not diminish the perfection of Christ's divine excellences. In "The Excellency of Christ," he acknowledges that affirming a category of excellences distinctive to human creatures might risk compromising a Christian view of God as goodness itself and as having all goods properly connected to God's own being. He maintains that the incarnate Christ contains all human perfections but that these cannot logically be said to add to his divine perfections: Christ's human excellences "indeed are no proper addition to his divine excellencies."[74] Divine excellence, Edwards explains, is "infinite." Christ possesses human excellences as well because these are means through which humans may perceive his greatness, but human excellences do not add to the excellent qualities of the divine.[75] Edwards, then, strives to uphold Christ's perfect possession of human excellences (and, as a necessary counterpart to this claim, to affirm that there exist qualities that can properly be called excellences of creatures) while simultaneously showing that these excellences do not add to or compete with the virtue and merit of God.

Yet although Edwards is explicitly concerned to protect the integrity of Christ's divinity, in presenting Christ as the archetype for divine and natural virtues he necessarily brings these virtues into close relation so that the divine nature can, in a limited sense, be said to embody perfect humility. This is particularly evident when we recall that Edwards situates his defense and explication of Christ's perfect virtue in the context of redemption. Christ's virtues function, in part, as a means through which redemption is accomplished, and consequently cannot be entirely detached from Christ's divine nature, even in the case of creaturely virtues. Edwards is clear that the incarnate Christ's activity upon earth was redemptive only because Christ is God and because Christ's activity can therefore be attributed to the divine nature. In discussing the salvific character of the atonement in "The Free and Voluntary Suffering and Death of Christ," Edwards explains that the atonement accomplished redemption only because we affirm it as an intentional act of the divine God in Christ: "The life that was laid down was not the life of the divine nature; but notwithstanding it was the life of a divine person that was laid down. . . . The offering up the life of Christ, though it was only of the human life, yet the offering was made by Christ not only as man but as God-man. It is that which renders the act meritorious, because it is not only the act of Christ as man, but also as God."[76]

Although Edwards is speaking here of the atonement rather than specifically of Christ's virtue or merit, the point is nevertheless significant because it indicates that he believed that Christ's divinity must be at work in all the activity of the incarnation for human redemption to be accomplished through it. Because virtue, in turn, is part of redemption, the virtues that Christ redemptively possesses and exemplifies must in some sense be possessed and exemplified by Christ's divine nature.

Indeed, because both the atonement and the practice of virtue are part of Christ's redemptive and meritorious activity, Edwards's discussion of the interplay between the divine and human natures during the atonement can compellingly be viewed as a model for how he is likely to have conceived the relation between Christ's divine and human natures in the practice of creaturely virtues. He affirms that it was only Christ's human nature that was killed, just as it was only Christ's human nature that can fully be said to have practiced humility: "It was not the divine life but the human life of that person [Christ] that was laid down." At the same time, however, he is quick to maintain that the action undertaken by Christ at this point was an act of his divine nature as well as of his human nature: "There was the act of Christ as God in it as well as man. It was not only the human nature of Christ that was concerned in offering up that sacrifice to God." The reason that he reiterates this point is that he recognizes that an activity that is redemptive must be accomplished by God: "If Christ had offered the sacrifice only as man, and it were to be looked upon as the act of the manhood, it would not have been meritorious, nor would it ever have availed for our salvation."[77] It therefore follows that, as part of redemption, Christ's meritorious practice of creaturely virtues must in some sense be an activity of God.

In one sense, then, it is Christ's humanity that enables him to practice those virtues most properly ascribed to creatures. Had Christ not become human, he could not have assumed these human excellences. At the same time, however, Edwards emphasizes the unity between the human and divine in Christ to such a degree that it would be artificial to deny any link between Christ's divine nature and the virtues that the incarnate Christ practices. Indeed, such a denial would be damaging to Edwards's soteriology. Even if Christ's divine nature is technically unable to practice a virtue such as humility, the unity of the divine and human natures in Christ's salvific activity would make it questionable to rely too heavily on a distinction between virtue practiced by the human nature of Christ and virtue practiced by the divine nature. By explaining that it is Christ's human nature to which humility is properly attributed, he avoids the potential problem of undermining Christ's divinity, but he also ensures that God, in Christ, is the moral exemplar even for this virtue. A characterization of Christ as the moral exemplar for humility locates the perfections of the divine and human virtues in the person of the incarnate Christ and thereby establishes an intricate connection between creaturely virtue and the divine virtue that is constitutive of God's being.

Merciful Condescension as Divine Humility

The incarnation, I have suggested, ensures a type of unity between divine and human virtues. In turn, a closer look at humility reveals more specifically how divine and human virtue are drawn together in the person of Christ. For Edwards, I contend, this unity is established through a typological relationship; human excellences are types or images of God's own virtue, even though these human excellences (in their precise contours) are qualities that God cannot strictly possess. The incarnation reveals that the virtues that appear most proper to creatures in fact retain a particular relation to true virtue in God and, correlatively, to God's being. An exploration of the relation of Edwards's humility to the divine quality he calls "condescension," which I will suggest is best viewed as one specific component of divine mercy, demonstrates the typological relation between divine virtue and human excellences.

In the previous section, I noted that Edwards affirms that Christ's human excellences do not add to his divine excellences because his divine perfections are infinite. In the course of defending this argument, he suggests that Christ's human virtues are images of his divine excellences. Though the glory of Christ appears in both divine and human excellences as he embodies these qualities, human excellences are in some ways simply reflections of divine perfections:

"His human excellencies are but communications and reflections of his divine; and . . . this light [of Christ's human excellences], as reflected, falls infinitely short of the divine fountain of light, in its immediate glory." Human excellences retain some qualities of divine excellences, but only in a limited sense; human excellences have "a semblance of the same divine beauty [of divine excellencies], and a savor of the same divine sweetness."[78] These statements suggest that Edwardsean virtues that are in one sense creaturely are, in another sense, reflections of divine virtue that are meritorious because they image and communicate divine beauty.

The suggestion that creaturely virtues are images of divine virtue is further corroborated through passages in Edwards that seem to describe a certain kind of humility that God does practice. In "The Excellency of Christ," Edwards praises Christ's condescension, a quality that seems remarkably similar to humility but that differs from humility in that it is proper to the divine nature. Condescension, as Edwards describes it, is a merciful disposition that is expressed through a type of self-renunciation, just as humility is. Both condescension and humility involve a willingness to subject oneself to a low state. God, whose nature is inherently good, practices condescension as an ultimate manifestation of the divine mercy constitutive of his being. As an act of self-renunciation, this divine condescension is parallel to the virtuous humility that Christ practices, and, like Christ's humility, models for us the merit of self-renunciation.

Edwards's willingness to attribute condescension to God is striking because it suggests that condescension, unlike humility, is compatible with divine self-glorification. Condescension involves an awareness of one's own desert, and an intentionality in forgoing that desert, that exceeds even the intentionality of the humility practiced by Christ's human nature. Christ's human nature renounces its desert, but the deserts it renounces are limited because Christ's human nature is simply human. To some degree, Christ's humility functions as an acknowledgment of what is true; the human nature of Christ is not God and is therefore not as worthy of honor as God is. But in practicing condescension, Christ's divine nature renounces the deserts of a divinity, a renunciation even more excessive and unmerited than that which Christ's human nature practices as part of humility. Just as Christ's humility exceeds that of creatures, so does Christ's condescension exceed his humility, and, in doing so, demonstrates the excessive and unmerited character of divine mercy. Indeed, though Edwards does not say as much, it could be suggested that condescension is the means through which God glorifies himself most fully: Just as Christian fortitude is exercised in humility, so is the glory of God exercised in condescension.

Edwards does not specifically compare humility with condescension in "The Excellency of Christ," but he does praise Christ's practice of both qualities in a manner that suggests that the incarnate Christ practices humility and condescension through the same activities. Christ's meritorious condescension is revealed in the very act of becoming human and subjecting himself to low circumstances while human: "[The conjunction of excellences in Christ] appears in what Christ did in taking on him our nature. In this act his infinite condescension wonderfully appeared; that he that was God, should become man; that the Word should be made flesh, and should take on him a nature infinitely below his original nature! And it appears yet more remarkably, in the low circumstances of the incarnation, . . . His infinite condescension marvelously appeared in the manner of his birth."[79]

Condescension here is a morally excellent quality embodied by Christ's divine nature in its assumption of human nature. As Edwards discusses the specific events of the incarnation, he conjoins condescension and humility in a manner that highlights the parallels between them. Christ's willingness to live in discomfort is a manifestation of both his condescension and his humility: "Christ dwelt on the earth in mean outward circumstances, whereby his condescension and humility especially appeared."[80] These passages suggest an account of condescension as a divine quality that creaturely humility images or mirrors.

It should be noted that Edwards does implicitly distinguish Christ's humility from humility in creatures, and it is useful to recognize that Christ's perfect humility more truly images God's excellence than does the less perfect humility that creatures may possess. For Edwards, Christ's embodiment of humility will never be matched: Christ "is not only become man for you, but far the meekest and most humble of all men, the greatest instance of these sweet virtues, that ever was, or will be."[81] In making this point, Edwards is recognizing a fundamental difference between Christ's practice of these creaturely excellences and the manner in which God's creatures, even after God's revelation of these virtues' content, are logically able to practice them. Christ's perfect humility involves the renunciation of honors that he deserves, both because of his sinlessness and because of his status as God's Son. Our humility, in turn, may involve the renunciation of honor that we in one sense deserve; but at the same time, Edwards's view of original sin is such that we do not strictly deserve *any* moral merit or honor for ourselves because we cannot practice virtue independent of God. Moreover, even independent of the Fall, our finitude prevents us from deserving as much honor as God does. In the strictest sense, then, only Christ practices humility in its most perfect form: the renunciation of honors that he truly deserves. This form of humility is most fully an image or type of divine condescension (and hence, I will argue, of divine mercy), although the humility of the elect can be seen as less perfectly imaging this divine quality.

My argument that Christ's perfect humility images divine condescension is underscored by recognizing that in *A History of the Work of Redemption*, Edwards goes so far as to describe as "humility" the same divine quality that he calls condescension in "The Excellency of Christ." He affirms that Christ demonstrates humility in his willingness to descend from a loftier place than the angels to a lower place: "The proper trial and evidence of humility is stooping or complying with those acts or circumstances when called to it that are very low and contain great abasement. But none ever stooped so low as Christ, if we consider either the infinite height that he stooped from, or the great depth to which he stooped."[82] Though Edwards does not attribute this descent specifically to the divine nature, it must be the divine nature to which he refers, for Christ's human nature did not descend from an "infinite height."

Moreover, Edwards deems various activities of Christ as "manifestations of humility"—Christ's willingness to submit himself to the torture and ridicule of violent humans and to be wrongfully accused—and suggests that Christ's divinity heightens the significance of his willingness to undergo humility. Christ's humility is greater because of his righteousness and because he does not deserve suffering, and it is Christ's divinity, rather than simply the moral character of his human nature, that secures his infinite worthiness: "Such was his [Christ's] humility that though he knew his infinite worthiness of honor, and of being honored ten thousand times as much as the highest prince on earth, or angel in heaven, yet he did not think it too much when called to it to be bound as a cursed malefactor, and to be the laughing stock and spitting stock of the vilest of men."[83] Christ's divine nature, then, is not inactive in his practice of humility. In *A History of the Work of Redemption*, Edwards presents an account of humility that must logically be practiced by divine and human natures together, for it is Christ's divinity that gives him the merit and desert that makes his humility greater.

Recognizing that God in Christ practices condescension is significant for Edwards's theory of the virtues because it reveals a close relation between excellences proper to creatures and the virtue of God. Creatures embody the excellences proper to their natures when they practice humility by following the example of the incarnate Christ. Yet the true nature of Christian humility is revealed to be a component of Christ's character, and of humans only insofar as God has created them in God's image. Creaturely humility, as it is embodied in its most perfect form in Christ, is an image or type of divine condescension, and this condescension, in turn, is a component of God's mercy. It is divine mercy that motivates the incarnation, God's supreme act of condescension. In *A History of the Work of Redemption*, Edwards affirms that love for the church is Christ's motive for redemption: "All this great work [redemption] is for them [the church]. Christ undertook it for their sakes, and for their sakes he carries it on from the Fall of man to the end of the world. 'Tis because he has loved them with an everlasting love."[84] God's act of redemption is evidence of God's constant and faithful mercy exercised toward the church; in considering redemption, "we may see the stability of God's mercy and faithfulness to his people, how he never forsakes his inheritance, and remembers his covenant to them through all generations."[85]

Edwards's sermon "Sinners in Zion" similarly presents the incarnation as a supreme act of mercy: The sin of those who are in the church is particularly grievous because those who exercise it "sin against so much greater mercy. They have the infinite mercy of God in giving his own Son often set before them. They have the dying love of Christ, have this mercy, this glorious Savior, and his blood and righteousness, often offered to them."[86] "The Sorrows of the Bereaved Spread before Jesus," a sermon with a different tone, exhorts those who are mournful to turn to Christ for comfort; his incarnate life has given evidence of his disposition to be merciful and loving: "By the bowels of his mercies, the love and tenderness of his heart, he is disposed to help those that are in affliction; and his ability is answerable to his disposition."[87] In condescending to become incarnate, then, God in Christ is exercising the mercy proper to his divine being. Condescension is a means through which mercy is practiced supremely.

Humility is linked to divine mercy through its typological relation to divine condescension. This connection between humility and mercy, in turn, draws together the humility that represents a human moral excellence and the true virtue that is God's very being. Edwards's humility is a type of divine mercy, an expression of love that involves the active renunciation of self in favor of others. A humble moral agent renounces her own worth and gives of herself excessively. Moreover, she is inclined to esteem others better than they deserve and thereby, in a sense, to forgive their sins, or at least to treat them with love even though they may not be said to deserve it. In these actions, a humble moral agent images the inherently merciful God. The creaturely practice of humility is the reflection of the divine mercy constitutive of God's very being. Thus even these virtues that Edwards defines as human excellences can be understood properly only in relation to God's being; these human virtues are types or images of divine virtue.

Conclusion

In his account of humility, Jonathan Edwards demonstrates that he recognizes that certain virtues can more aptly be called excellences proper to creatures than excellences proper to God. At the same time, he develops an understanding of these virtues that presumes an integral relation between these human moral ideals and God's moral excellences. His account of creaturely virtues reveals that even virtues proper to humans can only be truly understood in relation to the perfections of God. The incarnate Jesus Christ is a moral exemplar for creaturely virtues such as humility because of his perfect human nature, and his exemplarity draws the practice of these virtues into intricate relationship with divine excellencies, and, indeed, with God's very being. At the same time, the incarnation reveals that this interplay is inherent in the relation of these human virtues to divine virtue itself. The perfect forms of human virtues are types of divine mercy, and as such they image God's virtue, so much so that it is in fact God in Christ who perfects the creaturely virtue of humility. God's relation to the moral order is secured through Edwards's view of the incarnation, because his Christology reveals that even virtues such as humility are images of the moral qualities of the divine.

Notes

1. E.g., William Danaher's *The Trinitarian Ethics of Jonathan Edwards* (Louisville: Westminster John Knox Press, 2004) contends that the doctrine of the Trinity is essential to understanding Edwards's key ethical texts and his overall vision of the moral life. Edwards's virtues, he suggests, reflect the triune God's nature and character (p. 117), and that theosis is central to Edwards's understanding of the moral task (pp. 119, 153–54). Stephen Wilson's *Virtue Reformed: Rereading Jonathan Edwards' Ethics* (Leiden: Brill, 2005) likewise develops an account of Edwards's virtue that is closely connected to God's activity in salvation, sanctification, and the life and practices of the church. Additionally, I would suggest that a version of this claim is implicitly assumed in James Gustafson's appeal to Edwards as that thinker who informs his "theocentric" ethic in *Ethics from a Theocentric Perspective*, 2 vols. (Chicago: University of Chicago Press, 1984).

2. Jonathan Edwards, "The Excellency of Christ," in *The Works of Jonathan Edwards* (hereafter *Works*) (New Haven, Conn.: Yale University Press, 1957–2006), vol. 19 (2001), ed. M. X. Lesser, 567–68.

3. I use the term "excellence" to stand in keeping with contemporary literature in virtue ethics. Edwards himself uses the term "excellency" to speak of Christ's divine and human perfections. In quoting Edwards, I retain his use of the term "excellency" but use the term "excellence" to speak about his position.

4. For further discussion of this point, see Amy Plantinga Pauw, *The Supreme Harmony of All* (Grand Rapids: William B. Eerdmans, 2002).

5. Edwards, "Excellency of Christ," 567–68.

6. George Marsden, *Jonathan Edwards: A Life* (New Haven, Conn.: Yale University Press, 2003), 482.

7. Stephen Holmes, *God of Grace and God of Glory* (Edinburgh: T. & T. Clark, 2000), 115–16.

8. Jonathan Edwards, *A History of the Work of Redemption*, in *Works*, vol. 9, 512.

9. Ibid., 524.

10. Ibid., 304–5.

11. Ibid., 295.

12. Holmes, *God of Grace*, 142–43.

13. Edwards, *History of the Work of Redemption*, 305.

14. Ibid., 309.

15. Ibid., 320.

16. Ibid., 309.

17. Jonathan Edwards, "Like Rain upon Mown Grass," in *Works*, vol. 22, 309.

18. Jonathan Edwards, *Original Sin*, in *Works*, vol. 3, 200.

19. Edwards, "Like Rain," 309.

20. Paul Ramsey makes this claim in his "Editor's Introduction" to Edwards's *Ethical Writings*. Though Ramsey does not address the virtue of humility or discuss the distinction between divine and human virtues at length, he does argue that Christ's redemption reveals God's love, joy, and wisdom to us; he therefore contends that Edwards's ethic is "Christological"; "Editor's Introduction," in *Works*, vol. 8, 25–26.

21. Conversion, for Edwards, involves God's gift to the elect of a faculty or disposition that enables them to know and pursue truly virtuous dispositions and actions. Chapter 1 of Roger Ward's *Conversion in American Philosophy: Exploring the Process of Transformation* (New York: Fordham University Press, 2004) offers a helpful overview of Edwards's position.

22. "'Tis an exceeding difficult thing for a wicked man, destitute of Christian principles in his heart, to guide him, to know how to demean himself like a Christian, with the life, and beauty, and heavenly sweetness of a truly holy, humble, Christlike behavior. He knows not how to put on these garments; neither do they fit him." Jonathan Edwards, *The Religious Affections*, in *Works*, vol. 2, 284.

23. "God, who knew the human nature, and how apt men are to be influenced by example, has made answerable provision. His infinite wisdom has contrived that we should have set before us the most amiable and perfect example, in such circumstances as should have the greatest tendency to influence all the principles of man's nature, but his corruption. . . . Men are apt to be moved by the example of others like themselves, or in their own nature; therefore this example was given in our nature. Men are ready to follow the examples of the great and honorable: and this example, though it was of one in our nature, yet it was one of infinitely higher and more honorable than kings or angels. . . . Men are very apt to follow the example of their friends; the example of Christ is of one that is infinitely our greatest Friend." Edwards, *Original Sin*, 199.

24. The idea that we require God's work in Christ in order to pursue a life of virtue complements Roland Delattre's argument that for Edwards there is a "Christological path" to humanity's participation in the divine life and pursuit of divine virtue. See pages 93–98 in "The Theological Ethics of Jonathan Edwards: An Homage to Paul Ramsey," *Journal of Religious Ethics* 19 (Fall 1991): 71–102.

25. Edwards, *History of the Work of Redemption*, 320.

26. Edwards's account of true virtue as love to God and to the universe as a whole is detailed in *The Nature of True Virtue*, in *Works*, vol. 8.

27. *History of the Work of Redemption*, 320–21.

28. Ibid., 321.

29. Ibid., 323.

30. The perfect love of Christ is also a theme central to many of Edwards's sermons and to his revival text *The Distinguishing Marks of a Work of the Spirit of God*. Edwards consistently affirms the great love and compassion that the incarnate Christ practiced, and his sermon "The Sorrows of the Bereaved Spread before Jesus" suggests that Christ "has the same compassion now that he is ascended into glory" (*Works*, vol. 22, 467). Similarly, both "Excellency" and *Marks* present Christ's character as epitomizing true virtue for humans in a manner that suggests that Christ's love reveals to humans how we may act virtuously. In "Excellency," Edwards affirms that Christ possesses all God's attributes and reveals them to us in the incarnation (*Works*, vol. 19, 565). In turn, our recognition of Christ's revelation of love is used as the basis for moral exhortation in *Marks* (*Works*, vol. 4, 258).

31. Jonathan Edwards, "The Sweet Harmony of Christ," in *Works*, vol. 19, 443.

32. Edwards, "Excellency of Christ," in *Works* v. 19, 569.

33. Jonathan Edwards, *The Distinguishing Marks of a Work of the Spirit of God*, in *Works*, vol. 4, 258.

34. Edwards, "Excellency of Christ," 568.

35. Edwards, *History of the Work of Redemption*, 321.

36. Ibid., 320; see also Jonathan Edwards, *The Life of David Brainerd*, in *Works*, vol. 7, 91.

37. "Christ is full of grace; and Christians all receive of his fullness, and grace for grace: i.e., there is grace in Christians answering to grace in Christ, such an answerableness as there is between the wax and the seal." Edwards, *Religious Affections*, 347.

38. Edwards describes natural virtues in Christians in a manner that indicates that they must logically reflect Christ's virtues: "Christians that shine by reflecting the light of the Sun of Righteousness, do shine with the same sort of brightness, the same mild, sweet, and pleasant beams. . . . It would be strange if Christian should not be of the same temper and spirit that Christ is of; when they are his flesh and his bone, yea are but one spirit (I Cor. 6:17)." Edwards, *Religious Affections*, 347.

39. This argument is somewhat contested. Wilson's *Virtue Reformed* argues that there are greater affinities between Edwards and Aristotelianism than scholars have heretofore recognized (pp. 17–23). Certainly Wilson is right to acknowledge Edwards's exposure to Aristotelian ideas through such thinkers as Malebranche and the Cambridge Platonists, but it is nevertheless the case that Edwards clearly and explicitly rejects particular features of Aristotle's thought, such as his account of habituation. Edwards's resistance to an Aristotelian view of moral formation is evident in *Religious Affections*, 341–43, and *Original Sin*, 191, 224–29. Danaher discusses this feature of Edwards's thought as well; see *Trinitarian Ethics*, 143, 151–54.

40. E.g., Edwards opposes pride to humility in the following texts: "Excellency of Christ," 567; *Distinguishing Marks*, 258; "Keeping the Presence of God," in *Works*, vol. 22, 531; Jonathan Edwards, "Continuing God's Presence," in *Works*, vol. 19, 413–14; "Mary's Remarkable Act," in *Works*, vol. 22, 397; and *History of the Work of Redemption*, 321.

41. Jonathan Edwards, *Some Thoughts Concerning the Revival*, in *Works*, vol. 4, 414.

42. Ibid., 415.

43. Ibid., 414.

44. Ibid., 414, 417.

45. In *Some Thoughts Concerning the Revival*, Edwards explains that spiritual pride is a powerful force. It is hidden and functions in secret ways: "Spiritual pride in its own nature is so secret, that it is not so well discerned by immediate intuition on the thing itself, as by the effects and fruits of it" (pp. 417–18). Even the exercise of humility, its opposite, can be distorted by pride and used to its own advantage, for a moral agent can be proud of her humility and thereby undermine that humility's practice: pride "perverts and abuses everything, and even the exercises of real grace and real humility, as an occasion to exert itself" (p. 417). Spiritual pride, then, is to be avoided at all costs so that we can practice humility and emulate the "Spirit of the Lamb of God" (p. 416).

46. In loving creatures, God loves himself: "God's virtuous disposition, appearing in love to holiness in the creature, is to be resolved into the same thing with love to himself." Jonathan Edwards, *End*, in *Works*, vol. 8, 456.

47. "That which this [any] person looks upon as his interest may interfere with or oppose the general good. Hence private interest may be regarded and pursued in opposition to the

public. But this can't be with respect to the Supreme Being, the Author and Head of the whole system: on whom all absolutely depend." Edwards, *End*, 452.

48. Edwards, *History of the Work of Redemption*, 322–24.

49. Ibid., 322.

50. Ibid., 323.

51. Edwards, *Some Thoughts Concerning the Revival*, 418.

52. Edwards, *Religious Affections*, 334–35.

53. Thomas Aquinas, *Summa theologiae* (herafter *ST*), II.II, q. 162, a.1, a. 2.

54. *ST*, II.II, q. 129, a.1, a. 2. In her article "Aquinas and the Challenge of Aristotelian Magnanimity," *History of Political Thought* 14, no. 1 (Spring 2003): 37–65, Mary M. Keys cogently argues that Aquinas subtly transforms Aristotelian magnanimity in theologically significant ways. She explains that whereas Aristotelian magnanimity is "the virtue of claiming the greatest of honors, when one rightly judges oneself deserving of them" so that the chief concern of the magnanimous man is his own greatness (pp. 39, 42–43), Aquinas focuses instead on the ways in which magnanimity can lead us toward good actions that serve the community and God (pp. 43–44).

55. *ST*, II.II, q. 161, a. 1.

56. *ST*, II.II, q. 133.

57. *ST*, II.II, q. 133, a. 2.

58. Edwards, *History of the Work of Redemption*, 320–21.

59. Ibid., 322–23.

60. "No man ever met with such provocations as Christ did when he was upon earth. . . . And yet how meek was he under all, how composed and quiet his spirit, how far from being in a ruffle and tumult; when he was reviled he reviled not." Ibid., 323.

61. Edwards, *Distinguishing Marks*, 258.

62. Edwards, *Religious Affections*, 350.

63. Ibid., 350–51.

64. Ibid., 350.

65. Ibid., 351.

66. "And never was the patience, meekness, love, and forgiveness of Christ, in so glorious a manifestation, as at that time. Never did he appear so much a lamb, and never did he show so much of the dovelike spirit, as at that time. If therefore we see any of the followers of Christ, in the midst of the most violent, unreasonable and wicked opposition, of God's and his own enemies, maintaining under all this temptation, the humility, quietness, and gentleness of a lamb, and the harmlessness, and love, and sweetness of a dove, we may well judge that here is a good solider of Jesus Christ." Ibid.

67. Hauerwas and Pinches are critical of such indifference and link it to Stoicism, in which they perceive a type of "fatalism" to be at work. Stanley Hauerwas and Charles Pinches, *Christians among the Virtues: Theological Conversations with Ancient and Modern Authors* (Notre Dame, Ind.: University of Notre Dame Press, 1997), 175, and see also 216 n. 29.

68. Edwards, *Distinguishing Marks*, 257.

69. Ibid.

70. Ibid., 258.

71. Edwards, "Excellency of Christ," 568.

72. Edwards, "Sweet Harmony of Christ," 443.

73. Edwards, "Excellency of Christ," 569.

74. Ibid., 590.

75. "Christ has no more excellency in his person, since his incarnation, than he had before; for divine excellency is infinite, and can't be added to: yet his human excellencies are additional manifestations of his glory and excellency to us, and are additional recommendations of him to our esteem and love, who are of finite comprehension." Ibid.

76. Jonathan Edwards, "The Free and Voluntary Suffering and Death of Christ," in *Works*, vol. 14, 497.

77. Ibid.

78. Edwards, "Excellency of Christ," 590.

79. Ibid., 573.

80. Ibid., 574.

81. Ibid., 590.

82. Edwards, *History of the Work of Redemption*, 322.

83. Ibid.

84. Ibid., 526.

85. Ibid., 525.

86. Jonathan Edwards, "Sinners in Zion," in *Works*, vol. 22, 279.

87. Edwards, "Sorrows of the Bereaved Spread before Jesus," 468.

Caritas as the *Prae-Ambulum* of All Virtue: Eberhard Schockenhoff on the Theological-Anthropological Significance and the Contemporary Interreligious Relevance of Thomas Aquinas's Teaching on the *Virtutes Morales Infusae*

William McDonough

JEAN PORTER RECENTLY ASKED, IF CHRISTIANS "SEE MEN AND WOMEN OF every religious belief, and none, displaying what we can only regard as . . . charity, . . . how can we deny that the Spirit of God is present when we see its fruits?" She says that the development of a more interreligiously open Christian theology of the "infused moral virtues" is a task for our day. This essay accepts Porter's question and suggests that the German Catholic theologian Eberhard Schockenhoff, in his 1987 study of the foundations of Aquinas's virtue ethics, has already largely given us the renewed approach that Porter seeks. This essay is a presentation of Schockenhoff's thought on the matter.

Preamble: Why? Virtue and the World in Which Christians Live and Act

Why yet another essay on Aquinas and the virtues? In a word, because English-speaking Christian ethics remains in a high state of disagreement about the meaning and relevance of Aquinas's teaching on virtue. For Christians to talk about virtue as somehow both acquired by human effort *and* infused by divine love is to talk about the world in which Christians live and act. Without oversimplifying, we can say that two ways of conceiving that world have predominated in (English-speaking) Christian ethics in the last half century or so. And we can further say that neither approach fully describes the world in which Christians live and act.

The first description, perhaps less in favor now than twenty or thirty years ago, sees Christians (like everyone else) as acting in the "natural" world. The

Catholic philosopher Robert Sokolowski says "transcendental Thomism" views Christian life in this way, seeing us as living in the same world as all others while also seeking "a kind of fulfillment of what is anticipated in natural moral activity. Human nature is said to be inclined from the beginning toward the activities it achieves in faith, hope, and charity. The distinction between the natural and the supernatural is deemphasized; the Christian message is said to be that which everyone is more or less waiting for, at least obscurely, and the power of human thought and desire to transcend any particular object is taken as an anticipation of Christian revelation, of the Christian understanding of God, and of the Christian questioning of the world as a whole."[1]

At a far distance from the transcendental Thomists, Stanley Hauerwas and a school of theorists influenced by him understand us Christians as not living "in the same world" as those outside the faith: "[To say] there is no difference between what the good person and the Christian should do in the concrete . . . is unsatisfactory. . . . The person whose life is lived in love and peace with God simply does not live in the same world as the person whose life is not. . . . They inhabit different narrative contexts."[2]

These thinkers describe this difference of context as the difference between acquired and infused virtue: Most "men of virtue" (sic) live in the world of acquired virtue, but Christians must leave that world behind. In fact, say these authors, Christians experience a "problem of divided narratives . . . our present selves are yet constituted by two narratives," because we have not yet fully left the world of virtue acquired by our own effort and entered into the world of grace.[3]

In many ways, the transcendental Thomists and the followers of Hauerwas could not be further apart in their understanding of the "world" in which Christians act. For the first group, we live and act where all others live and act, in the world of human nature seeking God; for the latter group, the whole point of Christianity is to leave this world behind.

Yet a fundamental similarity unites these opposed understandings of the Christian moral life. That is, they share the view that there exists a natural world in which most human beings live and act. Sokolowski, whose position is more like Hauerwas's than that of the transcendental Thomists, perhaps unwittingly demonstrates the underlying agreement in the two positions by calling the naturally acquired virtues "those that we normally experience, those that provide the stability and guidance for human life, those that are the first kind of virtue that we encounter and name as virtues, . . . [those] we begin with in human experience."[4]

For Hauerwas and company, Christians begin our lives here, and we are being led toward another world. For the transcendental Thomists, we begin here and develop into believers. What is most problematic in both views is this one point on which they agree: namely, that there is any such "natural" world.

Eberhard Schockenhoff, the German Catholic ethicist whose interpretation of Aquinas on virtue is this essay's focus, gives a name appropriate to both Hauerwas's and the transcendentalist approaches. They comprise a "pyramid" view of the world(s) in which we live the moral life. In such a view, "the intellectual, moral, and theological virtues . . . form . . . an ascending pyramid, the summit of which is love. . . . So it gives the impression that Thomas saw love as only the final crowning virtue of the canon . . . as an appendix following after a self-enclosed presentation of the ethical life."[5]

Surely Hauerwas would see the pyramid's capstone of love differently than would the transcendentalists, but what both see on the way to love is a world of "preceding steps capable of existing independently of this last and highest one."[6] The French Dominican theologian Jean-Pierre Torrell puts the problem with such a view of the world most succinctly: "Thomas teaches that . . . human nature has never existed without sanctifying grace. . . . When grace was driven out by sin, the whole edifice was affected."[7]

Torrell's statement cuts like a two-edged sword through both the Hauerwasian and transcendentalist views of the world. Its first part, about human nature never having existed without grace, challenges Hauerwas's view of a "narrative of good persons" separated from grace. This is a picture of the world that Thomas specifically rejected when he contradicted Bonaventure and the common medieval position that God first created human beings and then, in a second act, raised them to grace. Aquinas held instead that God created human beings in grace (I, 95.1).[8] Hauerwas's view of a natural world of good people separate from grace is not Thomas's world. No one has ever lived in such a world.

But the second part of Torrell's statement—"by sin the whole edifice was affected"—cuts through the view of the transcendentalists. Here Torrell is referring to Thomas's teaching that the nature we live now is corrupted: "In the state of corrupt nature (*natura corrupta*) the human being falls short of what he could do by nature, so that he is unable to fulfill it by his own natural powers" (I-II, 109.2). So no one lives in the world of the transcendental Thomists, either. Since sin entered into the life of human beings, none of us has been able to live virtuously by our own efforts.

In what world, then, do we live and seek to act virtuously? More fully answering this question is the task of this essay, but a brief further word of context setting is appropriate here. Our guide, Schockenhoff, stays with the building metaphor for the virtues, but he modifies it to see in Thomas's treatise on the virtues not a pyramid but the central staircase of a beautiful building. One ascends this staircase to arrive at the "keystone" of the whole structure (in the presentation of *caritas* as the key to the whole *ordo perfectionis*; see I-II, 62.4) and then to look again over all one has thought to have seen along the way:[9] "To read in an unbiased way the texts [after I-II, 62.4] that wait to be interpreted is to have the irresistible impression of Thomas being led into a new room of theological reflection opening itself up to him, at the threshold of which Thomas must leave behind piece by piece all that he himself had up till now positively recognized under the lead of Aristotle and a broad philosophical tradition. . . . Thomas interprets the whole . . . way through the field of the natural virtues anew in light of faith, hope, and love."[10]

To complete the metaphor: We must say that the entire moral life of every human being is lived on a stairway coming down out of heaven to us from God; not a single step of that stairway is constructed from the ground up by us.

The aim of this essay is to follow Schockenhoff in disclosing a fuller understanding of the "world" than the one normally seen in summaries of Thomas Aquinas on the virtues. With Schockenhoff, this essay holds that Thomas saw a different, fuller, and more universal world than the one(s) seen by most English-speaking theorists of Christian ethics. He came to see anew the one world, broken by sin and being restored by grace, in which all human beings live and act. He came to see that the world Aristotle described does not and never did exist.

This essay thus summarizes Schockenhoff's presentation of Thomas on virtue. It does so with the further purpose of employing Schockenhoff's understanding in service of English-speaking Christian ethics' need more fully to engage interfaith ethical dialogue. In Hauerwas's description of Christians in a "different world" from others, no real engagement is possible. And in the transcendentalist view, no engagement is really needed, for grace is simply presumed to work mysteriously in all. Again, Torrell shows in general the way we are to go:

> Thomas thinks that it is not possible to achieve successful moral action without the healing effected by grace, for the human being, detoured from his true end by sin, is not able to be clear on the very beginning of his moral way. In order to act effectively in the moral order, the human being must take God again as her end; and that is impossible without grace, for this moral order is supernatural from its very beginning in the creation of the human being in grace. If, then, in taking up again the case of the pagan who is observant of the law [see I-II, 109.4 ad 1], the theologian observes a similar success, she is right to suggest not only that grace is not far away, but that it is right at work there, even if in an anonymous way.[11]

Torrell is right to point out that Thomas can imagine a "case" of a non-Christian acting through grace. Yet a more explicit reflection is probably not to be found in Thomas (or in Torrell).[12] The great strength of Schockenhoff's exposition and interpretation of Thomas on the virtues is that he shows us how to think more thoroughly about grace at work in human beings. It works through *caritas* and the moral virtues infused with it. Grace works to heal all human beings by inviting us into the work of being remade in all our human capacities—mind, will, and affections. This is the one world in which all human be-ings live and must learn to act well; the aim of this essay is to describe it.

Contemporary English-Speaking Christian Ethical Theorists on Infused Moral Virtue and Their Reluctance to Engage Interfaith Ethical Dialogue

A brief survey suggests that many contemporary English-speaking Christian theological ethicists who are eager to speak about Thomas Aquinas's idea of the infused moral virtues are more reluctant to apply the idea to non-Christians. Bonnie Kent, a moral philosopher, presents Christianity's understanding of in-fused moral virtue in a way reminiscent of the "pyramid view" of the world we saw above in the preamble. She says Thomas Aquinas and the Christian tradi-tion accept "pagan virtues as genuine virtues" but that Christianity's real focus is more inward, on how believing Christians are to live their day-to-day lives: "Thomas firmly resists any attempt to reduce life to some dreary waiting room on the train route to heaven. . . . Thomas envisions what might be described as the sanctification of a Christian's everyday life in human society. . . . A Chris-tian's daily conduct in selling cars, caring for patients, or teaching philosophy, and likewise, her routine behavior with family and friends, can express both her love for strictly human good *and* her love for God."[13]

The Christian's most mundane actions, done through the working of the in-fused moral virtues, are done for the sake of God; and thus they are aids to sal-vation. It does not occur to Kent to ask whether non-Christians might love God, and come under the influence of infused virtue.

Some contemporary Catholic ethicists do specifically wonder about the rela-tionship between "pagans" and the infused virtues, only to reject that non-Christians experience those virtues. That is, such theorists make explicit what is implicit in Kent's presentation: Christians live the infused moral virtues, whereas non-Christians live the naturally acquired moral virtues. A recent doctoral thesis in philosophy at the University of Notre Dame by Angela McKay puts this argu-ment most strongly: "It seems fair to assert that the pagan, by cultivating the ac-quired virtues, disposes himself for the initial gift of grace."[14]

Need a theory of infused virtue be so exclusivist? The Catholic theologian Michael Sherwin is more open in this regard, but he is concerned that talk about the infused moral virtues (and the theological virtue of *caritas* with which they are infused) not be divorced from these virtues' grounding in Christian faith:

> Thomas can affirm that love of God "presupposes knowledge of God." Since this knowledge is mediated to us by faith, this means that in this life charity depends on faith for its very existence. . . . All are saved through faith in Christ (II-II, 2.7). But Aquinas's position is nuanced. He recognizes, for example,

that those who lived before Christ were saved by merely having an "implicit" or "veiled" knowledge of Christ (II-II, 2.8). Yet, what about those who, although born after Christ, still have no knowledge of him? . . . From Thomas's principles, we can affirm that such persons' response to grace, if it is to be a human response lived in charity, requires some conceptual, even if limited, understanding of God's love revealed to us in Christ.[15]

Sherwin's teacher, Jean Porter, more openly defends the interreligious reality of infused moral virtue but sees "theological difficulties":

> The relevant conception of happiness [for a Thomistic ethic] . . . is to be identified with the practice of the infused virtues, including faith, hope, and charity as well as the infused cardinal virtues. . . . What are the implications of this approach for the status of those who do not share Christian beliefs? . . .
>
> We conceive the infused virtues in terms of distinctively Christian beliefs and practices—and properly so, since apart from this context the distinction between infused and acquired virtues would have no point. But this is a conceptual link, not an assertion of a set of necessary and sufficient conditions. Nothing prevents us from acknowledging that these same virtues might appear, in different but recognizably analogous forms, in other contexts. This implies, of course, that grace is operative in those contexts—even though, as the [Second Vatican] Council [in *Gaudium et spes*, par. 22] so carefully puts it, the exact mechanisms of grace are known only to God. . . . We see men and women of every religious belief, and none, displaying what we can only regard as exemplary moral goodness, and even charity. How can we deny that the Spirit of God is present when we see its fruits? We can affirm this much, while leaving further theological difficulties for another day.[16]

Porter articulates these "theological difficulties" specifically in respect to the theory of religious pluralism offered by the great Catholic interreligionist Jacques Dupuis, whom she admires. She says Dupuis seems to be "more sympathetic to a Rahnerian analysis of grace than I am." She points to the section of Dupuis's 1997 book citing Karl Rahner's (transcendental Thomist) understanding of the "supernatural existential," whereby all human beings live the "'transcendental' history of salvation." Porter is rightly afraid such an approach "downplays the distinction between nature and grace, . . . [which] is not Aquinas's view."[17]

From this too-brief survey of contemporary views, we can conclude that English-speaking Christian ethicists are interested in the idea of the infused moral virtues, but they are at least cautious about the range of the theory. Could too much emphasis on it endanger Christian ethics' connection to Christian faith in Jesus? Porter, who wants to defend the interreligious nature of infused moral virtue, proposes to wait for "another day" to work through the difficulties.

I propose that this "other day" actually arrived twenty years ago in the 1987 Tübingen dissertation of the German Catholic scholar Eberhard Schockenhoff, *Bonum Hominis: The Anthropological and Theological Foundations of Thomas Aquinas's Virtue Ethic*.[18] Though Schockenhoff's subsequent essay on *caritas* as friendship with God and his book *Natural Law and Human Dignity* both have been translated into English,[19] neither directly takes up the question of infused moral virtue. The earlier, still untranslated, work addresses the topic directly, but it has received very little attention in the writings of English-speaking ethicists. Writes Schockenhoff:

> For Thomas to give up on the reflection on *virtus moralis infusa* would mean, not jettisoning superfluous baggage that only unnecessarily complicates theological thinking, but jumping over the anthropological binary structure of human action [i.e., in its intrinsic principles of the powers and habits of the human soul and its external principles of law and grace] that he wants to work through. That he remains so decisively steadfast in his thesis about the infused moral virtues is not to betray . . . the underlying concern of his whole virtue ethic. Rather he remains loyal to it precisely where he, as a theologian, asks how the call of grace reaches the human being in the natural structure of her actions.[20]

This essay first gives a close reading of Schockenhoff's interpretation of Thomas Aquinas's teaching on infused moral virtue, and then it shows how Schockenhoff's approach gives full support for a Christian theology of the interreligious working of infused moral virtue. I develop my summary of Schockenhoff in three points: first, on the place he assigns to the theory of the infused moral virtues within Aquinas's theology as a whole; second, on the specific relationship he sees between the infused and the acquired moral virtues in an individual's moral life; and third, on his synthesis of Thomas's whole theological virtue ethics, with *caritas* as the preamble (*prae-ambulum*[21]) of all genuine virtue ever lived by any human being anywhere. Although the implications of this theory for recognition by Christians of the infused virtues in the lives non-Christians remain largely implicit in the body of this essay, I will return explicitly to the topic in the essay's conclusion by proposing Schockenhoff's theory as completely adequate to the task Porter asks theology to take up in our day.

Virtus Infusa est Virtus Incompleta: Schockenhoff on Infused Moral Virtue in the Full Scope of Aquinas's Theology

Moral theologians are used to asking a whole series of questions when the conversation turns to the infused moral virtues. Among them: How do the "new" infused virtues relate to natural virtues already gained by natural human effort?

Do they join together with these virtues or build a parallel structure? What function could acquired virtue continue to have alongside the new God-given habits? Schockenhoff is not much impressed by these questions: "That later theological discussion has become enflamed with such questions that were never of direct interest to Thomas can only serve as a warning for those attempting to appropriate Thomas's thought. Instead of trying to build some self-standing system of 'supernatural virtues,' one should try . . . to present the same understanding that Thomas had of his thesis and to understand why he spent no time ruminating on these questions that later broke out."[22]

Schockenhoff thinks we miss the point when we try to prove the existence of infused moral virtues, by arguing either from metaphysical necessity (viz., there must be infused moral virtues because the supernatural potency infused into us by grace needs a supernatural form in which to work) or from theological "fittingness" (viz., it is fitting that God should operate in the supernatural order in a way that is at least as intricate as the way God operates in the natural order; so, if there are moral virtues in the natural order, they should be there in the supernatural as well). Thomas makes both these arguments along the way, but Schockenhoff says they are far from his central concern.[23]

Schockenhoff suggests we enter into the issue instead by first taking the two ideas—*virtus* and *infusa*—separately, and then asking what Thomas meant in combining them. Thus, with respect to the terms, Aquinas understood *virtus* as Arisotle did: as a *habitus*, with its three marks of "spontaneity, ease, and joy."[24] To understand the term *infusa*, Schockenhoff says our "primer . . . is the relationship between divine and human action in the treatise on grace in the *Summa Theologiae*."[25] Aquinas used *infusa* to connect ethics to his theology of grace.

And in respect to his combining the terms, Schockenhoff says Thomas had a twofold purpose: first to agree with Aristotle that "it is the spontaneous self-regulating joy at what is good that is the most unerring sign of virtue";[26] and, second, to show that it is precisely this "unerring sign" of virtue as a *habitus* that is missing from the *habitus* infused in us by God, from infused moral virtue. "Reflection on the work of God in human life cannot block the truth that the efficacy of grace in the psychic structures of the human being is not given as an immediately experienced quality. . . . Precisely, the '*delectatio*' of acquired virtue is not given with infused virtue. . . . The experience of the motivating power of good as an experience of joy is not given; at least not at the beginning. So at the beginning action arising from '*virtus infusa*' must make do without the '*delectatio*' that is identified with the life of acquired virtue."[27]

Schockenhoff asks, "What meaning could it have to call both the infused and the acquired habits "virtues," when the infused lack precisely that characteristic which is most characteristic of the acquired?" His answer is that infused virtue is one that is not yet perfected in a human being; it is "*virtus incompleta*."[28]

It is Thomas's theology of grace that is driving the understanding of infused virtue as incomplete: "God comes to meet the human person in all of her dimensions. The return of the human Spirit to God impresses itself even in the lowest layers of her soul, so that the *conversio ad Deum* can become an all-encompassing anthropological reality. . . . The working of God's call in grace must reach all the way down into the deep strata of the person becomng permanent in a way that is true to the work of the new quality of soul in the human being."[29]

In the *Prima Secundae*, Aquinas understands grace as a *motio* of God, effecting the "*iustificatio impii*" by working in the soul of the sinful human being a *motus in contrarium*.[30] Though grace effects a complete new beginning in an instant, its work through the whole of the human person is not instantaneous. The infused virtues are *virtutes incompletae* because they are in complete opposition to the old (sinful) habits, which are weakened, but not destroyed. Schockenhoff concludes that Thomas's theory of the infused virtues constitutes a theological anthropology of grace: "Only from this center do the lines go out toward a theological-ethical reflection about the perfection of the human being in the call of God. Only in that Thomas is drawing further these thoughts into the anthropological structure of the human being marked for perfection, does he go to the insight about the necessity of the theological virtues and then about that of the infused moral virtues."[31]

In this section of the essay, we have come to see that talk about infused moral virtue has everything to do with the depth of the work of God in the lives of human beings. *Virtus infusa* as *virtus incompleta* is a way to speak about conversion that is always (and necessarily) incomplete in a human being. In this section of the essay, we have also seen Schockenhoff rescue infused virtue from its placement within an overschematized moral theology and reset in a central place within a theological anthropology of grace.

Two further moves are in order now. First (and following Schockenhoff's organization of his thesis), this essay shifts its attention back to what the distinction between infused and acquired virtue means in the practice of moral living. Then the third section of the essay looks at Schockenhoff's synthesis of infused virtue's place within Aquinas's theological virtue ethics as a whole.

Acquired Virtue Is also *Virtus Incompleta:* Schockenhoff on the Working of Virtue in Lived Moral Decision Making

Before summarizing Schockenhoff's moral theological understanding of the relationship of infused and acquired virtue, we should pause over his argument for virtue ethics' superiority as a moral method. Our doing so, in fact, will only make his theological point clearer. Thus, for moral as well as theological reasons, it is right to think not only about the reasonable goods but also about "how the good known to reason carries across the psychic energies of the person and mobilizes his own contribution to the success of good action." Schockenhoff quotes Thomas's argument that virtue serves to make action as "completely good as possible" (*ultimum complementum bonitatis*) because it works its way through all the cognitive, affective, and sensual powers of a person. Morality must not be reduced to asking what is morally good but must also and especially ask: How can morally good action happen?[32]

A purely normative ethic misleads one into thinking that moral goodness is a fully cognitive affair, when in fact the true *bonum hominis* becomes known in the practice of the virtues. As Schockenhoff puts it, making reference to a text from the II-II: "The concrete good that justice seeks to do in a particular situation shows itself to the just person through her own becoming just; as she does what is just, and continues to do it, an affective ability to judge (a '*cognitio affectiva seu experimentalis*') ripens in her that allows her to come to recognize what is just by connatural agreement."[33] In sum, there is no way of coming to true moral judgments except through the "organic" process of virtue. (Schockenhoff finds the word used by Aquinas himself!) And we have seen that the idea of infused virtue brings such an organic approach to Thomas's theology of grace as well.[34]

But now we must ask how and where these two organic understandings of ethics and of theology meet in the life of the human being. For we must not allow any "unhappy separation . . . [between] the theological and the ethical [leading to] the double danger of a faithless praxis and a faith that is a stranger to praxis."[35]

Schockenhoff says that it is completely correct, "in the realm of high abstraction," to speak separately about the "pure forms" of infused and acquired virtues. But then he makes a simple and strong assertion (and repeats it three times over the course of twenty pages): in actually existing moral practice in the real world, pure forms of infused and acquired moral virtues do not exist and have never existed:

> Neither *virtus acquisita* nor *virtus infusa* accomplish good action in the pure form under which they are analyzed in the study of essences in "thought laboratories." In a theological view like the one Thomas adopted in the *Summa theologiae*, acquired virtue (like every natural power of the human being) does not appear in a neutral, undecided status with respect to grace. It exists instead in the life of a concrete human being, who stands either open to the call of grace through a free decision or an unaware readiness, or closed to that call. In respect to the answer given by God's spiritual creature to the love of God calling out from eternity there is no such thing as a stance of undecidedness by any human being. In the life of his rational creation God is always confessed in the mode of either loving affirmation or of rejection. Practical

action stands in a necessary ordering to its last end, an ordering that it can accomplish through acceptance or aversion but cannot suspend. . . . Moral actions arising purely through *virtus acquisita* in the concrete order of salvation simply do not exist.[36]

Schockenhoff understands Thomas to hold that infused and acquired virtue either exist in "complementary togetherness" in the concrete life of a person or, when not, that neither of them exists fully. Schockenhoff reads Thomas's claim that acquired virtue can exist without *caritas* (see I-II, 65.2; II-II, 23.7) as a reference to the lives of sinners in which virtues "can be realized only incompletely and fragmentarily. . . . On their own such virtues fall below their natural determination and tend to return over the long run to being mere dispositions."[37]

For Schockenhoff, the question is not *whether* infused and acquired virtues function together but only *how*. For both infused and acquired virtue are incomplete and each needs the other: "Since both infused and acquired virtue, each in a different way, are *virtus incompleta*, lacking either the perfected ease and joy or the inner directedness to the last end, not only are they able to exist together in one power of the soul, but also to work together from their shared anthropological setting in such a manner as to produce acts that bear the specific imprint of each of them, without one being able adequately to divide which portion of such acts was brought forward by the one or the other."[38] To the commonly accepted "incompleteness" of infused virtue, Schokenhoff adds that of acquired virtue as well, because alone acquired virtue cannot reach the final end of the human being. This mutual incompleteness is Schokenhoff's ground for positing a necessarily complementary relationship between the two in one human action.

If this mutual incompleteness is so clear, why did Thomas never make the argument himself? Because, says Schockenhoff, "in the place where most commentators raise the question Thomas cannot see any problem because he thinks he has already solved the problem elsewhere [in his discussion on grace]."[39]

Schockenhoff knows the solution proposed here by George Klubertanz in 1959, namely, that acquired virtue provides the material cause of the one moral action, while infused virtue provides its formal cause.[40] And though he accepts it, he wants to push further than Klubertanz. For Schockenhoff, Thomas does not raise the issue of material and formal causality of acquired and infused virtue at this point because he understands himself to have settled the question already in his treatise on grace and God's justification of the sinful human being.

Here the themes of this second section of the essay begin to come together with those of the first. For the mutual and complementary relationship of infused and acquired virtue is a mirror of the mutual and complementary relationship between the grace of God and the free consent of the human being in the act of justification. From the very beginning of his writings, according to

Schockenhoff, Thomas resisted any unidirectional understanding of the movement from God to the human being and back again in the sinner's justification by grace. Schockenhoff cites Thomas's short formula, *Deus non sine nobis nos iustificat*, adding that in Thomas's earlier writings the complementary relationship of God's grace and human consent in justification is the relationship between formal and material cause.[41]

So, again: It is not on the basis of some metaphysical necessity that Thomas argues for the existence of infused and acquired moral virtues together, but out of respect for the freedom-respecting God. The mutual, complementary relationship of infused virtue (as formal cause) and acquired virtue (as material cause) in the generation of every action of a justified human being is an application in practical ethics of Thomas's profound theological vision. On the analogy of prudence being in two powers of the soul "not on an equal footing, but in a certain order" (I-II, 56.2), Schockenhoff writes: "If two different powers are able to bring forward one common act, then there is nothing to argue against infused and the acquired virtue in the same complementary structure being at work in one power of the soul. That the '*virtus infusa*' brings forth the same common effect together with acquired virtue '*non ex aequo, sed ordine quodam*' means their complementary relationship and the subordination of acquired to infused virtue is sufficiently guaranteed."[42]

Schockenhoff concludes that infused moral virtue may be at work in a person who is subjectively aware that all her "partial goals" are ordered to her final goal in God; or, it may be equally at work "alongside the person's own immediate *finis* in acquired virtue, objectively functioning as an end intermediate to the final end whether or not the acting subject is subjectively aware of the '*finis ultimus.*'"[43]

There is a further point to be made about Schockenhoff's presentation of infused and acquired virtue in relationship to grace. That is, he says Thomas's understanding of the relationship of God and the human being in justification matured in his later writings, particularly in the *Summa theologiae;* he dropped the language of formal and material causality to describe the workings of grace, and used instead the analogy of motion: "The infusion of grace is now understood wholly as the outgoing motion of the divine mover; the *infusio* comes entirely from the *ipsa Dei moventis motio*, preserving God's absolute primacy in the whole process of movement in a stronger way than the relationship between form and matter. The turning of the *liberum arbitrium* to God in second place as a *motio ipsius mobilis* is itself sustained by the first movement of grace."[44]

Even in his changed understanding of grace, Thomas refused to drop his teaching that God's grace can only effect the justification of the sinner when it is accepted by a free decision of the human being. Schockenhoff says Thomas is "at the borders of what can be expressed in language and concepts" with this understading of grace as "motion." Thomas puts it this way: The free will's movement precedes the reception of grace but follows the infusion of grace.[45]

Thomas does not push the form–matter analogy further in respect to virtue in the way he does with respect to grace. "In the grace-teaching, motion is predominant. In the reflection on virtuous action, the analogy of *habitus*-form remains predominant. . . . They remain next to each other in open tension."[46] But, says Schockenhoff, it is no contradiction that Thomas did not revise his understanding of the relationship of the infused and acquired virtues in light of his further thinking about grace:

> We are at the boundaries of the understandable when we say that the responsible act of consent given by a human being in a free decision is at the same time the work of his grace-giving God; and there is no passing through this limit by further conceptual explication. Just here we are at a different theoretical situation than one of unsolvable paradox. The fact that reflection must check itself here, because there is no further explication possible through theological inquiry, is precisely what can be seen as a result of the inquiry itself. The border that theology's understanding is brought to, however, is seen in all its clarity as soon as we ask *how* such an occurrence should be thought about and presented conceptually. The beginner's optimism that led Thomas to think that he could cross over this boundary with the help of the Aristotelian categories of matter and form became ever more questionable to Aquinas in the course of his theological work. The special suspense that remains in his theological thought about grace even after his shift to the overriding *motio* analogy is thus also an indication of his growing skepticism in regard to the all too wide reaching attempts at explanation, that are sought for in isolated conceptual schemas within theology.[47]

Schockenhoff says there is no "cheap solution" in thinking through the implications of a theology of grace for a practical ethics of virtue. But he sees Thomas as having already gained much by resituating Christianity's language of virtue within theology (as outlined in the first section of this essay), and then by calling theology back to to a more organic understanding of how moral virtue works in the lives of real human beings (as seen in the second section). Now it is time for a more formal synthesis between theology and the ethics of virtue, which is the heart of this essay.

Shockenhoff's Synthesis of Aquinas's Theological Ethics of Virtue: *Caritas* Is the Preamble (*Prae-Ambulum*) of All Virtue

So far, we have seen Schockenhoff give us a way to understand our "partial acts" of goodness as participating in the life of God, that is, as manifestations of *caritas*. Why not, then, move from this directly to the affirmation for which Porter was seeking theological warrant at the beginning of this essay, namely, that people outside the Christian faith are included in the dynamic of charity and the infused moral virtues? First, Sherwin's concern needs to be addressed. The circle from *caritas* back to faith has to be closed, for as Thomas says curtly, "*Non potest habere . . . caritatem, nisi fidem habeat*" (I-II, 65.5). This third section of the essay shows how Schockenhoff's understanding of the connection between faith and *caritas* will indeed allow us to make Porter's affirmation.

This part outlines Schockenhoff's understanding of love's origins in faith, and then turns to his understanding of how faith is visible in love. Schockenhoff starts from Thomas's claim at the beginning of the II-II that the formal object of faith is "*veritas prima*" (II-II, 1.3): "In faith the human being experiences himself as called by God to participate in God's eternal truth; this is the first and most fundamental definition of Thomas toward which all other meanings of *fides* point. In faith the 'first truth' itself becomes the 'object' of the highest life expression of the human spirit, who recognizes his final goal in it. Thus, the right interpretation of this *veritas prima* provides the key to understanding Thomas's theology of faith as also of the systematic frame of its accompanying virtue ethic."[48]

What is our "participation" in the *veritas prima* of God? Schockenhoff says it must not be reduced to "a purely intellectual acceptance of a set of propositions,"[49] but he also insists on giving faith real intellectual content:

> Thomas sees . . . the whole universe as ordered to the truth of God, but that truth shines above all as a light on the human being as God's spiritual creature, a light which makes known to him the goal of his life and lets him see where he is underway to with the eyes of faith.
>
> Precisely for the sake of its ethical relevance, the cognitive nature of faith must not be underemphasized. Certainly every act of assent to the world as the creation of God is implicitly an act of faith, even if it does not rise to the level of clear consciousness and reflexive certainty. Such an understanding, however, only begins to articulate the actual function of faith. It is not as a necessary act of trust toward and first affirmation of life that makes faith, faith; but that the human being becomes certain of the truth of that which alone is worthy of his trust [is the essence of faith]. Only when the assent of the believer is sustained by the light of the self-manifesting "first truth" of God, does faith remain an act corresponding to the dignity of the spiritual and thus ethically responsible creature.[50]

What is the intellectual certainty reached by faith? Schockenhoff says its content per se consists in "only what immediately orders the human being to eternal life; of explicit faith nothing more is demanded than what leads the believer to his last end."[51] Then Schockenhoff gets more direct: Thomas' most profound contribution to Christianity's understanding of faith is in seeing it as an "inchoate" certainty about our future. The essence of faith is "a habit of the mind, whereby eternal life is begun in us, making the intellect assent to what is non-apparent."[52] Schockenhoff summarizes: "That faith, the 'inchoative' beginning of eternal life, reveals what the perfecting goal of life is and that faith also grasps it in a beginning way, is something Thomas saw in a way that none of his predecessors and none of his immediate successors saw; above all, in his interpretation of the eschatological structure of '*fides*' lies his personal contribution to faith-theology in the middle ages as a whole and in particular to its recognition of faith's practical relevance."[53]

To bring this eschatological emphasis home, Schockenhoff cites Thomas's allegorical reading of Exodus 13.21: "The Lord went before them by day in a pillar of cloud to lead the way." Writes Thomas: "Like a cloud, faith involves obscurity, because it deals with enigma; a dissolving [quality], because it is pulled upward; fluidity, because it excites toward devotion."[54] Faith is a certain knowledge, but one characterized by *obscuritas, aenigma, umiditas, et dissolutio.* Faith is an "imperfect knowledge" that dissolves into the enigma of God. Schockenhoff sums up Thomas's understanding of faith as a "twofold insight, with two poles between which his interpretation moves": "[First,] faith does not receive its worth from its confirmation in practical life, but only from the fact that in grace it touches the eternal truth of the revealing God. This position, which Thomas never abandoned, is crucial in order to keep ethics from being overloaded and burdened. But, [second and] at the same time, . . . faith is only a 'foretaste of the vision' (*praelibatio visionis*) and a beginning of eternal life in us because *caritas* lets it be adequate to its goal and leads faith to its full form in which, for the sake of *caritas, fides* becomes active and includes the wide arena of the moral life within its affirmation of divine truth."[55]

Just the opposite of divorcing our actions from their dependence on faith, Schockenhoff's view that infused virtue can be at work in a way unknown to those in whom it is working *depends on* this theological-eschatological understanding of faith itself. Faith unfolds as *caritas*, and that is the second point we need to take up in summarizing Schockenhoff's understanding of the infused moral virtues. And here we come to the heart of not only this section but also this whole essay. For Schockenhoff cites a remark of Thomas's in the *De Caritate* to argue for the "consummation of the canon of the virtues in *caritas*."[56] *Caritas* is the *prae-ambulum* of all virtues, including faith: "Friendship toward God [*caritas*], insofar as God is blessed and the cause of blessedness, needs to stand ahead of (*praestitui*) those virtues that order us towards blessedness. That is why, since it does not follow, but comes before (*praeambulum*), the other virtues, as I have shown, it needs to be a virtue."[57]

To call *caritas* faith's *preamble* is not to say it precedes faith (it never does) but that it "walks out ahead" of faith and all the infused moral virtues. Schockenhoff delightfully plays on the word *prae-ambulum*:

> In an incidental remark Thomas calls love the preamble of the virtues and thus indicates its place of pre-eminence in the canon of virtues. . . . The moral

life is always empowered by the word of love, though one is often lost along the way of trying to order life and its claims rightly in life's steps and partial advances. . . . Thus despite all its possibilities for error and despite all the actually committed errors, one's way is itself not an erring way. Having already hurried ahead (*prae-ambulare*) to the goal love has brought back news from there; in this way love lights the way, so that the still hidden way of moral action is seen as a *via perfectionis* leading the human being to his eternal goal in the community of the infinite Godhead.[58]

The fundamental theological-ethical claim of this essay can now be articulated, namely: Faith always *precedes* virtuous action in the world, and the full presence of faith *only* makes itself known in a life of the infused moral virtues ordered to *caritas;* for *caritas* and the infused moral virtues *run ahead* of faith toward the consummation of our lives in friendship with God. That statement is the heart not only of this essay but also of Schockenhoff's 1987 presentation of Aquinas's theological ethic of virtue.

There is much to be filled out with regard to the practical ethical implications of this claim, and Schockenhoff begins to do that work in his thesis, though much of the work is taken further in his subsequent writing. For our purposes, it is enough to indicate three practical implications Schockenhoff sees his presentation of virtue ethics to have. I sketch each here briefly, referring to the specific places in Schockenhoff's translated work where each can be found.

First, for Schockenhoff the moral life is primarily one of friendship with God, the "concentric middle" formed by the theological virtues. The truest *bonum hominis*, says Schockenhoff at the end of his book, is life with God:

> The *beatitudo* offered to us by God appears as the highest and actual good of the human being. This exceeding perfection of the human being, one which the human being does not reach by his own powers and which leads him beyond those natural powers, is in this perspective the *bonum hominis principale*, or simply the highest absolute instance of human being, the *optimum hominis.* This utmost perfection of human action is not only a goal unreachable in this life. It is also a goal to which every intermediate goal and every fragmentarily reached form of the good life witnesses; and a goal in which faith, hope and love are already inchoatively taken hold.[59]

This *optimum hominis* means that the life of virtue has no upward boundary; it is simply the invitation into deeper, more "intense" friendship with God.[60]

The second practical moral implication of this view of virtue is one Schockenhoff only begins to get at in his 1987 study. This same life of friendship with God has clear lower borders. At the end of his dissertation, Schockenhoff writes: "Moral commands designate only an entry-securing lower-boundary for the moral life: below that boundary it makes no sense to speak about love."[61] What Schockenhoff establishes here is that love is only able to work "all the way down" in a human being because it works through the requirements of moral virtue: "Love does not neglect or overrun the right standards of the ethical; it moves the lover to an ever growing readiness to be lead by those standards."[62]

Working out the relationship between the absolute "lower borders" of love and its borderless entry into the *via perfectionis* is the work of Schockenhoff's book *Natural Law and Human Dignity*. This book works theoretically through the relationship of love and justice, contending that "there is no competition between justice and love."[63] For this essay, for now, it is enough to see that Schockenhoff's claim that love "walks ahead" of all the virtues does not mean all their acts are reduced to acts of love.

The third practical ethical implication of love walking ahead of all virtue to friendship with God is that this friendship is the ground of the autonomy of ethics. Schockenhoff says that Thomas had this view of the matter in mind from the start of the *Summa theologiae*: "Not one of its questions" is unrelated to Thomas's claim that *caritas est quaedam amicitia hominis ad Deum.*[64] When Thomas wrote in the prologue of I-II that the human being is the image of God in that she is the cause of her own action (*ipse est suorum operum principorum*), Schockenhoff insists that Thomas already had in mind what he would say in the discourse about *caritas* in II-II, 23.1: "It is written (John 15:15): 'I will not call you servants . . . but my friends.' Now this was said to them by reason of nothing else than *caritas*." Schockenhoff writes on the second-to-last page of his book: "For Thomas moral autonomy is the freedom of the friend of God, who no longer needs any outside law because she has already accepted God's assent to everything that is good as her own law; [it is the freedom of one who] on the basis of being invited into the friendship of God, freely shares God's love for everything that is worthy of it. Such a theological understanding of freedom can give ethical autonomy its rightful home within a Christian reflection on faith, since it does not accept freedom . . . as a stranger; rather faith sets that freedom free on its [faith's] own theological grounds."[65]

Schockenhoff takes this issue of ethics' autonomy much further in his later book as an argument in support of natural law ethics.[66] That argument finds its presuppositions in the theological understanding of virtue presented in this essay: Not despite but because of its grounding in faith's "enigmatic" understanding of God, this virtue ethic will look for virtue wherever it is to be found in the world.

But my main concern is to see the specific possibilities of this theological understanding of virtue for grounding an understanding of infused virtue at work interreligiously. I turn to that now in the conclusion.

Eschatological Faith and the Humble Certainty of Infused Virtues' Operation beyond the Christian Church

In this essay's introduction, we saw the reluctance of some contemporary English-speaking Christian ethicists with regard to infused moral virtue's connection to a Christian theology of religious pluralism. That reluctance involves the desire of Christian ethicists to protect something of the specificity of Christian ethics: of its relation to Christian faith (Sherwin, in particular), and of a Christian understanding of grace (Porter, in particular). Though Schockenhoff's book does not directly address the presence of the infused virtues beyond Christianity, I contend that the theology of the virtues developed here fully responds to these grounds for reluctance.

With respect to faith, Sherwin wrote of the need for those who possess infused virtue to have some "conceptual, even if limited, understanding of God's love revealed to us in Christ." Schockenhoff's presentation of Aquinas's theory of infused virtue accepts Sherwin's claim about virtue's connection to the knowledge of faith but outbids it theologically. The eschatological nature of faith means that the knowledge we are given now by God's gift is a felt and known *inchoatio* of eternal life. It is an intellectual conviction about our safety in God. On theological grounds, we should be careful against overstating the conceptual or propositional nature of faith's knowledge. Schockenhoff gives Thomas's allegorical reading of faith as the pillar of cloud leading the Jews in the desert. Faith's knowledge is certain; it is enough for the journey . . . and it is *obscura, aenigmata, dissoluta, et excitans ad devotionem.*

Faith's knowledge is a cloud that goes ahead of the believer as guidance, but its concepts "evaporate." What they evaporate into is the devotion of *caritas* and the infused moral virtues, which become faith's preamble, announcing its presence. Schockenhoff says that faith's first practical function in the lives of human beings "is to let us know the goal that, even unaware, we are stretching toward in all our actions."[67]

Schockenhoff's understanding of faith's knowledge evaporating into love meets well the Dominican theologian Herbert McCabe's reading of John 14.5, "No one comes to the Father, but by me." Writes McCabe:

> In Jesus . . . we do not understand God but we can watch God understanding himself. God's understanding of God is that he throws himself away in love, that he keeps nothing back for himself. God's understanding of God is that he is a love that unconditionally accepts, that always lets others be, even if what they want to be is his murderers. God's understanding of God is that he is not a special person with a special kind of message, with a special way of living to which he wants people to conform. God's understanding of God could not appear to us as someone who wants to found a new and better religion, or

recommend a special new discipline or way of life, a religious code laid upon us for all time because it is from God. God's understanding of God is that he [*sic*] just says: 'Yes, *be;* be human, but be really human; be human if it kills you—and it will.[68]

A Christian understanding of faith visible in love could find much to theologize about in the "socially engaged Buddhism," whose spokesperson Thich Nhat Hanh describes the movement's goals "in his etymological analysis of the word 'comprehend,' which means to pick something up and be with it. . . . The strength to continue the intense involvement (in caring for people in their sufferings) can only come from a deep, inner peace born of meditation, of practicing mindfulness in each moment of our daily lives."[69] I am not trying to claim Thich Nhat Hanh for Christianity. I am saying that his life is evidence that what Christian theology calls infused virtue is at work outside Christianity. Not despite our faith would we say this, but because of it.

And what of Porter's concern that an interreligiously open theory of infused virtue could obscure the distinction between nature and grace? Porter is right to critique any hint of understanding grace as somehow built into the "existential horizon" or "transcendental" nature of human beings. (In fact, Schockenhoff shares the critique.[70]) But perhaps this concern is already answered in the *prae-ambulum* text. The *caritas* infused in us by God walks ahead of faith as its surest sign; it is not we who walk ahead, at least not on our own. In describing Thomas's use of Aristotle's friendship teaching to describe our relationship with God, Schockenhoff says the teaching gets "turned on its side . . . moved a quarter turn, ninety degrees from the horizontal to the vertical, . . . set on a new axis . . . by means of a bridge built by God."[71]

Referring to Thomas's understanding that the *ordo caritatis* is maintained in eternal life (for according to Thomas, in eternal life we will still love most those who are most closely related to us), Schockenhoff adds that "humility of thought forbids Thomas from thinking about particulars of who will be loved most in eternal life for 'all the reasons for loving are incomparably surpassed by the reason of closeness to God (*Incomparabiliter praefertur ratio dilectionis . . . ex propinquitate ad Deum'*"; II-II, 26.13). Closeness to God in charity is the "incomparably preferable" reason for us to love another human being. And, adds Thomas, "the quantity of *caritas* in us depends on nothing except the will of the Holy Spirit."[72]

Doesn't the same humility require us not to make exclusivist claims for Christianity with regard to the life of infused moral virtue? And with regard to Porter's concern about the theology of grace at work in Dupuis's interreligious openness, we could look to his last book, written in 2003, to answer the concerns of the Vatican's Congregation for the Doctrine of Faith about the very 1997 book about which Porter was also concerned. In Dupuis's last book, the earlier references to a "supernatural existential" of grace are gone, as are references to the transcendence of the person. In their place, Dupuis writes of Christianity's deepest impetus toward interreligious pluralism:

> On what basis, then, can the affirmation of a religious pluralism "in principle" be based? The appeal to faith in a plurality of persons in the one God is not in itself a sufficient reason for it; a simple appeal to the "plural" character of all reality would be even more inadequate. Nor will it do simply to point to the variety of ways in which human beings, in the diversity of cultures in the world, have given expression to their search for the divine Mystery. . . . If, however, religion and the religions originate in a self-manifestation of God to human beings, the primary foundation for the principle of multiplicity is the superabundant riches and variety of God's self-manifestation to humankind. . . . Religious pluralism in principle is then based on the immensity of a God who is Love and communication.[73]

In none of this do I mean criticism of Porter, who herself is seeking deeper theological reasons to support Dupuis. What I have tried to do in this essay is suggest that the reasons we seek are already given in Schockenhoff's 1987 dissertation at Tübingen. There are no references to interreligious dialogue in that dissertation, but its theological foundation in a Christian theology of infused virtue is there. It should not surprise us, then, that in his 1996 book (2003, English translation), Schockenhoff gives voice to a theory of interreligious dialogue. He articulates his theory in reference to the biblical tradition of vicarious representation, in which the chosen people thought of themselves as standing in for all humanity; and he relies specifically on the eschatological nature of Christian faith:

> The truth which is discovered and lived (doubtless in a fragmentary and imperfect manner) within the faith community of the church does not seek to replace the paths of ethical experience in the other world religions; it wishes to lead these to grasp the highest possibilities which they possess and to set them free to realize their own inherent fullness. This is why Christian truth need not disqualify those aspects of successful human existence which have been further developed or better preserved in other cultural spheres than in the Western civilization which bears the imprint of the Gospel message. On the contrary, the model of . . . a vicarious existence on behalf of others suggests that we should be able to learn from the ethical traditions of the other peoples. Their testimony reminds the church that she is the eschatological community of salvation to which God has entrusted the revelation of his love, and that she is always *in via* towards full knowledge of the truth.[74]

If Schockenhoff articulates this eschatological affirmation in this later work, it is because he had already laid out its foundation in his 1987 treatment of the infused and acquired virtues. We English-speaking and -writing Christian ethicists who are interested in infused virtue as an interreligious reality would do well do study that earlier work.

Notes

1. Robert Sokolowski, *The God of Faith and Reason: Foundations of Christian Theology* (Notre Dame, Ind.: University of Notre Dame Press, 1982), 89.

2. Stanley Hauerwas and Charles Pinches, *Christians among the Virtues: Theological Conversations with Ancient and Modern Authors* (Notre Dame, Ind.: University of Notre Dame Press, 1997), 127–28.

3. Hauerwas and Pinches, *Christians among the Virtues*, 128.

4. Sokolowski, *God of Faith and Reason*, 78, 100.

5. "Die bisher dargestellten intellektuellen, moralischen, und theologischen Tugenden . . . bilden . . . eine aufsteigende Pyramide, deren Spitze die Liebe ist. . . . So kann sich in der Tat der Eindruck aufdrängen, Thomas sehe in der Liebe nur die abschließende Krönung seines Tugendkanons . . . nur als Appendix verstehen, der einer in sich geschlossenen Darstellung des ethischen Handelns nachträglich." Eberhard Schockenhoff, *Bonum Hominis: Die anthropologischen und theologischen Grundlagen der Tugendethik des Thomas von Aquin* (Mainz: Matthias-Grünewald Verlag, 1987), 286–87. English translations of Schockenhoff's *Bonum Hominis* are mine.

6. "Die vorangehenden Stufen ohne diese letzte und höchste sein können." Schockenhoff, *Bonum Hominis*, 286.

7. "La grâce étant chassée par le péché tout le reste de l'édifice se trouve atteint. Thomas enseigne donc . . . che la nature humaine n'a jamais existé sans la grâce sanctifiante." Jean-Pierre Torrell, "Nature et grâce chez Thomad d'Aquin," *Revue Thomiste* 1001 (2001): 199. (In my translation, I switch the order in which the two phrases appear in Torrell's essay without any change in their meaning.)

8. The debate is well summarized by Torrell, *Nature et grâce chez Thomad d'Aquin*,168–69. Thomas's *Summa theologiae* is cited parenthetically within the body of this essay; Thomas's text will be cited according to the "Blackfriars Edition" (New York: McGraw-Hill, 1964 and ff.)

9. "In den theologischen Tugenden und innerhalb des unter ihnen waltenden *'ordo perfectionis'* in der *'caritas'* (I-II, 62.4) hat Thomas den Schlußstein des ganzen Bauwerkes seiner Tugendethik gefunden." Schockenhoff, *Bonum Hominis*, 284.

10. "Liest man die nun zu interpretierenden Texte unbefangen, so kann man sich des ersten Eindrucks nicht erwehren, von Thomas in einen neu sich öffenden Raum des theologischen Nachdenkens geführt zu werden, an dessen Schwelle man Stück für Stück all das zurücknehmen muß, was unter Berufung auf Aristoteles und eine breite moralphilosophische Tradition auch er selbst bislang ausdrücklich anerkannte. . . . [Thomas] interpretiert den ganzen . . . Weg durch das Feld der natürlichen Tugenden neu im Licht von Glaube, Hoffnung und Liebe." Schockenhoff, *Bonum Hominis*, 287–88, 285.

11. "Thomas pense qu'il n'y a pas de réussite morale achevée sans le guérison apportée par la grâce, car l'homme, détourné par le péche de sa vraie fin, n'est plus au clair sur le principe meme de sa vie morale; afin de pouvoir agir efficacement dans l'ordre moral, l'homme doit donc prendre de nouveau Dieu pour fin, et c'est cela qui n'est pas possible sans la grâce, car de fait cet ordre moral est aussi surnaturel dès son origine par la creation dans la grâce. Si

donc, pur reprendre le cas du païen observeant la loi, le théologien observe une semblable réussite, il se trouve en droit de supposer non seulement que la grace n'y est pas étrangère, mais qu'elle est bel et bien à l'œuvre, fût-ce de façon anonyme." Torrell, *Nature et grâce chez Thomad d'Aquin*, 197.

12. Alongside this text acknowledging grace outside of Christianity, there surely exist many Thomistic texts that presuppose non-Christians to be living in mortal sin—most egregious perhaps is II-II, 10.8, on compelling unbelievers to accept Christianity. Though these texts will not be directly dealt with in this essay, it would perhaps be fruitful to think of Thomas as holding the time-limited and wrong assumption that failure to become a Christian is a failure to have faith. If the necessity of faith can be separated from faith's historical forms (as Schockenhoff will help us do), we are in a better position to accept the profound and provocative truth of Thomas's teaching that the first actual sin a person commits has to be a mortal sin—a rejection of God (see I-II, 89.6). Then the question becomes whether Christians really want to claim that people of other faiths have rejected God, or whether we do better to wonder if our practice of faith might mask a deeper rejection of God in our own lives.

13. Bonnie Kent, "Habits and Virtues (in the *Summa Theologiae*)," in *The Ethics of Aquinas*, ed. Stephen J. Pope (Washington, D.C.: Georgetown University Press, 2002), 125–26.

14. Angela McKay, "The Infused and Acquired Virtues in Aquinas' Moral Philosophy" (PhD diss., Department of Philosophy, University of Notre Dame, 2004), 195. The dissertation is available online from University of Notre Dame Electronic Theses and Dissertations at http://etd.nd.edu/ETD-db/theses/available/etd-04152004-125337.

15. Here is Sherwin's argument in its fuller context: "Thomas can affirm that love of God presupposes knowledge of God. Since this knowledge is mediated to us by faith, this means that in this life charity depends on faith for its very existence. Thomas advances the traditional Catholic doctrine of the centrality of Christ in the work of salvation: all people are saved through Christ. Yet, in the context of Aquinas' teaching on the role of knowledge in one's love for God, does this mean that to be saved one must have explicit knowledge of Christ? . . . All are saved through faith in Christ (II-II, 2.7). But Aquinas's position is nuanced. He recognizes, for example, that those who lived before Christ were saved by merely having an 'implicit' or 'veiled' knowledge of Christ.(II-II, 2.8). Yet, what of those who, although born after Christ, still have no knowledge of him? Vatican II, GS 22. The challenge for the theologian is to construct a theology of grace that explains how this offer is given by the Spirit and freely responded to by the individual.

From Thomas's principles, we can affirm that such persons' response to grace, if it is to be a human response lived in charity, requires some conceptual, even if limited, understanding of God's love revealed to us in Christ. This conclusion appears necessary once we grasp the relationship between knowledge and love in the act of living faith. It would, no doubt, be an 'implicit' and 'veiled' knowledge of Christ. Yet, from the Thomistic perspective, the Holy Spirit's veiled offer would nevertheless entail a colloquy between God and the rational creature, a colloquy of knowledge and love, offer and response. St. Thomas's understanding of charity's relationship to knowledge of God, therefore, raises questions for both soteriology and missiology that merit further reflection." Michael Sherwin, *By Knowledge and by Love: Charity and Knowledge in the Moral Theology of St. Thomas Aquinas* (Washington, D.C.: Catholic University of America Press, 2005), 233–35.

16. Jean Porter, *Nature as Reason: A Thomistic Theology of the Natural Law* (Grand Rapids: William B. Eerdmans, 2004), 396–98.

17. See Porter, *Nature as Reason*, 397 n. 81, for the statement on Dupuis's Rahnerian understanding of grace; see Porter, *Nature as Reason*, 383–84, for the critique of Rahner's understanding of grace. Porter is indeed accurate that Dupuis defends this Rahnerian notion of grace in his 1997 book. The text cited above in the paper is from Louis Dupuis, *Toward a Christian Theology of Religious Pluralism* (Maryknoll, N.Y.: Orbis Press, 1997), 218.

18. See the full citation above in note 5. The ony two references to Schockenhoff's dissertation I have seen in English language treatments of virtue simply acknowledge its existence; they do not analyze it. See: Romanus Cessario, *The Moral Virtues and Theological Ethics* (Notre Dame, Ind.: University of Notre Dame Press, 1991), 158 n. 6; and Jon Inglis, "Aquinas's Replication of the Acquired Moral Virtues: Rethinking the Standard Philosophical Intrepretation of Moral Virtue in Aquinas," *Journal of Religious Ethics* 27/1 (1991): 4 n. 2. I have not been able to locate any English language reviews of his book. But see the extended review by Servais Pinckaers in *Freibürger Zeitschrift für Philosophie und Theologie* 37 (1990): 253–62.

19. Eberhard Schockenhoff, *Natural Law and Human Dignity: Universal Ethics in an Historical World*, trans. Brian McNeil (Washington, D.C.: Georgetown University Press, 2003); and Eberhard Schockenhoff, "The Theological Virtue of Charity," in *Ethics of Aquinas*, ed. Pope, 244–58.

20. "Auf das Reflexionsglied der '*virtus moralis infusa*' verzichten hieße für Thomas nicht, einen überflüssigen Ballast abwerfen, der das theologische Denken nur überflüssig kompliziert, sondern die anthropologische Binnenstruktur des menschlichen Handelns überspringen, die er gerade herausarbeiten möchte. Wenn er so entschieden auf seiner These von den eingegossenen moralischen Tugenden beharrt, dann verrät er nicht . . . das tragende Anliegen seiner ganzen Tugendethik. Er bleibt ihm vielmehr dort treu, wo er als Theologe danach fragt, wie der Anruf der Gnade den Menschen in der natürlichen Struktur seines Handelns erreicht." Schockenhoff, *Bonum Hominis*, 307–8.

21. The word *prae-ambulum* is taken from a text in Thomas's *De Caritate*; its import will become clear later. See note 57 below.

22. "Er selbst hat darin freilich weit weniger Schwierigkeiten gesehen als die meisten seiner späteren Kommentatore. Wie die 'neuen' eingegossenen Tugenden sich zu den bereits im Menschen vorhandenen erworbenen verhalten, ob sie in ihrer das Handeln prägenden Wirkung an diesen anknüpften oder eine parallel in der Seele tätigen Tugendorganismus von völlig eigener Struktur bilden, welche Funktion unter oder neben der von Gott geschenkten '*virtus*' schließlich die durch den Menschen erworbene Tugend behält, all das is für Thomas fast nur am Rande. . . . Daß sich die spätere Diskussion mit Vorliebe an solchen Fragen entzündet, die für Thomas nicht unmittelbarer Gegenstand seines Nachdenkens sind, kann dem Versuch einer interpretierenden Aneigung der thomanischen These nur zur Warnung dienen: Statt der Gedankengang des Thomas zu einer verselbständigten Systematik der 'übernatürlichen Tugenden' auszubauen, versucht sie . . . daß sie das eigene Verständnis darlegt, das Thomas von seiner These hat, und nach dem Grund sucht, warum ihm die meisten der später aufgebrochenen Probleme noch kein Kopfzerbrechen bereiten." Schockenhoff, *Bonum Hominis*, 308–9.

23. See Schockenhoff, *Bonum Hominis*, 293–300, esp. 299–300.

24. See ibid., 311.

25. "Als Leitfaden auf der Suche nach der authentisch thomanischen Antwort soll dabei das Modell der Verhältnisbestimmung zwischen göttlichen und menschlichem Wirken dienen, das der Gnadentraktat der STh entwickelt." Schockenhoff, *Bonum Hominis*, 309.

26. "Das '*delectabiliter operari*' ist die zugespitzte Pointe des Tugendbegriffes, der die natürlichen, erworbenen Tugenden im Auge hat; es ist die spontan sich einstellende Freude am Guten, die das gute Handeln vollendet und zum untrüglichen Zeichen der '*virtus*' wird." Schockenhoff, *Bonum Hominis*, 311. In note 74 on that same page, he cites Thomas's *De virtutibus in communis*, article 1: "Ex hic potest patere quod habitus virtutum ad tria indigemus. Primo ut sit uniformitas in sua operatione. . . . Secundo ut operatio perfecta in promptu habeatur. . . . Tertio, ut delectabiliter perfecta operatio compleatur."

27. "Die Reflexion auf das Wirken Gottes am Menschen kann sich der Tatsache nicht verschließen, daß die Wirksamkeit der göttlichen Gnade in den psychischen Strukturen des

Menschen nicht unmittelbar als seelische Erlebnisqualität gegeben ist. . . . Genau dies [die *'delectatio'*] aber ist bei den eingegossenen Tugenden noch nicht der Fall. . . . Es ist ihnen nicht gegeben, die Motivkraft des Guten als erlebbare Freude verspüren zu lassen; zumindest im Anfang entbehrt ein nur der *'virtus infusa'* entspringendes Handeln der *'delectatio'* die der erworbenen Tugend zu eigen ist." Schockenhoff, *Bonum Hominis*, 312–13.

28. "Welchen Sinn hat es, die von Gott geschenkte und die von Menschen erworbene Tugend mit dem gleichen Begriff der *'virtus'* zu bezeichnen, wenn der *'virtus infusa'* gerade das Deutungselement abgeht, das den praktisch erfahrbaren Ertrag der *'virtus acquisita'* ausmacht? . . . Die eingegossene Tugend ist . . . eine *'virtus incompleta.'*" Schockenhoff, *Bonum Hominis*, 313, 315.

Jean Porter speaks about infused virtue in a similar way in her 1992 study. It is Aquinas's "subversion" of Aristotle's perfectionstic theory of virtue. See Porter, "The Subversion of Virtue: Acquired and Infused Virtues in the *Summa Theologiae*," *Annual of the Society of Christian Ethics*, 1992), esp. 30–33.

29. "In allen seinen Dimensionen wird der Mensch Gott zugewandt; die Hinkehr seines Geistes zu Gott prägt sich auch dem unteren Schichten der Seele auf, so daß die *'conversio ad Deum'* eine umfassende anthropologische Wirklichkeit wird. . . . Muß die Wirkung von Gottes berufender Gnade auch bis in diese Tiefenschichten hinabreichen und dort in der Art einer dem Menschen wahrhaft zu eigenen Neuen Seinsqualität bleibend gegeben sein." Schockenhoff, *Bonun Hominis*, 319, 301.

30. The text is from I-II, 113.1; it is cited at Schockenhoff, *Bonum Hominis*, 319 n. 104.

31. "Nur von diesem Zentrum her entfalten sich die Linien seines theologisch-ethisches Nachdenkens über dieVollendung des Menschen unter dem Anruf Gottes. Nur indem Thomas die dort entspringenden Linien weiter auszieht und sie bis in die anthropologische Struktur des zur Vollendung bestimmten Menschen hinein verfolgt, gelangt er zur Einsicht in die Notwendigkeit der theologischen und schließlich auch der eingegossenen moralischen Tugenden." Schockenhoff, *Bonum Hominis*, 301–2.

32. "Die Frageebene, auf der eine Tugendethik ihre genuine Leistungsfähigkeit entfaltet, ist erst dort eröffnet, wo die ethische Analyse zu erhellen versucht, wie sich das von der Vernunft erkannte Gut auf die willentlichen Energien und psychischen Handlungskräfte des Menschen überträgt und deren eigenen Beitrag zum Gelingen des guten Handelns mobilisiert . . . . Das *'ultimum complementum bonitatis,'* die letzte Perfektionierung, die das menschliche Handeln zu seiner im Gedanken der *'virtus'* anvisierten Zielgestalt führt, erwächst aus einem Zusammenspiel aller seelischen Kräfte, in dem die Fähigkeit zur rationalen Handlungsorientierung in die anthropologisch tiefer verwurzelte Bereitschaft zum spontane, freudigen und konstanten Tun des Guten überführt wird." Schockenhoff, *Bonum Hominis*, 579; see note 15, quoting Thomas *De virtutibus in communis*, a.4, ad 2.

33. "Das konkrete Gut, das zu verwirklichen die Gerechtigkeit in einer ganz bestimmten Lage fordert, zeigt sich dem Gerechten durch sine eigenes Gerecht-Sein an; indem er das Gerechte tut und es immer wieder tut, reift in ihm ein affektives und durch Erfahrung gewachsenes Urteilsvermögen (*'cognitio affectiva seu experimentalis'*) heran, das ihn das Gerechte aus konnaturaler Übereinstimmung erkennen läßt." Schockenhoff, *Bonum Hominis*, 580–81.

34. The text is from *De Caritate*, 11 ad 12: "Qui consistit in his quae organice ordinantur ad perfectionem caritatis." Cited at Schockenhoff, *Bonum Hominis*, 554 n. 289.

35. "Sie läßt die unglückliche Diastase erst gar nicht aufbrechen, die Theologie und Ethik voneinander trennt und die doppelte Gefahr einer glaubensloser Praxis und eines praxisfremden Glaubens heraufbeschwört." Schockenhoff, *Bonum Hominis*, 583–84.

36. Schockenhoff repeats his assertion three times: "Weder die *'virtus acquisita'* noch die *'virtus infusa'* prägen den praktischen Vollzug guten Handelns in der Reinform, die sich im

Gedankenlaboratorium der Wesenanalyse erkennen lassen. Einer theologischen Betrachtung, wie Thomas ihr in der STh folgt, zeigt sich die erworbene Tugend wie jedes natürliche Vermögen des Menschen nicht mehr in einem neutralen, hinsichtlich der Gnade noch unentschiedenen Status. Sie ist vielmehr in einem konkreten Menschen gegeben, der sich dem Anruf der Gnade in freier Entschiedenheit oder unbewußter Bereitschaft öffnet oder aber sich ihm gegenüber verschließt. In Anbetracht der die Antwort seiner geistigen Kreatur von Ewigkeit her suchenden Liebe Gottes gibt es für keinen Menschen den Stand der Unentschiedenheit. Gott ist im Leben sein vernünftigen Geschöpfe immer im Modus liebender Bejahung oder der Ablehnung zugegen; das praktische Handeln steht zu seinem letzten Ziel in einer notwendigen Hinordnung, die es nur in Annahme oder Abwendung vollziehen, nicht aber aufheben kann. . . .

Reine, nur durch die '*virtus acquisita*' in ihrem ursprünglichen Leistungsvermögen geformte sittliche Akte sind in der konkreten Heilsordnung nicht gegeben; sie stehen entweder bereits unter dem Einfluß der göttlichen Gnade und entspringen damit zugleich der '*virtus infusa*,' oder aber sie unterliegen noch der alten Schwächung durch die Sünde, aus der sich der Mensch nicht aus eigenen Kräften befreien kann."

At the end of this section, Schockenhoff repeats the conviction a third time: "Diese im Tun des Gute erlebbare Lust am Guten kommt dem aus der eingegossenen und der erworbenen '*virtus*' gemeinsam geprägten Handeln zu. Nur in abstrakter Analyse läßt sich die fundamentale Ermöglichung dazu auf die '*virtus infusa*' und das Moment der Leichtigkeit auf das Wirken der erworbenen Tugend zurückführen." Schockenhoff, *Bonum Hominis*, 327–28, 347.

37. "Wenn die erworbenen Tugenden des Sünders so auch in sich wahre Tugenden sind, so verwirklichen sie ihr Wesen doch nur unvollkommen und gebrochen; was ihnen ursprünglich an natürlicher Vollkommenheit zugedacht war, das erreichen sie nur mehr in eine durch die Gnade Gottes geheilter Natur. Das aber heißt: Nur in Verbindung mit der '*virtus moralis infusa*' gewinnt die '*virtus acquisita*' die ihr ursprünglich zu eigene Stärke zurück; auf sich allein gestellt bleibt sie hinter dem, was ihre natürliche Bestimmung ist, zurück und tendiert auf die Dauer . . . auf die Stufe einer Disposition zurück." Schockenhoff, *Bonum Hominis*, 328–29.

Schockenhoff thinks Thomas's description in I-II, 65.2, of a (very limited) existence of the moral virtues without *caritas* represents an abandonment of his earlier, more Aristotelian position: "Den Satz aus dem Sentenz Kommentar, daß in gleicher Weise, wie die eingegossenen Tugenden durch die Liebe geformt sind, auch die durch den Menschen erworbenen Tugenden die '*perfecta ratio virtutis*' erfüllen, sofern sie von der Klugheit geleitet sind, kann Thomas an dieser Stelle der STh offenbar so nicht mehr wiederholen." Schockenhoff, *Bonum Hominis*, 288.

38. "Da beide, die eingegossene wie die erworbene Tugend in einem jeweils verschiedenen Sinn eine '*virtus incompleta*' darstellen, der entweder die vollendete Leichtigkeit und Freudigkeit oder die innere Ausrichtung auf das letzte Ziel abgehen, können sie nicht nur in einer seelischen Potenz zusammen existieren, sondern auch gemeinsam wirken und die aus ihrem gemeinsamen anthropologischen Sitz hervorgehenden Akte in eine Weise formen, daß sie die spezifische Prägewirking beide zukommt, ohne daß in den hervorgebrachten Akten selbst noch der jeweilige Anteil der einer oder der anderen adäquat zu trennen wäre." Schockenhoff, *Bonum Hominis*, 337–38.

39. "Warum [hat] Thomas selbst in einer Sache, die solchen Aufwand erfordert, so wenig verläßliche Vorarbeit gelesitet? Mangelt es ihm an Problembewußtsein? Übersieht er gar nicht die Konsequenzen, die seine Theorie der eingegossenen sittlichen Tugenden mit sich führt? . . . Müßte nicht, bevor solches zumindest implizit unterstellt wird, die näherliegende Möglichkeit geprüft werden, daß Thomas an der Stelle, an der seine Kommentatoren danach suchen, kein Problem mehr sehen kann, weil er es bereits anderswo gelöst zu haben glaubt?" Schockenhoff, *Bonum Hominis*, 331–32.

40. "Nous dirions que les (vertus naturelles) sont comme la matière, et les (vertus surnaturelles) comme la forme, en celui qui pratique la vertu en état de grace." George Klubertanz, "Une théorie sur les vertus morales," *Revue Thomiste* 59 (1959): 571.

Bonnie Kent thinks Klubertanz's solution "especially" deserves to be looked at here, but asks: "How, exactly, can one agent be directed to two ends? If he desires the happiness of this life only for the sake of eternal happiness, the happiness of this life seems to lose its status as an end; but if he desires both worldly happiness and eternal happiness, how does he reconcile the two ends in practice?" Bonnie Kent, *Virtues of the Will: The Transformation of Ethics in the Late Thirteenth Century* (Washington, D.C.: Catholic University of America Press, 1995), 33 and note 71 on the same page. See Schockenhoff's response to Klubertanz at *Bonum Hominis*, 332 n. 137.

41. The text from Thomas is from I-II, 111.2 ad 2, and is cited at Schockenhoff, *Bonum Hominis*, 333 n. 142.

Here is Schockenhoff's outline of the complementary relationship between grace and free will in justification: "Ist zur *iustificatio impii* auch eine Bewegung des freien Willens auf seiten des Menschens gefordert? (see I-II, 113.3). . . . Gott bewegt alle Dinge gemäß ihre natürlichen Eigenart; er achtet die ihnen wesenhaft zu eigene Wirkweise und tut ihnen keinen Zwang an. . . . Erst recht gilt dieses Prinzip seines Wirkens unter den Geschöpfen, wenn er in freier Liebe an seiner geistigen Kreatur handelt. Er bewegt den Menschen zur Gerechtigkeit, wie es seiner Natur entspricht. Damit alle Gewaltsamkeit von der Aktivität Gottes ausgeschlossen bleibt, handelt er so am Menschen, daß dieser zugleich handelt; er bewegt ihn in der Art, daß es zugleich des Menschen freie Bewegung ist. Gegenüber dem gerechtmachenden Handeln Gottes nimmt die freie Bewegung des Menschen des Charakter des *Konsenses* an . . . Ohne die Zustimmung gibt es keine Gerechtmachung; Gottes Handeln an seiner Schöpfung ist, wo es dem Menschen als seiner freien Kreatur gilt, immer ein Handeln das die Aktivität des Menschen einschließt. . . . Für die hier vor allem anvisierte Zuordnung von '*infusio gratiae*' und Zustimmung des '*liberum arbitrium*' bedeutet dies, daß beide im Verhältnis einer *reziproken Priorität* zueinander stehen; unter jeweils verschiedener Rücksicht gebührt sowohl dem Handeln Gottes wie auch dem Konsens des Menschen der logische Vorrang. Die doppelte Bewegung des '*liberum arbitrium*' (Hinkehr zu Gott und Abwendung von der Sünde) geht [im Thomas Frühwerk] als '*causa materialis*' der '*infusio gratiae*' und der '*remissio peccatorum*' voraus, folgt ihr aber nach, sobald der ganze Vorgang der '*iustificatio*' von seiner '*causa formalis*' her beleuchtet wird; hinsichtlich der Formalursächlichkeit, deren Wirken die Gerechtmachung des Menschen trägt, kommt ausschließlich der Eingießung der Gnade und mit ihr zusammen dem Nachlaß der Sünde Priorität zu." Schockenhoff, *Bonum Hominum*, 333–34.

42. "Wenn schon zwei verschiedene Potenzen einen gemeinsamen Akt aus sich hervorgehen lassen können, dann ist nicht einzusehen, weshalb die eingegossene und die erworbene Tugend in derselben komplementären Struktur, in ein und derselben Potenz nich das gleiche bewirken sollen. Daß die '*virtus infusa*' zusammen mit der erworbenen Tugend den gemeinsamen Effekt '*non ex aequo, sed ordine quodam*' hervorbringt, ist durch ihre wechselseitige Zuordnung und die Subordination der erworbenen unter die eingegossene Tugend zur Genüge gewährleistet." Schockenhoff, *Bonum Hominis*, 338.

43. "Die '*virtus acquisita*' kann der eingegossenen Tugend unterstehen, insofern der Handelnde selbst das Ziel seines sittlichen Tuns dem Richtungssinn der '*virtus infusa*' einfügt und eine subjektive Subordination der Ziele konstituiert. Ebenso kann im gemeinsamen Wirken der '*virtus infusa*' und der '*virtus acquisita*' aber auch eine objektive Unterordnung gegeben sein, insofern nämlich die letztere auf ihr eigenes Ziel ausgerichtet bleibt, das neben seiner Funktion als unmittelbarer '*finis*' der erworbenen Tugend zugleich als ein Zwischenziel fungiert, das auch unabhängig von der subjektiven Aufmerksamkeit des Handelnden dem '*finis ultimus*' untersteht." Schockenhoff, *Bonum Hominis*, 337.

44. "Die Eingießung der Gnade wird nun als ganz von dem göttlichen Beweger ausgehende Bewegung verstanden; die '*infusio*' wird in strenger Identität zur '*ipsa Dei moventis motio,*' die noch stärker, als es in der Überlegenheit der Form über die Materie zum Ausdruck kommt, den absoluten Primat im ganzen Bewegungsvorgang bewahrt. Die an zweiter Stelle stehende Hinwendung des '*liberum arbitrium*' zu Gott ist als '*motio ipsius mobilis*' selbst von Grundbewegung der Gnade getragen." Schockenhoff, *Bonum Hominis,* 341.

45. "Et ideo motus liberi arbitrii naturae ordine praecedit consecutionem gratia, sequitur autem gratiae infusionem." I-II, 113. 8 ad 2. Cited by Schockenhoff, *Bonum Hominis,* 342 n. 173. Schockenhoff comments: "Aber es fällt schwer, begrifflich exakt anzugeben, wo die genaue Unterscheidungsgrenze zwischen der '*infusio*' und der '*consecutio gratiae*' verlaufen soll." Schockenhoff, *Bonum Hominis,* 342.

46. "In der Gnadenlehre entfaltet die Bewegungsvorstellung ihre Stärke, in der Reflexion auf die das Handeln prägende '*virtus*' bleibt dagegen die '*habitus*' / Form Analogie vorherrschend. . . . Sie bleiben in einer offenen Spannung nebeneinander bestehen." Schockenhoff, *Bonum Hominis,* 345.

47. "Daß der vom Menschen in freier Entschiedenheit verantwortete Akt der Zustimmung zur Gnade zugleich das Werk des seine Gnade schenkenden Gottes ist, führt an eine Grenze des Verstehbaren, die durch keine weitere begriffliche Explikation zu überschreiten ist. Doch ist dies eine andere denkerische Situation, als sie ein unauflösbares Paradox bezeichnet. *Daß* es sich so verhalten muß, wie es der nicht mehr weiter auflösbare theologische Satz ausdrückt, vermag das theologische Denken noch einzusehen; die Grenze, die seinem Verstehen gezogen ist, tut sich aber in aller Schärfe auf, sobald danach gefragt wird, *wie* eine solche Koinzidenz zu denken und begrifflich darzustellen ist. Sein anfänglicher Optimismus, diese Grenze mit Hilfe des aristotelischen Verstehensansatzes von Materie und Form übersteigen zu können, ist Thomas im Verlauf seines theologischen Arbeitens immer fraglicher geworden. Die eigenartige Schwebe, in der sein gnadentheologisches Denken nach dem Übergang zur vorherrschenden Analogie der *motio* verbleibt, ist deshalb auch das Indiz einer gewachsenen Skepsis gegenüber allzu weitreichenden Erklärungsansprüchen, die im Raum der Theologie von isoliert gebrauchten Begriffsschemata erwartet werden." Schockenhoff, *Bonum Hominis,* 343–44.

48. "Im Glauben erfährt sich der Mensch, das ist die erste und grundlegende Aussage des Thomas, die allen weiteren Bestimmungen der '*fides*' die Richtung weist, als von Gott zur Teilhabe an seiner ewige Wahrheit gerufen; im Glauben wird die erste Wahrheit selbst zum 'Gegenstand' der höchsten Lebensäußerung des menschlichen Geistes, der darin sein letztes Ziel erkennt. Die richtige Interpretation der '*veritas prima*' bildet deshalb den Schlüssel zum Verständnis der thomanischen Glaubenstheologie ebenso wie zu ihrer Einordnung in den systematischen Rahmen der sie umgebenden Tugendethik." Schockenhoff, *Bonum Hominis,* 358.

49. "[*Fides*] tranzendiert die reine intellektuelle Zustimmung zu einer Reihe von Glaubenssätzen und dargebotenen Erkentnnisinhalten." Schockenhoff, *Bonum Hominis,* 371.

50. "Unter aller Kreatur, mit der er Anteil hat an der Ur-Bewegung, durch die Gott seine Schöpfung zu sich heimholt, weiß er sich allein dazu berufen, das Ziel seiner Sehnsucht beim Namen zu nennen und ihm in dem geistigen Urakt freier Bejahung zuzustimmen, der das Wesen des Glaubens ausmacht. Auf die Wahrheit Gottes sieht Thomas die Welt alles Lebendigen, ja das ganze Universum hingeordnet (*Oportet . . . veritatem esse ultimum totius universi.*" *Summa Contra Gentiles*—Prologus), aber dem Menschen als Gottes geistiger Kreatur leuchtet sie als ein Licht voran, das ihm das Ziel seines Lebens schon jetzt kundtut und ihn mit den Augen des Glaubens sehen läßt, wohin er unterwegs ist." Schockenhoff, *Bonum Hominis,* 376.

He continues in footnote 98 on the same page: "Gerade um der ethischen Relevanz des Glaubens darf deshalb sein kognitives Element nicht unterschlagen werden. Gewiß ist, wie

W. van der Marck . . . in seiner Interpretation der thomanischen Glaubentheologie besonders hervorhebt, bereits jeder Akt der Zustimmung zur Welt als der Schöpfung Gottes implizit ein Akt des Glaubens, auch wenn er nicht zur klaren Bewußtheit und reflexen Gewißheit aufsteigt. Die eigentliche Funktion des Glaubens wird in einer solchen Analyse aber nur ansatzweise zur Sprache gebracht. Nicht daß der Glaube notwendig ein Akt des Vertrauens und der Ur-Bejahung des Lebens ist, macht ihn zum Glauben, sondern daß der Mensch der Wahrheit dessen gewiß wird, der allein seines letzten Vertrauens würdig ist. Nur wenn die Zustimmung des Glaubenden vom Licht der sich selbst manifestierenden Ur-Wahrheit Gottes getragen ist, bleibt der Glaube ein der Dignität der geistigen Kreatur entsprechender und damit ethisch verantwortlicher Akt." He is referring to Van der Marck's, "The Object of Faith in St. Thomas," *Recherches de Théologie Ancienne et Médiévale* 43 (1976): 160–66.

51. *"Per se* gehört nur das zum Glaubensgut, was den Menschen unmittelbar auf das ewige Leben hinordnet; an explizitem Glauben ist nicht mehr gefordet, als was den Glaubenden zu seinem letzten Ziel führt." Schockenhoff, *Bonum Hominis,* 360.

52. The citation is from II-II, 4.1: "Habitus mentis, qua inchoatur vita aeterna in nobis, faciens assentire intelletum non apparentibus." Schockenhoff thinks it is "erstaunlich" that this text makes no mention of a *"duplex hominis bonum."* See Schockenhoff, *Bonum Hominis,* 389–90.

53. "Daß der Glaube der inchoative Beginn des ewigen Lebens ist, der das Ziel der Vollendung erkennen läßt und es bereits anfanghaft ergreift, das hat Thomas wie keiner seiner Vorgänger und unmittelbaren Nachfolger gesehen; in der Interpretation der eschatologischen Struktur der *'fides'* liegt sein persönlicher Beitrag zur mittelalterlichen Glaubenstheologie überhaupt und zur Deutung ihrer praktischen Relevanz im besonderen." Schockenhoff, *Bonum Hominis,* 417.

54. The allegory comes from the prologue of Thomas's *Lectura super Epistolam ad Ephesios:* "'Dominus autem praecedebat eos, ad ostendendam viam per diem in columna nubis': Fides enim ad modum nubis habet obscuritatem, quia cum aenigmate; dissolutio, quia evacuatur; humiditatem, quia excitat ad devotionem." Cited at Schockenhoff, *Bonum Hominis,* 353; see also 381: "Obscuritas enim quam aenigma importat ad genus cognitionis pertinet."

55. "Sie enhält doch in nuce bereits die doppelte Einsicht, zwischen deren beiden Polen die thomanische Interpretation sich bewegt. . . . Der Glaube empfängt die ihm eigene Würde nich aus seiner Bewährung im praktischen Leben, sondern allein daraus, daß er im Licht der Gnade den sich offenbarenden Gott in seiner ewigen Wahrheit berührt; gerade diese von Thomas niemals angetastete Aussage der Glaubenstheologie ist ein wichtiger Ertrag für das ethische Denken, der dieses vor einer reflexiven Überfrachtung des ethischen Anspruchs bewahrt und insofern entlastende Funktion ausübt. Ebenso wahr . . . ist aber auch, daß der Glaube nur deshalb bereits *'praelibatio visionis'* und Beginn des ewigen Lebens in uns ist, weil die *'caritas'* ihn nach seinem Ziel auslangen läßt und zu der Vollgestalt führt, in der die *'fides'* um der Liebe willen tätig wird und das weite Feld des praktischen Lebens in die Ur-Bejahung der göttlichen Wahrheit einschließt." Schockenhoff, *Bonum Hominis,* 396. On faith as "imperfect knowledge," Schockenhoff cites Thomas's *Commentary on the Sentences of Peter Lombard:* "*Illa imperfectio . . . est substantia fidei.*" Cited by Schockenhoff, *Bonum Hominis,* 381 n. 122.

56. This is the title of the last chapter of Schockenhoff's book, "Zehntes Kapitel: Die Vollendung des Tugendkanons in der Liebe." Schockenhoff, *Bonum Hominis,* 476.

57. "Sed amicitia quae est ad Deum, in quantum est beatus et beatitudinis auctor, oportet praestitui ad virtutes quae in illam beatitudinem ordinant; et ideo, cum non sit consequens ad alias virtutes quae in illam beatitudinem ordinant; et ideo, cum non sit consequens ad alias virtutes, sed praeambulum . . . oportet quod ipsa sit per se virtus." *De caritate* 2, ad 8. Cited at Schockenhoff, *Bonum Hominis,* 570 n. 363.

Some English translations render *praestitui* and *praeambulum* as "precede." See, e.g., *Saint Thomas 'On Charity,'* trans. Lottie H. Kendzierski (Milwaukee: Marquette University Press, 1993), 31. Such a translation does not seem helpful. In fact, the objection is raised in II-II, 4.7 obj. 5, that "*caritas praecedit fidem.*" But in answering the objection, Thomas does not accept this view: "*Actus voluntatis caritate . . . presupponit fidem.*" Moreover, *praestitui* does not indicate that love precedes faith; the word indicates that love is to be counted more excellent than any of the other virtues. It "stands ahead" of them.

58. "In einer beiläufigen Bermerkung nennt Thomas die Liebe einmal die Präambel der Tugenden und kennzeichnet damit treffend ihre Vorrangstellung im Tugendkanon. . . . Das ethische Handeln ist stets auf Etappen und Wegstücken damit beschäftigt, die konkrete Vielfalt des Lebens zu ordnen und ihrem Anspruch gerecht zu werden, doch erfährt der in der Not konkreter Entscheidung und Abwägung sich oft verlierende Wanderer durch das Wort der Liebe, das ihm wie eine immer zum Ziel zurückführende Wegbegleiterin mitgegeben ist, daß sein Weg trotz aller Irrtumsmöglichkeiten und trotz aller wirklich begangenen Irrtümer kein Irrrweg ist. Die Liebe läßt, als sei sie bereits zum Ziel vorausgeeilt ('*prae-ambulare*') und als brächte sie von dort her Kunde, den noch verborgegen Weg des Handelns als die '*via perfectionis*' aufleuchten, die den Menschen zu seinem ewigen Ziel in der Gemeinschaft des unendlichen Gottes führt." Schockenhoff, *Bonum Hominis*, 570–71.

59. "Die von Gott angebotene '*beatitudo*' erscheint als das höchste und eigentliche Gut des Menschen; diese äußerste Gestalt des menschlichen Sein-Könnens, die der Mensch nicht aus sich erreicht und die ihn über seine natürlichen Grenzen hinausführt, ist in dieser Perspektive das '*bonum hominis principale*,' oder einfach der Höchstfall des Menschseins schlechthin, das '*optimum hominis.*' Diese äußerste Vollendung ist dem menschlichen Handeln jedoch nicht nur als eine in diesem Leben unerreichbare Grenze gesetzt; sie ist zugleich ein Ziel, das jedem erreichten Teil-Ziel und jeder fragmentarischen Form gelungenen Lebens vorausleuchtet und in Glaube, Hoffnung, and Liebe bereits jetzt inchoativ ergriffen wird." Schockenhoff, *Bonum Hominis*, 582–83.

60. On the moral life as friendship with God, see Schockenhoff's essay on *caritas* in *Ethics of Aquinas*, ed. Pope. This essay largely translates material found in *Bonum Hominis*, 501–26.

61. "Im Wachstum der Liebe findet das sittliche Leben zu seiner Vollendung und zu seiner inneren Einheit. Ihre Gebote formulieren nur eine ihren Einsatz sichernde Untergrenze, jenseits derer es keinen Sinn mehr gibt, von Liebe zu reden." Schockenhoff, *Bonum Hominis*, 571.

62. "Die Liebe übergeht nicht das rechte Maß des Ethischen, sie bewegt den Liebenden dazu, sich in immer größerer Bereitschaft von ihm leiten zu lassen." Schockenhoff, *Bonum Hominis*, 564.

63. "There is no competition between justice and love, as if love would begin only where justice ceased, or justice meant that love would have to be extinguished in order to make possible the establishment of a neutrally objective social order. Rather, justice and love are related to each other like two *concentric circles* which enclose all the individual commandments of the Decalogue in both a narrower context and a broader horizon." Schockenhoff, *Natural Law and Human Dignity*, 253. For further reflections on love and justice, see especially pages 287–307 of that same book.

64. The text is from II-II, 24.2. Schockenhoff says: "Es gibt in den 512 von Thomas selbst verfaßten Quaestionen seines Hauptwerkes nicht einen theologischen Gedanken, nicht einen niedergeschriebenen Satz, der unabhängig von dem Ur-Geschehen der Liebe wahr wäre." Schockenhoff, *Bonum Hominis*, 478.

65. "Sittliche Autonomie ist für ihn die Freiheit des Freundes Gottes, der keines fremden Gesetzes mehr bedarf, weil er sich die göttliche Bejahung alles Guten zum eigenen Gesetz

gemacht hat und aufgrund des ihm geschenkten Zugangs zur Freundschaft Gottes dessen Liebe zu allen, was ihrer würdig ist, frei nachvollzieht. Ein solches theologischen Freiheitsverständnis kann den Gedanken der ethischen Autonomie innerhalb der christlichen Glaubensreflexion Heimatrecht verschaffen, denn es übernimmt ihn nichts als einen . . . Fremdkörper, sondern entläßt ihn aus seinem eigenen, genuin theologischen Begründungsgang." Schockenhoff, *Bonum Hominis*, 584.

66. See, e.g., his long chapter on the "universal claim of natural law." Schockenhoff, *Natural Law and Human Dignity*, 121–223.

67. "Als das erste und vornehmste praktische Funktion des Glaubens muß deshalb gelten, daß er uns das Ziel erkennen läßt, nach dem wir unbewußt in allem Handeln ausgreifen." Schockenhoff, *Bonum Hominis*, 394.

68. Herbert McCabe, OP, "Nobody Comes to the Father but by Me," in *God Still Matters* (New York: Continuum, 2002), 104–5.

69. Thich Nhat Hanh is quoted here by Bradley S. Clough in "Altruism in Contemporary Buddhism: Thich Nhat Hanh's Socially Engaged Buddhism," in *Altruism in World Religions*, ed. Jacob Neusner and Bruce Chilton (Washington, D.C.: Georgetown University Press, 2005), 119–20.

70. See, e.g., Schockenhoff's strong critique of any theology of hope that grounds itself in the human longing for transcendence. See Schockenhoff, *Bonum Hominis*, 473.

71. "Der unendliche Gott von sich aus die Brücke zur Kreatur schlägt. . . . Das Zueinander der Begriffskoordinaten der aristotelischen Analyse ist geblieben, aber die Achse, um die alles gruppiert ist, wendet sich aus der Waagerechten auf und ragt nun steil nach oben. Es ist die geniale und doch höchst einfache theologische Intuition des Thomas, daß er nur einer Vierteldrehung nach rechs oder links bedarf, um aus der philosophischen Freundschaftstheorie des Aristoteles ein Verstehensmodell der dem Menschen von Gott geschenkten 'caritas' zu gewinnen." Schockenhoff, *Bonum Hominis*, 512, 516.

72. "Die Demut des Denkens verbietet es Thomas jedoch, solche Vollendung im einzelnen zu denken, denn er muß damit rechnen, daß alle jetzt zutage liegenden Gründe, die Menschen liebenswert machen können, in unvergleichlicher Weise durch die unmittelbare Gegenwart Gottes überstrahlt werden." Schockenhoff, *Bonum Hominis*, 550. He cites Thomas's text at note 277 on that page.

Schockenhoff also cites Thomas's teaching in II-II, 24.3: "Caritas, autem, cum superexcedat proportionem naturae humanae . . . non dependet ex aliqua naturali virtute, sed ex sola gratia Spiritus Sancti eam infundentis." Schockenhoff, *Bonum Hominis*, 555 n. 292.

73. Jacques Dupuis, *Christianity and the Religions: From Confrontation to Dialogue* (Maryknoll, N.Y.: Orbis Press, 2003), 255.

74. Schockenhoff, *Natural Law and Human Dignity*, 284.

Liturgy and Ethics: The Liturgical Asceticism of Energy Conservation

Margaret R. Pfeil

THE CONCEPT OF LITURGICAL ASCETICISM SERVES TO RELATE LITURGY and ethics as seen in the case of energy conservation. Disciplined practices undertaken to limit energy consumption can deepen contemplative awareness of God's creative energy as work in the world and the moral significance of human cooperation with it as an expression of one's baptismal commitment rooted within a particular faith community. The liturgical location of the moral agent who engages in such *askesis* implies a sacramentally informed epistemology as a way of knowing oneself in relation to God and all of created reality that imbues conservation practices with eschatological meaning.

Twenty years after writing his seminal essay on the relationship between liturgy and ethics, Don Saliers observed that "there *ought* to be a profound inner connection between worship and service, between love of God and love of neighbor, between our prayer and the lived pattern of moral life. But is this so? How is this so?"[1] One of the particular challenges he raised for consideration was the role of liturgical formation in light of the pervasive effect of consumerism in society.

The concept of liturgical asceticism provides fruitful ground for addressing his concern, suggesting a process of moral formation involving *praktikê*, ascetic struggle, as the Christian worshipper's graced and free response to God's gratuitous love celebrated in Christian liturgy. First, liturgical asceticism springs from and seeks to nourish the life of the Christian worshipping community, and second, it implies an eschatological horizon in which the ultimate *telos* of *askesis* consists in the fullness of life in God. These features distinguish it in purpose from theories of *askesis*, both ancient and contemporary, that place emphasis upon individual moral advancement in relation to a philosophical ideal.[2]

Liturgical asceticism encompasses not only the disciplines of liturgical worship but also those sustained practices of daily life undertaken with a conscious awareness on the part of the moral agent of the way in which these disciplines express one's baptismal commitment rooted within a particular faith community.

Journal of the Society of Christian Ethics, 27, 2 (2007): 127–149

Thus, a liturgically rooted *askesis* suggests a broadened conception of sacramentality beyond formal ritual worship to include intentional acts of asceticism such as virtuous habits of energy conservation.

The multivalent meaning of liturgical asceticism offers the possibility of making a liturgically based ethical argument for energy conservation practices that flows from a pneumatological understanding of creation within which the sacramental, ecclesiological, eschatological, and anthropological dimensions of liturgical life inform ethical action. In particular, I suggest that the discipline of energy conservation as liturgical *askesis* involves the cultivation of ecological humility as a virtue that inclines the practitioner toward the reduction of energy consumption as a form of loving self-gift in relation to the rest of God's creation. By establishing the notion of personal sacrifice as a good, liturgical asceticism provides an ethical and theological hermeneutic that represents a new contribution to interdisciplinary discourse on energy conservation.

Although I believe that liturgical asceticism offers a promising approach to reducing energy consumption, this claim requires some caveats. First, it is admittedly a limited and modest suggestion, particularly given the scope of the global environmental crisis. However, I hope that these reflections might contribute to the ongoing formation of ecologically attuned consciences in Christian ecclesial communities at the local level, which I take to be the sine qua non of any credible and effective effort on the part of Christian churches to bear witness to the integrity of creation in a U.S. sociocultural context so profoundly marked by consumerism.

Second, in this essay, I have intentionally taken the U.S. context as my departure point, principally because, as I show below, much of the ethical responsibility for present patterns of global climate change rests with the wealthiest nations, among which the United States currently is the leading carbon emitter.[3] This sign of the times, which endangers all biotic systems on the planet, will continue unabated without significant lifestyle changes leading to reduced energy consumption among the world's highest-income peoples. By adopting this focus, in no way do I intend to reinforce U.S. elitism vis-à-vis the particular contexts of socioeconomically poor countries. On the contrary, I seek to affirm Andrew Simms's argument that, in fact, the wealthiest nations, and the United States in particular, owe an "ecological debt" to the rest of the world.[4]

Third and finally, I recognize that widespread practices of reduced energy consumption at the local level would likely have correlative effects at the macroeconomic level. The position I am proposing here bears affinity with Wendell Berry's argument for the idea of a local economy. Over against almost automatic forces of economic globalization driven by "supranational corporations," without meaningful input from the affected populations, Berry advocates solidarity at the local level to restore the organic relationship between local producers and consumers of goods and services, akin to what Leonardo Boff has called "participatory politics." Global free trade's promise of high economic tides of prosperity that would lift all boats has stranded some of the world's most vulnerable peoples.[5] In response, local communities around the globe have developed alternative economic practices, from fair trade coffee cooperatives in El Salvador to community-supported agricultural initiatives in the United States.

Following this same logic, local efforts to reduce energy consumption may well disrupt dominant patterns of corporate-driven "free-market" economies, but they may also engender other ethical goods in the process. These might include, for example, fostering a more direct relationship between energy consumers and the sources of energy consumed as well as contributing to the overall flourishing of creation. Faced with the real possibility of planetary ecological systems failure, it seems that any short-term negative socioeconomic effects of reduced energy consumption would be far outweighed by the obvious advantages of sustaining a global climate capable of supporting life on Earth.

The Ethics of Energy Conservation: Framing the Question

The phrase "energy conservation" enjoys a wide range of interpretation. Some theorists use the term "energy efficiency" to mean the maximization of work or service produced by each unit of energy, reserving "energy conservation" to denote reduction in overall demand for energy.[6] Brenda Boardman of Oxford's Environmental Change Institute argues for the salience of this distinction in light of current manufacturing trends leading to products that tend to be more energy efficient while also superseding their predecessors in size or volume, resulting in an increase in the actual amount of energy consumed.[7] Plasma-screen televisions, for example, have become increasingly popular in the United States and are as energy efficient as current technology permits. Still, a plasma screen model uses 450 watts, compared with 75 watts for its typical predecessor.[8] While appreciating her point, in this essay I follow the more common practice of interpreting "energy conservation" broadly to include both the actual reduction of energy consumption and more efficient use of energy, because I wish to show that the concept of liturgical asceticism applies to both of these energy practices and provides an ethical hermeneutic linking efficiency measures to reduced energy consumption and giving priority to the latter.

Forging the connection between efficiency and consumption takes on greater significance in light of prevailing public attitudes in the United States, where this twofold understanding of conservation has been conspicuously absent from public discourse about energy. As Paul Roberts argues: "In spite of high energy prices and rising concerns about energy security, consumers and policymakers alike have all but stopped talking about the ways we use energy, how much we waste, and what can be changed."[9] Even with the recent spike in awareness generated by Al Gore's Oscar-winning documentary film *An Inconvenient Truth* and the latest sobering report of the Intergovernmental Panel on Climate Change, U.S. public discussions of energy continue to focus mainly on seeking alternatives to fossil fuel and increased efficiency rather than reducing energy consumption.

When they do surface for consideration in the public forum, these dual aspects of conservation are sometimes held in tension, with efficiency measures cast as the balanced alternative to energy cuts perceived as a threat to economic productivity. As the oil crisis of the 1970s deepened, President Jimmy Carter became the oft-satirized icon of draconian energy curtailment practices, appearing on national television bundled in a sweater to ask Americans to reduce their energy consumption by making personal sacrifices.[10] Conservation pioneers like Arthur Rosenfeld have distanced themselves from countercultural austerity such as Carter's by insisting that improved efficiency measures would not require citizens of the world's wealthiest country to trim their consumption habits. "With the right technologies, regulations, and financial incentives," he maintains, "energy waste could be cut unobtrusively, without affecting how people worked or lived."[11]

As a member of the California Energy Commission, Rosenfeld has spearheaded the implementation of statewide end-use efficiency policies such as the adoption of building energy codes and appliance efficiency standards over the past three decades. Such measures have enabled California's per capita energy use to remain nearly level at about 7,000 kilowatt-hours from 1974 to 2001, while the rest of the country experienced nearly a 50 percent increase from 8,000 to 12,000 kilowatt-hours over roughly the same period.[12] Prima facie, the data would seem to confirm Rosenfeld's assertion that efficiency measures alone, without lifestyle changes, are sufficient to meet energy demands.

John Holdren, a respected scholar of energy policy and former White House climate adviser, affirms Rosenfeld's line of argument, pointing to end-use efficiency measures as a relatively expedient means of addressing this century's urgent energy challenges: "Increasing the efficiency with which energy is converted into the goods and services that people want—comfort, mobility, illumination, refrigeration, the powering of industrial processes, and so on—is equivalent to an energy source, because kilowatt-hours or liters of fuel saved in one application can be used for another. Such end-use-efficiency improvements are (and are destined to remain for some time to come) the cheapest, cleanest, surest, most rapidly expandable energy option we have."[13]

Notably, Holdren does not mention the option of reducing overall energy consumption. Like Rosenfeld, he assumes as a policy goal the satisfaction of consumer desire and then establishes the corresponding need for energy-efficient products, without considering the possibility of distinguishing wants from needs and reeducating consumer desire. This conceptual lacuna ultimately translates into higher energy demand, as Boardman's research shows, and it seems to reflect a broader cultural reticence about reducing consumption. Recent polls in California and across the nation indicate that the vast majority of the respondents perceive global warming as a serious threat, but "polling organizations have asked little about the potentially painful sacrifices that may be required."[14] In the nation responsible for 22.2 percent of global primary energy consumption in 2005, this silence speaks volumes.[15]

Five ethical implications of the culturally dominant approach to conservation—emphasizing energy efficiency without reference to reduced consumption—are worth considering at this point because they help to establish the context within which liturgical *askesis* appears to offer a valuable approach to energy conservation. First, the replacement of older equipment with more efficient units produces energy savings over the life cycle of the item but requires the availability of capital to cover higher initial expenses, making it very difficult for the economically poor to avail themselves of the efficiency option. The energy consumption of the average U.S. refrigerator model, for example, has decreased from 1,800 kilowatt-hours a year in 1974 to the federal standard of 450 kilowatt-hours a year established in 2001.[16] As Roberts notes, however, the public will to generate comprehensive energy conservation policies has been largely lacking, and without the public consciousness required to support subsidies, it is highly unlikely that a low-income family will buy a new, energy-efficient refrigerator when older, less efficient versions are readily available secondhand for little or no cost.

Second, Boardman's observations find confirmation in history: Gains in energy efficiency typically have been outstripped by increased energy consumption at the macroeconomic level.[17] The British economist Stanley Jevons noted in 1865 that the relatively high efficiency of Watt's steam engine proved many times more efficient than the best alternative model, but its growing popularity correlated with a sharp rise in coal consumption.[18] More recently, technology has facilitated production of lighter, more fuel-efficient cars, but the demands for engine power and comfort help account for the fact that U.S. automobiles "consumed 35 percent more energy in 2000 than they did in 1980."[19] With the growing popularity of sport-utility vehicles and minivans, the average fuel economy of new cars and light trucks actually decreased by 2 miles a gallon from 1987 to 2002.[20] Likewise, the trend toward energy-efficient home heating and appliances has been matched by a 50 percent increase in the average size of homes over the last thirty years.[21]

Third, placing emphasis on energy efficiency alone can convey the impression that current levels of energy consumption are environmentally sustainable, a dangerous message in light of global climate change. Projections indicate that "by the year 2100, the world's ten billion people will need something on the order of fifty terawatts of electricity, or around four times what we produce to-day." Carbon-free energy sources cannot be developed at a rate or power density sufficient to meet such demand, Roberts warns, and even if it were possible, it would not be environmentally sustainable.[22]

Increasing emissions of carbon dioxide, widely regarded as the most critical anthropogenic greenhouse gas, constitutes the principal cause of rising tropospheric temperatures.[23] In June 2006, after an intensive examination of the most recent climate studies, the U.S. National Research Council confirmed "with a high level of confidence" that the global average surface temperature was higher in the last decades of the twentieth century than in the previous four hundred years.[24] In the first volume of its *Fourth Assessment Report* (2007), the Intergovernmental Panel on Climate Change estimates a global average surface temperature increase of 1.8 to 4.0 degrees Centigrade by the end of the twenty-first century.[25] Preventing global climate change from becoming irreversible will require reductions in greenhouse gas emissions by 60 to 90 percent in the twenty-first century.[26]

In the United States, fossil-fuel consumption accounts for about 90 percent of total energy use and almost all its carbon dioxide emissions.[27] It remains the largest single-country source of fossil-fuel-related carbon dioxide emissions, responsible for 1,580 million metric tons of carbon output in 2003, or 28 percent more than China, the second-highest national producer of carbon dioxide.[28] Overall, greenhouse gas emissions in the United States increased by almost 16 percent from 1990 to 2004. That period also yielded a 19.6 percent increase in carbon dioxide emissions, principally caused by fossil fuel combustion.[29]

U.S. energy consumption is predicted to grow 36.5 percent from 2003 to 2030.[30] To meet its energy demands, it has become the world's leading consumer of oil, with 5 percent of the world's population accounting for 26 percent of global oil consumption. Though the United States produced 70 percent of the oil it consumed in 1985, presently it imports more than half its oil, and that figure is projected to climb to 62 percent by 2030, raising a fourth concern about the rhetoric of energy efficiency without sacrifice.[31] Without a serious public effort to curb consumption, oil will continue to serve as a geoecological form of power driving what some theorists have called "petroimperialism," an energy policy predicated on the use of armed force.[32] In a recent article in *Foreign Affairs*, the energy researcher Daniel Yergin warned that the United States needs to redouble its efforts to secure the global energy supply chain and infrastructure to ensure adequate availability of fossil fuels to meet demand.[33] Giving a nod to the positive impact of energy efficiency measures that allowed a lighter, more service-based U.S. economy to expand by 150 percent, while energy consumption grew only 25 percent in the last three decades, Yergin did not mention perhaps the surest form of energy security: the possibility of curtailing consumption.[34]

Finally, even if it were possible to locate and secure supplies of fossil fuels sufficient to satisfy anticipated energy demands, the projected rate of consumption would not be replicable globally. Historically, high energy consumption has correlated closely with industrial economic development. By the end of the twentieth century, affluent nations, making up 20 percent of the global population, consumed 70 percent of the Total Primary Energy Supply (TPES). The United States alone used 27 percent of the TPES in 2000, in contrast to the poorest quarter of the world's population, which consumed 2.5 percent of the TPES.[35] To provide perspective, Simms invites us to consider that "beginning from the stroke of New Year, as they sit down to their evening meal on 2 January, a U.S. family will already have used, per person, the equivalent in fossil fuels that a family in Tanzania will depend on for the whole year."[36] The wealthiest industrial nations, he argues, owe an "ecological debt" to the rest of the world.

If global climate change predictions are borne out, that debt will soon take on flesh and blood: The United Nations Millennium Ecosystem Assessment warns that the adverse effects of climate change will fall more heavily on the world's poorest regions due to factors such as increased drought and reduced food consumption in drier areas, while noting that "the buildup of greenhouse gases has come overwhelmingly from richer populations as they consume more energy to fuel their higher living standards."[37] In the process of accruing capital, the world's wealthiest nations, measured by gross domestic product, together with the elites living in socioeconomically poor countries, have adopted energy consumption habits that in themselves are not environmentally sustainable, let alone replicable by the world's economically poor majority. Thoughtful energy efficiency measures can contribute to sustainable global energy use, but, ultimately, the widespread curtailment of absolute energy consumption will be required to meet that goal.[38] The available evidence prompts the energy scholar Václav Smil to conclude that "*future energy use in the affluent world is primarily a moral issue, not a technical or economic matter.*"[39]

Liturgical Asceticism

As the image of President Carter bundled up in a chilly White House suggests, practices to curb energy consumption connote ascetic discipline, embodying the single-minded purpose and physical effort reflected in the ancient Greek understanding of *askesis* as a sort of training directed toward the cultivation of virtue as an end. A liturgically based asceticism shares the Hellenistic concept of *askesis* as disciplined practice but, springing from the context of Christian monasticism, it identifies a distinctive *telos* for ascetic action. Since the fourth century, Christian monks have sought not their own moral perfection as an end in itself but rather growth in relationship with God through virtuous living in community and in cooperation with grace.

Writing in the early seventh century, Maximus the Confessor emphasized the significance of *praktikê*, ascetic struggle, as an essential and abiding feature of the human spiritual journey toward union with God, the free and graced response to God's kenotic love poured out in Jesus Christ, the Incarnation.[40] For Maximus and other Christian monks, the ultimate goal of ascetic practice is radical surrender to the rhythm of God's healing grace at work in one's life, in the church, and in the world.

Seeking to emphasize this sort of *askesis* as a theological category, David Fagerberg has coined the term "liturgical asceticism," distinguishing it from moral, religious, civic, and athletic varieties of disciplined training by the end to which it is directed.[41] "If liturgy means sharing the life of Christ (being washed in his resurrection, eating his body)," Fagerberg writes, "and if *askesis* means discipline (in the sense of forming), then liturgical asceticism is the discipline required to become an icon of Christ and make his image visible in our faces."[42] The specific *telos* of *liturgical* asceticism is participation in Christ as a member of Christ's Body. Unlike Max Weber's antinomy pitting asceticism against mysticism and action against contemplation, *liturgical* asceticism involves a contemplative awareness of the practices of the worshipping community as *leitourgia*, the work of the people of God at the service of the world.[43]

The context of liturgy bears with it multivalent theological meaning that shapes the interpretive lens of the one who participates in Christian worship. As contemplation in action, liturgical practice both takes root in and nurtures an epistemology that allows members of the ecclesial community to see themselves in relationship with all of God's creation and to understand the practices of their quotidian lives in the world as a means of sacramental cooperation with God's ongoing creative activity.

A liturgically based asceticism of energy conservation, I suggest, flows from a pneumatological understanding of creation that allows liturgical life to inform ethical action in four ways. First, the sacraments invite worshippers to cultivate what John Hart calls "creatiocentric" consciousness, "a holistic understanding that the Creator, abiotic creation, and the biotic community are interrelated."[44] Second, the notion of the sacramentality of creation finds support in the broad ecclesiological self-understanding of Christian worshipping assemblies as *leitourgia*, a community gathered in Jesus Christ to minister in his name. Third, the eschatological *telos* of Christian liturgical life provides the ethical horizon for practices of liturgical asceticism. Fourth and last, liturgy implies a particular anthropology, establishing the context for each member of the assembly and the community as a whole to strive toward fulfillment of the Christian aspiration to holiness, becoming ever more like the God they worship.

Pneumatology

Love, Teilhard de Chardin asserted, constitutes "the physical structure of the universe."[45] His bold claim rested on a pneumatological understanding of divine energy at work in creation, one enjoying firm roots in the Christian tradition. As the Orthodox Ecumenical Patriarch Bartholomew I observes, Eastern Christian patristic writers recognized the significance of energy as an ontological category:

> About fifteen centuries before the quantum theory of modern physics, the Greek Church affirmed that matter is energy, a "concurrence of logical (*logokoi*) qualities," a created result of the uncreated divine Energy. The difference in essence between created and uncreated does not preclude or hinder what is created from being energised as a *logos* of the uncreated, from revealing the creative energy and the hypostatic otherness of the personal God-the-Word (*theos logos*). . . . Only when people approach matter and the whole of nature as the creation of a personal Creator, only then does the use of matter and of nature as a whole become truly a relationship and not a narrow sovereignty of man over physical reality. . . . The *logos* of the beauty of created things is a call which God addresses to man, a call to personal relationship and communion of life with him.[46]

The disciplined practices of liturgical life nourish a personal and communal understanding of the radical relationality of material creation with its Creator. Through liturgical celebration, the Christian community bears witness to God's energy at work in creation through the Holy Spirit, rendering the church a sacrament of trinitarian love. Liturgy, Fagerberg suggests, "is participating in the eternal circulation of love between the Father and the Son which is the Holy Spirit. The very Son of God installs us in that circuit of love and the very Spirit of God animates us by it. The Spirit of God is holy love. The mark of the Holy Spirit is love."[47] Liturgical life provides the narrative context for the graced human response to God's invitation to cooperate freely in the dynamism of divine love drawing all creation toward the Reign of God.

Liturgy: Celebrating the Sacramentality of Creation

The sacraments celebrate this graced encounter of love between God and God's creation. Jean Corbon elucidates the pneumatological wellspring of the sacramental life of the church in terms of a threefold movement of the Spirit's manifestation of Christ, the Spirit's transforming action in Christ of the ecclesial community's offering, and finally the dynamic synergy between the life-giving power of the Holy Spirit and the Christian worshipper's graced response of free will, a total self-gift of one's energies to the work of God's love. For Corbon, the "sacramentality of the Church means that, in her everything is the joint energy of the Spirit and of the humanity he transfigures. This synergy constitutes the liturgy."[48] Through liturgical participation, Christians willingly become *synergoi*, or cooperators, coworkers, with God.[49]

The liturgical asceticism of Christians as *synergoi* with God springs from the waters of baptism and recalls the original meaning of the word "sacramentum," the soldier's vow upon entering military service. Analogously, believers fulfill their baptismal commitments through liturgical practices of *askesis*.[50] This asceticism flows from the theological virtues of faith, hope, and charity infused through baptism, and, writes Fagerberg, it constitutes the discipline "by which the Christian can participate in the liturgical life this sacrament initiates."[51]

Christian worship locates table fellowship at the center of liturgical life. The ecclesial community's sacramental practice of the Eucharist connects the act of thanksgiving for God's creation with the responsibility to participate in God's saving activity in the world. It bears witness to the assembly members' beliefs about their communal role in the world and about the value of the material creation that liturgy celebrates, uniting humanity to the fruits of the Earth, bread and wine, flesh and blood. Receiving the Body and Blood of Jesus Christ in the Eucharist, the members of the community enact their belief that in so doing, they receive what they are, as Augustine put it, the sacrament of God's presence as the Body of Christ in the world.[52] The liturgical anamnesis of God healing, reconciling, and uniting creation to God's self in Christ effects what it signifies: As Maximus perceived, the liturgical celebration restores the unity of creation with Creator, both within the heart of each member of the assembly and in the cosmos that the liturgy celebrates.[53]

Ecclesiology: An Epistemology of Relationality

Precisely through the *askesis* of liturgical practice, the Christian community embodies an ecclesiology and an epistemology of relationality. This way of being in and seeing the world calls to mind the original meaning of the Greek term "*leitourgia.*" As Alexander Schmemann notes, it carried a fundamentally communal and public connotation: "It meant an action by which a group of people become something corporately which they had not been as a mere collection of individuals—a whole greater than the sum of its parts. It meant also a function or 'ministry' of a man or of a group on behalf of and in the interest of the whole community. . . . Thus, the Church itself is a *leitourgia*, a ministry, a calling to act in this world after the fashion of Christ, to bear testimony to Him and His kingdom."[54]

Through liturgy, the worshipping community becomes more than the sum of its parts; it becomes the Body of Christ. Through ministry, members of the ecclesial community become *synergoi*, cooperators in Jesus Christ's mission to give himself for the life of the world. Like the first disciples to whom Jesus sent his Spirit, the ecclesial community, enlivened by the Spirit through the graced discipline of sacramental worship, takes up a twofold task. First, the Spirit invites Christians to enter into communion with one another in ways befitting their call to become a new creation in Christ; and second, the Spirit leads them to enter into restorative relationship with all of God's creation.

An Eschatologically Rooted Anthropology

This dual ecclesial mission ultimately has one single *telos*, the Spirit-driven restoration of the integrity of God's creation. Toward this end, liturgical life shapes an eschatological consciousness, training the Christian community's attention not on the last things but rather on "the *lastness of* things." Viewed against the ultimate horizon of the *eschaton*, things appear in their true significance before God, affording a glimpse in the here and now of the fullness of reconciliation of all creation as one in God.[55] Eschatological vision encompasses the scope of the future and holds it together with contemplative attention to the present. As Gustavo Gutiérrez explains: "More precisely, this tension toward the future lends meaning to and is expressed in the present, while simultaneously being nourished by it."[56] All the things comprising the present moment thus become bathed in the light of an eschatological hope that sustains the assembly in *praktikê*, the ongoing ascetic struggle to live into the fulfillment of God's promise.

Eschatology provides the overarching *telos* of liturgical asceticism, and it also implies a particular anthropology. With the eschatological horizon in view, the moral agent seeks through *askesis* to become a human being disposed to enjoy the plenitude of life in God. Liturgical asceticism both expresses the practitioner's desire to become ever more like God, a process referred to as "deification" in the Orthodox Christian tradition; and, through grace, it also gradually forges a path toward the fulfillment of that desire. Over time, practices of liturgical *askesis* change the person who undertakes them, beginning with his or her worldview. The liturgical ascetic comes to envision creative ways of relating to the rest of God's creation from the perspective of the lastness of things.

Energy Conservation as Liturgical Asceticism

The foregoing overview of the theological underpinnings of liturgical asceticism presents the ethical ideal for liturgical practice as a wellspring of rightly ordered action on the part of the Christian community. As any honest disciple of Jesus will attest, actual Christian liturgical experiences often fall regrettably short of realizing such lofty aspirations. With regard to the particular issue of the environmental integrity of creation, Christian worship practices historically have failed to facilitate the theological connections in support of the sacramentality of creation that I am suggesting here. As James Nash acknowledges, "Anthropocentrism has been and remains a norm in the dominant strains of Christian theology and piety, and it has served as both a stimulus and a rationalization for environmental destruction in Christian-influenced cultures."[57] The fact of Christianity's questionable environmental legacy provides all the more reason to plumb the theological depths of Christian worship as a resource for ethical insight into the integrity of creation.

In relation to the particular environmental challenges of energy consumption, for example, the concept of liturgical asceticism offers an ethical hermeneutic capable of linking Christian worship to the discipline of energy conservation. First, it trains practitioners in virtue so that they might distinguish wants from needs and to examine carefully the nature of their desires. Second, it provides a theological, liturgically nourished rationale for conceiving of personal sacrifice as a graced, free, and loving response to trinitarian divine love. Finally, it leads the liturgical ascetic to embrace both aspects of energy conservation while giving clear priority to reducing consumption over end-use efficiency.

In the remainder of this essay, I make the case, first, that liturgical asceticism accomplishes these tasks through the cultivation of ecological humility as a virtue. As Nash has indicated, a number of virtues bear ecological salience, such as sustainability, adaptability, relationality, frugality, equity, solidarity, biodiversity, and sufficiency. In this essay, while attending to relationality and solidarity, I devote sustained attention to the virtue of ecological humility because I take Nash's point that it serves as "a guiding norm" for the other virtues mentioned.[58] The practice of ecological humility also functions normatively to mediate the theological commitments of liturgical asceticism—pneumatology, sacramentality, eschatology, and anthropology—enabling practitioners to incarnate the relationship between liturgy and habits of energy conservation.

Second, a number of liturgical practices could potentially shape a Christian discipline of energy conservation as liturgical *askesis*. I focus specifically on the liturgical form of mystagogy because it lends itself quite well to the formation of Christian consciences regarding energy conservation through the cultivation of discursive consciousness.

Ecological Humility: The Process of Reeducating Human Desire

The eschatological horizon of liturgical asceticism allows the practitioner to interpret quotidian practices, such as habits of energy conservation, as forms of *askesis* rooted in the worship life of the ecclesial community. A liturgically based discipline of energy conservation involves deliberate cultivation of awareness regarding the relationship of particular practices and the eschatological *telos* of the reconciliation of all creation in God. Making an epistemological connection between climate change and the sacramental integrity of creation provides an ethical framework within which to consider specific actions of energy conservation as expressions of liturgical asceticism.

Within the graced context of sacramental life, the theological virtue of charity directs the liturgical ascetic toward the supernatural end of divine love, providing support for his or her desire to love creation as God loves it. Motivated by love, the ascetic can find reason to conserve energy based on fidelity to the mutuality of communion drawing all God's creation into relationship. Ordinary conservation practices become expressions of liturgical asceticism by incarnating the truth of those relational ties as sacramental expressions of God's ongoing, creative love at work in the world. But, as the concept of *askesis* implies, God's gracious love awaits free human response; the process of becoming a liturgical ascetic does not automatically follow from participation in Christian worship. Even with the grace of the sacraments, as Maximus insisted, the ascetic struggle remains a constant feature of the Christian journey.[59]

Cultivating the disciplined practices of energy conservation as virtuous habits involves the ongoing education of intellective desire in the deliberative process.[60] Behaving virtuously, the liturgical ascetic will choose a conservation practice based on the coherence of the intentional objects with his or her intellectual apprehension of the good that it represents. Liturgically based asceticism trains the practitioner in the apprehension of the ecological good against the eschatological horizon of sacramental life, with liturgy providing the context for the moral agent's ongoing formation toward the supernatural end of life in God. "As we are educated toward this end," writes Diana Fritz Cates, "we will be re-educated toward our natural human end, which means that our ordinary understanding and experience of ourselves and the ultimate significance of our chosen action and passion will be altered."[61]

The *askesis* of reeducating human desire away from patterns of consumption that devour ever-increasing amounts of energy and toward ends more consonant with the integrity of creation requires the cultivation, in particular, of ecological humility as a virtue. As part of temperance, Thomas Aquinas observed, humility serves to restrain the movement of passion evidenced "by preoccupation with earthly greatness."[62] Humility "mainly concerns a man's subjection to God, for whose sake he also submits himself to others."[63]

Stemming from the root "humus," meaning "ground" or "earth," humility recalls the human being to his or her organic origin in the earth, leading to a rightful sense of his or her own creatureliness within God's creation. Conceiving of humility as steps of spiritual progress on the ladder of earthly life leading toward that "*perfect love* of God which *casts out fear*" (1 Jn. 4:18), Benedict of Nursia contrasted the ascent in humility with the downward journey of pride.[64] Becoming detached from a false sense of self, the humble person becomes available for relationship with the rest of God's creation, mindful of the "lastness of things" in God.

The virtuous quality of ecological humility is characterized by the interior freedom to be true to oneself in relationship to God through identifying one's own good with the well-being of God's creation. Integrity and humility amount to "practically the same thing," Thomas Merton suggested, and ecological humility implies awareness that the journey of personal integration unfolds of a piece with the whole weave of God's creation.[65] The humble practitioner of energy conservation as liturgical *askesis* undertakes "a way of tenderness and integration with oneself, with each other and with creation . . . consciously aware that the problem of pollution can not be sharply distinguished from the problem of inner alienation."[66] Maintaining this connection between personal integrity and the well-being of creation lies at the heart of the Catholic social teaching concept of the "planetary common good."[67] Ecological humility disposes the practitioner toward fulfillment of this *telos*.

Humility, rooted in charity, informs a spirit of sacrificial self-gift in response to God's gratuitous love lavished upon creation, most abundantly in the Incarnation, as Maximus noted. As a model of the sort of sacrifice required for but sorely missing from contemporary environmental action, Patriarch Bartholomew I offers an extended reflection on the Orthodox liturgy of January 6, celebrating the Feast of Theophany, Jesus' baptism in the Jordan:[68]

> The Great Blessing begins with a hymn of praise to God for the beauty and harmony of creation:
> "Great are You, O Lord, and marvelous are Your works: no words suffice to sing the praise of Your wonders. . . . The sun sings Your praises; the moon glorifies You; the Stars supplicate before You; . . . You have stretched out the heavens like a curtain; You have established the earth upon the waters; You have walled about the sea with sand; You have poured forth the air that living things may breathe. . . ."
> Then, after this all-embracing cosmic doxology, there comes the culminating moment in the ceremony of blessing. The celebrant takes a cross and plunges it into the vessel of water. . . . The cross is our guiding symbol in the supreme sacrifice to which we are called. It sanctifies the waters and, through them, transforms the entire world. . . . Such is the model of our ecological endeavors. Such is the foundation of any environmental ethic. The cross *must* be plunged into the waters. The cross *must* be at the very center of our vision.[69]

The cross of Jesus, the ultimate sign of Christian humility, bears with it the promise of radical interior freedom from desires that distort the sacredness of all creation as gratuitous divine gift. With the cross as its central narrative thread, the Christian community possesses within it the self-understanding needed to give what it has been freely given. Plunged into the baptismal waters along with the cross, the Christian worshipper emerges with a personal commitment, communally mediated, to live with a view toward the lastness of things, with a willingness to take up the cross, giving oneself completely in bridging the chasm between that eschatological vision and the reality of material creation, including the Christian community itself, as it actually is, fragile and marked by sin.

Mystagogy as Discursive Consciousness

With the cross anchoring the baptismal commitment to strive toward the Reign of God, the liturgical life of the Christian community provides the narrative context and ethical hermeneutic necessary to conceive of habits of energy conservation as disciplined training in liturgical asceticism, guided by the virtue of ecological humility. The environmental sociologist Gert Spaargaren has demonstrated the significance of narrative context for the formation of human beings in the habits of sustainable consumption. Using Anthony Giddens's structuration theory, he has examined consumption as a practice taking shape from social norms and lifestyle choices as well as societal institutions and structures.[70] Choices to conserve energy, he finds, are inherently social in origin and scope, emerging from the rich fabric of one's life story.

Spaargaren also draws upon Giddens's distinction between practical and discursive consciousness as a helpful conceptual tool for tracing habitual formation in sustainable consumption. Practical consciousness comes into play in accomplishing repetitive tasks almost automatically, with routine behaviors like turning off lights upon leaving a room often dating back to one's early development.[71] Discursive consciousness, conversely, involves the moral agent's deliberations about the meaning of his or her behavior, typically after the fact. Having engaged in a particular action, the agent then reflects back upon and articulates his or her intention.[72]

Drawing upon Spaargaren's work, the Global Action Plan (GAP), a highly effective independent nonprofit based in the United Kingdom, has structured its energy conservation programs to include the grassroots formation of small groups designed to encourage the exercise of discursive consciousness regarding energy consumption practices.[73] GAP has found that "social interaction is absolutely vital in bringing those routinised behaviours that help to structure the individual's environment from 'practical' to 'discursive' consciousness," thus preparing the way for each member of the group to reflect upon and develop practices of sustainable consumption.[74]

GAP's approach bears resonance with the early Christian liturgical discipline of mystagogy now being retrieved in forms of sacramental practice such as the Rite of Christian Initiation of Adults.[75] Thus, within its own narrative context of worship, the Christian community possesses a structured means of cultivating discursive consciousness to ground the *askesis* of energy conservation. Reflecting mystagogically upon their ritual celebration of the Feast of Theophany, for example, a local ecclesial community might discern that one particular expression of ecological humility could entail fasting from certain forms of energy consumption precisely as an act of celebrating the goodness of God's creation. Fasting, as Olivier Clément has observed, "signifies a radical change in our relation with God and with the world. God—not the self—becomes the centre, and the world is creation, a dialogue amongst ourselves and with the Creator. Fasting prevents us from identifying ourselves with the world in order merely to possess it, and enables us to see the world in a light coming from elsewhere. Then every creature, every thing, becomes an object of contemplation."[76]

Fasting as a part of the liturgical *askesis* of energy conservation can attune Christian practitioners to the ways in which other parts of nature may be bearing witness to the integrity of God's creation. Relationality implies mutuality in communication patterns, and liturgical asceticism "clears the channel of communication from the world to us" by purifying human perception.[77] Like the rituals of liturgy, natural systems reveal the possibility of wholeness as a way of being, as well as the real fragmentation that marks its absence. "Great are You, O Lord, and marvelous are Your works," the liturgy of the Feast of Theophany proclaims by way of preparing to submerge the cross in the baptismal waters: What might a Christian mystagogical reflection group, contemplating this feast, make of the increasing rate of melting along the ice shelves of the Antarctic Peninsula, regarded as a significant proxy indicator of global climate change?[78]

Taking up the cross in the context of a Christian community that is cosmically attuned grows from and shapes a discursive consciousness of liturgical asceticism, training practitioners to order their material desires to the needs of creation. Given the stark data linking carbon dioxide emissions with climate change, might the members of an ecclesial community discern their transportation needs together? Could they consider fasting from the use of private vehicles or from air travel? When they deem it necessary to fly to a destination, could they pledge to one another, as an expression of their baptismal *sacramentum*, to purchase carbon credits to offset the harmful effects of that particular trip? Liturgical ascetics of energy conservation might become as familiar with the amount of carbon dioxide (0.83 tons) emitted for every three thousand miles of air travel as the prevailing culture is accustomed to accumulating frequent flyer miles through credit card purchases.[79]

These deliberations of discursive consciousness manifest a distinctive intentionality that marks them as practices of liturgical asceticism. First, the virtue of ecological humility inclines the liturgical ascetic to prioritize the reduction of consumption over end-use efficiency. Before opting for a carbon offset, he or she will ask whether car or air travel is necessary in a particular situation. Before choosing the most efficient form of lighting for home and office space, he will already have determined how much illumination is actually necessary.

The intentionality expressed through ecological humility resonates with Maximus's mystagogical reflection on the nature of God's creation as "cosmic," that is, as one ordered and coherent whole.[80] His conception of the "cosmic liturgy" involved free human cooperation "with God in a communion of intentionality" in the dynamic movement toward the integrity of creation in God.[81] The simple practice of turning off lights upon leaving a room takes on deeper meaning when the liturgical ascetic understands it as her grateful, free, and material cooperation with God's creative love at work in the world. He or she values the energy saved and directed toward other (it is hoped more generative) uses as a concrete form of witness to the power of the divine energy at work in creation.

Second, the intentionality of energy conservation as liturgical *askesis* finds its center of gravity in the liturgical life of the ecclesial community. Liturgical asceticism can and ought to be nourished by mystagogical reflection groups to foster discursive consciousness regarding energy conservation, but it does not necessarily require the formation of church environmental action committees. Though not problematic in themselves, Elizabeth Theokritoff argues that special interest groups nevertheless imply "a narrowing of horizons"; "the parish appears thereby to be given some aim, some goal other than being the Church. Ultimately, however, the message of the environmental crisis to the church community is simply this: Become what you are!"[82] Far from insulating the Christian community from the social and global challenges of energy conservation, liturgical *praktikê* impels worshippers to embrace their ecclesial mission as part of their baptismal *sacramentum*. Strengthened through liturgical worship in their own identity as members of Christ's Body, they take up the cross, "becoming what they are." In so doing, a community formed mystagogically to notice the connection between their worship life and reduced energy consumption will take their normative guidance from the fruits of their communal deliberations rather than from prevailing cultural standards of consumption.

The distinctive countercultural emphasis of the liturgical ascetic's approach to energy conservation emerges clearly in light of what is likely the most prevalent factor driving conservation strategies in the United States: cost-effectiveness. The State University of New York (SUNY) Buffalo, for example, has undertaken an extensive energy conservation program, even going so far as to appoint an energy officer, Walter Simpson, to oversee policy development and implementation. He calculates that SUNY Buffalo's strategies have resulted in $60 million in energy savings since they were implemented in the late 1970s, at a current annual rate of about $9 million.[83] Though SUNY Buffalo's approach has involved education around climate change, its primary goal has been monetary savings. That policy *telos*, in turn, has set the tone for technology choices and for direct action by members of the university community. Considering ways to encourage students to save energy in their dormitories, Simpson concludes, "Nothing will induce behavioral change better than charging residents for the energy they use."[84]

Economic motivation alone, though, has proven relatively weak in sustaining energy-saving habits. As the social psychologist Paul Stern notes, "When real energy prices fell in the 1980s, the first conservation gains to disappear were those from resetting home temperatures."[85] Faced with the same circumstances, by contrast, a practitioner of liturgical asceticism would continue to cultivate habits of energy conservation, emphasizing the value of reducing absolute energy consumption regardless of cost-effectiveness. Moreover, with a view toward the eschatological horizon of the lastness of things, he or she would persevere in these practices in every social setting, whether at home, in church, or in a public, secular workplace like SUNY Buffalo.

For the liturgical ascetic of energy conservation, the cultivation of ecological humility and the communal worship practice of mystagogy as an exercise of discursive consciousness also serve as an expression of the value of "participatory politics" at the local level, involving a balance between the principle of subsidiarity and the virtue of solidarity. Given that discrete energy practices may have multivalent consequences affecting the whole world, the principle of subsidiarity indicates the need for thoughtful environmental policy decisions at the highest level of social organization, superseding even the structures provided by the nation-state system.[86] At the same time, the virtue of solidarity serves to ground such supranational deliberations in grassroots participation. Treating interdependence as a moral category, John Paul II proposed solidarity as a way of seeing others "not just as some kind of instrument, . . . but as our 'neighbor,' . . . to be made a sharer, on par with ourselves, in the banquet of life to which all are equally invited by God."[87] The liturgical ascetic of energy conservation commits himself or herself to solidarity as an expression of participatory politics, celebrating a banquet of life that includes all creation and extends from the cosmic liturgy of the eucharistic table to all the forms of life threatened by rising tropospheric temperatures. "Great are You, O Lord, and marvelous are Your works. . . ."

Conclusion

By cultivating habits of energy conservation as liturgical *askesis*, the Christian community takes up the cross as an expression of its baptismal commitment in the world. With an eschatological appreciation of the lastness of things in the present historical moment of material creation, the liturgical ascetic willingly strives to exercise the virtue of ecological humility, which inclines him or her to order material desires toward the good of creation and to prioritize the reduction of energy consumption over energy efficiency. Rooting the notion of sacrificial self-gift in the context of liturgical life as a sacramental celebration of love between creation and its Creator, the ecclesial community practicing energy conservation as liturgical *askesis* can offer a countercultural moral witness, modeling the sort of interior detachment from material goods that sustainable global energy use requires.

Notes

I am very grateful to the editors and anonymous reviewers of the *Journal of the Society of Christian Ethics* as well as to David Fagerberg, Cynthia Moe-Lobeda, Jame Schaefer, Timothy Brunk, Christiana Peppard, Elizabeth Groppe, John Sniegocki, and Charles Wilber for their insightful comments on a draft of this essay.

1. Don E. Saliers, "Afterword: Liturgy and Ethics Revisited," in *Liturgy and the Moral Self: Humanity at Full Stretch*, ed. E. Byron Anderson and Bruce T. Morrill (Collegeville, Minn.: Liturgical Press, 1998), 210. In this essay, I follow the established practice of liturgical theology by using "liturgy" in the singular to encompass a wide variety of Christian worship practices. By taking up David Fagerberg's term, "liturgical asceticism," I am suggesting that the scope of liturgical influence on ethical action extends beyond the limits of a discrete worship experience.

2. For a helpful survey of various contemporary approaches to *askesis*, see Maria Antonaccio, "Contemporary Forms of *Askesis* and the Return of Spiritual Exercises," *Annual of the Society of Christian Ethics* 18 (1998): 69–92.

3. In this essay, I choose not to invoke the language of "developed" and "underdeveloped" countries because these terms fail to take into account the flourishing of all creation, particularly in its most vulnerable dimensions. In addition, they tend to reinforce an economistic bias, as Lourdes Benería insightfully argues in *Gender, Development, and Globalization: Economics as If All People Mattered* (New York: Routledge, 2003), 1–29.

4. See Andrew Simms, *Ecological Debt: The Health of the Planet and the Wealth of Nations* (London: Pluto Press, 2005).

5. See Benería, *Gender, Development, and Globalization*, for a helpful overview of this phenomenon.

6. Brenda Boardman, "New Directions for Household Energy Efficiency: Evidence from the UK," *Energy Policy* 32, no. 17 (November 2004): 1922.

7. Ibid., 1923.

8. Ibid.

9. Paul Roberts, *The End of Oil: On the Edge of a Perilous New World* (New York: Houghton Mifflin Company, 2005, orig. pub. 2004), 216.

10. Cf. Jimmy Carter, "The President's Proposed Energy Policy" (televised speech, April 18, 1977), *Vital Speeches of the Day* 43, no. 14 (May 1, 1977): 418–20.

11. Roberts, *End of Oil*, 218, based on personal communications with Rosenfeld.

12. Howard Geller, Philip Harrington, Arthur Rosenfeld, Satoshi Tanishima, and Fridtjof Unander, "Policies for Increasing Energy Efficiency: Thirty Years of Experience in

OECD Countries," *Energy Policy* 34, no. 5 (March 2006): 569–70, and Danylo Hawaleshka, "California's New Power Diet Plan," *Maclean's* 119, no. 13 (March 27, 2006): 36.

13. John P. Holdren, "The Energy Innovation Imperative. Addressing Oil Dependence, Climate Change, and Other 21st Century Challenges," *Innovations: Technology, Governance, Globalization* 1 (Spring 2006): 4.

14. Felicity Barringer, "California, Taking Big Gamble, Tries to Curb Greenhouse Gases," *New York Times*, September 15, 2006.

15. *BP Statistical Review of World Energy 2006*, 40, www.bp.com/liveassets/bp_internet/globalbp/globalbp_uk_english/reports_and_publications/statistical_energy_review_2006/STAGING/local_assets/downloads/pdf/statistical_review_of_world_energy_full_report_2006.pdf. "Primary energy" refers to energy derived from commercially traded fuels.

16. Arthur H. Rosenfeld, Tina M. Kaarsberg, and Joseph Romm, "Technologies to Reduce Carbon Dioxide Emissions in the Next Decade," *Physics Today* 53 (November 2000): 31.

17. Roberts, *End of Oil*, 232. See also Václav Smil, *Energy at the Crossroads: Global Perspectives and Uncertainties* (Cambridge, Mass.: MIT Press, 2005; orig. pub. 2003), 317, 332–35; and UN Millennium Ecosystem Assessment, "Living beyond Our Means: Natural Assets and Human Well-Being: Statement from the Board," March 2005, 22, available at www.Maweb.org.

18. Smil, *Energy at the Crossroads*, 332.

19. Ibid., 333–34.

20. Geller et al., "Policies for Increasing Energy Efficiency," 563, cite a decrease from 25.9 to 23.9 miles per gallon.

21. Smil, *Energy at the Crossroads*, 333–34.

22. Roberts, *End of Oil*, 223.

23. Smil, *Energy at the Crossroads*, 3.

24. U.S. National Research Council, "Surface Temperature Reconstructions for the Last 2,000 Years," (2006), 3, at www.nap.edu/catalog/11676.html.

25. Intergovernmental Panel on Climate Change, "Climate Change 2007: The Physical Science Basis," 13, in *Fourth Assessment Report*, 2007, vol. 1, www.ipcc.ch/SPM2feb07.pdf.

26. Simms, *Ecological Debt*, 99.

27. Rosenfeld et al., "Technologies to Reduce Carbon Dioxide Emissions in the Next Decade," 29.

28. G. Marland, T. A. Boden, and R. J. Andres, "Global, Regional, and National CO_2 Emissions," in *Trends: A Compendium of Data on Global Change* (2006), available online from the Carbon Dioxide Information Analysis Center, Oak Ridge National Laboratory, U.S. Department of Energy, at www.cdiac.ornl.gov/trends/emis/meth_reg.htm.

29. Office of Atmospheric Programs, Environmental Protection Agency, "The U.S. Inventory of Greenhouse Gas Emissions and Sinks," April 2006, table 2, "Energy Consumption by Sector and Source," at www.epa.gov/globalwarming/publications/emissions.

30. U.S. Department of Energy, "Annual Energy Outlook 2006 with Projections to 2030," www.eia.doe.gov/oiaf/aeo.

31. Ibid., table 11, "Petroleum Supply and Disposition Balance."

32. See Nayna J. Jhaveri, "Petroimperialism: U.S. Oil Interests and the Iraq War," *Antipode* 36, no. 1 (2004): 2–11; and Michael Watts, "Petro-Violence: Community, Extraction, and Political Ecology of a Mythic Commodity," in *Violent Environments*, ed. N. L. Peluso and M. Watts (Ithaca, N.Y.: Cornell University Press, 2001), 189–212.

33. Daniel Yergin, "Ensuring Energy Security," *Foreign Affairs* 85, no. 2 (March–April 2006): 76–78.

34. Ibid., 80–81.

35. Smil, *Energy at the Crossroads*, 49–50.

36. Simms, *Ecological Debt*, 98–99.

37. UN Millennium Ecosystem Assessment, "Living beyond Our Means."

38. Cf. United Nations Development Program, *World Energy Assessment Overview: Update 2004*, ed. Jose Goldemberg and Thomas Johansson (New York: United Nations Development Program, 2004), 64.

39. Smil, *Energy at the Crossroads*, 370; emphasis in the original.

40. Andrew Louth, *Maximus the Confessor* (London: Routledge, 1996), 51–52, 69.

41. David Fagerberg, *Theologia Prima: What Is Liturgical Theology?* 2nd ed. (Chicago: Hillenbrand Books, 2004), 20.

42. David Fagerberg, "A Century on Liturgical Asceticism," *Diakonia* 31, no. 1 (1998): 41.

43. Cf. Max Weber, *The Protestant Ethic and the Spirit of Capitalism*, trans. Talcott Parsons (London: Routledge, 2004; orig. pub. 1930), 100–1; and *The Sociology of Religion*, trans. Ephraim Fischoff (Boston: Beacon Press, 1964; orig. pub. 1922), 166–83. See also Richard Valantasis' critique of Weber's approach, "The Social Function of Asceticism," in *Asceticism*, ed. Vincent L. Wimbush and Richard Valantasis (New York: Oxford University Press, 1998), 544–52.

44. John Hart, *Sacramental Commons: Christian Ecological Ethics* (Lanham, Md.: Rowman & Littlefield, 2006), 17.

45. Pierre Teilhard de Chardin, *Human Energy*, trans. J. M. Cohen (New York: Harcourt Brace Jovanovich, 1969; orig. pub. 1962), 72.

46. Patriarch Bartholomew, "The Orthodox Faith and the Environment," *Sourozh* 62 (1995): 23–24. In support of this insight, he points to the work of Eastern Christian authors Maximus the Confessor, Gregory Palamas, and Gregory of Nyssa.

47. Fagerberg, "Living Christ's Life By Sacrament and Holy Spirit," *Diakonia* 33, no. 1 (2000): 40–41; see also 28–29, where he refers to Paul Evdokimov's description of *perichoresis*, in "Saint Seraphim of Sarov," *Ecumenical Review* 15 (April 1963): 273.

48. Jean Corbon, *The Wellspring of Christian Worship*, trans. Matthew J. O'Connell (San Francisco: Ignatius Press, 1988; orig. pub. 1980), 113; see also 17, 38, 101, 143, 218.

49. For this interpretation of *synergoi*, I am following Kallistos Ware, "Lent and the Consumer Society," in *Living Orthodoxy in the Modern World: Orthodox Christianity and Society*, ed. Andrew Walker and Costa Carras (Crestwood, N.Y.: St. Vladimir's Seminary Press, 2000), 66.

50. Fagerberg, "Century," 41.

51. Fagerberg, *Theologia Prima*, 30.

52. Augustine, Sermon 272, in *The Works of St. Augustine*, ed. John E. Rotelle (Hyde Park, N.Y.: New City Press, 1993), 300–1.

53. See Maximus the Confessor, "The Church's Mystagogy," in *Maximus the Confessor: Selected Writings*, trans. George C. Berthold (New York: Paulist Press, 1985), 2–5; and Andrew Louth's commentary, "Apophatic Theology and the Liturgy in St. Maximos the Confessor," *Criterion* 36, no. 1 (Autumn 1997): 4–5. See also Louth, *Maximus the Confessor*, 77.

54. Alexander Schmemann, *For the Life of the World: Sacraments and Orthodoxy* (Crestwood, N.Y.: St. Vladimir's Seminary Press, 1973), 25.

55. Elizabeth Theokritoff, "Embodied Word and New Creation: Some Modern Orthodox Insights Concerning the Material World," in *Abba: The Tradition of Orthodoxy in the West*, ed. John Behr, Andrew Louth, and Dimitri Conomos (Crestwood, N.Y.: St. Vladimir's Seminary Press, 2003), 228; and John Chryssavgis, "The World as Sacrament: Insights into an Orthodox Worldview," *Pacifica* 10 (1997): 4. See also Vigen Guroian, "Liturgy and the Lost Eschatological Horizon of Christian Ethics," *Annual of the Society of Christian Ethics* 20 (2000): 227–38.

56. Gustavo Gutiérrez, *A Theology of Liberation*, rev. ed., trans. Caridad Inda, John Eagleson, and Matthew J. O'Connell (Maryknoll: Orbis Books, 1988; orig. pub. 1971), 95.

57. James Nash, *Loving Nature: Ecological Integrity and Christian Responsibility* (Nashville: Abingdon Press, 1991), 74.

58. Nash, *Loving Nature*, 67.

59. Louth, *Maximus the Confessor*, 69.

60. Cf. Diana Fritz Cates, *Choosing to Feel: Virtue, Friendship, and Compassion for Friends* (Notre Dame, Ind.: University of Notre Dame Press, 1997), 19; and Thomas Aquinas, *Summa theologiae* (New York: Blackfriars and McGraw-Hill, 1963), I-II, 14.1 ad 1. Subsequent references to this source will be abbreviated *ST*.

61. Fritz Cates, *Choosing to Feel*, 44. See also Olivier Clément, *The Roots of Christian Mysticism: Texts and Commentary* (London: New City Press, 1993), 136. This process of reeducating desire resonates with what Maria Antonaccio has called a nondogmatic, naturalistic form of asceticism. See "Asceticism and the Ethics of Consumption," *Journal of the Society of Christian Ethics* 26, no. 1 (2006): 90–91.

62. *ST* II-II, 161.5 ad 4; cf. 161.4 *sed contra*.

63. *ST* II-II, 161.1 ad 5.

64. *The Rule of St. Benedict in English*, ed. Timothy Fry (Collegeville, Md.: Liturgical Press, 1982), 7.67; emphasis in original. Applying systems theory to ecology, Gregory Bateson offers a similar affirmation of the role of humility in shaping humans' attitudes toward nature in "Form, Substance, and Difference," in *Steps to An Ecology of Mind* (Chicago: University of Chicago Press, 1972), 467–68.

65. Thomas Merton, "Integrity," in *New Seeds of Contemplation* (New York: New Directions Books, 1972; orig. pub. 1961), 99.

66. Chryssavgis, "World as Sacrament," 21.

67. U.S. Catholic Conference, "Renewing the Earth," Pastoral Statement, November 14, 1991, in *"And God Saw That It Was Good": Catholic Theology and the Environment*, ed. Drew Christiansen and Walter Grazer (Washington, D.C.: U.S. Catholic Conference, 1996), 232.

68. Roman Catholics celebrate the Epiphany on January 6, followed a week later by the Baptism of the Lord. For Orthodox Christians, the Epiphany and Baptism coincide in the Feast of Theophany.

69. Patriarch Bartholomew, "Sacrifice: The Missing Dimension," closing address to the Fourth International and Interreligious Symposium on the Adriatic Sea, June 10, 2002, in *Cosmic Grace, Humble Prayer: The Ecological Vision of the Green Patriarch Bartholomew I*, ed. John Chryssavgis (Grand Rapids: William B. Eerdmans, 2003), 307–8; emphasis in the original.

70. Cf. Tim Jackson, "Motivating Sustainable Consumption: A Review of Evidence on Consumer Behaviour and Behavioural Change," a Report to the Sustainable Development Research Network (2005), x, at www.sd-research.org.uk/documents/MotivatingSCfinal.pdf; and Gert Spaargaren, "Sustainable Consumption: A Theoretical and Environmental Policy Perspective," *Society and Natural Resources* 16 (2003): 687–701. As used here, "lifestyle"

means a particular moral agent's social practices as well as the accompanying narrative. See Spaargaren, "Sustainable Consumption," 689; and Anthony Giddens, *Modernity and Self-Identity* (Cambridge: Polity Press, 1991), 81.

71. Cf. Jacquie Burgess, "Sustainable Consumption: Is It Really Achievable?" *Consumer Policy Review* 13, no. 3 (May–June 2003): 81.

72. Jackson, "Motivating Sustainable Consumption," x–xi, 91.

73. Burgess, "Sustainable Consumption"; and see also Jackson, "Motivating Sustainable Consumption," 116. As Burgess explains, GAP draws heavily upon the conceptual model of consumption that G. Spaargaren and B. van Vliet have developed using Giddens's structuration theory in "Lifestyle, Consumption, and the Environment: The Ecological Modernisation of Domestic Consumption," *Society and Natural Resources* 9 (2000): 50–76.

74. Burgess, "Sustainable Consumption," 83.

75. See Kathleen Hughes, *Saying Amen: A Mystagogy of Sacrament* (Chicago: Liturgical Training Publications, 1999); and Enrico Mazza, *Mystagogy: A Theology of Liturgy in the Patristic Age*, trans. Matthew J. O'Connell (New York: Pueblo, 1989).

76. Clément, *Roots of Christian Mysticism*, 141. His insight bears resonance with Louis-Marie Chauvet's notion of dispossession. See Louis-Marie Chauvet, *Symbol and Sacrament: A Sacramental Reinterpretation of Christian Existence*, trans. Patrick Madigan and Madeleine Beaumont (Collegeville, Minn.: Liturgical Press, 1995; orig. pub. 1987), 168.

77. Theokritoff, "Embodied Word," 236.

78. National Snow and Ice Data Center, "State of the Cryosphere," http://www.nsidc.org/sotc/iceshelves.html.

79. A useful carbon calculator can be found at www.carboncounter.org.

80. Cf. Kallistos Ware, "The Value of Material Creation," *Sobornost* 6, no. 3 (1971): 158.

81. Myroslaw Tataryn, "The Eastern Tradition and the Cosmos," *Sobornost* 11 (1989): 48; cf. Maximus, "Church's Mystagogy," 2.

82. Elizabeth Theokritoff, "From Sacramental Life to Sacramental Living: Heeding the Message of the Environmental Crisis," *Greek Orthodox Theological Review* 44 (1999): 522.

83. Walter Simpson, "Energy Sustainability and the Green Campus," *Planning for Higher Education* 31 (March–May 2003): 157.

84. Simpson, "Energy Sustainability," 153.

85. Paul Stern, "What Psychology Knows about Energy Conservation," *American Psychologist* 47 (October 1992): 1226, citing data from U.S. Department of Energy, *Energy Conservation Trends: Understanding the Factors That Affect Conservation Gains in the U.S. Economy* (Washington, D.C.: Office of Policy, Planning, and Analysis and Office of Conservation and Renewable Energy, 1989).

86. Here, I am taking Nash's argument for subsidiarity and solidarity at the level of the international community one step further to emphasize the need for a global environmental consciousness that transcends the narrow interests of nation-states and allows the voices of those often marginalized in discussions among the nations to be heard, e.g., nongovernmental organizations and displaced peoples. See Nash, *Loving Nature*, 65–66.

87. John Paul II, *Sollicitudo rei socialis* (1987), in *Catholic Social Thought: The Documentary Heritage*, ed. David J. O'Brien and Thomas A. Shannon (Maryknoll, N.Y.: Orbis Books, 1992), paragraph 39.

Sex in 3-D: A Telos for a Virtue Ethics of Sexuality

Lisa Fullam

AS WITH OTHER CONSIDERATIONS FROM AN ETHICS OF VIRTUE, DISCERN-
ing the ends of sexual activities requires a careful examination of the particularly
human dimensions of sex. By asking, "What do you want from, what are your
hopes, what are your ends for your sex life?" three dimensions of excellent sex
emerge: a feel for incarnation, an ability for intimacy, and an eye for insight.

I have a question: What do you want from your sex life? What are your
hopes? To speak philosophically, what is the end, the telos, of your sex
life?

It is not a simple question. There are few human experiences that carry as
broad a range of meanings and values as sex. Sex can be everything from a monetary transaction without emotional meaning, to a profound experience of loving union between partners. Sex can be celebratory or can be solace in sadness.
Sex can help us develop a deeper understanding of ourselves, our partners, and
God. Sex can be tender or violently abusive; it can heal and can deeply wound.
It can be solitary, shared, or abstained from altogether. Sex can signify acceptance and mutuality, or it can be a competition to demonstrate prowess and to
gain one's own pleasure unconnected to that of our partner. Sex is the occasion
of what is arguably the greatest pleasure flesh is heir to—orgasm is climactic, after all. And sex is the usual way we procreate, and in so doing seek to perpetuate
ourselves in another iteration of humanity who we hope will grow to live and
love in turn. One of the ways that sex may be understood is that it can symbolize
a close relationship between people. "Are they having sex?" is one question people ask to find out if a couple is serious; additionally, sexual intimacy serves to
deepen a relationship by opening the couple to otherwise unknowable aspects
of the partner. In other words, sex can help to effect the intimacy that it symbolizes. Part of the challenge of thinking about goals or ends for sex and sexuality is
the breadth of sexual experience and its meanings.

We need definitions before going further. "Sex" is a biological category
like male or female, and "sex" also refers to the panoply of human erotic acts.[1]

Sexuality is a much broader term, shaping the totality of how we understand ourselves and how we relate to others, physically and more generally. A UN World Health Organization international technical consultation in 2002 employed this definition: "Sexuality is a central aspect of being human throughout life and encompasses sex, gender identities and roles, sexual orientation, eroticism, pleasure, intimacy and reproduction. Sexuality is experienced and expressed in thoughts, fantasies, desires, beliefs, attitudes, values, behaviours, practices, roles and relationships. While sexuality can include all of these dimensions, not all of them are always experienced or expressed. Sexuality is influenced by the interaction of biological, psychological, social, economic, political, cultural, ethical, legal, historical, religious and spiritual factors."[2]

Sexuality, then, is connected to the fulfillment of erotic desires, though it is not limited to the erotic. In short, the human person is intrinsically a sexual being, and our sexuality permeates our self-understanding and our relationships with others, including our relationship with God. Sex is one expression of sexuality, and perhaps the most focused and intense expression of sexuality. And it is precisely in its connection to sexuality that sex becomes more polyvalent in meaning, more likely to be a powerful force in our lives, and more connected to our humanity overall. In that connection, questions of sex reach beyond matters of biology and technique to include the realm of feelings, meaning, and desire. And this is where sex becomes morally interesting, at the level of whole persons in our lives and loves.

Sex cannot be reduced to its biological data or elevated to a mystique of the erotic. To reduce sex to the biological facts of copulation ignores the fact that we can bring far more to sex and sexual relationships than a merely physical account can convey. At the same time, to elevate sex to a mysteriously powerful Eros ignores the fact that, even in the best of sexual relationships, sex can sometimes be not much more than two tired people falling into each others' arms, finding more an experience of simple physical release than one of profound physical and spiritual union. Even an extraordinarily intense and loving sex life includes mostly "ordinary" sex—neither the worst nor the best, but the whole spectrum of healthy sexual engagement. In other words, in looking at sex, we should avoid both biological minimalism but also an unwarranted and unreal romanticism about sex. Sex can mean very little, or a great deal, and usually for most couples a given sexual encounter means something in between.

So my opening question "What do you want from your sex life?" might be rephrased "How do you hope to celebrate, fulfill and express your sexuality, especially in intimate relationships involving sex?" Here, I outline a vision for excellent sex, a tripartite suggestion of a telos for sexual relationships. I approach this question via an exploration of how happiness and virtues inform each other in an Aristotelian-Thomistic approach to virtue ethics. This form of virtue ethics has been particularly influential in the contemporary retrieval of virtue-based morals in Roman Catholic (and other) circles, and though in need of some updating in its details (as we know now, for example, that women are not defective men), it remains a powerful methodology for ethical reasoning. In this view, virtues are acquired gradually by practice and are constitutive of happiness. In addition, our progress in a particular virtue allows us to grasp more deeply and broadly the full scope of that virtue for the moral life. Thus, the telos in an ethics of virtue, whether construed narrowly (as, e.g., the telos of a particular endeavor like becoming a musician) or broadly (the overall excellence of human living), is something discovered in its pursuit, even as it serves as the end that directs our striving. The life of virtue, then, is a continuing dialectic of telos and the current state of virtue in the soul, each shaping the other. With this understanding of the function of a telos for virtue ethics, I suggest a tripartite telos encompassing (1) a feel for incarnation, (2) an ability for intimacy, and (3) an eye for insight that might guide us in constructing a virtue ethics of sexuality.

There have been several virtue- or justice-based approaches to sexual ethics in the recent literature. John Grabowski, in *Sex and Virtue*, constructed sexual ethics in light of the virtues of covenant fidelity and chastity. Raja Halwani, in *Virtuous Liaisons: Care, Love, Sex and Virtue Ethics*, explored an ethics of care and love in relationship to sexuality. Karen Lebacqz added appropriate vulnerability to the traditional norms of procreation and union as a guiding norm for sexual relationships. Marvin Ellison and Sylvia Thorson-Smith invoked justice love as a guiding principle for Christian sexuality. Most recently, Margaret Farley's 2006 book *Just Love: A Framework for Christian Sexual Ethics* constructs sexuality in light of a single composite norm of justice and love.[3]

However, none of these approaches seems to catch the wide array of meanings of human sexuality. Grabowski's chastity approach seems to risk ignoring larger social questions about sexuality, such as the culturally sanctioned sexual abuse of women or children. Halwani's care ethics shares the strength and weakness of a "love and do what you will" approach in general; it seems to lack normative force even to the degree that a virtue ethic will permit such. A justice-inflected framework is a very good starting-point for addressing critical questions of equality, mutuality, social justice, and sexual abuse, but it is less useful when it comes to ordinary sexuality and questions concerning sexual pleasure, and in general it is less focused when we begin to seek a maximalistic vision of sex. Farley's vision for just love provides a richer engagement between the two categories of justice and love—her framework calls for "justice *in* loving" as the norm that serves as a principle for sexual relationships.[4] I would suggest that loving needs further parsing in addition to the category of justice.

James Keenan, in his article "Virtue Ethics and Sexual Ethics," recognized the tradition's emphasis on chastity as the chief virtue for sexual relations then argued for a more thoroughgoing virtue approach to sexual ethics, which he modeled in keeping with his tetrad of cardinal virtues construed relationally: prudence, justice, fidelity, and self-care.[5] This construction of cardinal virtues provides what he describes as a "skeletal" framework for a sexual ethics, which is then fleshed out differently in different cultural contexts. For example, he suggests that "justice, fidelity and self-care in a Buddhist culture have somewhat similar and somewhat different meanings than they do in a liberal or Confucian context."[6] He cites some of the possible functions of each cardinal virtue but does not begin to specify the cardinal virtues into what I will call subsidiary virtues (as, e.g., distributive justice is a subsidiary virtue of justice generally.)[7]

Keenan's approach has a number of advantages. First, it is comprehensive, in that it covers all the logically possible realms of human relationship.[8] At the same time, it avoids the morass of needing to defend a set of cardinal virtues as encompassing an adequate, timeless, and self-contained account of human nature as such, a pitfall in some readings of Thomas Aquinas. It would add to a framework like Farley's norm of justice in loving both an explicitly virtue-ethical approach to sexual ethics and a thicker parsing of the other virtues of loving besides justice in loving, namely, fidelity in loving, self-care in loving, and prudence in loving. Keenan's construction engages the powerful insights and potentials of relationality/responsibility ethics while remaining fundamentally virtue based, and it privileges relationality rather than a more abstract quality like rationality as central to human being in the world.

But to move from his call for cardinal virtues in sexual ethics to a more specific account of virtues for sexual ethics requires another intermediate methodological step. Virtue ethics is teleological. When we begin to move from the realm of cardinal virtues to that of more specified or contextual virtues, that process brings focus to the telos in those realms of human life that may be guided by those subsidiary virtues. This focus makes sense because the virtues, at least in an Aristotelian-Thomistic virtue ethics, are constitutive of the telos, not merely a means to it. First, then, I explore the relationship of telos to virtues in Aristotle and Aquinas, with a brief glance at Plato along the way.

The Function of the Telos in Aristotle's *Nicomachean Ethics*

Aristotle begins his *Nicomachean Ethics* with the assertion that everything we do is done with some purpose. But what is the highest good, the purpose to which all particular ends are ordered? Here Aristotle finds his starting point in a consensus that immediately becomes a new problem: "Most people virtually agree; for both the many and the cultivated call [the ultimate end] happiness, and they suppose that living well and doing well are the same as being happy. But they disagree about what happiness is, and the many do not give the same answer as the wise" (1095a).[9]

Aristotle dismisses several common notions of what happiness consists of (e.g., pleasure, wealth, and honor), and he dismisses as well Plato's form of the Good as the last end, because it does not seem to be accessible enough or practical enough to serve as a functional last end in moral life: "Moreover, it is a puzzle to know what the weaver or carpenter will gain for his own craft from knowing the Good Itself, or how anyone will be better at medicine or generalship from having gazed on the Idea Itself. For what the doctor appears to consider is not even health [universally, let alone good universally] but human health, and presumably the health of this human being even more, since he treats one particular patient at a time" (1097a; brackets in original).[10]

Aristotle moves easily between the realm of particular ways of life and the happiness that is complete without qualification, that is, the happiness of the most excellent human life overall, and extending over the whole of one's life. The reason is simple; to be an excellent carpenter, weaver, or whatever is a subcategory of human excellence overall, presuming that the particular way of life chosen is not itself inimical to human excellence overall. The excellent practitioner is a particular type of excellent human being overall, and we know the function by seeing it at work in the excellent practitioner:

> Now we say that the function of a [kind of thing]—of a harpist, for instance—is the same in kind as the function of an excellent individual of the kind—of an excellent harpist, for instance. . . . Moreover, we take the human function to be a certain kind of life, and take this life to be activity and actions of the soul that involve reason; hence the function of the excellent man is to do this well and finely. Now each function is completed well by being completed in accord with the virtue proper [to that kind of thing]. And so the human good proves to be activity of the soul in accord with virtue, and indeed with the best and most complete virtue, if there are more virtues than one. Moreover, it must be in a complete life. For one swallow does not make a spring, nor does one day; nor, similarly, does one day or a short time make us blessed and happy." (1098a, brackets in original)

Here, we must be careful not to read Aristotle through a puritanical or deontological lens. Happiness is not the reward for a life of virtue, as though if we struggle against nature to be prudent and magnanimous and brave that we will then be granted happiness like a Girl Scout earning a merit badge for an activity she finds onerous. Happiness, rather, consists in a life of virtue. Happiness is activity that arises out of the stable habits of character that Aristotle calls virtuous. And if that weren't enough, because virtues are perfections of natural human capacities, virtuous living is also pleasant. For Aristotle, virtue is its own reward:

> Moreover, the life of these active people is also pleasant in itself. For being pleased is a condition of the soul, [and hence is included in the activity of the

soul]. Further, each type of person finds pleasure in whatever he is called a lover of; a horse, for instance, pleases the horse-lover, a spectacle the lover of spectacles. Similarly, what is just pleases the lover of justice, and in general what accords with virtue pleases the lover of virtue. Now the things that please most people conflict, because they are not pleasant by nature, whereas the things that please lovers of the fine are things pleasant by nature. Actions in accord with virtue are pleasant by nature, so that they both please lovers of the fine and are pleasant in their own right. Hence these people's life does not need pleasure to be added [to virtuous activity] as some sort of extra decoration; rather, it has its pleasure within itself." (1099a)

Thus, for Aristotle, virtue and pleasure exist in a reciprocal correlation between activity and state; one cultivates in oneself the habits or virtues that are deeply pleasing—that constitute happiness, incipiently or completely—when we act in accord with them. And the fullest happiness available in human living is life in accord with complete virtue, the array of perfections of human nature. Virtue, then, is a matter of striving, but happiness (and pleasure) comes with its acquisition. Athletic activity is a good example of this dynamic correlation at work, by dint of practice, sometimes arduous or onerous practice, a basketball player acquires skills that become more and more reflexive, and in practicing the player becomes more and more fit. In playing, whether in practice or in games, he or she finds a certain ease and skill that carries pleasure, and even joy, along with it. As though by nature, the player dribbles the ball, stops, pivots, fakes, jumps shoots, and sinks the shot, all with the ease and sense of physical rightness of the fit athlete whose body responds to the command of athletic reason because that is an excellence for which it was created. In sex, too, we become adept at the skills that enhance pleasure, at everything from becoming a more dexterous lover to becoming better at the kind of emotional and spiritual openness that builds intimacy. We find ease and enjoyment in ourselves and our partners as we become lovers, for sexual loving is an excellence for which we were created.

There is also another aspect of this dynamic. Virtue and happiness are known or understood more deeply as they are acquired. The telos is that according to which we orient our striving, while at the same time we come to understand the possibilities of virtue, its challenges, rewards, and its pleasures, only in the process of practicing it. A beginning pianist concentrates to place his or her fingers on the right keys, and eventually "Chopsticks" comes clearly, with a measure of joy, or at least a sense of accomplishment. But with further practice, the pianist begins inchoatively to experience the self-expression that is possible in more complex music, the kind of expression that can be heard in the recordings of the excellent, and the pianist strives to incarnate this in playing. The excellence of piano playing, then, comes both in and through the physical skills acquired by the practice that the art requires. The art then reveals the depths of beauty in ways that only music can achieve, displayed most fully where technique is masterful, even where the piece played may not push the player to his or her technical limits. And therein lies an expansive happiness that invites the pianist deeper into the art, and the listener to perhaps begin his or her own first blundering moves toward—well, toward "Chopsticks" first. We experience and acquire happiness in glimmers and hints as we acquire virtue, and we see its range of possibility more clearly in that process.

Aristotle describes this process in *Nicomachean Ethics* obliquely in terms of the difference between actions and states of character like virtues. Though our actions set us on the path to acquire a given virtue, the shape of that aspect of our character is unknown in its acquisition. Yet the choice to shape our characters is still ours. "We are in control of actions from the beginning to the end, when we know the particulars. With states, however, we are in control of the beginning, but do not know, any more than with sickness, what the cumulative effect of particular actions will be. Nonetheless, since it was up to us to exercise a capacity either this way or another way, states are voluntary" (1114b30).

And of course this choice is also how virtues become personal, in that they are excellences of individuals with given degrees of talent, enabled or limited by particular contingencies. The piano player practices, perhaps thinking: "I want to play like Billy Joel!" In the end, the only way to know what piano playing will mean for him is in the playing, and in the end, he will not be Billy Joel, but will be the piano player he can be. Otherwise, he never moves beyond mimicry to art. Likewise in sex; though we look to great lovers for models of how to be sexually excellent, ultimately we strive to become ourselves as the best lovers we can be, bringing our own gifts and limitations to art. Where we look for models of excellence matters, too; one shortcoming of pornography is that it tends to suggest that sexual excellence is merely a matter of physical endowment or technique, rather than a personal encounter of body and spirit, whereas erotica tends to present sexual encounters more holistically.

One of the great curiosities of the *Nicomachean Ethics* is the lack of systematization in Aristotle's presentation of the virtues. The force of his argument would seem logically to lead to a description of the human person, then to a list of virtues that would perfect the human person in toto. And he does offer a brief moral anthropology (1102a ff). But when he starts to describe particular virtues, he deliberately avoids those categories, preferring to describe what I am calling subsidiary virtues, because they go closer to providing guidance for particular actions and therefore are truer in his view.[11] Aristotle's account of particular virtues is scattershot, consisting of a random-seeming list of virtues that, as has been widely noted, seem to reflect the values of Athenian gentlemanly society rather than human perfections more generally. In keeping with his inductive methodology, when proposing virtues, it seems that Aristotle set out merely to observe the qualities of those who seemed happiest, and from there began to sort out what some of the most notable virtues might be.

A Thomistic Turn: A Synthesis of Aristotelian and Platonic Uses of Telos

It was Plato who proposed the notion of cardinal virtues, a move that Thomas Aquinas would recover when working out his own virtue ethic. In the *Republic*, Plato recounts Socrates' search to define justice. Because he argues that it is easier to see things writ large (i.e., socially) than in individuals, Socrates first described the ideal or beautiful city as comprising three classes: the ordinary citizens (who produce and consume what is essential for life), the guardians, and the rulers. Justice was the happy state in which each class fulfilled its function harmoniously and obediently to the ruler's wise oversight. In book IV of the *Republic*, Socrates recapitulates the isomorphism of city and citizen: "We are pretty much agreed that the same number and the same kinds of classes as are in the city are also in the soul of each individual."[12] In the individual, then, there are three parts: the appetites, the spirited part, and the rational part. Justice in the individual is the happy state in which the intellect rules the spirited part, which rules the appetites. In the *Republic*, we see virtue framed in an anthropology—virtues inhere in the basic facets of the human person described analogously to the polis as a whole, all under the guidance of reason.

Like Plato, Thomas Aquinas will also schematize his virtues in an anthropological frame, but Aquinas begins where Aristotle begins, in a consideration of human happiness. For Aquinas, the happiness that fulfills the human person is twofold, natural and supernatural, imperfect and perfect. True and perfect happiness consists in the beatific vision. Because God is the origin and end of all our human desires, nothing short of God can truly fulfill us, and God will fulfill us entirely. However, short of heaven, there is true though imperfect happiness. First there is the life of grace that finds its completion in the beatific vision. Both the beatific vision and the life of grace on Earth are gifts of God, not achieved by human effort or merit. These are supernatural, precisely because they exceed our natural capacities and strivings. But even though the beatific vision is the perfection of human happiness, the concept does little or no moral work for Aquinas. He seems to be invoking the beatific vision as an analogue to the form of the good in Plato, while at the same time he seems to have accepted Aristotle's scathing critique of that ultimate Good as useless for moral discernment.

The other form of happiness, the natural or imperfect kind, for Aquinas consists in a life of virtue. In his account of natural happiness expressed as an ethics of virtue, he adopts Aristotle's inductive natural law method, in which reason reflecting on humanity yields moral insight, but he schematizes his virtues according to Plato's paradigm. He arrives at his account of the four cardinal virtues in two ways, first as requisites of a formal rationalist schema and then as an anthropology constructed on happiness and human flourishing:

> [From a rationalist schema,] things may be numbered either in respect of their formal principles or according to the subjects in which they are: and either way we find that there are four cardinal virtues. For the formal principle of the virtue of which we speak now is good as defined by reason; which good can be considered in two ways. First as existing in the very act of reason: and thus we have one principal virtue, called Prudence. Secondly, according as the reason puts its order into something else, either into operations, and then we have Justice: or into passions, and then we need two virtues, [Temperance and Fortitude] (I IIae, q. 61.1c.).[13]

> [From an anthropological perspective, we] find the same number if we consider the subjects of virtue, for there are four subjects of the virtue we speak of now, viz. the power which is rational in its essence, and this is perfected by Prudence; and that which is rational by participation, and is threefold, the will, subject of justice, the concupiscible faculty, subject of temperance, and the irascible faculty, subject of fortitude (I IIae, q. 61.1c.).

Aquinas's synthesis structures his account of the cardinal virtues after Plato's anthropological schema (which also coheres with the rationalist formal schema of virtue) rather than Aristotle's more scattershot inductive modality. The anthropology he employs differs from Plato's principally in seeing justice perfecting a distinct faculty (the will) rather than as harmony among the other faculties. But like Plato, he derives his cardinal virtues from an anthropology that he regards as comprehensive. At the same time, his overall approach in the *Summa* is Aristotelian and inductive—we must begin with what is available to us, what we can observe and ponder.

The logical link that unifies rather than merely juxtaposes the Platonic-deductive and Aristotelian-inductive accounts of virtue is a theological claim. Aquinas's natural law approach reflects his confidence that God is ultimately and perfectly rational, and that human reason, while liable to error, retains enough competence of its own to gain glimpses of the mind of God. Our reason is the imperfect image of God's reason, so what is true to human reason (which truth must be rigorously winnowed in recognition of our fallen and temptible state) participates, if distantly, in the eternal law, the truth as it is known completely to God. It would follow, then, that carefully looking at the human person should yield not just a random collection of disconnected virtues but would reveal a structured and reasonable moral anthropology. We can work from the realm of pure reason to the four cardinal virtues, or we can induce the four cardinal virtues from a careful reading of the capacities of the human person—and if we reason correctly, they will agree.

What does this have to do with sex and sexual ethics? First, one persistent critique of natural law ethics of this sort is that it is increasingly questionable whether it is possible to construct a complete moral anthropology of the sort Plato and Thomas offered. Here, I side with Jean Porter's insight that to make natural law claims need not attain to comprehensiveness: "It is not difficult to set forth a cogent concept of human nature, so long as we do not hold ourselves to the unattainable standard of a complete, fully articulated and nonrevisable concept. We cannot hope to reach this ideal until the biological and human sciences attain a level of development proper to a perfected science in the Aristotelian sense, and they are very far from that point, if indeed they could attain it at all. Nonetheless, even now we can attain—indeed we actually have—a concept which is to some degree implicit and certainly provisional, but adequate for most purposes."[14]

In short, even if we cannot claim an overarching account of human nature, that does not require us to toss out the natural law endeavor entirely but only that we understand a posited telos as true but liable to revision and expansion in light of new understandings, especially new scientific understanding. In fact, because scientific knowledge of all kinds, philosophical insights, and new understandings of scripture and previous Christian tradition are continually raising challenges to traditional Christian sexual teaching, such openness to new knowledge and new understandings of what it means to be human is essential if sexual ethics is to be credible to contemporary Christians and relevant to their lives.[15] So we must seek what is true of human nature but in a flexible and responsive way, with a strong dose of the kind of epistemological humility that Porter recommends.

Second, understanding the telos in a more Aristotelian, inductive vein, that is, to begin by looking for those who seem to have achieved happiness and then strive to discern and acquire the virtues they possess would bring to sexual ethics an experiential warrant that has been underplayed or absent from most Roman Catholic sexual ethics until recently. To be sure, the Catholic sexual ethical tradition has claimed a natural law basis, but one that has been widely critiqued as tending toward physicalism. That framework for sexual ethics has underplayed the distinctiveness of human sexuality in all its layers of meaning. Here especially, in issues such as contraception and gay unions, the voices of Christians in relationships reveal something of true human flourishing that challenges the tradition to discern norms by observing the lives of those who are happy in these relationships.[16] A natural law framework is always revising itself in light of new insights, including those of human experience.

Therefore, the virtues that one strives for in order to realize this happiness may be discerned inductively from, or in light of, a moral anthropology that is always open to revision, expansion, and correction by reflection on experience. The structure of cardinal virtues, in this view, becomes a heuristic device for categorizing virtues rather than a debatable claim about human nature completely. If Aquinas is correct in his theological and philosophical presumption that all truths participate in the one ultimate truth of the Eternal Law, then these two lenses for the telos—one that is based on a provisional moral anthropology that describes an array of proper human perfections and the other that is inductively arrived at by observing happiness and by enjoying the subtler pleasures of incipient and deepening happiness—must cohere for determinations of the good and the right. As I show in the next section, the notion that these two lenses participate in one ultimate truth means that we can see them as a dynamic and mutually informing dialectic of induction, deduction, and the cycling back again.

Subsidiary Virtues and the Specification of the Telos

In returning to classic texts of virtue ethics, we saw that Aristotle provided the method in which virtues are constitutive of natural human happiness, while Plato provided the anthropological structure of virtues in Aquinas's moral theology. If we reduce Plato's claim of anthropological comprehensiveness to a more modest claim of "true but provisional," as Porter does, we can begin to see emerging a dialectical dynamism between telos and virtue. Our happiness consists in living most fully as we were created to live, the meaning of which we discover as we progress. It is as though we are building the boat we sail in as we sail in it. The gradual discovery of the range of possibility of virtues means, moreover, that though we may have begun with a plan for the boat, the plan itself may be affirmed, modified, radically revised, or limited by contingencies as we build it. Moreover, the building we do may be done well or badly, because we are also learning to build in the building.

When we begin to specify, or, in Keenan's terms, to enflesh or thicken cardinal virtues into subsidiary virtues, this dialectical dynamic of telos and virtue becomes clearer still. It is here that we begin a process that takes us closer to particular actions or circumstances than the very abstract cardinal virtues do. For example, "fidelity is the virtue that nurtures and sustains the bonds of those special relationships that humans enjoy whether by blood, marriage, love, citizenship or sacrament."[17] (I would extend this virtue to include other special close ties, e.g., that between doctor and patient.) But the virtues or practices that participate in fidelity between spouses (e.g., here I would invoke the practice of sexual exclusivity) are quite distinct from those that are operative in a citizenship relationship (though some might say that faithful citizenship might invite us to buy American-made cars, it cannot be said to require that we have sex only with other Americans).

When we move from the realm of cardinal virtues to subsidiary virtues and to prudential practices, the particular construction of the telos of the agent becomes more salient. When Aristotle moved easily from the excellence of the harp player to human excellence generally, he downplayed the specificity of the excellences proper to the harpist. Though the cardinal virtues are perfections of human capacities generally, and so are understood universalistically, the particular virtues sought, and the prioritization of those virtues, may be seen to reveal the fundamentally dialectical relationship between the human telos when it describes a narrower realm than "human excellence" generally and the virtues that constitute that excellence particularly.

Consider, for example, the excellent physician. From a virtue perspective, a person studying to become a physician is seeking to incarnate not just the cardinal virtues as universally applicable to all human persons but a particular specification and hierarchy of virtues. For example, one specification of fidelity for physicians is trustworthiness, which includes such practices as respect for confidentiality, devotion to continuing education, and not exploiting patients for sex or undue profit. And though courage is a virtue for medical practice (including questions such as when to take a patient to surgery and when to stand up to a superior's unwise decision), it is generally less central to daily medical practice than trustworthiness. Similarly, if a physician cheats on her taxes, that tax evasion may make her less trustworthy as a citizen but perhaps will have little effect on trustworthiness as a physician. Though it is a truism in virtue ethics that virtues and vices spread from one area of human endeavor to another (the tax-cheating physician may indeed become more likely to cheat in other aspects of life), there is no simple or direct translation of virtues and practices from one realm to the other.[18]

The specification of the virtues, then, constitutes a telos for what an ideal physician would be—trustworthiness is more central than courage, and medical courage takes forms different than battlefield courage. Physicians in training observe and imitate the practices of those they regard as excellent in light of the telos they perceive, but they reconstruct what it means to be a physician in their own practices, which then shapes medical tradition, in MacIntyre's sense of that term: "A living tradition then is an historically extended, socially embodied argument, and an argument precisely in part about the goods that constitute that tradition."[19]

A Proposed Triune Telos

Alasdair MacIntyre's seminal 1984 book *After Virtue* begins with a powerful myth of a postscientific age in which scientific knowledge is shattered into small shards of information without consensus as to their meaning or of a method by which they might be tested. Scientific terms lose specified meanings and are used randomly according to linguistic affectations that cannot respect their original contexts. He argues that because we live in a world without a common vision for human moral life, ethics exists only as those contextless shards.

The situation in sexual ethics may be paradigmatic of the kind of absence of common telos that MacIntyre posits. It certainly seems to be the case of issues concerning sexuality that are roiling the churches far beyond other topics. Surely the Episcopal Church has deeply held divisions on questions like the rightness of American military action in Iraq, access to medical care, poverty, violence in the streets, and such; but it is the issue of gay unions and partnered gay clergy and bishops that threaten to split the denomination and divide the Anglican Communion worldwide. The 2006 synod of American Catholic bishops released four documents—two on sexual issues, one on norms for Holy Communion, and one on the Iraq war. The combined length of the two sexual statements was more than ten times that of the one on the war. The Presbyterian Church (USA), the Evangelical Lutheran Church in America, and some large evangelical groups and churches have been in the middle of contentious debates and the occasional scandal concerning matters of sexuality.

I speculate that one cause of the tumult about sexual issues is that we seem to have lost sight of a convincing account of a telos for human sexuality—if indeed, the Christian tradition ever really possessed one. And the wide range of human meanings for sexuality with which I started this essay makes such a project both complex and necessary. If we want to move beyond minimalistic, rule-based teachings on sexuality that seem to receive nearly universal indifference from the Christian faithful, then perhaps an account of a telos for sexual relationships would be a useful starting point. Also, given the dialectical relationship of telos to virtues, to indicate such a telos would seem to be essential for a virtue ethics of sexuality.

Here I suggest one way we might envision what sexual flourishing means, what it might mean to fulfill the aspects of our nature in which our sexuality is especially engaged. I offer here a telos for excellent sex in terms of the three dimensions of incarnation, intimacy and insight. The key here is that this telos is triune; each aspect is addressed separately, but they are intertwined in the human person.

In keeping with Porter's reminder to maintain epistemological humility in making any anthropological claims, however, I disavow from the outset that this is a complete account of human sexual nature. What I hope I am doing here is pointing to dimensions of human sexual flourishing that I believe can be used to start to lay out a sexual virtue ethics that is personalistic, optimistic, and coherent with the experience of Christians in their sexual relationships.

A Feel for Incarnation

Incarnation is a central motif of Christian anthropology. We speak of Jesus as God incarnate, but the very notion that God can be human, fully human, like us in all things but sin is a bold proclamation of the dignity and ineradicable goodness of human embodiment generally—not just Jesus' incarnation but our own as well. We are not spirits trapped in matter; nor are we mere matter that has stumbled into self-awareness. Rather, Christian tradition holds that we are incarnate spirit, an indivisible body-soul-spirit composite. For example, we do not look to the afterlife for a kind of "liberation" from our bodies, but we look for the resurrection of the body, because apart from our bodies we cannot be fully human.

In sex, we are aware perhaps more than any other time in our lives of our bodily nature. (I speculate that other candidates for this kind of intense awareness of our embodied nature include childbirth, severe pain, and death.) When we are lost in sexual passion, there is usually not a lot of thinking going on—we are taken up in our bodiliness. Certainly pleasure is one of the obvious ends we hope for in our sex lives. Besides orgasm, of course, there is a huge array of other sexual pleasures, and pleasure by proxy, as it were, when we delight in the delight of our partner. Christine Gudorf has unpacked sexual ethics in terms of a norm of mutual pleasure: "Sexual pleasure is a good because it enhances our sense of well-being by satisfying some basic human needs: for touch, for excitement, for physical release, for companionship. But sexual pleasure can also be a means to the satisfaction of other human needs and desires, through its ability to bind persons together in intimacy. A Christian sexual ethic should encourage sexual pleasure in sex, emphasizing its social as well as its individual functions. A Christian sexual ethic should make mutuality in sexual pleasure normative."[20]

To develop a feel for incarnation includes mutual pleasure in sex but goes beyond that to encompass aspects of our bodily nature as such. A sense of our incarnate selves leads us to pay attention to our overall physical, emotional, and spiritual well-being. In our culture generally, there is a strong emphasis on fitness; but generally where that is connected to sexuality, we tend to reduce the question pretty quickly to matters of access or technique—in other words, people want to be fit to attract a sexual partner and to be healthy enough to satisfy their partner and themselves sexually. In contrast, some models of Christianity have emphasized a body-denying asceticism that seeks to ignore the legitimate needs of the body in an attempt to become more wholly spiritualized. Neither stance is sufficient. A feel for incarnation means that we seek general health in recognition that we are incarnate and to be good stewards of ourselves and our partners. The access and technique goals are fine, but not enough, and a little asceticism is a good thing, but, as Aquinas observed, "To afflict the body immoderately . . . is to offer a sacrifice of stolen goods."[21] A feel for incarnation, then, calls us to be kind to our bodies for their own sake.

A feel for incarnation also means that, contrary to social messages that reduce the worth of persons to their sexual desirability, we seek from our sexual relationships to grow closer to our partner in his or her totality. We are called to love ourselves and others as incarnate persons—not just bodies, not just minds, and not just spirits. The epidemic of life-threatening eating disorders, and the more subtle forms of self-loathing that come from poor body image, point in part to a greater need for us to be aware of ourselves and our partners in totality. I am not suggesting that it is a sufficient response to a person with an eating disorder to say "love yourself as you are!" The condition is far more complex than that. But the fact that we see an explosion of eating disorders in our culture—rather than, say, "Holy Fasting" or extreme, obsessive, or pathological religious practices like sitting on pillars, wearing barbed wire around one's thigh, or walling oneself off in a church—might reflect in part our reduction of the worth of the person to his or her physical attributes.[22] A feel for incarnation means we understand that we are bodies but are not only bodies and that our ineradicable human dignity lies in the whole human person.

Here again, we see the potential for the opposing tendency to be at work. If it is incomplete to value people only, or even chiefly, for their bodies, it is also incomplete to ignore the beauty of the human body, our own and others'. In traditional sexual ethics, a lot of time is spent discussing lust. The problem is that we tend to equate lust with sexual desire. But sexual desire is a normal and holy aspect of our embodied humanity, and as such it cannot be wrong in itself, any more than hunger for food cannot be wrong in itself. Hunger—sexual or dietary—simply means that the body is recognizing its wants and needs in a healthy way. The essence of lust, however, and what makes lust wrong where sexual desire itself is not, is that lust seeks only the body of the other—like saying: "I want me some of that!" The problem is not that we desire sexually attractive people. Let us face it, to not notice sexually attractive people would be like not perceiving color; we could negotiate the world in shades of gray, but how much different life is in color. A feel for incarnation means that we appreciate the beauty in the people around us, celebrate beautiful bodies, and seek in our relationships to perceive human beauty holistically—body, mind, and spirit.

An Ability for Intimacy

Intimacy is a central goal of sex. Like developing a feel for incarnation, intimacy is something that can deepen with attentive practice. Intimacy, then, is not a yes-or-no question but a matter of depth and degree. After all, people who remain sexually and emotionally contented in very long relationships tend to say that they continue to learn new things about their partner—they keep on growing in their knowledge of the other. Here we begin to see another kind of problem with a rule-based, minimalist sexual ethics. In a minimalist ethics, so long as you meet the criteria for permissible sex, all guidance ceases. Is merely establishing minimal standards—"under these circumstances, sex is not a sin"—all that Christian theology can say about sex?

The tendency to construe sexual ethics in terms of rules that ought not be broken seems too often to miss the point, and the point that is missed is often about intimacy. In many cases, when people are involved in breaking some sexual rule, the deeper problem is less that they have let an unruly appetite run away with them than that they have failed to ask enough of sex. A person who pursues many emotionally shallow sexual experiences, for example, breaks a traditional rule against fornication. But the real sadness here is not that a rule has been broken but that the encounter is incomplete—the human encounter of deep care, loving concern, and interpersonal acceptance is ignored as a goal for sex, leaving the participants perhaps physically satisfied and sometimes also with a deep loneliness that has not been satisfied. One risk of a habit of shallow sex is that our sex partners and, over time, people we meet in general might be seen chiefly as means to the (selfish) end of our own satisfaction. This reduction of persons to means or the objects of our pleasure-seeking ends can hurt us reflexively, too, and we can find ourselves caught by sexual performance anxiety, nervous that we might fail to meet someone else's standards. The presence of at least a foundation of intimacy provides a security that does not require Olympian performance every time to have a great sexual relationship. Not only that, but both men and women report overall greater sexual satisfaction in steady relationships than in casual encounters.

Now let us be clear about the role of the telos here, lest we fall into the opposite error from moral minimalism with regard to sex. Some contemporary approaches to sexual ethics, especially those from more conservative Christian circles, are very willing to envision excellent sex in terms not too different from what I am proposing here. The difference is that they then set that ideal as the minimal standard for any sexual encounter. This standard is still a minimalist approach, but a "high-bar" minimalism instead of "low-bar" minimalism. The high-bar standard requires that every sex act must meet the criterion of perfection to be morally acceptable. In the Roman Catholic tradition, for example, sex must always be an act of total self-gift in the deep loving union of Christian marriage and open to procreation or it lapses into sin for failing to be perfect.

What intimacy as an aspect of the telos in a virtue ethics does, conversely, is not so much to condemn or approve particular acts but to help us remember to keep an eye on the whole relationship, our entire sex life, and not to settle into patterns of stasis, boredom, and perfunctoriness that fail to keep looking for ways to make sexual relationships better. In virtue ethics, the ideal should invite and inspire us, not judge or depress us. Also, remember the dynamic character of virtue ethics—it is not about being perfect but about striving—taking a step, a half step, or whatever we can, to get there.

Intimacy as one of the three dimensions of excellent sex is related to incarnation—sex expresses a personal reality, not merely a bodily one. At the same time, it calls us to an emotional and psychological openness and vulnerability that can be far more challenging than just physical sex. This challenge in turn contributes to the third dimension of excellent sex, which is insight.

An Eye for Insight

Insight means more than just perception, but it implies a deeper level of cognition, or what has been called "evaluative knowledge" as compared with "conceptual knowledge." Conceptual knowledge is objective or knowledge of things outside ourselves, whereas evaluative knowledge includes relevant conceptual knowledge and goes deeper. Though an observation such as "She moved out" is a matter of conceptual knowledge, a fairly clear objective fact, the evaluation "She doesn't love me anymore" is a deeper awareness of the fuller and here more painful human meaning behind the observed act.

Without insight, incarnation and intimacy alone lack a rich aspect of human self-awareness that transcends the more obvious levels of bodily and psychic/emotional intimacy. It is insight that invites us to see the echoes of our relationships beyond the immediacy of partners to include family, society as a whole, and our relationship to God, individually and communally. Insight allows us to come to better understanding of how sexual relationships have played out in our lives in the past and how we might use that experience in present and future relationships. Insight calls us to compassion for our own mistakes and others' and to be committed to what sustains stronger intimate relationships for ourselves and others. Insight reveals connections that may not have been apparent and sharpens our vision of what might be.

Insight includes the intellectual comprehension of the connection of sexuality and other aspects of our lives but is not reducible to linguistically expressible concepts or merely intellectual conceptualizations. Insight includes that flash of joy and felt rightness in the arms of a lover, and the supra-verbal "yes" of appropriate sexual abandon. The desire to cuddle and protect our lover is an aspect of insight that cherishes the particular intimacy of that relationship and recognizes its preciousness and fragility. This is not unlike the depth of self-understanding reported by some parents on first holding their newborn child and experiencing the wonder, deep love, and fierce protectiveness of that moment.

In particular, insight is how we begin to grasp the spiritual resonances of excellent sex. After all, spirituality, like sexuality, is an inherent aspect of being human in the world. For centuries, Christian tradition has tended to conflate serious spiritual practice with sexual abstinence, which hardly seems appropriate; why should two different but potentially deeply powerful realms of human experience necessarily be incompatible? To the contrary, the two should have something to say to one another.

As one example, I would suggest that it is in our closest relationships, and perhaps most best of all in intimate sexual relationships, that we most closely imitate the way God loves human beings. God, after all, certainly has a feel for incarnation in creating us as embodied spirits and inspirited bodies. Beyond that, God seeks intimacy of a particularly intense form, most intensely in being immanent in each and every person. And God shows us intimacy in relationship, in that God throws a lot in with each of us, personally, individually (and also communally, yes, but uniquely with each of us, too) every day, trying to accept and navigate and respond to our human strengths and weaknesses, both the trivial and profound. God seeks each of us with the intense desire of a lover and invites us to respond from our own desire. God risks heartbreak with each of us, in much the same way lovers risk and dare with each other, saying "Yes, you, personally, are the one I want to be loved by, and will be hurt by if you cannot, will not, or do not love me back."

We learn how to love God partly from our direct experiences in growing in loving God, but we also learn how to love God by learning how to love well in all the other realms of our lives. The two clauses of the great commandment of love of God and love of neighbor are not separable demands; each requires the other, and each shapes and can deepen the other. Further, we are created in the image of God; so, by strict Aristotelian logic, we fulfill our own nature when we grow in likeness to God. One way we grow in becoming more like God is when we seek to love others as God loves us, intensely and personally. We can do that nowhere better than in circumstances, such as in the pursuit of excellent sex, where we seek to make ourselves love, and make love in the world, as God is love and creates the world out of love for love.

Again, these three dimensions of excellent sex—a feel for incarnation, intimacy, and insight—are not discrete ends but three facets of a single unified end: the fulfillment of love and loving in the momentary concrete here and now as a foretaste of the love that awaits us in the glorified life. They are distinguishable, but inseparable, not unlike the way we speak of God as one being but three persons, distinguishable inseparable relationality.

Conclusion

In this essay, I have offered a possible construction of a telos for sexual ethics. A teleological ethics begins with a construction of the end, at least implicitly. As Aquinas puts it, "The principle in the intention is the last end; while the principle in execution is the first of the things which are ordained to the end."[23] In other words, if we do not have some notion where we are going, we cannot start to go there. Nor will we have any way of judging whether we are on the right track or not. In keeping with Porter's caveat about claiming too much for an account of human nature, this telos may be affirmed or revised in light of considered reflection on human lives and increasing scientific understanding as well.

At the same time, it might serve—for now—as an end toward which to strive, knowing that we discover and revise and refine our understanding of the telos along the way as we grow in virtue.

Notes

1. This definition is circular. But consider: sex acts include acts that are solitary or not, loving or not (or even violent,) genital or not, pleasurable or not, orgasmic or not, reproductive or not, etc. In general, an act is sex if it aims at the sexual gratification of at least one person engaged in it.

2. See www.who.int/reproductive-health/gender/sexual_health.html.

3. See John S. Grabowski, *Sex and Virtue: An Introduction to Sexual Ethics* (Washington, D.C.: Catholic University of America Press, 2003); Raja Halwani, *Virtuous Liaisons: Care, Love, Sex and Virtue Ethics* (Chicago: Open Court, 2003); Karen Lebacqz, "Appropriate Vulnerability: A Sexual Ethic for Singles," in *Sexuality: A Reader*, ed. Karen Lebacqz with David Sinacore-Guinn (Cleveland: Pilgrim Press, 1999); and Margaret Farley, *Just Love: A Framework for Christian Sexual Ethics* (New York: Continuum, 2006). See also Marvin Ellison and Sylvia Thorson, eds., *Body and Soul: Rethinking Sexuality as Justice-Love* (Cleveland: Pilgrim Press, 2003).

4. Farley, *Just Love*, 207; italics in text.

5. James Keenan, "Virtue Ethics and Sexual Ethics," *Louvain Studies*, 30, no. 3 (2005): 180–97.

6. Keenan, "Virtue Ethics," 192.

7. Thomas considers virtues to participate in cardinal virtues in three ways, as he explains in II IIae, q. 48: "Parts are of three kinds, namely, integral, as wall, roof and foundation are parts of a house; subjective, as ox and lion are parts of animal; and potential, as the nutritive and sensitive powers are parts of the soul. Accordingly, parts can be assigned to a virtue in three ways. First, in likeness to integral parts, so that the things which need to concur for the perfect act of a virtue are called the parts of that virtue. . . . The subjective parts of a virtue are its various species. . . [and] the potential parts of a virtue are the virtues connected with it, which are directed to certain secondary acts or matters, not having, as it were, the whole power of the principal virtue" (II IIae, q. 48). I am using the term "subsidiary" to include all these senses, but most specifically the subjective.

8. Asked by a student which of Keenan's cardinal virtues would include one's relationship with God—the student doubtless was recalling H. R. Niebuhr and Charles Curran's relationality/responsibility tetrad of relationship with God, neighbor, world, and self—I suggested that relationship to God is immanent in all four of Keenan's virtues, in keeping with a Rahnerian "supernatural existential."

9. Aristotle, *Nicomachean Ethics*, 2nd ed., trans. Terence Irwin (Indianapolis: Hackett, 1999). All citations in the text are by paragraph number.

10. Ibid.

11. His introduction to his list of virtues states: "For among accounts concerning actions, though the general ones are common to more cases, the specific ones are truer, since actions are about particular cases" (book II, chap. 7). Aristotle's virtues: bravery, temperance, generosity, magnificence, magnanimity, right relationship to small honors, mildness, friendliness, truthfulness, wit, justice, prudence, understanding, and wisdom.

12. Plato, *Republic*, trans. G. M. A. Grube (Indianapolis: Hackett, 1992), book IV, 441.c.

13. Thomas Aquinas, *Summa theologiae*, trans. English Dominican Province (Westminster, Md.: Christian Classics, 1913).

14. Jean Porter, *Nature as Reason: A Thomistic Theory of the Natural Law* (Grand Rapids: William B. Eerdmans, 2005), 141.

15. We see a counterexample of this at work in the Catholic magisterium's increasing intransigence regarding homosexuality. Recent documents on this subject speak more and more clearly of homosexual acts as the result of sinful choices out of objectively disordered inclinations, whereas contemporary biology and psychology point more and more to the category of sexual orientation as deep-rooted, at least partly genetically determined, normally variant in human populations, and difficult or impossible to change. Homosexual orientation is no longer regarded by credible psychologists as a mental illness. The two views are not absolutely irreconcilable—it is possible that a normal human variation could be the occasion of impulses that are invariably sinful. But such an anthropology raises questions of theodicy that lie beyond the scope of this essay.

16. On contraception, see, inter alia, Cristina L.H. Traina, "Papal Ideals, Marital Realities: One View from the Ground," in *Sexual Diversity and Catholicism: Toward the Development of Moral Theology*, ed. Patricia Beattie Jung and Joseph Andrew Coray (Collegeville, Minn.: Liturgical Press, 2001). On homosexuality, among many others, see Andrew Sullivan "Alone Again, Naturally," in *Theology and Sexuality: Classic and Contemporary Readings*, ed. Eugene F. Rogers Jr. (Malden, Mass.: Blackwell, 2002), 275–88.

17. Keenan, "Virtue Ethics," 190.

18. This touches on the question of the unity of the virtues, which is also a topic for another time. Suffice it to say for this essay that at the very least, the various virtues are linked by their common mediation by prudence or by a certain baseline goodness or striving to be more virtuous generally.

19. Alasdair MacIntyre, *After Virtue* (Notre Dame, Ind.: University of Notre Dame Press, 1984), 222.

20. Christine E. Gudorf, *Body, Sex and Pleasure: Reconstructing Christian Sexual Ethics* (Cleveland: Pilgrim Press, 1994), 139.

21. *Summa theologiae*, II IIae, 147.1. Thomas thought he was quoting Saint Jerome, but this dictum is not found in Jerome's works.

22. Part of the genesis of "Holy Fasting" was thought to be a mode of control for people who felt out of control of their lives or unable or prevented from controlling their lives, as, e.g., with women in centuries past, and too often now. I agree that self-assertion is also an important contributing factor to anorexia, but I raise the question whether it was a more prominent factor in centuries past than today. Nonpathological dietary self-control, of course, is also a means of expressing self-determination—but here again, why food and not some other obsessive act of self-determination (e.g., pilgrimage, sitting on pillars, walling oneself off in a church, or sexual abstinence?)

23. *Summa theologiae*, I IIae, q. 1.4.

Continuity and Sacrament, or Not: Hauerwas, Yoder, and Their Deep Difference

Gerald W. Schlabach

STANLEY HAUERWAS HAS FAMOUSLY TAKEN TO THE MENNONITES BE-
cause they constitute what appears to be an oxymoron—a tradition of dissent.
He launched his career endeavoring to restore the stuff of continuity to the Christian life. In contrast, John Howard Yoder launched his career arguing against the
assumption that traditions and organic communal life could carry practices of
authentic discipleship forward across generations. Here lies a fundamental difference between Hauerwas and Yoder that runs deeper than whether one of
them is more "for" or "against" the nations.

Stanley Hauerwas has taken to the Mennonites for what might be contradictory reasons. As successors to the Anabaptist or Radical wing of the
sixteenth-century Reformation, they constitute a tradition of *dissent*. But
they also constitute a *tradition* of dissent. Herein lies a tension, at the very least.

As a longtime colleague and close reader of John Howard Yoder, Hauerwas
encountered in his thought the best and most trenchant Mennonite argument
for principled dissent. Yoder—probably the most renowned Mennonite thinker
of the twentieth century—was Hauerwas's colleague at the University of Notre
Dame for many years and convinced him to swallow the "bitter pill" of Christian
pacifism.[1] In one of Yoder's earliest essays, he had labeled the very logic of Anabaptist ways of following Jesus as that of dissent, especially dissent from violent
ways of ordering the world and Christian accommodation with violence.[2] To be
sure, Hauerwas probably did not need much inspiration to dissent. He was already beginning to goad mainline Protestants and Roman Catholics into un-
muting a distinctive yet public voice shaped by specifically Christian convictions. Christians should be no more concerned that those convictions mesh with
dominant assumptions of the day—liberal, conservative, or whatever—than
Hauerwas himself was with using working-class Texan profanities in polite
company.

Of course, Hauerwas found Yoder's theology convincing, too, and it gave
him greater access to a living tradition that exemplified how all Christian

churches ought to constitute "communities of character."[3] Much to his initial surprise, "Yoder's account of the church fit almost exactly the kind of community I was beginning to think was required by an ethics of virtue."[4] Besides that, living in northern Indiana during his time at the University of Notre Dame piqued Hauerwas's interest in the actual Mennonite communities a few miles to the east. The Mennonites demonstrated concretely why Christians needed concrete practices more than just abstract principles to live faithful Christian lives.[5] Any thoroughgoing critique of the illusions of this age (or any age) required a community that holds and embodies an alternative narrative over the long haul, in turn shaped by the narrative of Jesus of Nazareth, the Christ.[6]

So what is the problem? The tension between dissent and tradition may be a contradictory, uneasy, or creative one—but a tension it is. Hauerwas has recognized the longitude in that Mennonite "long haul" to be far more crucial than Anabaptist-Mennonite theology has itself known how to name.[7] As we shall see, Yoder's early essay on Anabaptist dissent did not simply aim to place Mennonites in a dissenting posture vis-à-vis society at large or mainstream churches cozy with society's sources of power. It was also part of a radical program of church renewal challenging the very Mennonite leaders and institutions that had trained and shaped Yoder's generation. It relied on theological assumptions far deeper and more abiding than the youthful zeal that helped embolden it. It was deeply suspicious of settled community based on the continuities of family, ethnicity, and tradition—to say nothing of priestly office, apostolic and episcopal succession, or sacramentality. And it was equally suspicious of those formal church structures and institutions that might turn Mennonites into one more Protestant denomination.

Yet all these, at least in their particularly Christian shapes, are integral to the formative and sustaining practices that Hauerwas sees as necessary to constitute those Christian "communities of character" we call the church. Craftlike training at the hands of masters who have internalized a community's moral standards and purposes, apprentices who cannot know that moral craft until they learn it first by habit, ancient narratives retold across generations, saints and other mentors who are a bridge to Jesus across time, sacraments that reenact and re-present the fullness of his very life, moral disciplines learned through patient accountability both to the weakest in a community and to its authorities—all these are the stuff of continuity, character formation, and tradition. Dissenters almost always owe more to tradition than they know. And Hauerwas has noticed the debt that has made Mennonite dissent possible at all, even when dissenters have been relying on tradition far more parasitically than they dared admit.

A tradition of dissent, then, is nothing to take for granted. To trace the seam that makes it possible for courageous dissenters to form a tradition at all—and that then keeps such a tradition from tearing itself apart with the bad habits of dissent by which its virtue may turn to vice—is to help avoid what I call the

Protestant Dilemma. This dilemma is the tendency of Protestantism to undo itself whenever it makes what Paul Tillich called "the Protestant Principle" into an identity marker. Though Tillich and neoorthodox theologians are certainly right that all human realities and institutions fall short of God's will and must thus remain subject to continuing critique, a community that places such a principle at the core of its identity can hardly be sustainable.[8]

In the story that follows, some of the most influential Mennonite thinkers of the last half century questioned whether their faith should become a tradition at all; they doubted that the stuff of human continuity can ever embody the Gospel and argued that the very logic of Anabaptist discipleship is that of dissent, thus opening wide the Mennonite community to the Protestant Dilemma. And yet, whereas past Mennonites have hardly avoided their own successive rounds of schism, in this case Mennonite movements and leaders did manage to stay together, sometimes despite themselves. They may not altogether have avoided that more subtle form of schism that is modern individualism. Yet by drawing upon the strengths of their tradition precisely as they dissented from it, they left us a revealing irony for reflection. It is in the seam of that irony that we may discover the deep difference between Hauerwas and Yoder.

Mennonites amid the Acids of Modernity

Modernity, Hauerwas has remarked, "names the time of the loss of Christian habits." The Protestant Reformation in all its branches maintained greater continuity with popular practices of piety and charity among ordinary Christians in the "Roman Catholic" Church of the medieval period than we usually recognize. That continuity, argued Hauerwas, is why Protestantism continued to "work." Without these habits, "Protestantism has often found it lacks even the resources to know how to form those that wish to be Christian.[9]

U.S. and Canadian Mennonite communities have sometimes looked like proverbial canaries in the coal mine of modern life. Modernity is a complex phenomenon with many definitions.[10] But what all definitions do is mark the distance that much of the globe has traveled away from another more ecological kind of complexity—that tradition-shaped life of intimate, familial, and organic relationships in the village or *Gemeinde*, as the Germans have called it. Even Mennonites who have been ready to modernize have generally been more sensitive than most groups to the implications of modernity and keener to make sure they were adapting carefully and self-consciously.[11] What makes them the proverbial canaries is that if they cannot survive unscathed, then others are also surely vulnerable to the acids of modernity.

Against many of the markers of modernity, North American Mennonites actually seemed for many generations to do remarkably well at sustaining their communal identity. So concluded the lead researchers in extensive sociological surveys of five Mennonite denominations done in 1972 and 1989.[12] "Contrary to what some have predicted, [their] move to cities has not made Mennonites more secular, individualistic, and materialistic," wrote J. Howard Kauffman and Leo Driedger following the second survey.[13] Yet Kauffman and Driedger themselves did not seem altogether confident that what they called "the concomitants of modernization" would keep from corroding Mennonite communal identity over the long run. Might Mennonites not be spending down the capital of communal cohesion they had accumulated over generations? "The first generation of higher status, urban Mennonites may have sufficient religious commitment and community supports to combat countervailing forces," wrote Kauffman and Driedger. "Will this also be the case several generations later?"[14]

Four Strategies: The Debate That Was the "Goshen School"

If Mennonites have survived modernity relatively well to date, that may be precisely because they have worried about it long and hard. One center for Mennonite reflection about how to navigate the shoals of modern life and sustain authentic Christian community has been Goshen College, in Northern Indiana.[15] The middle decades of the twentieth century were a time of especially creative ferment at Goshen College, as leading thinkers forged an approach to Mennonite identity, history, theology, and peaceable alternative witness in society that would later come to be known as the "Goshen School."[16] Any lively school of thought, however, is really a conversation or even a bitter debate.[17] The Goshen School was in fact a conversation between four interlocking strategies for how Mennonites might relate faithfully to the modern world.[18]

Strategy One: Intentional Gemeinde

The setting for much of the creative ferment among Mennonites at midcentury, and the background to all four of the strategies whose debate constituted the Goshen School, was of course two world wars. World War I had created a bracing pastoral crisis among Mennonites. As World War II loomed, pressure both to negotiate legal options of conscientious objection for young Mennonite men and to demonstrate that the church as a whole was not impervious to the needs of society met with a still more sophisticated version of a standard charge: Military nonparticipants were "shirkers."[19] The rising American Protestant theologian Reinhold Niebuhr was glad to concede that groups like Mennonites were right to read Jesus as having renounced all violence and taught his disciples to do the same. But, he said, Jesus never intended this ethic as a guide for politics and government either. Christians could approximate Jesus' ethic in face-to-face relationships or a small community, a *Gemeinde*, but their very attempt to be faithful to Jesus rendered them politically irrelevant in more complex and impersonal institutions, which increasingly characterized modern life, to say nothing of the state.[20] So if military conscription prompted a very practical need for Mennonites to offer "alternative service," many felt a piercing existential need to demonstrate that their community offered an alternative way to serve their neighbors and society in socially responsible but Christlike ways.

Leading both the intellectual and practical response to this challenge was an unassuming yet tenacious professor of sociology and American history at Goshen College, Guy F. Hershberger.[21] Hershberger led churchwide committees negotiating a system of legal provisions, work camps, and other assignments that would allow conscientious objectors to perform alternative service in World War II. As an increasing number of Mennonites moved from farm to factory, Hershberger also guided negotiations to release Mennonites from labor union membership so long as they donated funds to charity that were equivalent to union dues, another kind of alternative service.[22] Meanwhile, though Hershberger was not a theologian per se, he consolidated biblical and ethical arguments for the Mennonite "peace position" in numerous articles and in a now-classic 1944 book, *War, Peace, and Nonresistance*.[23]

But there was more. The model of alternative service that Hershberger was formulating both required and provided a rationale for alternative community itself. In this respect, Hershberger was like another more famous leader of another stream of nonviolence, Mohandas (Mahatma) Gandhi. As the Hindu leader of India's independence movement, Gandhi is best known for his formulation of nonviolent thought and strategy, yet he actually put more of his time into human-scale economics and village-level community development in order to build and sustain the kind of social life that corresponded with his philosophy of nonviolence. So too with Hershberger, whose vision of a sustainable peace church, capable of offering a recognizable social witness to Christ's way of peace in the world, required not just a set of ideals or principles but a flesh-and-blood community living its life according to a self-conscious or intentional sociology.[24]

Hershberger, having been influenced by the same Weberian sociology that Reinhold Niebuhr took for granted, was ready to concur with one of Niebuhr's central premises, even as he took it to an opposite conclusion. Hershberger agreed that the ethic of Jesus is most practicable (perhaps only practicable) in the *Gemeinde*. The implication for him was not, of course, that he or his church must abandon Jesus' ethic of nonresistant love, but that precisely to stay faithful to it, they must also sustain community life at a small enough scale that employers and employees, for example, knew each other personally. This did not mean that all Mennonites must be farmers. Nor did it mean that Mennonites must shun their neighbors and relate only to one another in "separatist" communities. But it did mean that Mennonites had a long-term stake in the economic and cultural viability of the small towns in which, or around which, most of them still lived.

Above all it meant that church membership should not simply bring Christians together in the pews but should also tie them together through all kinds of economic practices and social bonds. Parallel to efforts such as the Catholic Rural Life Movement of the time, and sharing a confidence that such efforts could claim the eminent "social responsibility" of contributing to Jeffersonian democracy, Hershberger was the leading thinker behind a cluster of conferences, publications, and initiatives known as the Mennonite Community Movement. The movement directed postwar energy into creating new institutional mechanisms to provide mutual aid throughout "the brotherhood," for example, by facilitating the investment of better-off members via church institutions so that young families could acquire the credit they needed for land and businesses, rather than seeking employment at greater remove from their congregations.

In the face of modernizing forces, and Mennonite urbanization in particular, the efforts of Hershberger and the Mennonite Community Movement were not a striking success. (Here, too, Hershberger may parallel Gandhi.) The Mennonites themselves, especially Mennonite intellectuals, have criticized Hershberger for tying their social ethics too closely to a rural sociology. That is probably true, though in fairness, Hershberger never saw the preservation of rural and small time life as a quaint end in itself. The end was communal witness to the cause of Christ.

In service of that end, the strategy of intentionally using the rational tools of modernity, both intellectual and management tools, to strengthen the *Gemeinde* may actually have been savvier than the three other strategies we will shortly review.[25] It was keen to the relationship between what a Marxist would call superstructure and structure, the way that whole worlds of culture and ideas rest upon concrete economic and productive relationships. And it was keen to the truth of what many theologians now refer to as embodiment: In a faith where the incarnation of God in Jesus Christ is central, Christianity must take shape in social practices and community structures extended over time. Mennonites have named some of these practices "discipleship," but if this is not simply to bespeak an individual following Christ, it must necessarily issue in a culture. And then, despite all the ways that faithful Christianity must undermine rigid, hateful, and exclusivist forms of ethnic division, it may also mean the creation of some qualitatively new and permeable *ethnos* or people but an *ethnos* nonetheless.

Strategy Two: Denomination Building

Though the pace of Mennonite institution building picked up in response to the challenge of the two world wars, it hardly began then. Since the latter half of the nineteenth century, Mennonites had been building the structures that would make them into a number of denominations. Some sooner and some later, all but the most conservative Mennonite groups were forging the institutional apparatus of constitutions and minutes, mission agencies, and paid professional pastorates, as well as educational programs from Sunday school to colleges and eventually seminaries.

In his generation and throughout the midcentury decades of ferment, none was more involved in building either denominational or inter-Mennonite structures than Goshen's academic dean, Harold S. Bender. By the end of his career, Bender was simultaneously holding fourteen administrative positions in Mennonite institutions and boards.[26] He was the driving force behind his denomination's first seminary, also founded in Goshen in 1944, whereupon he became its first dean. In whatever his official role at Goshen, meanwhile, he was infamous for tapping promising young men on the shoulder, anticipating future positions in the church that would fit their intellectual or administrative talents, and insisting on the field and location of their graduate studies. When shoulder tapping felt more like arm twisting to some of the church's best and brightest, their resentment earned him the title of "the Mennonite pope."

Even Bender's work as a historian, however, served the project of denomination building in another way. By defending the legitimacy of their Anabaptist forebears against old charges that they were nothing but heretical rabble-rousers, Bender made a place for them on the denominational map of Protestantism. His articulation of the "Anabaptist vision" offered a path through Fundamentalist/Modernist controversies such as he had experienced in his youth. Anabaptism, after all, offered a third way that was biblical, orthodox, and evangelical yet also socially minded. Further, his vision gave young Mennonites a sense of identity and self-respect: inward-looking self-respect but also outward-facing respectability.[27]

Some of Bender's most conscientious students would eventually argue that the desire for denominational respectability and institutional growth had actually betrayed the witness of the Anabaptists and Bender's very "vision." But simply to accept the denominational map carried with it a subtle danger. In culturally Protestant America, a working understanding had developed that each denomination had its place expressing some essential truth of Christianity in its partial way.[28] But just what is the quasi-catholic whole of which each is a part? Protestant ecclesiology is generally vague. As a result, the whole of which Protestant denominations are a part has too often become Western civilization, American civil religion, or the nation-state itself.[29] Bender's Anabaptist vision certainly carried with it many checks against the seductions of nationalism. Denominationalism alone, however, had few such checks, and might even be a seduction itself.

Strategy Three: Historical Identity Made Portable

Though supportive of the Mennonite Community Movement, Bender was never so convinced as Hershberger seemed to be that the survival of Mennonite faith and practice depended on a rural or small town sociology.[30] If anything, Bender promoted the worldwide Mennonite community through an emerging Mennonite World Conference with the same persistence by which Hershberger promoted the local Mennonite community. Appropriately, Bender's definition of that "Anabaptist vision," which ought also be the core of Mennonite faith and practice, was more sociologically portable than Hershberger's strategy of intentional *Gemeinde*. In other words, it was capable of extraction, transport, and reinsertion into disparate cultures and social locales.

Inevitably, if not deliberately, therefore, Bender's Anabaptist vision was also more abstract. He summarized the "central teachings" of "genuine Anabaptism in its Reformation setting" with a succinct three-point outline of emphases or principles: "The Anabaptist vision included three major points of emphasis; first, a new conception of the essence of Christianity as discipleship; second, a new conception of the church as a brotherhood; and third, a new ethic of love and nonresistance."[31] As he elaborated, all three of these principles had practical implications, of course. He was in fact quite aware of the danger of reducing the life and faith of his tradition to principles so abstract that they might apply equally well to Western democracy as to the church.[32]

Yet Bender's phrasing here is symptomatic of a paradoxical abstraction.[33] Discipleship itself was an essence, if that is possible. Even while insisting upon a Christianity that must be performed and acted out in all of life, he turned often to the language of "principle," "concept," essence" and of course "vision" to make his case:[34] "First and fundamental in the Anabaptist *vision* was the *conception* of the *essence* of Christianity as discipleship."[35] Practice was a principle that required actual practice, he argued circuitously at one point.[36] Such terminology hints tellingly at precisely the role he was playing.[37] Still quite grounded in the concrete practices of traditional Mennonite community life, he was attempting to distill their essence to give new generations of Mennonites the guidance and self-understanding they needed to be faithful but versatile witnesses in the world.[38]

This greater portability was a great strength of Bender's Anabaptist vision. It was able to excite the imaginations and mobilize the service of successive generations. They could take it into cities and universities or apply it within new vocations. Since Bender's death in 1962, his work has appealed to new Mennonites of other races and cultures around the globe. Still, the capacity of a succinct three-point Anabaptist vision to pull up roots from the communal soil of Mennonite traditions and ethnicity would come to haunt Bender's final years.

Strategy Four: Heroic Pneumatology

In April 1952, seven young Mennonite intellectuals who were working or studying in Europe gathered for a two-week theological retreat in Amsterdam.[39] Their purpose was to analyze the devastating cultural, intellectual, and economic crises they were observing firsthand in postwar Europe, and to do so in light of their own fresh study of Anabaptist sources. When they turned to apply their conclusions to their home church in North America, their conclusions surprised them. And when they disseminated their findings first through correspondence and then in *Concern: A Pamphlet Series*, those conclusions deeply troubled their friends and mentors back home. At once devastating and invigorating, the lesson was that Mennonite reality fell far short of the Anabaptist vision and called for a radical movement of the Spirit to renew the church.[40] Mennonites could claim the Anabaptist legacy through their ethnic heritage but not their own heroic discipleship. And for a church formed by martyrs killed for living out their believers' baptism and its implication that every generation of the church must find and confess its faith anew, an ethnic claim to the Anabaptist legacy was no claim at all.

Though reticent to create a formal structure and thus repeat one of the very mistakes they saw their elders doing, the members of the Concern Group were nonetheless deeply indebted to their church's institutions.[41] The first three "Goshen School" strategies for navigating Mennonite faith and practice through the modern world had shaped all the men who met in Amsterdam in 1952. All were either working in denominational institutions or were among the students whom Bender was grooming for denominational leadership.[42] Those who could were doing their own historical research into Anabaptist sources; most were students of Bender at Goshen, and all seven were deeply shaped by his theological "vision."

Yet the Concern Movement was nothing if not an effort to turn the Anabaptist vision back upon both Mennonite ethnicity and Mennonite denominationalism. The movement's leaders looked back to sixteenth-century Anabaptists for precedents, yet they were deeply suspicious of all tradition, even those that connected them with the Anabaptists. John Howard Yoder was the intellectual leader of the Concern Movement, but Paul Peachey was nearly as influential as its publicist, and in this role he could sometimes exercise nearly as much influence as Yoder. Peachey's preface to the second *Concern* pamphlet stated the views of the group bluntly: "Denominational structures present themselves ever more clearly as a distortion of the Gospel. . . . If the supernatural redemptive reality of the Christian Church is again to break forth, if the "church" is to become the Church anew, it is clear that we must emerge from the strictures of dead traditions where we are bound by them. . . . Renewal will come only if the corn of wheat is ready to fall into the ground and die. The

Church of Christ will break forth anew if we are ready to receive her. This is *the* issue as we see it."[43] Tradition, in both its denominational and ethnic ways of passing down faith and practice, must always stifle the very freshness, spiritual renewal, critical edge, and vibrant church life by which Christianity engages the problems and crises of any age, they believed.

This spiritually fresh but socially critical edge is what the Concern Group saw in and sought to recover from both sixteenth-century Anabaptist and first-century Christian communities. Among themselves they sometimes debated whether and in what sense they wanted to claim a frankly "sectarian" posture.[44] But they had no doubt that even when the church stands most boldly "over against" the world, it must do so in service to the world. As the Mennonite historian Paul Toews has commented about the original Concern Group in Amsterdam, "After their nurture in parochial Mennonite environments, their European experience brought them into direct conversation with the ideological debates of a Western culture darkened by the shadows of Auschwitz and Hiroshima."[45] The wrenching failures of Western civilization, they believed, owed much to the compromised position of the church of Christendom. The Anabaptists had been a prophetic voice in the sixteenth century, heroically offering an alternative until persecution quenched that voice. What was especially tragic, however, was that the survivors of persecution had settled for and settled into quiescent ethnic enclaves that reproduced the patterns of Christendom, only on a smaller scale.

In Concern Group theology, pacifism, voluntary community, believers' baptism, a missionary impulse that burst through ethnic bonds, and a thoroughgoing social critique were all of a piece. Yoder's early 1950s essay "The Anabaptist Dissent" encapsulated arguments he would make throughout his career. He wrote: "Much of what is characteristic of western society results from the Constantinian liaison of church and world" by which Christians, since the time of fourth-century Roman emperor Constantine, had assumed that all of society could become Christian and cooperate with the state and its violence. "The church by her acceptance of the system became, not an autonomous moral force representing [in] the midst of the world the demands of God's righteousness, but simply the moral backbone, the morale-giver, the sanctifier of the society she was tied to."[46]

For the church to maintain the moral autonomy it needs if it is actually to offer society a qualitatively new witness or service, the church must ever constitute itself in a way different from the way that society sustains or reproduces itself. Not only must it reject "the sword" by which the state governs and protects itself. Infant baptism too is a subtle form of coercion, because the child becomes a member of the community involuntarily. But then, so too are the organic patterns of family and tribal life by which an ethnic group passes on its culture or faith to its children, even if it has eschewed infant baptism. Perhaps the most telling sign of how radical was the Concern Group's rejection of tradition, therefore, was its critique of Mennonite church schools, at least at elementary or secondary levels.[47]

In all this, the Concern Movement itself was seeking to recover a kind of *Gemeinde*, but here the trend in Bender's theology toward abstraction gathered momentum. As Concern Group members read the "crucial words of Christ in Matt. 18:20" about the gathering of as few as two or three in Christ's name, they believed they were discerning the very definition of the church.[48] Whatever its size, no congregation should stifle the authenticity of true Christian relationship among those "two or three" who gather for sharing, fellowship, mutual admonition, and mutual forgiveness. If congregations grew too large or if denominational structures grew so overbearing that the essential quality of face-to-face New Testament *koinonia* suffered, the church was already ceasing to be the church.[49] By advocating the formation of house churches and small group gatherings within congregations, the Concern Group advocated simple leadership patterns, warned against the professionalization of ministry, and emphasized "informality and naturalness."[50]

The stated ecclesiology of the Concern Group was almost entirely "pneumatic" from the beginning, understanding the church to be dependent on the renewing work of the Holy Spirit and sometimes, it seemed, on little if anything else. They certainly did not want to repeat the mistakes of the spiritualist wing of the Anabaptists by departing from the authority of the New Testament. When reporting on its 1952 meeting in Amsterdam, however, the introduction to the first *Concern* pamphlet placed the group's thinking entirely on one side of a series of dialectical oppositions. Over against "a church which becomes traditional or justifies the process of assimilation," was "the renewal and perpetuation of the true Christian community." And how to renew and perpetuate a church? Not through "conformity and organization in the institutional church" but through "freedom and necessity as expressed in the pneumatic church."[51]

Interlude: Heroic Pneumatology in the Later Yoder

To be sure, Yoder's later writings would temper his early views somewhat, and even in those early years of the Concern Group he was never quite so radical as his colleague Paul Peachey.[52] Still, even when Yoder affirmed a certain role for church structures as he wrote to clarify "our concerns" in the fourth Concern pamphlet, he continued to deny that institutions ever had any ecclesial status except as ad hoc tools in the service of local congregations, which were the only sure place to identify the presence of the church universal.[53] Yoder was also certain that American Mennonite churches "would be differently organized if they were more 'pneumatic.'" Prefiguring a later pattern, even when he acknowledged a role for church institutions, his caveats kept his position quite guarded. "The growth of conference and other machinery [was] not bad in itself," he wrote, for example, but it was a "poor substitute for the Spirit."[54] Of course, a certain youthful idealism animated the anti-institutionalism of the entire Concern Group. Yet too many of Yoder's lifelong arguments are present in that first paper from Amsterdam 1952, "The Anabaptist Dissent," for interpreters to isolate any of them without evidence to the contrary.[55] Concern Group presuppositions appear at the bedrock of Yoder's thought throughout his career, despite a more nuanced attitude toward tradition and the community-sustaining stuff of continuity, as well as attempts to come to terms with sacramentality.

Yoder's mature nuances did lead him to state the role of tradition in relatively positive ways. He sometimes described the role of the Christian scholar as an "agent of memory" by appealing to Matthew 13:52, where Jesus described the proper role of a "scribe who has been trained for the kingdom of heaven" as that of "the master of a household who brings out of his treasure what is new *and what is old.*"[56] He firmly rejected a naive restorationism that would attempt to restructure church life by jumping backward over centuries of development to mimic earlier forms.[57] Likewise, he disavowed the option of a formless "spiritualism" that imagined the church getting along without any structures at all.[58] More affirmatively, in the keynote to a conference where some were calling for an altogether distinctive approach to theology on the part of Believers' Church groups, he insisted on accountability to wider Christian traditions.[59] Perhaps most strongly and eloquently, in one 1990 essay he appealed to the principle of incarnation to insist that "God is the kind of God who takes on the risks of enfleshment. God takes on the available human shapes of community." Even in Old Testament eras when tribalism, holy war, and monarchy limited God's alternatives, the fact that it "*is* the *nature* of Jesus and of JHWH" to "take on the risks of history" means that God is not "diluted or denatured."[60]

Even as the mature Yoder cited God's ability to risk enfleshment in human institutions, however, he carried forward early Concern Group themes. For another author, a reminder of God's risky enfleshment might have abetted an argument for stable persistence within catholic Christianity, even of the Roman sort, despite the fallible vicissitudes of the medieval institutions he sometimes disparaged. He took the lesson in a different direction. The "human story of Jesus" meant that "God has entered historical relativity in a way that women and men everywhere are called and enabled to replicate by repenting, and by joining concretely accessible human communities of celebration, edification, service and proclamation."[61]

Note the word "replicate" here. Continuity for Yoder was the steady beat of recurrence, not a line of transmission that might proceed unbroken even for a while. Midcareer, a 1967 speech to the Mennonite World Conference had called upon Yoder to address the problem of valid change and continuity in the ongoing development of Christian theology. The punctuosity of congregation-alism was Yoder's answer at every point; only the local body could discern what was valid change and what was required continuity with tradition; supracongre-gational structures remained of purely instrumental value.[62] Twenty-five years later, Yoder's profound skepticism toward hierarchical priesthood, office, and classical understandings of sacrament could prove as sharp as ever, even or espe-cially when he attempted, in the final decade of his career, to state his own un-derstanding of the sacraments in his 1992 book *Body Politics*.[63]

The argument here is not that Yoder was necessarily wrong, a priori, at those points where he maintained a distance from Catholicism, much less where he differed from Hauerwas. What drove the Concern Group at the beginning and continued to animate Yoder throughout his career was something very right: a passionate concern for thoroughgoing church renewal issuing in authentic Christian discipleship and the active participation of all believers through mani-fold charisms of ministry. Free church theologians will surely do well to carry forward Yoder's arguments, and Christians of any tradition who share a like pas-sion for church renewal will benefit. Yoder was also surely right when he cut through old Protestant/Catholic formulas by insisting that the issue "is not tra-dition versus Scripture but faithful tradition verses irresponsible tradition."[64]

No, the argument here is simply that Yoder's mature nuances were precisely those—qualifiers, not major premises. They qualified arguments that almost al-ways continued to accent the need for dissent, critique, and corrective. The re-sult may even have been a version of the Protestant Principle that purged Tillich's version of its naive romanticism and filled it in with a far richer ac-count of social practices.[65] "It cannot or should not be argued that *any old* revi-sionism is better than tradition," Yoder remarked in 1993, "or that rebellion is in itself always morally imperative."[66] The balanced assessment by which he closed his essay "The Authority of Tradition" in his 1984 collection *The Priestly Kingdom* was that "we reconstruct [faithful tradition both] by critiquing and by remembering."[67] Nonetheless, when he framed this and other essays in his in-troduction to *The Priestly Kingdom*, he took pains to distinguish his position from many other views of how God carries forward God's project through time and history: "To be both more hopeful and more critical means finding more clear lines within the (particular, historical) orientation of the Christian move-ment and thereby being equipped to doubt (especially) those answers which have claimed a hearing because they were official."[68]

Yet again, we must insist that the point is not to deny that in many times and places suspicion and dissent from official positions may be necessary or morally imperative. Rather, the problem is that to continually stress such occasions and their exigencies will leave us with inadequate resources for discerning other moral imperatives—those of continuity, stability, and sustainability. An unpub-lished essay Yoder wrote in 1988 includes a tacit admission that his own theology had too little to say about these problematics. Over the years, many people committed to his vision of church life had written to him in moments of disillusionment, asking in effect, "Really now, have you ever seen a true church?" Yoder was thinking through his response to this continuing challenge.[69] Reminding his correspondent that the truth of the Gospel does not depend on a given person's experience of it anywhere any time, he nonetheless insisted that the phenomenon of church renewal recurs constantly through history. Still, he admitted: "That renewal vision has been less than fully successful in maintaining first-generation devotion in the second and third generation in the life of a restored community. That proves that there are yet unsolved theological and practical problems involved in understanding how the life of the church is supposed to continue."[70]

The heroic pneumatology of the early Concern Group, then, continued to supply Yoder's ecclesiological bottom line throughout his career. In his private memo, he put it this way: If any kind of proof from history can be expected to authenticate the true church, it is obviously not that any church is perfect; instead, "the proof that matters most must rather be that, where there is no such church at all, the idea of renewal can be seen to sprout again, and the reality of renewal can be seen to develop again in all its frailty and tentativeness."[71] Or, as he said in print near the end of his life: "The continuity that counts is that the same Gospel witness again and again evokes the same community-forming response, *even without* institutional connections."[72]

Freedom and Discipline: Lessons from an Unruly Synthesis, Despite Themselves

Too often, in too many churches, debates over the role of authority and dissent come to an impasse because they seem to pose a stark choice: "to obey, or not to obey?" One reason is that we have come to conflate authority with hierarchy, ignoring the possibility that those around us or before us might rightly exercise a guiding authority in our lives as surely as any king or pope, or that those "above" us may actually be representing those "around" or even "below" us. In fact, if we do recognize a proper role for authority in our lives, that will often be because we also see a role for mentors, social practices, institutions, and tradition. If ideals, principles, or the very work of the Holy Spirit are to be embodied in matter at all, over time and not just in spontaneity, these must arguably play a role. This is the stuff of continuity.

As we have noted, Hauerwas has been famously taken with the Mennonites because they constitute what might seem to be an oxymoron: a tradition of dissent. If he is right, they combine virtues needed to take a clear and courageous stand against the violence and conceit of the age with virtues needed to do so as a community enjoying sufficient discipline and cohesion to offer a collective witness sustainably over time. What he is seeing in them, however, is something about which they themselves are deeply ambivalent.

One way to arbitrate among the four strategies proposed within the Goshen School and to evaluate the Concern Movement's most contentious one is to use one of Peachey's own claims as a test. Peachey once noted favorably that sixteenth-century Anabaptism "can be viewed as a synthesis between Christian freedom and discipline rare in history. The fact that one and the same group could be variously accused of legalism and libertinism, as was the case in the six-teenth century, would illustrate the pronounced presence of both impulses. . . . Actually, as has been so well said recently: 'In the Anabaptist tradition, the free-dom of the Christian is combined with the utmost discipline in community.'"[73] This suggests a standard by which to assess Mennonite strategies for exercising faithful discipleship and community life amid modernity. If Peachey and the Concern Movement were right to argue that Mennonites could be more faith-ful by jettisoning ethnic, institutional, and tradition-bound ways of sustaining faithful practice, then the legacy of Concern should include a stronger "synthe-sis between Christian freedom and discipline." In other words, we should find Mennonites sustaining high ethical standards and consensus without relying on the stuff of continuity. Otherwise, we will have reason to suspect that Hauerwas instead is right to see something about Mennonite community that prominent Mennonites themselves have hesitated to recognize: that the moral vigor of the Concern Movement's heroic pneumatology actually depends on both commu-nal folkways and formal institutions for sustenance.

Now, obviously it is impossible for anyone other than God to judge faithful-ness definitively. What I can do is collect some signs and markers.

The first marker is that leaders of the Concern Movement sought to avoid, and did avoid, schism. Too often in their past, Mennonite internal dissent and renewal movements had issued in church splits. But the members of the Con-cern Group took pains to avoid such a fate from the beginning.[74] They contin-ued their service within formal church programs and determined not to take a "precipitous or sectarian action."[75] When a house church began to form right under the noses of Hershberger and Bender in Goshen, Concern participants maintained a tense but patient dialogue with the elders of the Goshen College Mennonite Church until the congregation commissioned them to form a new mission congregation in a low-income area of the city.[76]

Less happily, a second marker is that Concern Movement's ideas and models have hardly spared Mennonites from another kind of division—the "culture wars" that have buffeted other denominations in North America. Their chal-lenge, we may recall, has been to port the Anabaptist vision beyond the stric-tures of the organic village *Gemeinde* while seeking to maintain cohesive moral communities amid modern, individualistic, and increasingly urban life. One way that the Concern Movement attempted to hold "freedom" and "discipline" together in the process was to promote very intentional processes of moral discernment and discipline within small groups, house churches, and congregations.[77] These models have in fact proven influential among North American Mennonites. Yet it is not altogether clear whether this has helped or hurt the prospects for churchwide consensus or moral clarity.

In the last decade of the twentieth century and the first decade of the twenty-first, the two largest Mennonite denominations in North America were completing a historic merger. The process became significantly more complicated and painful as it coincided with conflicts over the status of homosexuals in the church, and over the status of congregations that accepted them as full members.[78] Mennonites thus found themselves trying to decide the moral issues surrounding homosexuality while also deciding on new structures for deciding. In some congregations, the ongoing influence of the Concern Movement inspired very careful processes of communal discernment. Results could sometimes be models of healing and community building, but other congregations who undertook such processes experienced standoffs and outright division. Churchwide, meanwhile, the Concern Movement's influence had been strengthening congregationalism in both denominations over previous decades. As merging Mennonites grew tired of their debates, and as leaders pressed to complete their denominational process of "integration," congregationalism increasingly provided a rationale for simply deciding not to decide. That resolution may have kept the peace in this historic peace church. But it would be hard to argue confidently that the process offered a marked demonstration of Spirit-guided moral discernment when just what Mennonites were actually discerning remained so uncertain.

However one assesses that question, a third marker for tracking whether the Concern Group legacy has held together freedom and discipline does indicate success, but only through a most telling irony. Kauffman and Driedger have provided evidence that the Anabaptist theological vision has done much to sustain a sense of Mennonite communal identity. These researchers correlated adherence to distinctive Anabaptist-Mennonite convictions concerning baptism, war, discipleship, and a Christian's relationship to the state with other indices.[79] Mennonites who were strong on this index of "Anabaptism" did just as well at resisting secularism as those who were strong on either orthodoxy or fundamentalism; they resisted individualism more strongly, and materialism even more strongly.[80] Alluding to Peter Berger's notion of a "sacred canopy" that once enveloped traditional societies with worldviews that integrated all of life, Kauffman and Driedger concluded that "because of the greater capacity of Anabaptist Mennonites to integrate their faith under the influences of modernization, Anabaptism appears to be the most viable engine for fueling the reconstruction of the Mennonite canopy, in a holistic way, amidst modern complexities."[81]

Neither the sociologists nor their data distinguish the role of Bender from the role of his Concern Movement students in promoting Anabaptist thought; the decades since the 1950s have in fact tended to merge their influence upon the church, and so we must credit both. What Kauffman and Driedger's work did make clear is the crucial role that ordained church leadership had played in spreading this influence: "In our examination of leadership we found considerable differences between the laity and leaders," they wrote. As compared with nonleaders, leaders "more strongly favored outreach through peacemaking, evangelism, MCC work, and service to the poor." And though clergy and laity did not differ much on personal morality, "the laity tended to be more independent, secular, individualistic, and materialistic," whereas the clergy's "Mennonite identity was stronger."[82] "Lay members reflect the dominant spirit of the modern world more fully than do the clergy," the researchers wrote in summary, whereas "Mennonite leaders tend to spearhead efforts to foster Anabaptist identity and outreach, and to serve as a break on excessive secularization, individualism, and materialism."[83]

The irony here may not be obvious until we recall the Concern Movement critique of the professional pastorate. Yoder played a larger and longer role here than did other Concern Group leaders. He may never have been quite so anti-institutional as Peachey, but this was only a matter of accent. For Yoder, "supercongregational bodies" like denominations and other institutions for Christian collaboration were useful as tools but no more than that; they were not churches nor the church itself and could claim no sociological or ontological continuity once they had outlived their ad hoc instrumental value.[84] Over the years, Yoder thus became the group's most prominent advocate for congregationalism and for a conception of Christian ministry that erased distinctions between lay and ordained leadership, tending to delegitimize the latter. Yoder's laudable intention was to release the "fullness of Christ" (Eph. 4:13) by returning to what he considered the Pauline vision of ministry; in such a vision, *all* members of the body of Christ are called to specific ministries and the ordination of certain offices does create the "heretical" "use of the word 'lay' to mean 'non-minister'" or "uninvolved."[85]

Yoder's hope was to push discernment and decision making downward until it resolved at the proper "unit of action and authority in the church [which] is the local congregation."[86] His arguments, however, had the effect of pushing authority and agency even farther downward, to the level of individual and increasingly individualistic believers. To be sure, this was not his intention. Writing with greater nuance in the early 1980s on "The Hermeneutics of Peoplehood," Yoder presented congregationally based discernment as an alternative to both authoritarianism and to individualism.[87] Recognizing the force of Catholic accusations that Protestantism was "incorrigibly individualistic," he noted that this was not the Reformers' intention "when they argued the perspicuity of

Scripture and the priesthood of all believers." Still, he insisted, "that openness to unaccountable individuality was potentially present in their logic."[88] But then it is fair to ask whether the logic of his own congregationalism might not have overridden his intention to avoid both authoritarianism and individualism. What logic prevented unaccountable congregationalism at best, and unaccountable cadres of "two or three" or even one individual within a congregation at worst, after all?

Despite Yoder's hope, many Mennonite pastors and church leaders now believe that his arguments have had exactly this effect; they have pushed authority and agency down to individual and increasingly individualistic believers. Yoder's critics in this regard are among those same leaders whom Kauffman and Driedger have credited with "spearhead[ing] efforts to foster Anabaptist identity and outreach." Yet they report hearing church members repeatedly citing "the priesthood of all believers" as a rationale for resisting the very leadership of their pastors.[89] By the 1980s and 1990s, some Mennonites were citing that phrase to claim an Anabaptist mantle for their individual "authority" as though they were invoking papal authority.[90] While recognizing that many different ideas cobbled together from the North American "religious supermarket" had contributed to this trend, pastors and pastoral theologians increasingly blamed Concern Group ecclesiology and Yoder's book *The Fullness of Christ* as having provided theological legitimization for the other influences.[91] Some took a second look at the Concern theology of ministry and argued that it grew less from New Testament models than from the very process of cultural assimilation that the Concern Movement thought it was countering.[92] Still, some ironies surrounding the Concern Movement are more welcome.

Continuity Anyway

Concern Movement thinkers have undoubtedly made a vigorous contribution to church renewal, but in some ways they have done so despite themselves. Or better: They have contributed so much despite the more radical and one-sided tendencies of their very ecclesiology. After all, they have done so in part by internalizing virtues within themselves of the very sort that Hershberger's Mennonite Community Movement and Bender's institution building were far more likely to celebrate: patience to continue working within the very church structures about which the Concern Group had such deep misgivings, rootedness in communities that continue needing all kinds of organic bonds in order to survive the corrosiveness of modernity while struggling together amid the tensions of North American culture wars, and formative practices capable of producing leaders who represent their traditions in themselves even when they doubted the priestly legitimacy of representational ministry. This suggests that Hauerwas has rightly perceived something that may not have been obvious to Mennonites caught up in their own internal debates: Namely, the dissenting witness of a Yoder is unintelligible apart from the communal and institutional practices of continuity that he and his Concern Movement peers were dismissing as mere ethnicity and stifling traditionalism.

In its principled dissent and its very case for a principle of dissent, the Concern Movement was articulating a Mennonite version of the Protestant Principle. Its most influential thinkers represented the Protestant Principle quite pointedly, though most problematically, through an anti-institutionalism that was almost metaphysical.

The Barthian theologian Jacques de Senarclens once articulated Tillich's "Protestant Principle" in a far more biblical and orthodox idiom. The church finds its sustenance not in "a continuing life owed to organization" but in the "continuing vitality" of Pentecost. The very "doctrine of the Holy Spirit challenges the Church and its authority," he wrote. "In itself the Church is no more lasting than manna" and must rely on the continual replication of Pentecost or else institutionalism immediately begins to set in." If manna or church lives on, it is because Jesus Christ in his faithfulness constantly gives anew and thus renews. The church is but "the effect of a living, actual, personal revelation of God by the Holy Spirit." Thus, "Whether in its Roman, Neo-Protestant or Orthodox form, institutionalism sins at this point. It finds truth in duration or tradition, not in the direct action of grace."[93]

Now, in what de Senarclens sought to affirm about our ultimate dependence on the work of God through Jesus Christ and the Holy Spirit, his argument should surely persuade. Still, it is unpersuasive in what it denies, paradoxically, at precisely the same point. For it would actually limit the power of grace and circumscribe the purview of God's Incarnation. The problem with this view is not that it trusts the work of Christ through the Holy Spirit too much, but that it actually trusts too little. For such a view determines in advance that the Holy Spirit cannot leave any trace in human habits, practices, social structures, or institutions.[94]

In one of the more polished statements of the Concern Movement agenda, published in 1957, Peachey articulated precisely the view of de Senarclens.[95] No truly Anabaptist missionary movement could break forth so long as Mennonites were "tied existentially to their culture as supposedly infused with a spiritual quality (and the same must be said of any other denomination or tradition)." Their prophetic impact and creativity had waned as soon as "their genius" had "crystallized into cultural tradition" as they developed "externally transmissible sub-culture systems." Those who said that a truly committed church of believers could only maintain its distinct character in the first generation were correct, concluded Peachey. Only unmediated existential authenticity seemed to count as Christian at all: "Even one's personal experience of yesterday may militate, as tradition does in the group, against the decision of today!"[96]

No infusion, crystallization, or transmission: Peachey certainly bore a deep commitment both to Christian community and to the work of the Holy Spirit. But he consistently rejected any metaphor that might have given him language to describe how God's work could abide in human affairs and thus survive to shape those affairs another day, even the very next day!

Peachey always articulated the heroic pneumatology and pneumatic eccle-siology of the Concern Group most starkly, yet this was in fact the logic that their writings shared. The only power on which the church may properly rely is prophetic not programmatic nor institutional at all, he had earlier insisted; it is thus a mistake for denominations to sustain themselves through "rational social organization."[97] The "universal people of God" does not become visible, nor is the "real presence of Christ" realized, except in the fellowship of the local church.[98] All bodily, ethnic, or territorial bonds have continually put the spiri-tual reality of the people of God "in constant jeopardy."[99] This was not to say that the church of the New Testament is "'merely' spiritual" and thus invisible, Peachey acknowledged, for "the believers are gathered together visibly, engage in observable activity, and live in visible discipleship, mutually submissive to one another."[100] Yet "precisely because the Church is visible, men confuse the visible expression with the reality itself," wrote Peachey.

Clearly, Peachey was struggling here to express the relationship between "Spirit and Form in the Church of Christ," as the title of another of his essays an-nounced.[101] Tellingly, "form" mainly evoked for him dead "formality," not the shaping or formation of human clay by which grace might perfect nature, thus imbuing the material stuff of "nature" with the supernatural. What he and others in the Concern Movement desperately needed was a *tertium datur*, a third option or category, for naming the possibility that the earthy stuff of human continu-ity—institutions, structures, offices, social practices, families, organic communi-ties, and not just intentional communities sustained through pure intentionality alone—might be capable of embodying the charismatic work of God.

No doubt there were some historical reasons why they failed to discover such a category: Neither Peachey nor his Mennonite peers denied the doctrine of Christ's incarnation, but theologians of their era had not yet made the notion of embodiment available in fresh ways. Likewise, the Second Vatican Council had not yet opened new theological exchanges with Catholicism, so Concern Group writers dismissed the category of sacrament out of hand.[102] Had it been avail-able, the category of sacramental practices might have offered a *tertium datur* transcending both an exclusionary, nonportable, and strictly ethnic form of em-bodiment, and an Anabaptism so strictly visionary as to become intellectualist and abstract. The Concern Movement needed some such category acutely.

Peachey, after all, was most sure of this: Confusion about the church's visible expressions results especially when Christians "believe that these expressions can be 'inherited from one generation to another' by external means and that the Spirit must adjust . . . to these 'cultural' structures."[103] In a telling lament near the very end of his 1957 statement of the Concern Group's agenda, Peachey noted that Christian parents inevitably "seek to throw a Christian influence about their children." Yes, lament—for the result Peachey bemoaned was that well-meaning parents "may well limit the 'chances' that theirs will be a daring, heroic faith." Alas, admitted Peachey, these were "fundamental facts of life." But realism dare not lead to any reevaluation of Anabaptist ecclesiology as the Concern Movement understood it. No, those fundamental facts did not "justify our transformation of the church of Christ into something which she essentially cannot be and was never intended to be."[104]

Peachey was not simply speaking for himself. At about this same time, *Concern* editors attempted to gather enough essays for a pamphlet on Mennonite "parochial" schools and colleges. Though they were unsuccessful, Yoder did write a major essay on Christian education that went unpublished. Every claim or assumption in Peachey's paragraph of lament finds fuller elaboration here. Just as Peachey resisted "fundamental facts of life," Yoder affirmed early Anabaptists not just for resisting but for "condemning" the sociological "Sect cycle" that tends to alter every Christian renewal movement after two or three generations.[105] Though Yoder's tone was less of a lament, the challenge he articulated for Mennonite education was likewise a dilemma: how to transmit the vision but not the sociology of previous generations?[106] Far from anticipating an answer in Hauerwas's recovery of Aristotelian "practices" for Christian ethics, Yoder insisted that "the Christian faith which we are interested in expressing, preserving, propagating, and passing on to our children is not first of all a behavior pattern."[107] Yoder was just as certain as Peachey that well-meaning parental attempts to transmit Christian faith to children could often backfire: "The possibility of exerting such pedagogical and psychological influences as to reproduce quite faithfully a desired behavior pattern is in fact not an aid to the propagation of true faith but often a hindrance, for those pedagogical and psychological influences can get in the way of faith."[108]

No starker statements could be found of the Concern Movement's radical rejection of the possibility that God's Spirit might use the earthy stuff of human continuity to embody the Gospel. And with it could be paired no more striking admission that such an ecclesiology is probably unworkable except perhaps for the most heroic and extraordinary of Christians. Yet such a view was far less uniquely "Anabaptist" than the Concern Movement assumed; in many ways, it was the logical implication of the Protestant Principle turned Protestant Dilemma.

In the years since Yoder's death in late 1997, a small cottage industry has begun among scholars delineating the differences between Hauerwas and Yoder.[109] Because Hauerwas did much to bring Yoder's thought to prominence far beyond Mennonite circles, some readers have equated the two. Scholars correcting the impression of unanimity have generally focused on the tone of their respective social ethics. Both have been prominent spokesmen for Christian pacifism, of course. But despite his call for churches to adopt a posture of frank and counter-cultural dissent, Yoder deliberately titled the last book he prepared for publication *For the Nations*, in contrast to Hauerwas's more contrarian *Against the Nations*.[110] Yoder was always more interested in politically engaged forms of Gandhian nonviolence than was Hauerwas, and he wrote more favorably of liberal democracy and Enlightenment ideals. All these points are valid, and on most of them I tend to side with Yoder. Yet none of them delves into the fundamental distinction that separates these two brilliant thinkers by the chasm of a hidden ravine.

It is this matter of continuity. Hauerwas launched his career endeavoring to restore the stuff of continuity to the Christian moral life—character development, habit and virtue, formative Christian social practices, and anything else that would help Christians sustain traditions of community. Thus would he help them reconnect the dots of discrete moral decisions and atomized lives within modernity. In contrast, Yoder launched his career as the intellectual leader of a movement arguing against the assumption that traditions and organic communal life could carry practices of authentic discipleship forward across time and generations, or that institutions ever had any ecclesial status except as ad hoc tools in the service of local congregations, which were the only sure place to identify the presence of the church universal.[111]

Though Yoder was never as radical as Peachey, his strongest affirmations for a principle of continuity tended to be intellectualist. Not long before his death, Yoder made a statement that could well mark his ultimate distance from the way that Peachey had sought to speak for the Concern Movement in 1957, when Peachey called into question the value of both tradition and yesterday's personal experience for today's discipleship decisions. "Without some thread through the past," wrote Yoder in 1995," any faith community is stranded in the present."[112] Yet even here, the thread of continuity that Yoder could most readily affirm was "the recovery of history," the work of those he had elsewhere called the church's "agents of memory." It is the intellect, not the organic habits of social practice, that carries the burden of such continuity.[113]

Although Hauerwas's first allegiance is to Jesus, not Aristotle, he has welcomed all the help Christians living amid the acids of modernity can get for those very practices through time that will sustain markedly Christian communities. Hence, Hauerwas has given far greater attention than Yoder to welcoming and forming children.[114] Hence, he has not joined Mennonites in rejecting infant baptism but has recognized it as a practice that incorporates children into Christian communities from the beginning.[115] Hence, and with even more certitude, he has insisted that liturgy and especially the Eucharist do not distract Christians from discipleship but ground and form discipleship.[116] Hence, he has rejected the assumptions of Weberian sociology and argued that office can be the bearer of charismatic authority rather than its antithesis.[117] Hence, he has even been willing to reconsider ways that some ethnic traditions on the one hand and some practices associated with Christendom on the other might help sustain a Christian witness within modernity.[118] Hence, he has sympathy for Catholic authority structures.[119]

Still, if in so many crucial ways Hauerwas is not Yoder, it is thanks precisely to these differences that he has seen something about Mennonite communities and practices that Yoder, his peers, and too many of his students were taking for granted and thought they could dismiss.[120] Thus he has highlighted the lines of continuity that show why the insights and impulses of Hershberger's Mennonite Community Movement, Bender's institution building as well as his theological vision, and the Concern Group's dynamism have needed each other all along. This is a service to a church tradition that has stressed Christ's call to be reconcilers but needed some reconciliation itself. And it should be a service to those in other church traditions who might only read inter-Mennonite debates as a curious case study were it not for their own need to hold together loyalty and dissent amid the acids of modernity.

Mennonites can thus be glad that the Concern Movement did not entirely live up to its theological ideal. The ecclesiology that in so many ways was the movement's strength was strong in part because it was parasitic—drawing strength from traditions, intergenerational practices, and church institutions whose very legitimacy it tended to deny. Participants were influential not just because they offered a cogent dissent at a critical juncture in the Mennonite Church. They were also influential because they stuck with their tradition even as they delegitimated traditions, stayed rooted in their church even though they disallowed ethnic means of continuity, and worked within its institutions even though their theology and ecclesiology discredited institutional forms of continuity.

If Hauerwas has urged Protestants and Catholics to be more Anabaptist, it is because the Concern Movement Mennonites who had such an impact on him stood in greater continuity than they themselves acknowledged with the Mennonite communities that formed them, thus constituting a tradition of dissent capable of maintaining a recognizably Christian witness amid the violent delusions of their age.[121] If Hauerwas has nonetheless urged Anabaptist-Mennonites along with more mainstream Protestants to be more Catholic, it is because the traditions and virtues needed to sustain their witness are nothing to take for granted. To think otherwise is itself nothing short of delusional.

Notes

1. See Stanley Hauerwas, *The Peaceable Kingdom: A Primer in Christian Ethics* (Notre Dame, Ind.: University of Notre Dame Press, 1983), xxiv; and William Cavanaugh, "Stan the Man: A Thoroughly Biased Account of a Completely Unobjective Person," in *The Hauerwas Reader*, ed. John Berkman and Michael G. Cartwright (Durham, N.C.: Duke University Press, 2001), 21–22.

2. John Howard Yoder, "The Anabaptist Dissent: The Logic of the Place of the Disciple in Society," *Concern: A Pamphlet Series* 1, June 1954, 45–68. See also John Howard Yoder, "The Prophetic Dissent of the Anabaptists," in *The Recovery of the Anabaptist Vision: A Sixtieth Anniversary Tribute to Harold S. Bender*, ed. Guy F. Hershberger (Scottdale, Pa.: Herald Press, 1957), 93–104.

3. See, of course, the title of one of Hauerwas's early collections of articles, *A Community of Character: Toward a Constructive Christian Social Ethic* (Notre Dame, Ind.: University of Notre Dame Press, 1981).

4. Hauerwas, *Peaceable Kingdom*, xxiv.

5. Stanley Hauerwas, "Why Truthfulness Requires Forgiveness: A Commencement Address for Graduates of a College of the Church of the Second Chance," in *The Hauerwas Reader*, ed. John Berkman and Michael G. Cartwright (Durham, N.C.: Duke University Press, 2001; orig. pub. 1992), 311–12; Stanley Hauerwas, "Reconciling the Practice of Reason: Casuistry in a Christian Context," in *Christian Existence Today: Essays on Church, World and Living in Between* (Durham, N.C.: Labyrinth Press, 1988), 67–87.

6. This is one way of summarizing a major theme running through the whole of Hauerwas's *The Peaceable Kingdom*, but see especially chapters 4 through 6. Also see Hauerwas, "Whose Church? Which Future?" where he wrote: "I am often accused of romanticizing both Catholicism and Anabaptist, and no doubt that is a danger. But the reason I am so attracted to those traditions is that they have managed to keep some practices in place that provide resources for resistance against the loss of Christian presence in modernity. For that is the heart of the matter—namely practices" (p. 67).

7. Though himself recognizing that it is an affront to the gospel whenever a church reproduces ethnic divisions ("Whose Church? Which Future?" 71), Hauerwas also chided Mennonites in the same essay for being too embarrassed about their ethnic identity: "[Today's] Anabaptists are embarrassed about their ethnicity, but it may be that 'ethnicity' is one way God provided and continues to provide for your survival as a people capable of remembering the martyrs who that have made you what you are. [Harold S.] Bender rightly understood that historiography is a theological enterprise, but discipleship, the voluntary nature of church membership, and nonresistance must be embedded in a thicker history if they are to continue to provide us with the skills of Christian faithfulness" (p. 73).

8. Paul Tillich, *The Protestant Era*, trans. James Luther Adams (Chicago: University of Chicago Press, 1948), xi, xxii, 163, 195–96, 202–5. But to confirm that his is not a particularly Tillichian view, see the lesser-known work of the Barthian Swiss theologian Jacques de Senarclens, *Heirs of the Reformation* (Philadelphia: Westminster Press, 1964), 85ff.

9. Stanley Hauerwas and Samuel Wells, "How the Church Managed before There Was Ethics," chap. 4 in *The Blackwell Companion to Christian Ethics*, Blackwell Companions to Religion (Malden, Mass.: Blackwell, 2004), 48. John Courtney Murray, SJ, a thinker with a very different view of the role of the Church in American society, concurred with Hauerwas's characterization of modernity in a way when he wrote: "My generalization will be that the political experiment of modernity has essentially consisted in an effort to find and install in the world a secular substitute for all that the Christian tradition has meant by the pregnant

phrase, the 'freedom of the Church.'" John Courtney Murray, *We Hold These Truths: Catholic Reflections on the American Proposition* (New York: Sheed and Ward, 1960), 201. The difference, of course, is that Hauerwas is more concerned about sustaining specifically Christian ecclesial practices, whereas Murray was more concerned about sustaining a Christian foundation for American civilization, which Hauerwas finds a dubious proposition.

10. See, e.g., Ernst Troeltsch, *The Social Teaching of the Christian Churches*, trans. Olive Wyon and introduction by Richard Niebuhr (Chicago: University of Chicago Press, 1981; orig. pub. 1931), 1010–12; and Robert N. Bellah, *The Broken Covenant: American Civil Religion in a Time of Trial—The Weil Lectures 1971* (New York: Seabury Press, 1975), 143. Apropos to Mennonites, also see Dennis D. Martin, "Nothing New under the Sun? Mennonites and History," *Conrad Grebel Review* 5, no. 1 (Winter 1987): 2. Bridging Hauerwas's concerns and impulses at work among some Mennonites are the provocative comments of Russell R. Reno, *In the Ruins of the Church: Sustaining Faith in an Age of Diminished Christianity* (Grand Rapids: Brazos Press, 2002), 15–26, where Reno finds surprising commonality in the Enlightenment philosopher René Descartes and the Anglican-priest-turned-Dispensationalist John Nelson Darby; their shared "strategy of separation" in search of conceptual or ecclesial purity in the face of the corruptions of the age "typifies the modern project" (p. 17).

11. Both among emerging Mennonite academics and among the sophisticated folk sociologists in the leadership of Anabaptist-Mennonite groups that have shunned higher education, anxieties and analyses of modernity could be found in almost any group and decade of at least the last century. Suffice then to note the subtitle of a major historical study of Mennonites in twentieth-century America by Paul Toews, *Mennonites in American Society, 1930–1970: Modernity and the Persistence of Religious Community—The Mennonite Experience in America, Volume 4* (Scottdale, Pa.: Herald Press, 1996).

12. Findings have been compiled and interpreted in J. Howard Kauffman and Leland Harder, *Anabaptists Four Centuries Later: A Profile of Five Mennonite and Brethren in Christ Denominations* (Scottdale, Pa.: Herald Press, 1975); and J. Howard Kauffman and Leo Driedger, *The Mennonite Mosaic: Identity and Modernization*, foreword by Donald B. Kraybill (Scottdale, Pa.: Herald Press, 1991).

13. Kauffman and Driedger, *Mennonite Mosaic*, 99. Urbanization had only a negligible effect on church participation or the practices of prayer and Bible reading that the surveyors called "devotionalism" (p. 83); it made them no less likely to support evangelism or community service, and a bit more likely to support the peacemaking and international development ministries of their church (pp. 182, 241). Not decisive either, on any of these counts, was a general rise in socioeconomic status, as indicated by education, income and occupational rank, or geographical mobility (pp. 83–84). Mobility and rising socioeconomic status actually appeared to have a positive impact both on church participation and wider community involvement (pp. 83, 182, 241). Predictably, all these "forces of modernization" did decrease the adherence of Mennonites to "general religious orthodoxy" a bit, lessened "fundamentalist beliefs" even more (though they actually increased "Bible knowledge"), and left a clear "trend toward theological pluralism" among Mennonites (pp. 46, 84, 256). The 1989 survey of Mennonites suggests that they were being pulled in those contrary directions that North Americans now know as the "culture wars" over moral issues such as abortion, homosexuality, and the role of women on the one hand, and over the moral priority of poverty, racism and social justice on the other (pp. 208–9). Just as the sociologist Robert Wuthnow famously noticed among all American denominations at about this same time, Mennonites were often diverging more within a given denomination than they were between denominations (pp. 209, 253–56); cf. Robert Wuthnow, *The Restructuring of American Religion: Society and Faith Since World War II* (Princeton, N.J.: Princeton University Press, 1988). Still, if sexuality, gender roles, and marriage have often seemed to define the front lines in the culture wars, Mennonite marriages in 1989 were staying together at a far

higher rate than in wider North American societies, even as patriarchal patterns gave way to somewhat greater egalitarianism (p. 124).

14. Kauffman and Driedger, *Mennonite Mosaic*, 100.

15. Since soon after its founding at the turn of the twentieth century, the college's very motto has hinted at the project it has carried forward. "Culture for Service" is emblematic of the attempt by many Mennonite leaders to engage their surrounding society and its best cultural resources in fresh but faithful ways: to modernize carefully, critically, and self-consciously for the cause of Christ and Christlike service in the world. This is my own interpretation, as an alumnus of Goshen College and the son of a faculty member. But see Susan Fisher Miller, *Culture for Service: A History of Goshen College, 1894–1994* (Goshen, Ind.: Goshen College, 1994), 1–3, 44–45.

16. That term has most often applied to an approach to sixteenth-century Anabaptist historical studies led by Goshen's academic dean and commanding presence, Harold S. Bender. Bender summarized his interpretation in his 1942 presidential address to the Society of Church History. Titled simply "The Anabaptist Vision," his paper not only won the respect of his fellow church historians but provided many Mennonites with a sense of self-respect, communal identity, and programmatic purpose. John Howard Yoder once characterized Bender's vision this way: "For Bender's generation the retrieval of his particular vision of the Swiss Brethren origins was not disinterested historiography; it was a weapon in the struggle for Mennonite identity in the face of the mid-century challenges of urbanization, acculturation, and global war"; John Howard Yoder, "Historiography as a Ministry to Renewal," *Brethren Life and Thought* 42 (Summer–Fall 1997): 218. Given the communal and programmatic function of the "Goshen School" even in its strictly historical sense, one may apply the term more broadly to the wider intellectual climate centered at midcentury Goshen College.

17. Complementing my own account of the Mennonite intellectual debate that centered in Goshen at midcentury are the following: Paul Toews, "The Concern Movement: Its Origins and Early History," *Conrad Grebel Review* 8, no. 2 (Spring 1990): 109–26; and Steven M. Nolt, "Anabaptist Visions of Church and Society," *Mennonite Quarterly Review* 69 (July 1995): 283–94.

18. The four major strategies that took shape in the creative debate that constituted the Goshen School were not mutually exclusive, although the last of the four turned one of the first three (Bender's very definition of "the Anabaptist vision") against the other two. Nor were they the only strategic options available to twentieth-century Mennonites. All four emerged against the background of two additional strategies, between which they all attempted to navigate. To one side was the theoretical possibility, at least, of frankly attempting to maintain Mennonite versions of village life with only the barest minimum of modernization. The Amish will come to mind for most readers, along with the Hutterites, for a few more. But I mean this strategy to be broad enough to include other "Old Order" groups that are Mennonite rather than Amish, as well as the kinds of communities in Western Canada and elsewhere that had literally transplanted entire Mennonite villages from Ukraine and Russia in the 1870s and after. On the former, see Theron F. Schlabach, "Keeping the Old Order," chap. 8 in *Peace, Faith, Nation: Mennonites and Amish in Nineteenth-Century America—The Mennonite Experience in America, Volume 2* (Scottdale, Pa.: Herald Press, 1988), 201–28. On the latter, note that Leo Driedger dedicates a chapter (no. 4) to what he calls "the Sacred Village" to provide a kind of sociological baseline for his contemporary study of *Mennonites in the Global Village* (Toronto: University of Toronto Press, 2000). To the other side of the "Goshen School" continuum was an option that stopped just short of outright assimilation by attempting to find a comfortable Mennonite niche within a larger mainstream religious culture. Again, I mean this category to be broad enough to include efforts to find a niche among both early-twentieth-century Fundamentalists and Modernists, and later among

both Evangelical and Liberal Protestants. The defining differences here are all important, yet they share the same basic strategy and differ mainly around which conception of the mainstream seemed most important to catch up with and join.

19. Theron F. Schlabach, "To Focus a Mennonite Vision," in *Kingdom, Cross and Community: Essays on Mennonite Themes in Honor of Guy F. Hershberger*, ed. John Richard Burkholder and Calvin Redekop (Scottdale, Pa.: Herald Press, 1976), 23–24.

20. See especially Reinhold Niebuhr, "Why the Christian Church Is Not Pacifist," in *Christianity and Power Politics* (New York: Charles Scribner's Sons, 1940), 1–32.

21. For a chapter-length biography of Hershberger, see Theron F. Schlabach, "To Focus a Mennonite Vision," in *Kingdom, Cross and Community*, ed. Burkholder and Redekop, 15–50. A book-length biography of Hershberger by Theron Schlabach is in preparation. The author's intention is to make his polished but most fully documented first draft available to Mennonite libraries, as a resource to scholars even after publication in a form and length more suitable for a general readership. The title has not been finalized at the time of this writing, but readers are advised to inquire at the Mennonite Historical Library, Goshen College, 1700 South Main Street, Goshen IN 46526; e-mail mhl@goshen.edu.

22. Schlabach, "To Focus a Mennonite Vision," 29–30, 32–33.

23. Guy F. Hershberger, *War, Peace, and Nonresistance*, 3rd ed., Christian Peace Shelf Selection (Scottdale, Pa.: Herald Press, 1969). Until John Howard Yoder's work began to become prominent, mainstream Protestant ethicists who wished to cite a representative of the Mennonite peace position would site this book by Hershberger; see Reinhold Niebuhr, "Why the Christian Church Is Not Pacifist," 4–5, 30–31; and John C. Bennett, *Christian Ethics and Social Policy*, Richard Lectures in the University of Virginia (New York: Charles Scribner's Sons, 1946), 41–46.

24. Nolt summarizes the movement's "fundamentally distinctive" approach to social ethics this way in "Anabaptist Visions": "The movement's method began with the affirmation that social ethics grow out of particular social settings and community patterns and that those particular settings must be the starting point for active Christian witness. Normative standards of scripture cannot be applied or understood theoretically apart from concrete human situations. Specific Mennonite communities, therefore, possessed ethical resources which were not only theological but also social and relational. As such, they offered not so much havens of withdrawal from the world but viable, valuable contexts in which to think ethically and to apply social justice principles in order to gain experience for subsequent engagement with surrounding society" (p. 286).

25. Nolt asks: "In light of some present Mennonite misgivings about the ahistorical and perfectionist irrelevance of the Anabaptist vision, and amid stirring among some Mennonites for a new communitarian approach to social ethics, might the Mennonite Community movement [*sic*] deserve a second look—not because the Community vision offered the right answers (often its answers were far too rurally oriented), but because it was beginning to ask the right questions and to employ helpful historical and contextual methods?" Nolt, "Anabaptist Visions," 293.

26. Albert N. Keim, *Harold S. Bender, 1897–1962* (Scottdale, Pa.: Herald Press, 1998), 13.

27. Against a range of other views of the Anabaptists, Bender wrote that "there is another line of interpretation which is being increasingly accepted and which is probably destined to dominate the field. It is the one which holds that Anabaptism is the culmination of the Reformation, the fulfillment of the original vision of Luther and Zwingli, and thus makes it a consistent evangelical Protestantism seeking to recreate without compromise the original New Testament church, the vision of Christ and the Apostles." "The Anabaptist Vision," in *Recovery of the Anabaptist Vision*, ed. Hershberger, 37; see also 41. The historiographic

claim here also offers a positive portrayal that might serve to buttress Mennonite self-respect. Bender's "Anabaptist Vision" first appeared in *Church History* 13 (March 1944): 3–24; and in *Mennonite Quarterly Review* 18 (April 1944): 67–88.

28. H. Richard Niebuhr expressed something of this approach in the opening pages of his book *Christ and Culture* (New York: Harper & Row, 1956). "The belief which lies back of this effort . . . is the conviction that Christ as living Lord is answering the question in the totality of history and life in a fashion which transcends the wisdom of all his interpreters yet employs their partial insights and their necessary conflicts." This was with reference to the various "types" of Christian involvement in the world that Niebuhr was to lay out. With regard to denominations per se, see H. Richard Niebuhr, *The Purpose of the Church and Its Ministry: Reflections on the Aims of Theological Education*, in collaboration with Daniel Day Williams and James M. Gustafson (New York: Harper & Row, 1956), 16–17. John Howard Yoder recognized this developing understanding of denominationalism by implicitly protesting it near the very start of his career, in the early 1950s. "The Anabaptist-Mennonite tradition, theologically understood, is seen to represent not simply a branch of Protestantism with a particular 'talent,' but a historical incarnation of an entirely different view of the Christian life, of the work and nature of the church, and fundamentally also of the meaning of redemption." Yoder, "Anabaptist Dissent," 57.

29. Though clearly uncomfortable with crassly nationalistic answers to Protestant uncertainty about the whole of which denominations are a part, H. Richard Niebuhr gave unmistakable evidence of that uncertainty in *The Purpose of the Church and Its Ministry*, 5–17, in a subsection titled "Denomination, Nation or Church?"

30. Keim, *Harold S. Bender*, 354–55.

31. Bender, "Anabaptist Vision," 42. Later, for his transition from his elaboration of point 1 to point 2, Bender wrote: "As a second major element in the Anabaptist vision, a new concept of the church was created *by the central principle* of newness of life and applied Christianity," a.k.a. discipleship (p. 47).

32. Though Bender was ready to agree with other historians that "the great principles of freedom of conscience, separation of church and state, and voluntarism in religion, so basic to American Protestantism, and so essential to democracy, ultimately are derived from the Anabaptists of the Reformation period," he also insisted that "in the last analysis" a concept such as freedom of religion "is a purely formal concept, barren of content; it says nothing about the faith or the way of life of those who advocate it, nor does it reveal their goals or program of action." Whatever the Anabaptists had contributed to the West's "development of religious liberty," such a concept "not only does not exhaust but actually fails to define the true essence of Anabaptism." Bender, "Anabaptist Vision," 30–31.

33. Gerald Biesecker-Mast also sees a tendency toward abstraction in Bender's "Anabaptist Vision," held in tension with an attempt to name essences that were in fact concrete practices rather than purely formal categories. See Gerald Biesecker-Mast, *Separation and the Sword in Anabaptist Persuasion: Radical Confessional Rhetoric from Schleitheim to Dordrecht*, C. Henry Smith Series, vol. 6 (Telford, Pa., and Scottdale, Pa.: Cascadia Publishing House and Herald Press, 2006), 48–50.

34. Bender, "Anabaptist Vision," 43; but see also 44–46.

35. Ibid., 42. Emphasis added.

36. The "practice of true brotherhood and love among members of the church" was a "principle" that should not express itself merely "pious sentiments, but in the actual practice of sharing possessions to meet the needs of others." Bender, "Anabaptist Vision," 49.

37. That is why one cannot write off Bender's vocabulary of essence to the intellectual climate of his day or attribute the lapses in his generally eloquent essay to the hasty

redaction that his overworked administrative duties required (according to Keim, *Harold S. Bender*, 310, 314).

38. In that sense, Bender was preparing the way for the Concern Movement of younger Mennonites influenced by Bender, who sought to break even more radically with ethnic and institutional ways of sustaining Mennonite community, as we will shortly see. One may also note a telling use of the language of "essence," e.g., in Paul Peachey, "What Is Concern?" *Concern: A Pamphlet Series* 4 (June 1957): 18 (calling for an "inner recovery of essence"); and Paul Peachey, "Spirit and Form in the Church," *Concern: A Pamphlet Series* 2 (1955): 16 (contrasting the New Testament's realization of the "spiritual essence of the people of God" with Jewish traditionalism, but no doubt using the latter as a foil for ethnic Mennonite traditionalism). Nolt also sees an increasing tendency to abstraction as one moves from Hershberger to Bender to the Concern Group; see Nolt, "Anabaptist Visions," 289–93.

39. These seven were Irvin B. Horst, John W. Miller, Paul Peachey, Calvin Redekop, David A. Shank, Orley Swartzentrudber, and John Howard Yoder.

40. The terms here come from the title of an essay that John Howard Yoder wrote a decade and a half later, "Anabaptist Vision and Mennonite Reality," in *Consultation on Anabaptist-Mennonite Theology: Papers Read at the 1969 Aspen Conference*, ed. A. J. Klassen (Fresno: Council of Mennonite Seminaries, 1970). From the beginning, however, the Concern Movement had been all about the strategy critically examining Mennonite reality in the harsh light of the "Anabaptist Vision."

41. The eighteen *Concern* pamphlets that this new generation of promising young church leaders published sporadically from 1954 through 1971 were, by intention, virtually their only quasi-institutional expression. The series thus gave them their unofficial name, the Concern Group or Concern Movement. Nomenclature is not standard, but when I refer to the Concern *Group* I will be referring to the original seven men who met in Amsterdam in 1952. When I refer to the Concern *Movement*, I will be referring to the larger group of friends, peers, and correspondents who contributed to *Concern* pamphlets in the following years.

42. The postwar relief efforts that had taken some of the seven in the original Concern Group to Europe were in direct continuity with the alternative service programs that church leaders like Hershberger had forged for conscientious objectors. The critique they refined in Amsterdam relied on training they had gotten from professors in the Mennonite Community Movement, which helped them critically examine their church's sociology in order to intentionally shape and sustain an alternative community.

43. Paul Peachey, "Preface," *Concern: A Pamphlet Series* 2 (1955): 3. Emphasis *sic*.

44. Their answer was yes, in the technical sense by which they believed authentic Christian communities must always stand over against the violence-rooted ways of a fallen world; Yoder, "Anabaptist Dissent." Probably insofar as this posture also forced the Anabaptists to break with established churches: "Epistolary: An Exchange by Letter," *Concern: A Pamphlet Series* 4 (June 1957): 9, 12–13. *No* in that they did not want to provoke a fresh schism in their own church: Peachey, "What is Concern?" 14. And their answer was no, in their desire to release themselves from parochial home communities and take their faith into robust engagement with the challenges of their age. Toews, *Mennonites in American Society*, 235, with hints of what he calls their rejection of "sociological sectarianism" in "Epistolary," 7, 10.

45. Toews, *Mennonites in American Society*, 232.

46. Yoder, "Anabaptist Dissent," 48.

47. Toews, "Concern Movement," 123. Whether out of convenience, lack of information, or common sense, Mennonite intellectuals of later decades under the influence of the

Concern Movement have generally ignored this part of the Concern program. The critique of Mennonite parochial schools appeared more often in the Concern Group's personal correspondence than in their published writings. I am thus indebted to the unpublished senior seminar paper of one of my peers at Goshen College in the 1970s; see Ronald S. Kraybill, "The 'Concern' Group: An Attempt at Anabaptist Renewal," History Seminar paper, Mennonite Historical Library, Goshen College, Goshen, Ind., 1976, 20–21. Nothing hints more clearly, however, that attitudes toward parochial schools mark a fundamental divide than this; Guy F. Hershberger apparently picked up on the significance of the point immediately. The decision-making process that had led to Mennonite church schools in recent decades, in keeping with the Mennonite Community Movement, was something he immediately sought to clarify and defend. See "Epistolary," 10–11.

48. John W. Miller, "Organization and Church," *Concern: A Pamphlet Series* 4 (June 1957): 35.

49. C. Norman Kraus and John W. Miller, "Intimations of Another Way: A Progress Report," *Concern: A Pamphlet Series* 3 (1956): 7–11.

50. Kraus and Miller, "Intimations of Another Way," 12–17, with quotation from 17. Toews has summarized Concern Movement advocacy of house churches and small groups within established congregations, which appeared especially in the 1956 issue of *Concern*, in this way: These would be "a place to recapture something of the fellowship, intimacy, empowerment, visibility, and purity of the New Testament ideal." Toews, "Concern Movement," 120.

51. "Introduction," *Concern: A Pamphlet Series* 1 (June 1954): 5–6. There were other oppositions in the series here. Standing over against "our own compromised life and at-home-ness in the world" was "the more complete discipleship of the early Christians coupled with a fervent expectancy of the *parousia*" (Christ's soon appearing). Over against "world conformity within church life conterminous [*sic*] with society" was "the validity of the Anabaptist dissent and 'exodus.'" Note that while this dichotomous formulation and the entire pamphlet introduction bears the marks of Peachey's authorship, the piece is unattributed and must be assumed to speak for all seven participants in the original Concern Group. Yoder made exactly this dichotomy between denominational "machinery" and the "'pneumatic'" character of the church proper in "Epistolary," 7.

52. I had the privilege of presenting an early draft of this paper in a seminar at Eastern Mennonite University (Harrisonburg, Va.) in April 2006. Present were two members of the original Concern Group, Peachey himself and Calvin Redekop. With Peachey nodding graciously, Redekop noted that these issues were continual matters for lively debate among the Amsterdam seven, and that Peachey represented an anti-institutional view that was on the far end of their continuum of positions. Yoder, said Redekop, stood somewhere in the middle.

53. See John Howard Yoder, "What Are Our Concerns?" *Concern: A Pamphlet Series* 4 (June 1957): 23–24, 29.

54. Yoder, "Epistolary," 7.

55. Though the following paragraphs trace the nuances of Yoder's later thought on tradition, dissent, and "continuity," the reader who knows his mature arguments about nonviolence, the "politics of Jesus," Constantinianism, counter-Niebuhrian notions of social responsibility, eschatology, and so on, will recognize the contours of his mature thought and career already taking marked shape in this essay. Note that Mark Thiessen Nation, a leading interpreter of Yoder's thought, concurs in finding an "amazing consistency" in Yoder from beginning to end of his theological career. See Mark Thiessen Nation, *John Howard Yoder: Mennonite Patience, Evangelical Witness, Catholic Convictions* (Grand Rapids: William B. Eerdmans, 2006), 75, as well as 77–78, 189, 197.

56. Emphasis added. See John Howard Yoder, "The Hermeneutics of Peoplehood: A Protestant Perspective on Practical Moral Reasoning," *Journal of Religious Ethics* 10–11 (1982–83): 52–53. Also note the allusion to this same text in John Howard Yoder, "To Serve Our God and to Rule the World," in *The Royal Priesthood: Essays Ecclesiological and Ecumenical*, ed. and introduction by Michael G. Cartwright and foreword by Richard J. Mouw (Grand Rapids: William B. Eerdmans, 1994), 139–40.

57. See John Howard Yoder, "Is There Historical Development of Theological Thought?" in *The Witness of the Holy Spirit: Proceedings of the Eighth Mennonite World Conference, Amsterdam, The Netherlands, July 23–30, 1967*, ed. Cornelius J. Dyck (Elkhart, Ind.: Mennonite World Conference, 1967), 379–88; John Howard Yoder, "The Authority of Tradition," in *The Priestly Kingdom: Social Ethics as Gospel* (Notre Dame, Ind.: University of Notre Dame Press, 1984), 70; John Howard Yoder, "The Kingdom as Social Ethic," in *Priestly Kingdom*, 86; and John Howard Yoder, *Body Politics: Five Practices of the Christian Community before the Watching World* (Nashville: Discipleship Resources, 1992), 10, 59.

58. Yoder, "Is There Historical Development?" 384–85. Also see John Howard Yoder, "A People in the World," in *Royal Priesthood*, ed. Cartwright, 68–73.

59. John Howard Yoder, "That Household We Are," keynote address at Conference on "Is There a Believers' Church Christology?" Bluffton College, 1980, 1.

60. John H. Yoder, "The Free Church Syndrome," in *Within the Perfection of Christ: Essays on Peace and the Nature of the Church—In Honor of Martin H. Schrag*, ed. Terry L. Brensinger and E. Morris. Sider (Nappanee, Ind., and Grantham, Pa,: Evangel Press and Brethren in Christ Historical Society, 1990), 174; emphasis is in the original.

61. Yoder, "Free Church Syndrome," 175.

62. Yoder, "Is There Historical Development?" 388–89. After a series of nine concluding theses, which all revolved around the congregation, Yoder concluded the essay with the following paragraph: "Thus the promise of the Spirit to lead the Church 'into all truth' has led us to examine not faith or order, doctrine or organization, in their own right, but rather to seek their rootage and their legitimation in the reality of the believing, forgiving congregation. It is because that Spirit is a permanent Presence in the church that bishops and synods, creeds and councils may be used of God; it is because the congregation is the locus of that presence that no creed or council, synod or bishop may stand in judgment over the congregation as in each age and in each place men gather around the Bible and confess that Jesus Christ is Lord."

63. Yoder, *Body Politics*. For skepticism of tradition as succession or priesthood, see pp. 51, 55, 60. For skepticism of classical understandings of sacrament, see pp. 1, 15, 21, 44, 72. In some of these instances, Yoder was reporting the view of free-church Protestants who associate the term "sacrament" with superstitious, mechanical, or magical workings of grace; and in other instances (pp. 3, 33, 71), he criticized Protestant theologies that would disallow any mediation of grace through the Christian community—but never did he distance himself at all from Protestant assumptions that classical sacramentalism is quasi-magical and thus unworthy of consideration. The sacramentality he affirms, wherein God is fully present in the distinctive yet public practices of the Christian community, certainly contributes important insights toward ecumenical understandings of the sacraments. And as an exercise in demonstrating how, as the subtitle puts it, "five practices of the Christian community" prove to be accessible public models "for a watching world," the book is quite successful. Still, any effort to translate Christian convictions into empirically verifiable, religiously neutral, language must risk reductionism, and it is not always clear that Yoder avoids a merely functionalist view of the Christian sacraments.

64. Yoder, "Authority of Tradition," 69. Thus, even those for whom continuity with tradition is a preeminent value, such as the leading Eastern Orthodox ethicist Vigen Guroian, have

been able to appropriate Yoder's suggestion that "the wholesome growth of a tradition" is more like a vine than an ever-growing tree, insofar as a vine needs regular pruning and new roots in order to extend fruitfully (pp. 69–70). Here, after all, is a considered approach to change and continuity that gives place to the dissent that would correct a tradition precisely through respectful accountability to it. Cf. Vigen Guroian, "Tradition and Ethics: Prospects in a Liberal Society," *Modern Theology* 7, no. 3 (April 1991): 217–18.

65. Note that Yoder began his important essay "The Hermeneutics of Peoplehood" by making an explicit cross-reference to Tillich's Protestant Principle. See Yoder, "Hermeneutics of Peoplehood," 40–41; and Yoder, *Priestly Kingdom*, 15.

66. John Howard Yoder, "The Burden and the Discipline of Evangelical Revisionism," in *Non-violent America: History through the Eyes of Peace*, ed. Louise Hawkley and James C. Juhnke, Cornelius H. Wedel Historical Series, no. 5 (North Newton, Kans.: Bethel College, 1993), 22. Emphasis is in the original.

67. Yoder, "Authority of Tradition," 79. I have already cited Yoder's faithful-tradition-as-vine metaphor from pp. 69–70 of this essay; another much-improved version of the Protestant Principle appears on p. 67. Still another example is John Howard Yoder, "Discerning the Kingdom of God in the Struggles of the World," in *For the Nations: Essays Public and Evangelical* (Grand Rapids: William B. Eerdmans, 1997), 237–45; the essay contrasts sharply with any kind of romantic Tillichian bias toward social movements outside the church.

68. Yoder, *Priestly Kingdom*, 3.

69. John Howard Yoder, "Methodological Miscellany #2: Have You Ever Seen a True Church?" historical mss. 1–48, box 187, section: ethics, 1938–1997, John H. Yoder Collection, Mennonite Church USA Archives, Goshen, Ind., 1988. I am most grateful to Mark Thiessen Nation of Eastern Mennonite Seminary for pointing out this document to me.

70. Yoder, "Methodological Miscellany #2," 4. Yoder's main point was that later disappointment does not refute a founding or renewing vision. Still, there is yet more circumspection in the following paragraph: "If the renewal vision is confirmed as real because renewal happens, but then it is lost in the second or the fourth [*sic*] generation, does that not prove it false after all? It may prove that the vision which triggers initial steps of renewal is not sufficient to face other questions of renewal. This I should insist on strongly. Yet to measure the second generation and third . . . by the idealism of the first generation is not a fair test either of the community or of the ideal, precisely because the situation of later generations poses new questions which are not automatically either answered or set aside by appealing to the truth of the earlier right answers." Though these remarks are part of a larger argument, they would seem to cast a retrospective judgment (probably unintentional) on the ways in the early Concern Group had in fact measured a later generation of Mennonites against first-generation Anabaptists. The younger Yoder had been little short of snide when he circulated the conclusions of the first Concern Group meeting in Amsterdam 1952 in his unpublished memo, "Reflections on the Irrelevance of Certain Slogans to the Historical Movements They Represent; Or, the Cooking of the Anabaptist Goose; Or, Ye Garnish the Sepulchres of the Righteous," historical mss. 1–48, box 6, file 1, John H. Yoder Collection, Mennonite Church USA Archives, 1952. Some of that same tone remained in the 1969 essay, "Anabaptist Vision and Mennonite Reality."

71. Yoder, "Methodological Miscellany #2," 3.

72. Yoder, "Historiography as a Ministry to Renewal," 219; emphasis is in the original. Interestingly, here and elsewhere Yoder's purpose was to counter a certain free church or believers' church impulse to trace an alternative underground line of unbroken apostolic succession of faithful dissenters who have remained faithful to the gospel. Believers' churches, by the very nature of their ecclesiological case, need not compete to authenticate

themselves in this way. Also see John Howard Yoder, "Anabaptism and History," in *Priestly Kingdom*, 133–34.

73. Paul Peachey, "The Modern Recovery of the Anabaptist Vision," in *Recovery of the Anabaptist Vision*, ed. Hershberger, 332.

74. Toews, "Concern Movement," 119–21; Nolt, "Anabaptist Visions," 287.

75. For both points, see Peachey, "What Is Concern?" 14.

76. Keim, *Harold S. Bender*, 469; John W. Miller, "Concern Reflections," *Conrad Grebel Review* 8, no. 2 (Spring 1990): 141, 144–45, 148.

77. Two expressions of this work that are readily accessible are John H[oward] Yoder, "The Hermeneutics of Peoplehood"; and John Howard Yoder, "Binding and Loosing," in *Royal Priesthood*, ed. Cartwright, 323–58.

78. The two merging denominations tended to locate ultimate decision-making authority at different places, congregations in one case and regional conferences of congregations in the other case.

79. Table 3-3 in Kauffman and Driedger, *Mennonite Mosaic*, 71, lists the following survey items as indicative of Anabaptist convictions: "Baptism is unnecessary for infants and children." "Should follow the lordship of Christ even if persecuted." "Church discipline is necessary for the unfaithful." "Christians should take no part in war." "Christians cannot perform in some government offices." "It is against God's will to swear civil oaths." "Must follow Jesus in evangelism and deeds of mercy." "Should not take a person to court even if justified."

80. Kauffman and Driedger, *Mennonite Mosaic*, 257. Not surprisingly, these respondents were also stronger on "peacemaking, service to others, and support for the work of Mennonite Central Committee" (p. 85). Furthermore, "Mennonites strongly committed to Anabaptism attended church and Sunday school more regularly, were more involved in church leadership, and showed stronger interest in serving their congregations" (p. 77).

81. Kauffman and Driedger, *Mennonite Mosaic*, 257.

82. All quotations to this point in the paragraph are from ibid., 271.

83. Ibid., 263.

84. Yoder, "What Are Our Concerns?" 21, 23–24, 29.

85. John Howard Yoder, *The Fullness of Christ: Revolutionary Vision of Universal Ministry* (Elgin, Ill.: Brethren Press, 1987), 9–17, 46–47, 66.

86. Yoder, "What Are Our Concerns?" 23.

87. Yoder, "Hermeneutics of Peoplehood," 48. This article also appears in *Priestly Kingdom*, 15–45.

88. Yoder, "Hermeneutics of Peoplehood," 48.

89. Over the last two decades, I have enjoyed close enough friendships with at least a half dozen Mennonite pastors that they have all confided their frustrations at some point. None are power-hungry authoritarian personalities; all are deeply committed to congregational, consensus-building discernment processes. One pastor's frustration reached its peak not when a church member objected to *his* decision but rather attempted to veto a decision the congregation had reached after months of processing. This kind of pastoral experience surfaces at various places in *Understanding Ministerial Leadership*, ed. John A. Esau and foreword by Ross T. Bender, Text Reader Series, no. 6 (Elkhart, Ind.: Institute of Mennonite Studies, 1995). Within this volume, see especially Esau, "Recovering, Rethinking, and Re-Imagining: Issues in a Mennonite Theology for Christian Ministry," 5, 12; Erick Sawatsky, "Helping Dreams Come True: Toward Wholeness—Articulating the Vision," 35; Marlin E. Miller, "Some Reflections on Pastoral Ministry and Pastoral Education,"

58–59; and George R. Brunk, III, "The Credibility of Leadership," 117–19. Crucial for re-assessing the claim that the notion of "the priesthood of all believers" as Mennonites were using it in the latter half of the twentieth century in fact could claim New Testament or sixteenth-century precedents was Marlin E. Miller, "Priesthood of All Believers," in *Mennonite Encyclopedia*, vol. 5 (Scottdale, Pa.: Herald Press, 1990), 721.

90. Esau, "Recovering, Rethinking, and Re-Imagining," 5.

91. Sawatsky, "Helping Dreams Come True," 32, 35. Also see Marlin E. Miller, "The Recasting of Authority: A Biblical Model for Community Leadership," in *Theology for the Church*, ed. Richard A. Kauffman and Gayle Gerber Koontz (Elkhart, Ind.: Institute of Mennonite Studies, 1997), 109–10; Brunk, "Credibility of Leadership," 117. Other non-theological influences that these leaders cited ranged from the egalitarian impulses of 1960s student movements, to business management models implying that church members were consumeristic clients, to the individualistic assumptions of the therapeutic culture that increasingly dominated North American religious life and ministry.

92. "What amazed me," wrote another Mennonite pastor turned seminary professor, "was the realization that the great theological shift in understanding ministry which we had defined as 'Anabaptist recovery' was in fact more rooted in the political, cultural, and sociological realities of the modern era." One clear indication came as he surveyed debates in other Christian traditions over how to discard older authoritarian models of clerical authority without inviting the dysfunctional patterns of a misguided egalitarianism: "The debates were the same; even the language was the same." Esau, "Recovering, Rethinking, and Re-Imagining," 11.

93. de Senarclens, *Heirs of the Reformation*, 125–26.

94. While de Senarclens's view is surely right that God in God's great faithfulness and stead-fast love renews creation every morning with new mercies, the biblical passage that affirms this so eloquently also proclaims that those mercies "never come to an end" (Lamentations 3:22–23). Thus, the work of God abides. That God must daily create manna to sustain God's people does not mean God leaves them utterly famished already before dawn the next day. Still less does it mean that God *only* creates manna but nothing else. And if something of God's old Creation abides into each new day, surely God's New Creation in the church has some durability as well, or more.

95. "The Modern Recovery of the Anabaptist Vision" was part of a festschrift for Harold S. Bender, and thus more "polished" and scholarly than any of the *Concern* pamphlets. Heightening its importance is its placement as the climactic chapter of the volume. The whole book may well be the single most serious scholarly project that Concern Movement leaders ever took up (cf. Keim, *Harold S. Bender*, 450–51, 469–70), though they did so in collaboration with Guy F. Hershberger, the named editor. As an effort to honor and perhaps mend fences with Bender, Concern Group collaborators were surely paying attention to how they would communicate. Peachey's essay seems to be the place where, after more historical and less programmatic essays, Hershberger allowed or they allowed themselves the luxury of coming back into the present, "The Modern Recovery of the Anabaptist Vision," cashing in on the capital they had built up through all the previous chapters, and offering an apologia for Concern agenda. Though the essay certainly bears the stamp of Peachey's own theological tendencies, his role as spokesman can hardly have been accidental, much less self-appointed.

96. Peachey, "Modern Recovery of the Anabaptist Vision," 339. On the next and final page, Peachey summarized: "I would therefore propose that the genius of the Anabaptist vision lies not merely in the heroic act of men who dared to abandon the apostate *Volkskirche* culture inherited and developed by medieval Christendom, but above all in the reassertion of the fact that *the church is always truly the church in the living existential community*" (p. 340, emphasis

added at end). More work needs to be done on the influence of philosophical existentialism on the Concern Group and Movement. Existentialism was in its ascendancy in the postwar years, and young Mennonites in Europe were experiencing the climate that favored it most. One of the group's other teachers of Anabaptist history was Robert Friedmann, who would later argue explicitly that Anabaptist theology was existentialist; see Robert Friedmann, *The Theology of Anabaptism: An Interpretation*, Studies in Anabaptist and Mennonite History, no. 15 (Scottdale, Pa.: Herald Press, 1973) and note his enthusiastic support for the Concern Movement in "Epistolary," 9–10. And yet explicit references to existentialism, or hints that the Concern Group was reading existentialist writers is rare.

97. Peachey, "What Is Concern?" 17, 16.

98. Peachey did not even say here that Christ's presence is realized in the local church but in the *fellowship* of the local church. Peachey, "What Is Concern?" 16.

99. Peachey, "Spirit and Form in the Church," 15.

100. Ibid., 21.

101. After all, the prospect that the church's visible expression is not its reality seemed to imply that the church's reality is invisible after all. See Peachey, "Spirit and Form in the Church," 24–25.

102. Cf. Peachey, "Spirit and Form in the Church," 19, 24. One correspondent, Paul Verghese, who described himself as "a Catholic (not a Roman one) by conviction," noticed the issue right away; see "Epistolary," 11.

103. Peachey, "Spirit and Form in the Church," 24. The "confusion" here is one that Peachey associated with centuries of "Catholic dogma."

104. Peachey, "Modern Recovery of the Anabaptist Vision," 339. For an account of internal debates and frustration among those within the Concern Movement over how to realize their ideals, see Toews, "Concern Movement," 121–22. Also note the chapter on the Concern Group in Keim's biography of Harold S. Bender; in relation to Concern Group idealism, see the chapter's final paragraphs, which end with these sentences: "In the 1950s Harold Bender and John Howard Yoder embodied the dilemma, but left it unresolved. The dilemma lay in the limits of Christian perfection." Keim, *Harold S. Bender*, 450–71.

105. John Howard Yoder, "Christian Education: Doctrinal Orientation," prepared as beginning of conversation about Mennonite Church–administered high schools, historical mss. 1–48, section 1, box 02, unpublished writings 1947–1997, John H. Yoder Collection, Mennonite Church USA Archives, 1958, 2.

106. Ibid., 4.

107. Yoder, "Christian Education," 5. Given the importance of discipleship and ethics in the Anabaptist-Mennonite faith, of course, Yoder did immediately clarify: "We believe, and rightly, that our Christian life *involves* a very specific behavior pattern"; emphasis added. Note that Yoder's alternative formulation of what was "first" in the Christian faith was not a propositional or creedal "set of truths" either; "Christian Education," 5. Rather, it was "a personal relationship of fellowship and obedience with God in Christ through the Spirit (p. 6).

108. Yoder, "Christian Education," 5.

109. Douglas K. Harink, "For or Against the Nations: Yoder and Hauerwas, What's the Difference?" *Toronto Journal of Theology* 17, no. 1 (Spring 2001): 167–85; Joseph J. Kotva Jr., "For or Against the Nations? John Howard Yoder vs. Stanley Hauerwas on the Nature of Christian Politics," conference presentation, Society of Christian Ethics, Chicago, 2001; Craig A. Carter, *The Politics of the Cross: The Theology and Social Ethics of John Howard Yoder* (Grand Rapids: Brazos Press, 2001), 227–28 et passim; Paul Doerksen, "Share the House:

Yoder and Hauerwas among the Nations," in *A Mind Patient and Untamed: Assessing John Howard Yoder's Contributions to Theology, Ethics, and Peacemaking*, ed. Ben C. Ollenburger and Gayle Gerber Koontz (Telford, Pa.: Cascadia Publishing House, 2004), 187–204; Craig R. Hovey, "The Public Ethics of John Howard Yoder and Stanley Hauerwas: Difference or Disagreement," in *A Mind Patient and Untamed*, 205–20.

110. Yoder, *For the Nations*; Stanley Hauerwas, *Against the Nations: War and Survival in a Liberal Society* (Minneapolis: Winston Press, 1985).

111. On this latter point, cf. Yoder, "What Are Our Concerns?" 23–24, 29.

112. John H. Yoder, "The Ambivalence of the Appeal to the Fathers," in *Practiced in the Presence: Essays in Honor of T. Canby Jones*, ed. Neil Snarr and Daniel Smith-Christopher (Richmond, Ind.: Friends United Press, 1994), 248.

113. Perhaps this is what has drawn an accusation by Patrick Madigan (who identifies himself as a pacifist) that Yoder's thought verges on gnosticism. See Patrick Madigan, "Review of John Howard Yoder, *The Jewish-Christian Schism Revisited*," *Heythrop Journal* 47, no. 2 (April 2006): 301–2. While I find Madigan's critique overwrought, he may be identifying a vulnerability to which Yoder's students should attend.

114. Hauerwas, *Community of Character*, 2; Hauerwas, "Character, Narrative, and Growth in the Christian Life," in *Community of Character*, 150. Cf. Hauerwas, "The Moral Value of the Family," in *Community of Character*, 155–66; Hauerwas, "The Family: Theology and Ethical Reflections," in *Community of Character*, 167–74; and Hauerwas, "Abortion: Why the Arguments Fail," in *Community of Character*, 212–29.

115. Stanley Hauerwas, "Response," in *On Baptism: Mennonite-Catholic Theological Colloquium, 2001–2002*, ed. Gerald W. Schlabach, Bridgefolk Series (Kitchener, Ont.: Pandora Press, 2004), 101–3.

116. Stanley Hauerwas, "The Liturgical Shape of the Christian Life: Teaching Christian Ethics as Worship," in *In Good Company: The Church as Polis* (Notre Dame, Ind.: University of Notre Dame Press, 1995), 153–68; Stanley Hauerwas and Samuel Wells, "Christian Ethics as Informed Prayer," chap. 1 in *Blackwell Companion to Christian Ethics*, 3–12.

117. Hauerwas has not made this critique of Weber in print, though he has done so in personal conversation. However, his rejection of a divorce between charismatic and official authority is evident in "Clerical Character," in *Christian Existence Today*, 133–48; and "The Pastor as Prophet: Ethical Reflections on an Improbable Mission," in *Christian Existence Today*, 149–67. "Clerical Character" also makes clear his assent to sacramental and priestly understandings of ministerial office, wherein office is understood precisely as a carrier of charism or grace.

118. Hauerwas, "Whose Church? Which Future?" 73. Cf. Hauerwas, "What Could It Mean for the Church to be Christ's Body? A Question without a Clear Answer," in *In Good Company*, 19–31.

119. Stanley Hauerwas, "The Importance of Being Catholic: Unsolicited Advice from a Protestant Bystander," in *In Good Company: The Church as Polis*, 94. For Hauerwas on authority more generally, see "The Moral Authority of Scripture: The Politics and Ethics of Remembering," in *Community of Character*, 60–63. Also note his juxtaposition of John Paul II and John Howard Yoder as two of the greatest witnesses to Christian truth and practice in the late twentieth century, in *With the Grain of the Universe: The Church's Witness and Natural Theology*, Gifford Lectures delivered at the University of Saint Andrews in 2001 (Grand Rapids: Brazos Press, 2001), 216–31.

120. Emblematic of this is Hauerwas's juxtaposition of John Howard Yoder's account of practical reasoning or casuistry with that of Mennonite farmer Olin Teague in "Reconciling the Practice of Reason," 72–82.

121. Here and in the following sentence I allude to my own suggestion that Hauerwas "wants Catholics to be more Anabaptist, and Anabaptists to be more Catholic, and Protestants to be both." This formulation of Hauerwas' position is one that he has endorsed for "say[ing] what I have been trying to say better than how I have said it." See Stanley Hauerwas, "The Christian Difference: Or, Surviving Postmodernism," in *A Better Hope: Resources for a Church Confronting Capitalism, Democracy, and Postmodernity* (Grand Rapids: Brazos Press, 2000), 43–44, as well as Stanley Hauerwas, *After Christendom?* 2nd ed., with new preface by author (Nashville: Abingdon Press, 1999), 7–8.

The "Elective Affinity" between Liberal Theology and Liberal Politics

John P. Crossley Jr.

MAX WEBER FURNISHES THE ANALOGY ON WHICH THIS ESSAY IS BASED: "This-worldly Protestant asceticism . . . acted powerfully against the spontaneous enjoyment of possessions; it restricted consumption, especially of luxuries. On the other hand, it had the psychological effect of freeing the acquisition of goods from the inhibitions of traditionalistic ethics. It broke the bonds of the impulse of acquisition in that it not only legalized it, but . . . looked upon it as directly willed by God."[1]

The relationship between the Calvinistic Protestant asceticism of the seventeenth century and the rapidly developing capitalism of the same period is, according to Max Weber, neither directly causal nor merely correlative but is a relationship of "elective affinity" (*Wahlverwandschaft*). That is, inner-worldly asceticism influences and encourages capitalism, whereas capitalism in turn influences the continuing development of this-worldly ascetic Calvinism. In this essay, I explore whether there is a similar "elective affinity" between modern (post–late eighteenth century) liberal theology and modern (post–U.S. independence) politics.

Exactly what we mean by liberal theology and liberal politics is the subject of the first two sections of the essay. However, it may be helpful at the outset to encapsulate the essential elements of liberal theology and liberal politics that point to a symbiotic relationship between the two. The essential element in liberal theology is the awareness that all attempts to capture in language the "divine" or "holy" or "transcendent" that religious persons sense in their inmost being are human constructs and therefore subject to change as human perceptions change. Similarly, the essential element in liberal politics is the awareness that all political arrangements designed to meet the human need to protect freedom in a secure environment are also human constructs and subject to change as circumstances change.

Journal of the Society of Christian Ethics, 27, 2 (2007): 209–226

Liberal Theology

The author who triggered the idea for such an undertaking is Peter Berger in *The Sacred Canopy*, so I begin with a brief analysis of its principal passages relevant to our topic. According to Berger, human beings are inveterate world builders, and the key to understanding this process is the dialectical relationship between human being (subjective) and society (objective).[2] The "three moments, or steps" of the dialectical process are "externalization," "objectivation," and "internalization." Externalization is the human projection of some idea of reality onto the world. Objectivation,[3] or objectification, is the transformation of the projected idea into a "facticity" of its own that now confronts the projectionist with a reality external to her or him. Internalization is the reappropriation of the external reality into the subjective consciousness of the person. Thus, the dialectic is the reciprocal relation between the human subject and the "external" world.[4] The ideal aim, never achieved in practice, is symmetry between the subjective and objective worlds. In Berger's words, "If one imagines a totally socialized individual, each meaning objectively available in the social world would have its analogous meaning given subjectively within his own consciousness."[5]

World construction is not limited to this finite world but extends to the cosmos itself. Human beings in their search for meaning seek to infuse the whole of reality with an orderliness beyond what society can provide. As Berger puts it, "Religion implies that human order is projected into the totality of being. Put differently, religion is the audacious attempt to conceive of the entire universe as being humanly significant."[6] The same dialectic that informs world construction in general applies also to religion.[7] The impetus for religious legitimation grows out of the subjective search for ultimate meaning and results in the objective postulation of a "sacred reality," which in turn is internalized as the truth of ultimate reality. As with the case of world construction in general, Berger has no intention of saying that the projection of the sacred or the ultimate is a pure reflection of the practical interests from which it arises,[8] that is, that it is a figment of the needy imagination, as in Feuerbach, Marx, or Freud. Rather, externalization in the case of religion is a matter of naming or identifying the ultimate reality in such a way that it becomes possible to internalize it as an objective reality that meets human needs. Berger is clear about the needs that religion satisfies—the need to explain evil, for example, and the need to legitimate finite social structures. But he is not very clear, at least in *The Sacred Canopy*, about the origin of any actual sense of an ultimate reality in the subjective consciousness prior to the externalization of that reality. He needs something like Friedrich Schleiermacher's sense of the infinite, or Otto's *tremendum fascinosum*, lest he be interpreted as the pure projectionist he is not.[9]

We come now to the point in Berger's analysis of religion that gave me the idea for this essay. This point concerns the relationship between religion and alienation. The basic idea is this: The more reified the absolute reality that human beings externalize becomes, the more human beings become alienated from the fact that it was they who originally projected the absolute reality they now regard as ultimate. Thus, one cuts himself or herself off from the subjective origin of ultimate reality and becomes dependent on something entirely other from the very self that brought the ultimate reality into consciousness in the first place. The result is self-alienation—a split within consciousness between the self, which projects ultimate reality, and the ultimate reality, which is now internalized as something entirely different from the self.[10] Berger makes the point that the more powerful religion is in overcoming anomie[11] (the threat of meaninglessness), the more it alienates the individual from her or his own subjective consciousness. There is an inverse proportion between alienation and anomie: The more alienated the individual, the more anomie is overcome, and, conversely, the more religion is able to overcome anomie, the more it alienates the individual from the subjective origins of religious truth.[12]

This is, of course, a situation that cries out for resolution, and, according to Berger, at least a partial resolution is possible. Religion can become de-alienating insofar as it brings into view a transcendent standpoint from which all reality is relativized.[13] In Berger's words, "Finally, and paradoxically, the entire web of mystifications thrown over the social order may, in certain cases, be drastically removed from the latter—*by religious means*—leaving it to be apprehended again as nothing but a human artifice."[14] If the social order is exposed by radical transcendence to be without divine sanction, what about radical transcendence itself? Isn't radical transcendence also the result of subjective objectification and therefore itself relative to whoever does the projecting? The answer appears for Berger to be both yes and no. On the one hand, the radical transcendence objectified in the original projection exposes that projection itself to be a human artifact.[15] That is, the human origin of transcendental reality is reaffirmed by transcendental reality itself. On the other hand, "it is impossible within the frame of reference of scientific theorizing to make any affirmations, positive or negative, about the ultimate ontological status of this alleged reality."[16] What we can know empirically is that whereas religion appears in history primarily as a world-maintaining force, it can also appear, especially in certain strands of mysticism and in the biblical tradition, as a revolutionary, world-shaking force.[17] Thus, while there is no proof that there is an ultimate force beyond the human projection of such a force, the relativizing power in history of such an ultimate force suggests a reality beyond all human attempts to describe it completely.

The idea that the ultimately real (if any) is not knowable in itself is not, of course, an invention of Berger in particular or of the sociology of knowledge in general. Thomas Aquinas, for example, recognizes that humans cannot know God "in Godself," but only by analogy. He states, "Things known are in the mind of the knower according to the mode of the knower,"[18] implying that all knowledge is filtered through a subjective lens. Phillip Melanchthon's statement to the effect that we know God, not in Godself, but in God's benefits to us, moves along similar lines. Immanuel Kant's distinction between phenomenon (the appearance of a thing) and noumenon (the thing-in-itself) appropriates the same fundamental insight. In Kant, an intuition (a knowing) is a result of the confrontation between an object as it gives itself to be known, and a mind that brings to the encounter the categories of space, time, and causality, not to mention its own particular social-situatedness. Thus, what is known is never the thing-in-itself, but the appearance of the thing as it is projected by the subjective mind.

In contemporary theology, one could cite the work of Gordon Kaufman in *The Theological Imagination* as a Protestant, theological application of Kantian epistemology. Kaufman understands Christian beliefs or doctrines not as timeless truths but as products of the human imagination and thus subject to revision as necessary.[19] In Catholic theology, David Tracy in *The Analogical Imagination* carries forward Aquinas's concept of analogy to explore newly meaningful ways to conceptualize God.[20] Thus, Berger's sociological theory of knowledge, and of religion in particular, has numerous antecedents in both theology and philosophy. What is new in Berger is the tying of his theory of alienation to his theory of religious epistemology. This connection maintains that the more ultimate reality or God is seen as an entity wholly other from the self that projected it as ultimate reality, the more the self is alienated from its own subjectivity. This alienation can be overcome nonreligiously simply by regarding the projection of ultimate reality as illusory. Whether one regards the illusion of ultimate reality or God as dangerous (Marx, Freud, secular existentialism) or as necessary for survival or flourishing (Feuerbach, Dostoyevsky's Grand Inquisitor) is irrelevant to the reintegration of the alienated self. Atheism of any stripe will do. As we have seen, however, alienation can also be overcome religiously, although Berger sees this as a rare occurrence in history.[21] For the self to overcome alienation religiously, ultimate reality or God must be perceived as radically transcendent, that is, as beyond human power to grasp conceptually. Any conceptualizations of such an ultimate reality or God must be understood as human projections. Thus, the subjective basis of religion is not obscured, as it is in alienation, but is openly acknowledged. That religious, unalienated human beings continue to believe in human perceptions of ultimate reality or God is, in my judgment, the very essence of liberal theology.

There are many aspects of liberal theology—a basic optimism with respect to human nature, respect for experience and reason, openness to culture and other religious traditions, flexibility in interpreting the texts and practices of its tradition, a positive attitude toward science, and so on—but the essence of liberal theology is the recognition that beliefs and doctrines are products of the human imagination, albeit a pious human imagination.[22] This recognition has given rise to much speculation about what it is in the human psyche that drives it to religious expression and practice, the most famous of which in the history of Protestant Christian thought is probably Schleiermacher's "intuition of the infinite,"[23] later expressed as "the feeling of absolute dependence."[24] It is quite proper that Schleiermacher should be known as the father of modern liberal theology, for he recognized that "the infinite" or God is in the first instance the "whence" of the feeling of absolute dependence and that consciousness of God has as its basis the consciousness of being absolutely dependent.[25] All doctrines or beliefs are at root expressions of the consciousness of being absolutely dependent. In the Christian tradition, the consciousness of being absolutely dependent is modified by the redemption wrought in Jesus of Nazareth.

There are starting points for religious projection other than that of Schleiermacher, of course. In the philosophical tradition, there is, for example, Kant's transcendental attempt to find an ultimate grounding for the ethical imperative. He projected God as a necessary postulate of practical reason and the categorical imperative. His *Religion within the Limits of Reason Alone* can easily be read as an ethical theology in which all beliefs and doctrines are under the control of the ethical imperative. There is also Georg Hegel's attempt to ground all thought in Absolute Spirit. From the sociological perspective, there is Émile Durkheim's search for security, in which gods (symbolized as totems) are projected to maintain the security of the society. Ultimately in Durkheim, the only "god" is society itself, so his is a purely immanent religion. And there are many other possibilities. I personally find Schleiermacher's idea of "a sense and taste for the infinite" to be the most compelling candidate for the religious impulse, as it appears both to be compatible with religious experience and capable of absorbing other starting points within itself.

To summarize, liberal theology is identifiable by two fundamental characteristics. The first is recognition of an innate human quest for the transcendent, that is, a quest for the source of human flourishing, a quest that goes beyond (but may include) the quest for security. There must be an indefeasible "something" in the human psyche that drives toward the source; otherwise, religion would be only a tool to attain security. The second is recognition that all conceptualizations of the transcendent or the source are human artifacts projected onto a cosmic screen and are subject to all the same biological and social influences and limitations characteristic of any human quest. The portraits human beings paint of their gods are no better (and no worse!) than the portraits they paint of anything that arouses their deepest feelings. Theologies that do not recognize that religion is grounded in a human impulse, or that do not allow that beliefs and doctrines are human creations, are alienating; that is, they so distance human beings from themselves that such theologies are incapable of relating the self to the transcendent.

Conversely, theologies that preserve the connection between human subjectivity and theological affirmations probably lose a little of religion's ability to overcome anomie. The price of preserving the subjective affirmation of theological truths, and thereby overcoming alienation, is a degree of objective uncertainty about theological truths, thereby necessitating living with a degree of anomie. Theologies that acknowledge a fundamental human religious impulse, and recognize that beliefs and doctrines are products of the human imagination—in other words, liberal theologies—are not thereby automatically "good" theologies, in the sense that they effectively convey the divine to the human. That remains, as with all things human, a matter of skill, tenacity, and good-heartedness to be proved.

Liberal Politics

Our task in this section is to see if there is anything in liberal politics that is analogous to our characterization of liberal theology, that is, if there is both an essence of liberal politics and an ability on the part of liberal politics to avoid alienation. To get our bearings, I turn to Franklin I. Gamwell's latest book, *Politics as a Christian Vocation: Faith and Democracy Today.*[26] Because Gamwell is a Christian theologian as well as a political analyst, we can also make use of his theological concepts to test Berger's theory of the social construction of beliefs and doctrines. Gamwell's project is not the same as mine, but there are some overlaps, and we can utilize a number of his definitions without our having to start from scratch.

Gamwell's principal concern is to contrast the Christian vision for society with the visions offered by what he calls "liberalism" and "conservatism," respectively, and to urge that a major aspect of a Christian's vocation is to attempt to implement the Christian vision politically. He sets the stage for this contrast by defining what he regards to be the fundamental basis of Christianity, on the one hand, and the fundamental basis of politics, on the other hand. To take the latter first, the fundamental basis of politics is what he calls the "humanistic commitment" or the "way of reason." At its core is the desire of people to rule themselves ("sovereignty of the people" or "government by the people"), subject only to the rule of reason in open argumentation. The humanistic commitment was suppressed for centuries by monarchical rule and became a live possibility during the Enlightenment of the eighteenth century. Gamwell defines the humanistic commitment as follows: "Our understandings of reality and ourselves can be validated or redeemed only through reasons authorized finally by our common human experience. If government by the people must be constituted as a full and free discourse, popular sovereignty is, we may say, the political form of this humanistic commitment."[27] Though Gamwell is not as interested as I am in trying to pinpoint the essence of the human impulse to self-rule, I infer that he regards the humanistic commitment to be the result of an indefeasible movement of the human spirit toward freedom. Thus, the democracy he advocates is driven by the innate quest for freedom.

From the perspective of his theology, Gamwell's summary definition of the essence of Christian faith, I argue, serves his liberal politics: "All worth or importance has its ultimate ground in the God whom Jesus Christ reveals as all-embracing love, and thus humans are called to unreserved commitment to or love for this God."[28]

Unreserved commitment to this God results in the creation of a "community of love."[29] The community of love is not the Christian community but the entire human community, of which the church is one part. The community of love is at the same time a community of justice. Gamwell rejects John Rawls's definition of justice because it is based on principles to which all must agree in advance; rather, for Gamwell, justice is always open to free discussion.[30] It should be clear that Gamwell is not interested in imposing a "Christian" view of community on the world; rather, he believes that Christians have the same rights and responsibilities as everyone else to bring forward their views of what constitutes a human community of love in a continuing, open dialogue.

It should now be apparent that Gamwell believes that "Christian faith prescribes democracy."[31] He spends many pages arguing this point in detail, but the bottom line is that the "community of love" that comes into view through Christian faith is the foundation of the "humanistic commitment" to which every human being feels drawn.[32] Thus, Christian faith is not only compatible with "the way of reason," Christian faith is the ground of the way of reason, whose political expression is democracy.[33] The Christian's public vocation is to bring to political reality through the democratic process the universal ideal of the community of love.

Gamwell sees this ideal threatened in the modern West by two distortions of community. One he calls the "liberal" ideal of community, the other, the "conservative" ideal of community.[34] The liberal ideal is freedom in the service of self-interest, especially economic self-interest. Community is merely instrumental to the freedom of the individual to pursue "success." Gamwell further divides the liberal ideal into what he calls "libertarian" liberalism and "welfare" liberalism.[35] Libertarian liberals believe that the pursuit of self-interest should be free from government interference, whereas welfare liberals believe that the government has a role to play in distributing wealth relatively equitably. Libertarian liberals and welfare liberals make common cause, however, in that both are interested in the acquisition of wealth to serve private interests. The conservative ideal, conversely, "is not focused on private interests but, rather, on cultivating and exhibiting private virtue."[36] Conservatism stresses "traditional values," which often means rigidifying codes of an earlier time, which, in turn, tends to stigmatize legitimate diversity, and often appears as racist or sexist. What liberalism of both stripes and conservatism have in common is an emphasis on *private*, whether this is construed as private self-interest, or the private cultivation of virtue. The emphasis on private enterprise, whether profit motivated or virtue oriented, is directly opposed both by the Christian ideal of a community of love, and the political ideal of the humanist commitment. Thus, "liberalism" and "conservatism" are distortions of the ideal of community, lead to alienation (to be discussed below), and need to be challenged by both Christian and political communitarians in the open marketplace of ideas that is central to Gamwell's program.

It is not my purpose to offer a full evaluation of Gamwell's overall argument but to make use of aspects of his analyses for purposes of determining whether there is an elective affinity between liberal theology and liberal politics. The most valuable aspect of his argument for our purposes is his analysis of what he calls the humanistic commitment or the way of reason. This analysis both assumes and develops a fundamental human aspiration for the freedom to govern one's own life under the rule of reason. I see this impulse toward freedom in the political realm as analogous to the impulse toward the infinite in the religious realm. In Schleiermacher's terms, the first impulse stems from a feeling of freedom; the second, from a feeling of dependence.[37] In Schleiermacher, the two are closely connected: no feeling of freedom without a feeling of dependence; no feeling of dependence without a feeling of freedom. For Schleiermacher, the feeling of dependence is prior to any feeling of freedom in such a way that one can speak of a feeling of absolute dependence but never of a feeling of absolute freedom. Gamwell's discussion of the priority of the Christian concept of the community of love over the political concept of the humanistic community parallels this strikingly, but I would not want to push the analogy too far in light of his dismissal of Schleiermacher's theology in general.

As for Gamwell's theology, because theological analysis and development are not central to his argument in this book, one simply has to piece together his basic theological position as best as one can. He does not discuss biblical authority, the Trinity, Christology, or many other doctrines central to Christian theology, so we have no way of knowing *for certain* whether his theology is liberal in the sense of regarding major beliefs and doctrines as human constructions and subject to modification or conservative in the sense that traditional beliefs and doctrines are true and permanent. I emphasize *for certain* because even though he does not open up his full theology for discussion, I feel comfortable interpreting his theology as liberal in the following ways. What we know is that his main theological emphases are on the love of God for all human beings as this love is manifested in Jesus Christ, and on the community of love that God's love for all human beings creates. We also know that his theology has a strong rationalistic bent along the following lines: "Perhaps Christian belief in God can also be fully validated by the way of reason. . . . We can offer reasons authorized by common human experience through which to warrant belief in this God. The argument proceeds from our nature as creatures who live with understanding and, therefore, decide in each present moment by evaluating as better or worse the alternatives for purpose given to us."[38]

The rational conclusion to be drawn from this line of argument is that Christian faith, with its emphasis on universal divine love and divinely ordained community, is in line with the kind of community for which the human spirit longs. In other words, though Gamwell does not focus any attention on the issue of whether his version of Christianity is an absolute given or is humanly constructed, what evidence there is suggests that it is humanly constructed. That is, he has *constructed* a version of Christianity that emphasizes its basic rationality and its core ideal of a universal community of love. Its "basic rationality" means that Christianity is always modifiable, or re-constructible, by reason.[39] Its core ideal of "a universal community of love" is intended to establish a standard of community that transcends, relativizes, and possibly criticizes all other concepts of community.[40]

I do not want to say that what Gamwell has done is exactly parallel to Berger's self-conscious construction of a religion of transcendence that relativizes all human attempts to capture transcendent reality completely in beliefs and doctrines, but I would conclude that both are on the same wavelength. Gamwell is not especially interested, in this book, at least, in exploring what it is that is at the core of the religious impulse. Because what that impulse leads to, however, is a rational religion and a perfect community, one could infer that his interests parallel Hegel's, or perhaps Alfred North Whitehead's (which he mentions frequently), and that the religious search is for ultimate meaning in the consummate community. Gamwell seems completely aware that political arrangements are human constructs and that their subjective origin lies in the human quest for freedom. Thus, all human political constructions are valid insofar as they facilitate self-rule, and they can never be legitimated by age, tradition, or any factor other than the humanistic commitment by way of reason.

There is one further point in Gamwell's project that can help us with our own. I suggest that his treatment of "liberalism," with its emphasis on private self-interest, and his treatment of "conservatism," with its interest on private virtue, can both be construed as examples of self-alienation in Berger's sense. "Liberalism" makes something that is surely a human construct, namely, the pursuit of profit, into an absolute ideal of community that contrasts both with the transcendent idea of community depicted in Christian faith and the humanistic commitment embedded in reason itself. This transcendent idea of community on the theological side, and humanistic commitment on the political side, also relativize and criticize "conservatism's" often piously enunciated emphasis on selected personal "moral" values. "Liberals" and "conservatives" would probably not consider themselves alienated in Berger's sense, but that is just the point. Self-interest for one group and personal morality for the other are so reified as external realities that internalizing them seems perfectly "natural," as though they were built into the structure of the universe. Because everything putatively built into the structure of the universe is actually a human projection, however, according to Berger, the person who does not recognize this is self-alienated.

It appears that there is indeed an elective affinity between liberal theology and liberal politics. Liberal theology is liberal essentially in that it keeps alive the connection between the subjective basis of theological beliefs and doctrines, and liberal politics is liberal in that it recognizes the essentially human basis of political arrangements. A liberal theologian would find it inconceivable to accept any political arrangement as absolute when no set of theological beliefs or doctrines themselves could be conceived as absolute, and a liberal politician could not possibly embrace a theology that considered itself capable of dictating an unchangeable set of beliefs and doctrines to the political community. Furthermore, because liberal theology understands its sense of ultimate reality to be expressible only in socially constructed terms, it is open to influence from the political dimension of life. Conversely, liberal politics, bent on making political arrangements that will enhance human freedom, is open to influence from theology, especially theology that offers a grounding for the freedom-in-community that liberal political theorists seek to realize in practice. Now it remains to be seen if such a theory of elective affinity between liberal theology and liberal politics is applicable in the work of other scholars who treat the relation between theology and politics.

Applications

Among the many theologians interested in politics from whom we could choose, I here select just three for a brief analysis of how they understand the relation between theology and politics. I have singled out these three because the positions they advocate exert considerable influence in the field. The three are Kathryn Tanner, professor of theology at the University of Chicago Divinity School; Stanley Hauerwas, professor of theology and ethics at Duke University Divinity School; and Jeffrey Stout, professor of ethics at Princeton University.

Kathryn Tanner

In her book *The Politics of God: Christian Theologies and Social Justice*,[41] which she published while she was still at Yale University Divinity School, Kathryn Tanner places herself in a long line of more-or-less orthodox Protestant Christian theologians—extending from the Puritans of the eighteenth century, through the Social Gospelers of the nineteenth century, through Reinhold Niebuhr and Karl Barth in the twentieth century, to the time of her own writing—who have found in Christian faith powerful resources for progressive social criticism. I say "more-or-less orthodox Christian theologians" because from the outset and throughout her book, she is critical of theologians who think that Christianity must revise its classic doctrines and accommodate them to a modern humanistic ethic to address the problems of contemporary societies. At first blush, this would seem to make her a less than ideal candidate for an elective affinity between liberal theology and liberal politics. As it turns out, however, she is indeed an ideal candidate.

While eschewing theological revisionism in order to make theology relevant to the sociopolitical order, she achieves a similar result by *choosing* which among the many Christian doctrines available she deems best applicable to the sociopolitical problems she thinks are the most serious. Most frequently, in order to make her criticisms, she calls on the doctrines of God's transcendence and providence. In her words, "The primary beliefs I recommend are, first, a belief in God's transcendence and, second, what I call a belief in God's universal providential agency. These are the Christian beliefs that I select for their progressive political potentials from among those that concern either God's nature or God's relation to the world."[42] Transcendence is primary, and providence as she utilizes it is broad enough to include the Christian belief in redemption. If one adds a well-worked-out doctrine of sin to this mix of beliefs, that addition pretty well covers the Christian "orthodoxy" that Tanner draws on to make her criticisms.

I want to draw attention, first, to her concept of choice in theology, and, second, to her choice of God's transcendence as the key doctrine to be utilized in sociopolitical criticism. "Choice" fits well into Berger's contention that the human factor cannot be omitted from theological construction without self-alienation, and it also signals that Tanner is doing more "theological construction" than she cares to admit. That is, anyone who feels free to pick and choose among the whole panoply of available doctrines, on the basis of a perceived worldly need, is pretty much in control of the theological material. As Rebecca Chopp puts it in the frontispiece to Tanner's book, "Tanner offers a *reconstruction* of Christian tradition as a prophetic challenge to the political status quo."[43]

Her choice of the transcendence of God as the primary doctrine utilizable in sociopolitical criticism[44] is a good example of the de-alienating power of "the radical transcendentalization of God in Biblical religion" of which Berger speaks.[45] Her theology may be orthodox in its essential elements, but as a sociocritical tool in her hands, her doctrine of the transcendence of God makes use of a "concept" of God that is beyond human capability to conceptualize. In other words, she bypasses all doctrines of God but one, namely, the doctrine of transcendence, which, as we have seen, is tantamount to admitting to the human inability to capture in doctrinal form the nature of God. At the same time, the doctrine of the transcendence of God is useful in sociopolitical criticism, especially in exploding any myths of divine sanction for humanly constructed injustices.

Sin, in Tanner's view, manifests itself in society in innumerable ways, but the forms of sin in which she is particularly interested are (1) those that attempt to preserve injustices by situating them in putatively divinely sanctioned "orders of creation";[46] (2) those that attempt to justify hierarchical models of human community, whether in politics or social and family relations, on the basis of God's presumed lordship over the world (a knotty but resolvable problem for advocates of divine transcendence);[47] and (3) those that disrespect differences among human beings.[48] She says nothing explicit about a Christian (or even merely human) justification for liberal democracy itself but simply assumes it, and she saves her Christian applications for violations of democratic freedom and equality. That she thinks her chosen Christian beliefs support her progressive politics is further testimony to the elective affinity between liberal theology and liberal politics, and proves that one does not have to be an avowed theological liberal to demonstrate such an elective affinity.

Stanley Hauerwas

Stanley Hauerwas, probably the most prolific and influential (at least in U.S. theological seminaries) theologian of the past thirty years, has written so much over such a long period of time that it is extremely risky to try to capture the essence of his thought on the relation between theology and the sociopolitical world in a short space. Nevertheless, precisely because of his outsized body of work and influence, we must try. From the beginning, he has sought to undermine the church's connection with democratic politics, primarily on the grounds that the church has lost its own soul by trying to make itself safe in a society defined by liberal democracy. Thus, the very words that are sacred in a liberal democratic society—"liberal," "democracy," "freedom," "social justice," and so on—are anathema to him, and the church must rediscover its own essential "community of character" and pay no further attention to liberal democratic society. These ideas were spelled out at least as early as 1981 in *A Community of Character: Toward a Constructive Christian Social Ethic*,[49] and more fully in 1983 in *The Peaceable Kingdom: A Primer in Christian Ethics*.[50] The basic ideas were already expressed in rudimentary form in his several books of the 1970s.[51]

Hauerwas's own theology is an attempt to recover a "true" "community of character," namely, the Christian community, which Christians should seek to perfect, as opposed to seeking "justice" in the larger society. The best contribution the church can make to the world is to model true community, and if it can do this, the world may sit up and take notice. Meanwhile, Christians are "resident aliens" (the title of one of his books) in the world and are to keep themselves uncorrupted from the world. He was heavily influenced by his colleague at Notre Dame, John Howard Yoder, and eventually bought into the latter's pacifism. Pacifism has become a cornerstone of Hauerwas's concept of true Christian community. The concept of "just war," therefore, is completely unchristian, and theologians who engage in speculation about just war reveal themselves to be apologists for liberal secular society, not Christian thinkers.

In spite of the fact that much of what Hauerwas has been saying for the last several years about the relation between church and world sounds sectarian, he strongly resists the designation,[52] but he does so without backing off from his criticism of liberal democratic society. The implication seems to be that his interest in liberal democratic society and the threat it poses to invade the Christian community cannot by definition be sectarian, because a true sectarian would not be interested in such a threat.

In terms of our interest in the elective affinity between liberal theology and liberal politics, it would be tempting to say that Hauerwas proves the point backhandedly by demonstrating an elective affinity between antiliberal theology and antiliberal politics. This is too simple a solution, however, for he is actually a liberal theologian according to Berger's theory of social construction. There is nothing orthodox, for example, about Hauerwas's pacifism; orthodoxy embraces just war theory. And there is nothing orthodox about his theory of Christian avoidance of political involvement; Calvin's *Institutes* IV, 20, proves that. His theology is actually quite innovative—quite socially constructed, as Berger would say. One gets no sense in reading Hauerwas that he is overwhelmed by revealed doctrines he can do naught but repeat. The sense is rather that he is constructing a theology that is as far removed as possible from the liberal political democracy he resents. His theological emphasis on the development of a sincere Christian community actually cries out for application to the sociopolitical world, much in the mode of Tanner or Karl Barth.

Barth is the theologian whom Hauerwas exalts in his recent Gifford Lectures, *With the Grain of the Universe*,[53] over William James and Reinhold Niebuhr, both of whom are regarded by Hauerwas as not finally really religious or Christian, respectively, but as liberal humanists in religious guise. If one grants Hauerwas's somewhat graceless comparison, the next question is: Why does he not also honor Barth's commitment to socialism or at least to a progressive social program? We have to conclude that Hauerwas's liberal theology should result in a commitment to liberal political ideals, and the fact that it does not must be attributed to his fear of the liberal political ideal itself and consequent resentment of it, unrelated to the actual content of his theology.

One way to explain the apparent disconnect between Hauerwas's liberal theology and his disinterest in liberal politics is by means of the manner in which he relates the church to the Kingdom of God. Ninety years ago in his *A Theology for the Social Gospel*, Walter Rauschenbusch called attention to the extreme neglect in theology of the Kingdom of God in favor of a focus on the church and of the dire consequences that flow from this shift away from the heart of the preaching of Jesus.[54] For Rauschenbusch, the Kingdom of God is coextensive with the world, and the church exists for the sake of the Kingdom of God, not vice versa.[55] As theology became preoccupied with the church instead of the Gospel in the world, "the movements for democracy and social justice were left without a religious backing for lack of the Kingdom idea."[56]

Hauerwas has certainly been a leader in our time in focusing the attention of theology on the church, and, I would say, in collapsing the Kingdom of God into it. It is not my intention in this essay, however, to mount either an analysis or critique of Hauerwas's theology of the church and the Kingdom of God but only to try to explain his indifference, and even hostility, toward liberal democratic politics when his liberal theology would appear to demand his embrace of liberal political ideals. It may be that Hauerwas, in focusing so intensely on the church, believes that in so doing he is focusing on the Kingdom of God and that the church's faithfulness to the Gospel will eventually spread to the world. If so, it may also be that his failure to connect his liberal theology with liberal political ideals is temporary. That is, the tension between church and world to which he repeatedly draws attention may be an impermanent tension, destined to free up as he connects his theology of the church more broadly with his theology of the Kingdom. In terms of the putative elective affinity between liberal theology and liberal politics, I would say that while the jury is still out on Hauerwas, the theoretical structure for an eventual wedding is in place.

Jeffrey Stout

The aim of Jeffrey Stout's newest book, *Democracy and Tradition*,[57] is completely different from the usual aim of trying to apply a particular kind of theology to sociopolitical issues. Stout is not a theologian but a pragmatic political philosopher. His commitment is to democratic politics, and his principal belief with regard to theology is that if it is too "traditional" ("tradition" is a euphemism for theology in his book), it either seeks to dominate political thought or to opt out of it and leave it to its own devices. (MacIntyre and Hauerwas, incidentally, represent, respectively, a philosophy and a theology that try to do both).[58] Stout is optimistic that theologians can be constructive participants in the democratic process he cherishes—but only if they drop their pretensions to know in advance where the democratic process should go or come down from their disengagement with discussions with ordinary citizens and genuinely open themselves up to the terms of the discussion. Stout is a thoroughgoing pragmatist who sees no need for any highfalutin theological (or philosophical) justification for ethics,[59] although he welcomes the rhetorical flourish of, say, a Martin Luther King Jr., who utilizes theological commitments to serve pragmatic ends.

In terms of an elective affinity between liberal theology and liberal politics, Stout would affirm it—but only on the grounds that theology is purely and simply a human construct and not without doubt pointed toward ultimate reality. That is, theological constructs represent the constructors' deepest convictions, not necessarily the divine. There is simply no need, in Stout's estimation, for the intrusion of any version of "ultimate reality" into the pragmatic discussion of adjudicating differences in the public square. Theologians are welcome, but only if they are willing to participate on equal terms with all other participants. They may and should introduce their theological commitments into the discussion, but such commitments cannot be introduced as discussion stoppers; they are, rather, legitimate opinions. Stout's real commitment is to participatory democracy, and the value of theology for him is directly proportional to its ability to enrich the discussion and inversely proportional to its tendency to wreck it. There is certainly no doubt in his mind that theology, à la Berger, is a human projection.

So, for that matter, is democracy. In one of the most interesting chapters in the book, Stout delineates the rise of modern democracy from its antitraditional beginnings in the eighteenth century to its becoming an "anti-traditional tradition" in its own right.[60] It is not as though democracy came into being in service of something outside itself—theological tradition, for example, as in some theologians, or the quest for freedom, as in Gamwell—but that democracy is its own origin and aim. That is, human community thrives on the democratic process itself, and democracy is not a means to something else but an end in itself. All human enterprises are evaluated according to their ability to serve the democratic process. In other words, the construction of democratic arrangements and all discussion within those arrangements are human constructs, but democracy itself seems in Stout to have some sort of primordial significance that "calls" human beings to its service. Analogous to Gamwell's drive for freedom or Schleiermacher's sense and taste for the infinite, the pull of democracy is universal. Even theologians must hear the call and bring their respective theologies to the table. Insofar as they are willing to subject their theologies to criticism in open discussion, they are liberals, and insofar as they contribute to the democratic process, there is an elective affinity between liberal theology and liberal politics.

Conclusion

The point of bringing theologians as different as Tanner and Hauerwas together with political philosopher Stout is to demonstrate that the elective affinity between liberal theology and liberal politics occurs in radically different contexts. Stout, for example, working in the context of pragmatic democratic politics, sees a place for theology in the political process—but only if it is liberal theology. Tanner, concerned to demonstrate the potential for certain Christian beliefs to have an impact on the political sphere, reconstructs theology to put its best foot forward and assumes the flexibility of democratic politics to be affected by this encounter. Hauerwas, in what I think of as his "political theology in progress," points his theology toward the purification of the church but with an eye beyond it on the church's potential to influence the sociopolitical realm. It appears that once a theologian becomes aware that the religious impetus expresses itself in socially constructed forms that are flexible and subject to revision, he or she can never embrace a politics that regards itself as absolute but will instead seek a politics that recognizes that the essential political drive for freedom and democracy constructs its own structures that are also flexible and subject to revision. Conversely, it appears that the only type of theology a liberal political theorist can welcome into the political discussion is a theology free from absolutism. I am hard-pressed to think of a circumstance in which the affinity does not hold, and I welcome readers' judgments about this.

Notes

1. Max Weber, *The Protestant Ethic and the Spirit of Capitalism*, trans. Talcott Parsons (New York: Charles Scribner's Sons, 1958; orig. pub. 1930), 170–71.

2. Peter Berger, *The Sacred Canopy: Elements of a Sociological Theory of Religion* (Garden City, N.Y.: Doubleday, 1967), 3–5.

3. Most analysts of Berger's work substitute "objectification" for "objectivation," because the latter appears to be an unnecessary neologism. Other words that would convey the same or a similar meaning are "reification" or "hypostatization."

4. Philosophically, Berger is not a subjective idealist or immaterialist. His interest is not in questioning the givenness of the objective world but in understanding how it is named and appropriated.

5. Berger, *Sacred Canopy*, 15.

6. Ibid., 28.

7. Ibid., 47.

8. Ibid., 41.

9. He has made this clearer in his books, *A Rumor of Angels: Modern Society and the Rediscovery of the Supernatural* (Garden City, N.Y.: Doubleday, 1969), and *The Heretical Imperative: Contemporary Possibilities of Religious Affirmation* (Garden City, N.Y.: Doubleday, 1979). In the latter, he writes: "The gods are indeed symbols of human realities. This insight, important as it is, does not necessarily imply that the gods are nothing but that. Religious experience insists that, over and beyond their capacity to become symbols, the gods inhabit a reality that is sui generis and that is sovereignly independent of what human beings project

into it" (p. 123). This awareness undoubtedly reflects Berger's appreciation of Schleiermacher, who has star billing in *The Heretical Imperative.*

10. Berger, *Sacred Canopy*, 81–87.

11. Berger spells it "anomy."

12. Berger, *Sacred Canopy*, 87.

13. Ibid., 96.

14. Ibid., 99.

15. Ibid., 100.

16. Ibid.

17. Ibid., 99–100.

18. Thomas Aquinas, *Summa theologiae*, II-II, Q. 1, "Faith," art. 2. "Dicendum quod cognita sunt in cognoscente secundum modum cognoscentis."

19. Gordon D. Kaufman, *The Theological Imagination: Constructing the Concept of God* (Philadelphia: Westminster Press, 1981), 21–24. See also his *An Essay on Theological Method* (Missoula, Mont.: Scholars Press, 1975), 28, 33–34.

20. David Tracy, *The Analogical Imagination: Christian Theology and the Culture of Pluralism* (New York: Crossroad, 1981), 405 ff.

21. Berger, *Sacred Canopy*, 96.

22. For fuller descriptions of liberal theology, see the articles by John P. Crossley Jr., "Liberalism," and Jeff B. Pool, "Liberal Theology," in *New and Enlarged Handbook of Christian Theology*, ed. Donald W. Musser and Joseph L. Price (Nashville: Abingdon Press, 2003), 294–97, 297–99.

23. Friedrich Schleiermacher, *On Religion: Speeches to Its Cultured Despisers*, trans. and ed. Richard Crouter (Cambridge: Cambridge University Press, 1988; orig. pub. 1799), 24.

24. Friedrich Schleiermacher, *The Christian Faith*, 2nd edition, ed. H. R. Mackintosh and J. S. Stewart (Edinburgh: T. & T. Clark, 1928; orig. pub. 1830), par. 4, art. 3, 16.

25. Schleiermacher, *Christian Faith*, par. 4, art. 4, 16–17.

26. Franklin I. Gamwell, *Politics as a Christian Vocation: Faith and Democracy Today* (Cambridge: Cambridge University Press).

27. Ibid., 49.

28. Ibid., 36.

29. Ibid., 82.

30. Ibid., 41. Later on in the book, Gamwell acknowledges his considerable debt to Rawls for his articulation of the "difference principle," 92 fn.

31. Ibid., 80. See also 106.

32. Ibid., 105.

33. Gamwell argues for the ultimate reasonableness of Christian faith against theologians such as Schleiermacher and Tillich, who think faith is something beyond reason. He appears to believe that Christian faith has to be justifiable rationally in order to anchor democracy (p. 105).

34. Gamwell, *Politics as a Christian Vocation*, 117.

35. Ibid., 118.

36. Ibid., 120.

37. Schleiermacher, *Christian Faith*, par. 4, art. 2, 13–15.

38. Gamwell, *Politics as a Christian Vocation*, 104.

39. Ibid., 104–5.

40. Ibid.

41. Kathryn Tanner, *The Politics of God: Christian Theologies and Social Justice* (Minneapolis: Fortress Press, 1992).

42. Ibid., 31.

43. Ibid., I; emphasis mine.

44. Ibid., 66–69.

45. Berger, *Sacred Canopy*, 99.

46. Tanner, *Politics of God*, 81–85.

47. Ibid., 145–56.

48. Ibid., 195–205.

49. Stanley Hauerwas, *A Community of Character: Toward a Constructive Christian Social Ethic* (Notre Dame, Ind.: University of Notre Dame Press, 1981).

50. Stanley Hauerwas, *The Peaceable Kingdom: A Primer in Christian Ethics* (Notre Dame, Ind.: University of Notre Dame Press, 1983).

51. Hauerwas's antiliberal rhetoric seems to have stepped up a notch following his association with antiliberal philosopher Alasdair MacIntyre, whose influential book, *After Virtue: A Study in Moral Theory* (Notre Dame, Ind.: University of Notre Dame Press, 1981), appeared in 1981.

52. Stanley Hauerwas, *Christian Existence Today: Essays on Church, World and Living in Between* (Durham, N.C.: Labyrinth Press, 1988), especially the first essay, in which he gives examples of how Christians can legitimately involve themselves in the world outside the church.

53. Stanley Hauerwas, *With the Grain of the Universe: The Church's Witness and Natural Theology*, The Gifford Lectures of 2001 (Grand Rapids: Brazos Press, 2001).

54. Walter Rauschenbusch, *A Theology for the Social Gospel* (Eugene, Ore.: Wipf & Stock, 1996; orig. pub. 1917), chap. 13.

55. Ibid., 143.

56. Ibid., 136.

57. Jeffrey Stout, *Democracy and Tradition* (Princeton, N.J.: Princeton University Press, 2004).

58. Ibid., chaps. 5 and 6.

59. Ibid., chap. 11.

60. Ibid., chap. 9.

John Locke's America: The Character of Liberal Democracy and Jeffrey Stout's Debate with the Christian Traditionalists

John Perry

RECENT STUDIES OF CHRISTIANITY'S RELATION TO LIBERAL POLITICS HAVE recognized the importance of specifying clearly what type of liberalism is being considered. Jeffrey Stout's critique is one such example. Unfortunately, Stout fails to engage the one thinker who arguably is the most influential in how Americans relate Christianity and politics: John Locke. Political arguments of today's Christians are premised, often unconsciously, on rival interpretations of Locke's political theology.

The subject of this essay is contemporary American political theology. But its main figure is not contemporary, not American, and—depending on whom you ask—not even a theologian. He was, rather, an English philosopher. But he is nonetheless relevant to the subject of contemporary political theology. Indeed, as Nicholas Wolterstorff puts it, he is indispensable to understanding "how we got to where we are in our thinking."[1] This English philosopher is, of course, John Locke.

If the subject of the essay is political theology in the United States, why is Locke its main figure? The reasons are complex but can best be explained by reference to one of the most prominent recent debates on the topic: the exchanges between writers such as Hauerwas, MacIntyre, Cavanaugh, Milbank, and Stout about the relation of Christianity to Western liberal democracy. Jeffrey Stout identifies such writers as Christian Traditionalists for their thoroughgoing critiques of democratic liberalism.

In the case, *Stout v. Traditionalists*, both parties claim to engage political liberalism and democracy as it is found in America today.[2] Unfortunately, both parties also offer largely idiosyncratic depictions of liberalism, ignoring forms more prominent in its historical development, as well as in political life today. My goal is to supplement and even refocus the debate by attention to a more "canonical" statement of liberalism. This is why John Locke is the main figure. As Philip Quinn puts it, it would hardly be canon if we excluded "Johannine liberal theory."[3]

My focus on Stout and the Traditionalists should be read as a kind of case study. I am arguing that Locke is *generally* important to how today's Christians relate religion and politics but is typically overlooked. What we find in the Stout-Traditionalists debate is thus a symptom of a wider problem, one that occurs even outside theological study, such as in the work of political scientists and philosophers.[4] As helpful as the work of these scholars has been in explaining how religion and politics interact in the United States, it also displays certain shortcomings. For example, the work tends to be insufficiently interdisciplinary and tends to be methodologically narrow.[5] I have elsewhere argued that there are five primary "spotlights" that best illumine how Christian and political thought interact in the United States.[6] In the present essay, I emphasize one of these spotlights in particular, shining it on the debate between Stout and the Christian Traditionalists. I am not arguing that Locke can help solve today's debates but rather that observing his influence helps us better perceive what, so far, lies in the dark.

To foreshadow my conclusion, Christian political arguments in the United States are frequently premised upon a certain harmonization of religious and civic loyalties—a harmonization definitively stated by Locke and appropriated by America's founders. Attention to this influence reveals much that is obscured by positions such as Stout's and Hauerwas's. To this end, I make three claims in this essay. First, the current debates among Christian ethicists about political theology purport to engage America's actual political context but fail to do so. They tend to rely on "minority reports" in defining liberalism, and this leads to certain problems. What we lack is a historically and theologically rigorous analysis of the American political context. Second, I suggest how future research could fill the void. I begin the task by briefly engaging with Locke's *Letter Concerning Toleration*.[7] Third, I conclude by reflecting on how the present debate would be reshaped by observing Locke's continuing influence.

In the course of the essay, I pay special attention to one of the most controversial issues touching on religion and politics: the debate about homosexuality and the law. This debate includes, most recently, gay marriage but has also involved debates about homosexuals as a protected minority group and the constitutionality of antisodomy statues. Though this need not be a religious issue per se, it is interesting that the debate persistently displays religious overtones. Indeed, the most recent major study of religious toleration in the early Enlightenment follows intolerance toward "sodomites" as a theme, tracing it from the patristic period and the High Middle Ages to Locke's day. Often, the terms "traitors," "heretics," and "sodomites" came to be used as a single designation, and support for the First Crusade was garnered partially by the claim that Muslims practiced sodomy. Arguments against heretics, such as Gregory IX's papal bull of 1233, were also bolstered by claims that the heretics concluded their meetings by extinguishing the lights and engaging in homosexual practices.[8]

The debate, as well as its close relation to religious persecution, is clearly not new. For all these reasons, it is a fitting example for this topic.

Stout versus the Traditionalists

Stanley Hauerwas and William Cavanaugh have argued that liberal political regimes such as America's are ill suited, if not incompatible, with a faithful expression of the Christian's political vocation.[9] Practice politics in America and you may begin to believe that Congress, not the church, is God's primary agent within human history. The politics of the state is the path to worshipping Caesar. As a practice of Christian discipleship, Christians should remind themselves that they are, in a sense, not full citizens of their respective nation-states but rather resident aliens. This argument has provided a much-needed corrective to those who too easily align Christian concerns with those of the United States.

Whatever the merits of this corrective, Stout and others have responded by pointing out that it is oversimplified.[10] It is not so clear that active engagement in liberal politics is as destructive to Christian faith as the Traditionalists suppose. Not only were many, if not most, of liberalism's founders themselves Christians, liberalism itself is very diverse and its development is historically complex. Certainly it is more diverse than Hauerwas suggests. In his much-maligned chapter, "Why Justice Is a Bad Idea for Christians," Hauerwas associates liberal politics exclusively with the early John Rawls. Though it may be incompatible with Christianity, it is a version of liberalism that few, not even the later Rawls himself, actually embrace.[11]

Stout's response has been to introduce an alternative strand of liberal democracy, one that is more richly traditional and less dismissive of religion.[12] (Stout prefers to speak of democracy rather than liberalism. I can see what he hopes to gain by the distinction, but I am not sure that it gains for him as much as he hopes, and so for simplicity sake I set aside the distinction here.[13]) In the years since *Democracy and Tradition* was published, these issues have dominated academic discussions of Christian political ethics, receiving sustained attention at meetings of the American Academy of Religion and the Society of Christian Ethics, and various other conferences and journal articles, including nearly an entire issue of the *Journal of Religious Ethics*.[14] The debate has, for the most part, proved fruitful. But there is at least one serious shortcoming. The heart of Stout's argument is that the Traditionalist critique of political liberalism fails on what we could call historical or factual grounds: The Traditionalists ignore the diversity of the liberal tradition, focusing instead on its most extreme, antireligious manifestation. As mentioned, the object of Hauerwas's critique is a version of Rawlsianism. But as Stout points out, liberalism is not limited to what

Rawls says it is. It is on similar grounds that Stout rejects Cavanaugh's position. The liberalism that Cavanaugh rejects is, he claims, Lockean liberalism. This is significant, given the focus of my essay. But Cavanaugh's is a controversial reading of Locke, one that makes him more or less indistinguishable from Hobbes. Thus Stout rejects Cavanaugh's interpretation of liberalism just as he had rejected Hauerwas's. Stout writes, "The story being told here is . . . flawed."[15]

That quotation pretty neatly sums up Stout's argument: If you are going to tell the story, at least get it right. On this, Stout is right. But this makes it all the more odd to observe what he does next. He does not, for example, correct Cavanaugh's reading of Locke's liberalism. Rather, Stout opens *Democracy and Tradition* by conceding, "I will not . . . be drawing mainly on liberal philosophy from John Locke to John Rawls."[16] He prefers, instead, Emerson and Whitman. Stout has his own good reasons for this move: He wants to present a political vision that attracts him and that he hopes will attract others, and he finds that vision in these thinkers. But such an approach risks being too historically disconnected for the same reasons that Hauerwas's and Cavanaugh's descriptions are too disconnected. Stout actually spends very little time arguing that his democratic heroes have continuity with the ethos of American political life, especially on controversial church–state issues. Yet it does seem to matter that there is continuity. Whatever Stout *wishes* the American political ethos were, if it *in fact* is closer to Hauerwas's depiction, then Stout's argument is undercut. We must get the story right. The story of political liberalism in America, especially in its interaction with religious perspectives, cannot be told if Locke is absent from stage. Is he the only character? No, but without him the story is incomplete. America's dominant political theory is neither Rawls's (as Hauerwas claims) nor Hobbes's (as Cavanaugh fears). But neither is it Emerson's (as Stout hopes).[17]

Because my focus in this essay is on the *effect* of Locke's influence, I cannot fully establish the historical basis of the claim that he *did* influence the early American political ethos, though I have done so elsewhere.[18] One of the characteristic features of Locke's political vision, as it has been appropriated in the United States, is that it holds out hope that religiopolitical conflict can be simply and neatly resolved so long as one properly limits church and state. In his words, "It [is] above all things necessary to distinguish exactly the business of civil government from that of religion and to settle the just bounds that lie between the one and the other."[19] Embrace this imaginative vision, Locke invites, and you can found a new order for the ages. This is precisely the vision the key American founders embraced, one that continues (often unobserved) to inspire the political thought of many American Christians today.

The legacy of Locke's vision has consequences for Stout's project, in terms not only of whether Christians can be as accepting of his proposal as he hopes but also of how Stout interprets what other Christians are saying. Read carefully, *Democracy and Tradition* does not actually offer Emerson, Whitman, and Dewey as models for Christian political theology. They are Stout's heroes, and he believes they represent a rich tradition of democratic discourse. But Stout never supposes Hauerwas is going to adopt them as his heroes. Rather, given that Emerson and Dewey make room for a richer political vocabulary, Stout takes this as evidence that there is room in American politics for distinctively Christian voices—something the Traditionalists have so far denied. The heroes that Stout hopes the Traditionalists will embrace are, in his words, "theologically conservative but politically progressive thinkers like Calvinist philosopher Nicholas Wolterstorff and Barthian George Hunsinger."[20] This is a good suggestion, but one that misses a very crucial step.

What happens when Wolterstorff's and Hunsinger's arguments are appropriated by Christians in political debate? Surprisingly often, though not always, what happens is exactly what the Traditionalists predict. Approaches in line with Wolterstorff and Hunsinger are easily and frequently subverted to the sort of nationalistic, unecclesial politics that Hauerwas fears. Two brief examples will be helpful.

In Wolterstorff's case, note that one of his favorite models for relating Christian and liberal politics is that of Abraham Kuyper, a Reformed theologian and onetime Dutch prime minister.[21] Wolterstorff concedes that there are problems with Lockean and Rawlsian liberalism, but he avoids siding with Hauerwas because he believes someone like Kuyper poses a genuine alternative: He avoids both the Rawlsian and the sectarian temptations. According to Wolterstorff, involvement in liberal politics *could* lead to the problems feared by the Traditionalists, but it need not if Christians critically engage liberalism, as did Kuyper. The language with which Wolterstorff makes this argument is unambiguously targeted at Hauerwas: "Christians are not resident aliens vis-à-vis the government of Holland or the United States; they do not carry green cards. They are citizens; they carry passports. Christians have dual citizenship. They are all, in the modern world, citizens of some state and also citizens of the institutional church. In Kuyper's own words, 'It is one and the same *I* who is a citizen of the country and a member of the church.'"[22] Wolterstorff believes that Kuyper provides a way for Christians to live responsibly as dual citizens, and Stout would like the Traditionalists to be open to this model.

Yet Kuyper has been appropriated increasingly by politically conservative American Christians for causes other than Wolterstorff would advocate, essentially by the Religious Right. For them, Kuyper's political theory provides a way to endorse the American political project, broadly conceived, while also providing a vehicle for the characteristic Religious Right policies, such as government support of religion and "family values."[23] Such uses of Kuyper make him appear more compatible with the liberalism of the founders than is in fact the case. Regardless of which appropriation is more faithful to Kuyper himself, this appropriation only confirms Traditionalist fears. Even Kuyper, who may indeed have much to offer, is easily co-opted.

Next, consider Stout's appeal to Hunsinger. Why can Hauerwas not be more like him? Drawing on Hunsinger, Stout points to Karl Barth's "Barmen Declaration."[24] Barmen, Stout says, is "a clear example of what it means for the confessing church to maintain the integrity of its theological commitments without defaulting on its urgent obligation to join with others in the struggle for justice and peace."[25] It is, in other words, a program to which Hauerwas should be able to subscribe. Where, Stout asks, is the Traditionalists' "Barmen Declaration"?

Hunsinger's original occasion for recommending Barmen was to counter the publication of Richard John Neuhaus's proclamation, "Christianity and Democracy."[26] In a scathing rebuke, Hunsinger argues that where Neuhaus falls short is in being insufficiently critical of American democracy and of suggesting that those who offer such criticisms betray their country.[27] According to Hunsinger, because of how Neuhaus argues within the American context, taking on its rhetoric and presuppositions, he loses critical purchase. He becomes what Traditionalists such as Hauerwas, Milbank, and Cavanaugh fear to become, and what they believe much of the church has already become.[28]

But notice an interesting detail: As everyone who has read the opening paragraph of "Christianity and Democracy" knows, Neuhaus wrote it to imitate "Barmen." Stout is wise to ask for an American Barmen, but by being inattentive to the nature of the American context, he does not see that Neuhaus has already met his request. Unless Christians first examine how American political arguments are uniquely shaped by certain political and theological presuppositions, future American Barmens may look just like the Traditionalist fear they will: thinly veiled defenses of American exceptionalism.

What, then, is the step Stout misses? He is correct that certain Reformed and Catholic voices have much to contribute to American Christian thinking on politics. Yet the Traditionalists are also correct that such proposals too often fall into the trap of exchanging the proper concerns of the church for those of the nation-state. What first needs to be done is to understand why and how this happens, particularly in America. In other words, we need a historically grounded, contextual, and theological reading of American political liberalism. Were that provided, Christian theologians could then set to work on the more constructive political theologies that Stout longs for, and which the Traditionalists fear (rightly at present) would be co-opted.

Returning to Stout's initial critique, there are three ways in which I hope to capture important details that his approach obscures. First, as already mentioned, Stout and the Traditionalists tend to rely on "minority reports" in defining liberalism. My focus on liberalism's founder avoids this, but it does not thereby exclude the minority reports. Having carefully examined Locke, it then remains open to others to qualify or restate his American influence. In a symposium on *Democracy and Tradition,* Stout actually opens the door to the sort of thing I am proposing when he briefly discusses the Constitution and Bill of Rights. He does not pursue this line further because, as he quite reasonably points out, "I am not a political theorist by trade."[29] But others can and should pursue this.

Second, my approach helps us see that Stout misidentifies certain thinkers as Traditionalists: Neuhaus remains very far from Hauerwas. It only confuses the matter to employ categories that align the two.[30] Third, it is not clear that the Traditionalist viewpoint is as pervasive among Christians as Stout believes. Recall that Stout is afraid the Traditionalists' influence in seminaries will trickle down to churches and will incite a Christian exodus from politics, threatening democracy itself. But why is Stout not similarly concerned with, say, the Hassidic Lubavitcher movement, which is arguably more a-liberal and sectarian than Christian Traditionalism? It ultimately comes down to raw numbers. There simply are not enough Lubavitchers for them to pose the same sort of political threat that Stout fears from Christian political withdrawal.[31] But if this is the case, it is vital to ensure, on Stout's own grounds, that the most politically influential are engaged. Except within a certain academic subculture, it may be that Hauerwas's influence is much less than Stout believes. Even in those seminaries where he is commonly studied, his rhetoric is greatly watered down by the time it reaches the pulpit. When it comes to relating Christianity to liberalism, we must, as Stout would say, get the story right. Although Stout is justified in pointing out that he is "not a political theorist by trade," the debate is ill served by not being more attentive to those forms of political theory that influence religiopolitical debates in the United States today. Among the most important theories to include is that of John Locke.

The Political Theology of John Locke

What is Locke's role, and how is the Christian understanding of American politics altered by recognizing Locke's place in it? Locke is significant, first and foremost, simply because he is the founder of political liberalism: that political theory that dominates Western democracies generally and the United States in particular.[32] But even granting Locke's status as founder, why should he matter to Christians today, three centuries after his death? Simply put, Locke was massively influential on the imaginative vision of the American founders, and on Christians and clergy of the founding period. The study of the founding period is complex, but much recent work by both historians and political theorists has demonstrated how Lockean thought amalgamated the Christian republicanism of the revolutionary era, *especially on the issue of religious toleration.*[33] The founding was not monolithically Lockean—far from it—but the importance of non-Lockean thought tended to be in areas besides religious liberty.[34]

If the founders' relation of religion and politics was as Lockean as I am suggesting, what is the source of today's widespread disagreements about the founding? Why can we not more easily determine what Locke and the founders would have done when faced with today's dilemmas? Time and again, today's disputes appeal to the founding for support. Now, the founding itself has become an object of dispute:

> For many, the key issues of American politics now are not issues of political structure or policy, but of "values"—family values, religious values, moral values, and so forth. The battle over these "values" often takes the form of a battle for custody of the founding. So, TV minister D. James Kennedy asserts that "Christians have a right to reclaim America because the nation was founded by Christians." To that, a liberal columnist responded by arguing that "our constitution [was] written by people—Christian, agnostic, atheist and otherwise—who believed uppermost in protecting the rights of the minority." For both, the questions involved . . . have direct and deep bearing on how we answer some of the most troubling questions of our current political life.[35]

What both sides in this custody battle affirm is that somewhere in the founding a solution exists. According to Kennedy, the solution is that Christians may participate fully in politics qua Christians; if they are to do this without feigned obedience, the state must support Christian "values." According to Kennedy's opponent, the original solution was quite the opposite, ensuring that nonbelievers need not feign loyalty to an established religion. Whatever their disagreements, they are both working in Locke's shadow, for it was Locke who passed on to the American founders a path to preventing "the pretences of loyalty."[36]

Thus, Locke's relevance for today is due largely to a peculiarity of American politics. The American founding possesses a certain kind of authoritative status such that appeals to the founders' vision are indispensable in today's debates. This is especially the case on controversial church–state issues, such as prayer in public schools, homosexuality and the law, and abortion, as well as some heated issues not always associated with religion, such as illegal immigration. The founding is important whether you are arguing on behalf of the American Civil Liberties Union or the Christian Coalition; the political positions with any viability today, at least in principle, share ground with the nation's founders.

But this is peculiar to the United States. However much is made of George Washington's piety and prayer, one rarely if ever hears about the religious life of John A. MacDonald, Canada's first prime minister. Canada's founding does not function mythically. Because of the rhetorical demand to make arguments in continuity with the founding, the terms of the founding continue to shape us today. Michael Sandel puts this well: "The public philosophy of contemporary

American politics is a version of this [Lockean] liberal tradition of thought, *and most of our debates proceed within its terms.*"[37] It is this rhetorical necessity that gives plausibility to the Traditionalists' fears that Christian commitments will be subverted to worldly ends. And it is this necessity that allows Wolterstorff's Kuyper and Hunsinger's Barmen to be co-opted once they arrive on America's political shores.

The importance of Locke is even confirmed, unintentionally, by the least likely of voices: Stanley Hauerwas. In a 2002 interview, Hauerwas was asked, "Since . . . Christians blew it regarding liberal democracy, what ought Christians to *do*?" At this question, all of those who have criticized Hauerwas for his lack of engagement with political theory ought to pay careful attention. How did he respond? "I am very sympathetic with people in the C. B. MacPherson school of political theory, . . . who have seen how liberal democracy, particularly exemplified in people like Rawls, is really the end of politics."[38] What Hauerwas does not say, but as every political theorist knows, MacPherson is most famous for his controversial reading of Locke.[39] That critique of liberal democracy—Hauerwas's—is premised upon a certain interpretation of Locke's work.

A Path between Jerusalem and Athens

Locke is perhaps most famous for his empiricist philosophy and his political theory. The second of his *Two Treatises* contains what is arguably the definitive statement of modern liberal rights-theory.[40] But Locke was not only a political theorist; he was also a political *theologian.*

A key goal of his political theology was to bring about a final, definitive resolution to the age-old tensions between religious and civic allegiance. His lifetime was a period of great religious violence; indeed, he wrote the *Letter Concerning Toleration* while in Amsterdam, amid the arrival of French Protestant refugees fleeing persecution.[41] But his concerns were bigger than the seventeenth century's wars of religion. He saw his work as having eschatological significance. This is the clearest in *Reasonableness of Christianity,* where he offers a grand historical narrative in which priests, magistrates, and philosophers all fail to deliver what he can provide: a basis of ethical thought not undermined by religious difference.[42]

Especially helpful is how Charles Taylor traces the historical developments that anticipated Locke. Taylor writes: "No ancient polis or republic existed in which the religious life was not bound up with the civic. It seemed axiomatic to them that religion must be one with the state. Anything else would threaten to undermine the allegiance of the citizens."[43] Yet this situation was altered by the coming of Christianity, which relativized the significance of the state by seeing it as merely a temporary stopgap for a sinful creation. And even when Christianity promoted a nobler view of the state, the Christian's universal allegiance always preceded national ones. What is more, the warrior virtues—so central to early republics—were generally dismissed as un-Christian. This created a tension between Christianity and republicanism, to which Machiavelli and Rousseau both called attention.[44]

This situation resulted in the crisis with which the modern world begins, and in which political liberalism was forged. The Reformation and ensuing wars of religion brought the crisis to a head, but its seeds were sown long before. In Taylor's words, "It is one of the legacies of Christendom that religion can neither be fully integrated in nor fully excluded from the state."[45] The peculiarity of the American founding, however, is that it begins not with a conflict between civic and Christian loyalty, but with their apparent resolution. Again, in Taylor's words, "For all the well-documented tensions between Christianity and the republican tradition, the United States starts its career by linking the two closely together."[46]

According to Taylor, the ancient city faced two alternatives in relating political and religious life. Either civic and religious loyalty were unified, such as by worshipping city-specific gods, *or* religious belief would threaten to undermine the allegiance of the citizens. Christianity posed a special problem because it rejected city gods and in many cases weakened civic loyalty in favor of the church. Machiavelli points out this conflict more openly than any previous writer: What will it profit a man to gain his soul, but lose his whole city?[47]

The tension posed by Christianity seemed only to deepen in the first century or so following the Reformation. Yet at the height of the violence, a possible solution emerged. As certain forms of Protestantism and republicanism interacted in seventeenth-century England, there arose the possibility of a "third way" between the alternatives of worshipping city-specific gods and religious belief undermining civic allegiance. This third way was most influentially and powerfully presented in the work of Locke.

This, then, is why we must study Locke: He appears to resolve the dilemma of Christian loyalty by reenvisioning politics and Christianity in new ways. His doctrine of natural rights and religious toleration builds on earlier thinkers, to be sure, but he also represents a distinctive new moment, in which just these ideas are brought together in just this way for the first time. He appears to have finally solved the age-old dilemma of the Christian's doubtful loyalty to his or her city. His political philosophy seeks to arrange loyalties in such a way that the good Christian and good citizen will always follow the same course.

"Preventing the Pretenses of Loyalty": Locke's Solution to an Ancient Dilemma

What are the key features of Locke's solution? How does he solve the dilemma of which Taylor speaks? It is a solution that is by now very familiar and eminently simple—or so it would appear: Church and civil government each have a certain goal, and their actions are limited to what achieves that goal. So long as each does not exceed its just bounds, the two will never conflict.[48] But on closer inspection, it is not nearly as simple as that—and Locke knows it.

The heart of Locke's argument is based on the distinction between government and religion. The state must tolerate diverse forms of religious expression, because its role is limited to securing the common good. On its surface, this is hardly unique to Locke, but he means something very particular by it, for he realizes there will be disputes about what does or does not help secure the common good. So he provides a mechanism for resolving such disputes: Government is limited to what will secure the individual, natural rights of its citizens, chiefly life, liberty, and property. He writes: A commonwealth is "a society of men constituted only for the procuring, preserving, and advancing their own *civil interests.*"[49] The "whole jurisdiction of the magistrate reaches only to these civil concernments": "man's rights." Obviously, Locke's strategy is to make government intolerance of religion logically impossible by showing government to be, by definition, limited. He gives three reasons why government "neither can nor ought . . . be extended to the salvation of souls."[50]

First, the care of souls never belonged to the magistrate in the first place. Government is "by the consent of the people," and the people never gave to the magistrate authority over their consciences.[51] This is a de facto claim; the magistrate *does not* have such power. Second, the magistrate *could not* have such power, because his power is limited to outward coercion. "Such is the nature of the understanding that it cannot be compelled to believe anything by outward force."[52] Third, Locke offers a prudential reason. It would be foolish for humans to turn over the care of their souls to the magistrate, because the magistrate does not necessarily have superior knowledge of religious matters.[53]

Locke has shown that the state must be limited in these ways, all of which leads to religious toleration. But he anticipates the objection that even if the civil government has no concern for its subject's souls, the church surely does. For his vision of toleration to succeed, he must not only show that the government's means are limited *to* external sanctions but also that the church is limited *from* them. He defines a church as follows. It is "a voluntary society of men, joining themselves together of their own accord in order to the public worshipping of God in such manner as they judge acceptable to Him, and effectual to the salvation of their souls."[54] The salvation to which Locke refers is otherworldly—what happens after death.[55] Whatever laws the church does impose on its members, those laws cannot have any civil consequences. So rigorous is his prohibition that even excommunications must be carried out with "no rough usage of word," lest those rough words lead to civil consequences, such as the loss of reputation or estate.[56]

It would appear, then, that Locke's solution is complete. There may be false conflicts between church and state, but never genuine conflicts. Should conflicts of loyalty arise, we can be sure that something has gone wrong "somewhere else in the system." The government is concerned with the common good in this life, and the church with salvation—bearing in mind, however, that by "common good" he means individual rights and by salvation he means only the afterlife. On the basis of this, Locke is able to give examples of the extent of his toleration. Theft, even for religious reasons, is of course intolerable because it threatens the individual right of property. Idolatry, by contrast, must be tolerated because it threatens only one's happiness in the next life, not to mention the fact, which he points out, that what is idolatry to one ruler will be piety to the next. Theft is intolerable while idolatry must be tolerated because, in his words, idolatry lacks "civil concernment."[57] But what happens when there is a dispute about whether a given act lacks civil concernment? In other words, what if citizens cannot agree about whether an act belongs to the theft-type or the idolatry-type?

As it turns out, this is a dilemma that Locke will not resolve for his readers and, more important, it is a dilemma that American Christians encounter repeatedly in today's culture war disputes. It is not going too far to say that this is what characterizes culture war and church–state disputes: They are disputes about whether something is, for example, more like theft—or more like idolatry. Does school prayer lack civil concernment? After all, its supporters say that it is essential to promoting a generally peaceful society and, ultimately, to securing basic rights. Precisely because Locke's solution was so influential among the founders, and is so pervasive in the American political imagination, it causes problems when the solution is pushed to its limits.

A Contemporary Example: Homosexuality and the Law

One of the most controversial issues touching on religion and politics is debate about homosexuality and the law. In principle, it seems as though Locke's approach should allow us to solve the dilemma of restricting sex acts. Those opposed to such restrictions argue that for all the reasons Locke gives about not prohibiting idolatry, we should similarly allow consenting adults to engage in whatever private sex acts they choose. It is my neighbor's right to sleep with whomever she chooses, so long as doing so does not infringe my rights. Religious believers may disagree about whether those acts are prohibited by God or threaten eternal salvation, but civil law cannot follow God's law on this point. Even if God forbids both homosexuality and idolatry, the magistrate may not. Thus it would seem that Locke's solution has indeed resolved a contemporary dispute related to civic and religious life.

But consider the counterargument, offered by various members of the Religious Right. It is generally thought that when Christians such as Jerry Falwell or Pat Robertson advocate laws against homosexuality, they are advocating a theocracy and reject classical liberal politics wholesale.[58] But a review of their arguments reveals something easily overlooked. When they advocate such laws *publicly*, they surprisingly often do so without reference to God's law or the Bible. Indeed, there is nothing in such arguments that would necessarily fall outside the bounds of the Locke's solution.

Observe this argument as it is presented by the Catholic political scientist J. Budziszewski. He encourages Christians to advance a "heterosexual public ethic" using, among other arguments, the claim that increased homosexual activity has led to an increase of colorectal injuries. This places an increased burden on medical resources, which ultimately reduces others' access to those resources, and so on.[59] Whatever the credibility of these medical and sociological studies, notice the form of the argument. Budziszewski does not argue that such sex acts violate God's law (though he believes they do), nor does he cite scripture. He is able to endorse the characteristic position of the Religious Right toward homosexuality fully *within* a Lockean framework. His argument does not violate the terms of Locke's solution—the same terms that, just previously, seemed to necessitate the opposite conclusion.[60] Where he disagrees is in seeing homosexuality as like theft but unlike idolatry, because it has, however indirectly, "civil concernment."[61]

The form of Budziszewski's argument appears to commit him to letting social scientific evidence (e.g., the medical facts he cites) be the arbiter in deciding the legitimacy of antisodomy legislation. But is that actually his position? For example, would he advocate repealing such legislation if it were revealed that the studies in question had been erroneous and, after recalculation, they supported the opposite conclusions?

If so, we would need to further press the question. Is homosexuality per se subject to legislation, or only certain forms of it—to use Budziszewski's examples, forms of it that are promiscuous or result in direct physical harm? On the one hand, it would seem as though only those particular acts could be prohibited, in which case the law would not even reference the gender of those involved in the act but only the acts themselves (and would thus ban equally promiscuous heterosexual sex). But on the other hand, Locke is unclear on the "directness" of the harm required to justify forbidding an act. Perhaps Locke's theory would allow outlawing homosexuality if social-scientific evidence could show a relatively direct link between it and the acts Budziszewski mentions. This would roughly be analogous to forbidding some form of idolatry because of evidence showing idolaters are likely to be thieves.

Locke's own passing comments on "sodomy" suggest that he was closer to Budziszewski's conclusion. Like theft but unlike idolatry, homosexual sex is subject to civil sanction. For today's "liberal" position—those who see such antisodomy laws as equivalent to prohibiting idolatry—Locke is simply being inconsistent on this point, but not in a way that undermines his principles. Perhaps beset by the prejudices of his own time, or perhaps unwilling to reveal the full implications of his solution, Locke treats homosexuality as theft, when re-ally (it is argued) it is more like idolatry. Thus according to this position, we must modify Locke's own position to make him more compatible with his own best intentions. For the rights secured by his theory to be of any lasting worth, they must be more than rights to do what is "objectively good"—precisely be-cause people disagree about what is objectively good. Indeed, his whole project seems prompted by such disagreements. Given such disagreements, we ought not to legislate about such matters. It is no matter to me whom my neighbor worships, much less whom he or she sleeps with.

To politically conservative Christians, this interpretation sounds very un-Lockean. It seems to them as though it is based not on Locke but on Justice Anthony Kennedy, striking down a Texas law banning same-sex intercourse: "These matters, involving the most intimate and personal choices a person may make in a lifetime, choices central to personal dignity and autonomy, are cen-tral to the liberty protected by the Fourteenth Amendment. At the heart of liberty is the right to define one's own concept of existence, of meaning, of the universe, and of the mystery of human life. . . . It is a promise of the Consti-tution that there is a realm of personal liberty which the government may not enter."[62]

However, in the *Letter* Locke writes something that could plausibly be seen as an antecedent of Kennedy's statement, even if it does not go quite as far: "In pri-vate domestic affairs, in the management of estates, in the conservation of bodily health, every man may consider what suits his own convenience, and *follow what course he likes best.* No man complains of the ill-management of his neighbor's af-fairs. No man is angry with another for an error committed in sowing his land or in marrying his daughter. Nobody corrects a spendthrift for consuming his sub-stance in taverns. Let any man pull down, or build, or make whatsoever expenses he pleases, nobody murmurs, nobody controls him; he has his liberty."[63]

Thus it is not that Locke sounds like Justice Kennedy so much as that Ken-nedy sounds like Locke—at least according to this interpretation. The tension within Locke's own thought seems only to deepen over time. In his *Second* and *Third Letters on Toleration,* he moves away from statements such as the above.[64] As John Marshall observes, "Locke increasingly came to stress in these *Letters* the magisterial promotion of a 'good life' and that the magistrates should hin-der the practices to which 'men's lusts' carried them."[65] Yet in a page of notes written late in life, Locke appears to move back toward the position of the first *Letter:* "For as for other men's actions, which is right and wrong . . . he is not concerned to know. His business is to live well himself and do what is his partic-ular duty."[66] These varying statements should not be seen as outright contra-dictions; but there is a tension between them. The precise path to navigate that tension is what occasions today's rival interpretations.

We can also see that further clarification is needed about how directly harm must follow from an action to justify regulating that action. For example, Locke seems to argue in the *Letter* that perjury but not lying ought to be illegal. But if enough people deceive enough of the time, would we not expect civil harm from even mere lying: a general reduction in civil stability and, ultimately, the security of individual rights? Locke had in mind that actions must meet a certain minimum standard of "directness" of harm to justify proscription. A given act of perjury may not threaten rights, but it is still criminal because, in general, perjury poses a more direct threat to rights and civil stability. A given act of lying may threaten rights, but it should not be made illegal because the harm, in general, is too indirect.[67] These points of disagreement help bring to light the "gaps" in Locke's theory.

Such gaps make it possible to conceive of *both* the "conservative" argument as well as the "liberal" counterargument as plausibly Lockean. Locke's argument, especially as it was implemented and modified by the American founders, owed much of its seeming effectiveness to that precise moment in history in which the gaps were less visible. Thus to implement Locke's solution today, *we need to ask questions such as* "Do Lockean natural rights differ from classical natural right such that government must be neutral with regard to the good?" and "How should social scientific evidence be used in justifying laws?" *But Locke and the founders did not ask these questions.* This is because they could take certain things for granted about the moral convictions of people of their day, such that different answers to these questions did not lead to differences in conclusions. However, when today's Christians, including Budziszewski and his opponents, make arguments such as those outlined above, they implicitly, sometimes subconsciously, take sides on these difficult interpretive questions.

The example of laws restricting homosexuality is particularly apt because of its prominence in current debates and also because of the interesting comparisons to what Locke says about idolatry. But any one of a number of other disputes could serve equally well to make this point. Especially significant in consideration of the American founders' thought would be the role of religious belief and practice as a *support* for civil stability. Even the most "liberal" founders, such as Thomas Jefferson, saw religious belief as important for maintaining basic morality among most citizens, for promoting civil order, and—ultimately—for securing individual rights. But the difficulties in how this should be implemented were largely invisible to the founders, perhaps because of the homogeneity of religious belief in their time; though disagreements separated the many sects and churches of seventeenth-century America, virtually all were Protestant. If government depends on widespread religious belief to fulfill its mission to secure rights, what may it do to foster that belief? We could thus say much the same things about this dispute that were said about homosexuality: Lockean arguments about religion and civic life could well lead to opposite conclusions, depending on how one interprets Locke's theory.

What this example suggests is that the political arguments made by today's Christians, *across the ideological spectrum*, are premised upon a certain harmonization of religious and civic loyalties. Both the "liberal" and "conservative" positions are broadly defensible on Lockean grounds, though they are based on rival interpretations of Locke. It is telling that the points at which Christians disagree on such matters are precisely those about which Locke's solution provides no clear guidance. I conclude by connecting this back to the contemporary debate among Christian ethicists, showing how attention to Locke reframes aspects of that debate.

John Locke's America: Political Theology in the Twenty-First Century

If Christians are to understand how their religious and political obligations interact in the United States, they must have a clear understanding of the character of that political world. I have argued that because of Locke's decisive role in the founding of political liberalism, and because of his influence on the American founding, this debate cannot proceed without attention to his thought. One of the key features of Locke's political theology is that it presents itself as ushering in a "new order for the ages," in which civic and religious loyalties are arranged so as to eliminate the possibility of conflict. He does this by distinguishing the realms of church and state in a particular way; but as we saw, his solution contains gaps that are present even in today's culture war debates.

One of the shortcomings of the debate between Stout and the Traditionalists is that, all intentions to the contrary, it fails to engage the sorts of influences and theories that are characteristic of American political liberalism. How does including Locke's voice reframe our understanding of Christianity's relation to liberalism? Recalling Taylor's narrative of the age-old tension between church and city, today's Christian positions are best distinguished by how they would answer the following question: Does Lockean liberalism, as appropriated in America, succeed or fail to resolve the tension of which Taylor speaks? Does he provide an authentic third way between worshipping city gods (i.e., nationalism) and potential disloyalty to one's city in obedience to God?

The answer Traditionalists such as Hauerwas and Cavanaugh would give is that Locke fails. Recall the interview quoted above, in which Hauerwas professes his support for the political theorist C. B. Macpherson; it should be no surprise that this is how Macpherson reads Locke as well. In fact, the Traditionalists would say that not only does Locke fail, his solution is actually harmful because it is based on theological error. Thus, they conclude, the only safe response is for Christians to shun American politics in favor of the politics of church practices.

But how do other Christians respond to the question of whether Locke's solution succeeds? The Traditionalist response is not the only one discernable in American politics; indeed, it is probably not even the dominant one. Far more common are responses that affirm the broad outlines of Locke and the founders' system but seek to amend it in certain respects. As we saw in the above example, members of the Religious Right fit squarely within the boundaries of Locke's solution, but they interpret Locke in such a way that he fits their ideological agenda—in this case, by arguing that homosexuality actually threatens individual rights.

Though this happens to be a politically conservative example, there are Christians closer to the political left who make parallel arguments. They affirm that the Lockean solution gives Christians room to faithfully practice their faith in a political context, but they interpret that solution in ways that make Lockean rights genuine spheres of immunity, which protect against the sorts of laws that would be supported by those of the Right. We cannot examine these in detail, but John Courtney Murray,[68] David Hollenbach,[69] and Brian Stiltner[70] all offer interpretations of Locke in this vein from a Catholic perspective. In addition, Nicholas Wolterstorff[71] and John Witte[72] offer such interpretations from a Reformed perspective. The thread that runs throughout the work of these writers is a willingness to justify their respective political visions by showing that they are merely correcting or amending Locke. The Catholic writers cited above argue for the fundamental compatibility of American and Christian political ethics, so long as we reinterpret Locke and the founders in line with Thomas Aquinas (Stiltner, Hollenbach, and Murray all do this explicitly). The Reformed writers premise this fundamental compatibility on Calvinist strands within Locke himself and non-Lockean within the founding (usually via John Adams). On the whole, these writers tend to be fairly careful; they are at least cautious in their willingness to share ground with Locke. By contrast, Budziszewski is naively optimistic about how Christian and civic obligations can be harmonized by Locke. Writers such as Neuhaus and Michael Novak are slightly less naive—but only slightly.[73] Novak in particular offers an extended interpretation of Locke and the American founders precisely in line with what I have described.[74]

This analysis results in a rather different portrait of American Christian politics than Stout's approach. Stout believes that the Traditionalist response fails because it misjudges the character of American liberalism. Recognizing Locke's significance, and observing how his political vision continues to hold influence, shows that the Traditionalist concerns are not unfounded, even if they are overstated. The way Kuyper and "Barmen" have been appropriated by the Religious Right confirms this. What Hauerwas was responding to in books such as *Resident*

Aliens, even if he did not realize it, is the force within American political life that presses in this direction, the "third way" out of the ancient conflicts described by Taylor.

Clearly, the willingness of today's Christians to make arguments in line with Locke's is due to the rhetorical appeal. These are the arguments that have plausibility in today's debates. But they are also accompanied by certain pitfalls, which tend to be of two types: Lockean reasoning is invoked in ways that are in tension with a thinker's other commitments (thus confusing herself), *or* Lockean reasoning is invoked in ways that disguise a thinker's other commitments (thus confusing her fellow citizens).

Though they have not engaged Locke or the American founders at length, the Traditionalists are concerned with avoiding the first of these two pitfalls. By taking on certain (often unseen) presuppositions, Christians subtly shift the basis of their own positions. Recall Budziszewski's argument against homosexuality based on sociological and medical data. But what, then, is the true basis of his opposition to homosexuality? Would he alter his position if the sociological data were to be revised?

If the Traditionalists are concerned with avoiding the first of these pitfalls, in a certain way Stout is concerned with avoiding the second. This is part of the reason why he spends an entire chapter of *Democracy and Tradition* critiquing John Rawls's and Richard Rorty's demand for secularized public debate.[75] When religious citizens are forced to employ "public" arguments that differ from their "private" arguments, this difference leads not only to resentment but also to confused civic debate. Again recalling Budziszewski, are his arguments against homosexuality *in fact* based on sociological and medical data, or are these merely politically expedient arguments offered because his real reasons are deemed publicly unacceptable? How can his fellow citizens engage him without knowing the true terms of the debate?

The combined effect of these pitfalls is that today's Christian political arguments often confuse Christians themselves, as well as their fellow citizens. As much as Stout hopes to avoid these pitfalls, it is not clear how easily this goal can be achieved. Most important, the first of the two pitfalls cannot to be taken lightly. The hope shared by Locke and the founders that Christian and civic loyalties need never be at odds has a powerful grip on the American imagination and greatly influences public discourse. For example, note that even if Stout can convince Rorty to abandon his demand for secular political discourse (and he has), the political discourse may simply be shaped in even subtler ways. In the very article where Rorty concedes to Stout that his earlier position was wrong, he reveals that he hopes to achieve the same goal but by different means. Rather than excluding religious discourse from political debate because of a *principle*, they will be eliminated by force of *custom* and social pressure.[76] In its way, the rhetorical force of Locke and the founders' vision is part of the custom that serves this purpose.[77] Yet as we have seen, this "custom" does not necessarily press toward secularization. It can (and by Rorty's reading it ought to), but it can also press toward a civil religion of the sort advocated by the Religious Right. Unfortunately, neither of these is a particularly attractive direction for Christian political theology; the one excludes theology's public contribution, while the other instrumentalizes it. It remains to be seen whether Stout's Emersonian vision is a genuine alternative to these or but a gentler form of them.

Conclusion

The primary goal of this essay is to prompt further research on those political and religious thinkers who have most influenced how church and state interact in the United States, as well as further research into how those thinkers shape today's debates. Pulling back the veil on Locke's overlooked influence reveals a possible response that is quite different from that of the Traditionalists. The greatest danger for Christians is simply being unaware of the forces in play, including the rhetorical demand to conform to Locke's solution. Where might such research lead?

First, it ought to begin with Locke, but it cannot end with him. A very strong argument can be made that his framework for relating church and state was the most influential for the founders and remains the most influential today. But there are other voices that must be heard, including Stout's heroes, Emerson, Whitman, and Dewey. How does their political vision relate to Locke's, Jefferson's, Madison's, and other founders'? Two particularly helpful writers on this topic are John Witte and Mark Noll.[78] They both show the interaction of Christian, republican, liberal, Puritan, and other strands of thought in the founding era. When today's Christians appeal to the founding in their arguments, they are in fact appealing to a complex amalgam of thought.

Second, the question, "Where should we go from here?" should lead us to revisit what the Traditionalists get right. To many observers, the Traditionalists propound a reactionary and dangerous critique of modernity. In fact, what actually lies at the heart of their arguments is a sense that the politics of the modern liberal state, especially the United States, is accompanied by a deep and powerful mythos. It produces its own rival doctrines of atonement, salvation, ecclesiology, and eschatology. In America, this mythos is often militaristic, materialistic, individualistic, and, above all, nationalistic. (It is many other things as well, including many good things, but the issues given here are the sources of concern.)

Having seen the influence this force holds throughout American churches, the Traditionalists raise their guard. If the American mythos is so powerful that it can supplant the church's mythos, perhaps Christians should stay safely away.

"Build a fence around the Torah," as the rabbis say. The Traditionalists raise their guard—or the fence—even higher when they read early modern writers such as Locke. Here is the mythmaker caught in the act, subverting the Christian story for this-worldly ends.

If this is indeed at the heart of the Traditionalist argument, it is on a certain level profoundly true—even if it is oversimplified. Writing as a Canadian, I do experience American politics as pervaded by a remarkably powerful mythos, one so all-pervasive that it can be frightening. Here, to pray for "those who are serving our country" *is* to pray for the military. Wolterstorff notices how this nationalistic mythos pervades education: "The ideology of the public schools became a religion of the democratic state, a religion whose object of veneration was American democracy. Repeatedly, it was preached that the main business of the schools was the inculcation of democratic values—whatever those might be. Thus, in a profound sense, American education began to resemble Marxist Russian education and Nazi German education and pagan Roman education. In all those cases a veneration of the state was the moving force in the educational system. Of course, different sorts of states were being venerated."[79] The common Traditionalist stories about American flags hung on church altars are not mere anecdotes. They suggest there is something gravely wrong with American Christianity. And if so, perhaps we ought to follow the rabbis' warning: Build the fence even higher.

The problem with this response is that it only increases the power of the myth. My response has been different; it is a form of demythologizing. We could even say that my examination of Locke is a demythologizing exegesis. For even though there *is* a powerful mythos surrounding contemporary American politics, when it is examined up close, there is nothing mysterious about it. What created this myth is not unexplainable or incomprehensible. It need not cause irrational fear. It is not something that must be fenced off to be controlled. It was created by the very ordinary responses of Christians and others to a long history of complex political and social problems.

What difference might this make for today's Christian political theologies? It suggests that it is possible to affirm *both* the Traditionalists' legitimate concerns about the mythic forces underlying liberal politics *and* an awareness that those forces need not be overly feared. Unobserved, they are powerful. But because they have been little understood, they have seemed more powerful than they are.

Notes

1. Nicholas Wolterstorff, *John Locke and the Ethics of Belief* (Cambridge: Cambridge University Press, 1996), i.
2. Here and throughout, I use America to refer to the United States, not North America.

3. Philip Quinn, "Can Good Christians Be Good Liberals?" in *God and the Ethics of Belief: New Essays in Philosophy of Religion*, ed. Andrew Chignell and Andrew Dole (Cambridge: Cambridge University Press, 2005), 249.

4. Interestingly, these can be best understood as comprising three different types of response to the work of John Rawls. Some challenge Rawls as being unfair for his restrictions on public discourse (e.g., Wolterstorff, Eberle), certain liberal theorists (e.g., Galston, Macedo, Sandel) critique Rawls's claim that liberalism ought to be "neutral," while others see Rawls as mistaken about the basic conditions necessary for genuine civic debate (e.g., "Deliberative Democracy"). See Robert Audi and Nicholas Wolterstorff, *Religion in the Public Square: The Place of Religious Convictions in Political Debate* (Lanham, Md.: Rowman & Littlefield, 1997); Christopher Eberle, *Religious Conviction in Liberal Politics* (Cambridge: Cambridge University Press, 2002); William Galston, *Liberal Purposes: Goods, Virtues, and Diversity in the Liberal State* (Cambridge: Cambridge University Press, 1991); Amy Gutmann and Dennis Thompson, *Democracy and Disagreement* (Cambridge, Mass.: Belknap Press, 1996); Stephen Macedo, *Liberal Virtues: Citizenship, Virtue, and Community in Liberal Constitutionalism* (Oxford: Clarendon Press, 1990); and Michael Sandel, *Democracy's Discontent* (Cambridge, Mass.: Belknap Press, 1996).

5. On the need for greater interdisciplinary awareness, consider that in Stout and Cavanaugh's disagreement about early modern political theory, both authors seem unaware that their positions parallel long-running disputes among certain political philosophers. Methodologically, approaches tend to be either theoretical (at the expense of historical engagement) or vice versa. On balance, my approach emphasizes the historical, an approach that Stout and Hauerwas tend to slight.

6. These five "spotlights" are as follows. (1) The Christian's dual loyalty to God and state is a source of enduring tension, not a passing phase that will be easily remedied. (2) The political theories of the Enlightenment responded to religious conflicts in part by attempting to "solve" that conflict. (3) Locke's solution to the religiopolitical problem is particularly influential for how subsequent thinkers understand the problem. (4) Locke's solution contains "gaps": questions to which Locke's solution provides no clear answer. These gaps often coincide with today's most contested culture wars debates. (5) Locke's thought is particularly important in the United States *across ideological lines*. Today's disputes are, then, a kind of Lockean family feud. By observing religio-political disputes today *in light of* these, we can understand the nature of the problem more clearly. For a full explanation, see John Perry, "Subverting the Republic: Christian Faithfulness and Civic Allegiance in John Locke's America" (PhD diss., University of Notre Dame, 2007).

7. John Locke, *Letter Concerning Toleration*, ed. Mario Montuori (The Hague: Martinus Nijhoff, 1963).

8. John Marshall, *John Locke, Toleration and Early Enlightenment Culture: Religious Intolerance and Arguments for Religious Toleration in Early Modern and "Early Enlightenment" Europe* (Cambridge: Cambridge University Press, 2006), 219.

9. William Cavanaugh, "A Fire Strong Enough to Consume the House: The Wars of Religion and the Rise of the State," *Modern Theology* 11, no. 14 (1995); William Cavanaugh, *Theopolitical Imagination* (Edinburgh: T. & T. Clark, 2002); Stanley Hauerwas, *After Christendom?* (Nashville: Abingdon, 1991); Stanley Hauerwas and William H. Willimon, *Resident Aliens: Life in the Christian Colony* (Nashville: Abingdon Press, 1989).

10. The key texts to which Stout responds include Hauerwas, *After Christendom*; Stanley Hauerwas, *A Better Hope: Resources for a Church Confronting Capitalism, Democracy, and Postmodernity* (Grand Rapids: Brazos Press, 2000); Stanley Hauerwas, *A Community of Character: Toward a Constructive Christian Social Ethic* (Notre Dame, Ind.: University of Notre Dame Press, 1981); Stanley Hauerwas, *Performing the Faith: Bonhoeffer and the Practice of*

Nonviolence (Grand Rapids: Brazos Press, 2004); Stanley Hauerwas, *Truthfulness and Tragedy: Further Investigations in Christian Ethics* (Notre Dame, Ind.: University of Notre Dame Press, 1977); Stanley Hauerwas, *Vision and Virtue: Essays in Christian Ethical Reflection* (Notre Dame, Ind.: University of Notre Dame Press, 1981); Alasdair MacIntyre, *After Virtue*, 2nd ed. (Notre Dame, Ind.: University of Notre Dame Press, 1984); John Milbank, *Theology and Social Theory: Beyond Secular Reason, Signposts in Theology* (Oxford: Blackwell, 1993); and John Milbank, Catherine Pickstock, and Graham Ward, *Radical Orthodoxy: A New Theology* (London: Routledge, 1999).

11. Hauerwas, *After Christendom?* chap. 2.

12. See Jeffrey Stout, *Democracy and Tradition* (Princeton, N.J.: Princeton University Press, 2004), chaps. 3–5.

13. So far as I can tell, what Stout advocates would be called "liberal democracy" by most any reader. Nonetheless, the distinction is worth noting because cases may arise where the difference is significant. Others have raised this point against Stout more forcefully. E.g., David Little observes that when Stout "goes on to disavow 'liberal' as a word 'blocking the path of inquiry,'. . . Stout inexplicably surrenders with one hand what he gained with the other. As I will argue, rescuing the 'word' liberal is no trivial undertaking, since the idea of '*liberal* democracy,' is indispensable both to the contemporary worldwide discussion of democracy, and, as a matter of fact, to much that Stout himself appears to favor about American democracy." David Little, "On Behalf of Rights: A Critique of Democracy and Tradition," *Journal of Religious Ethics* 34, no. 2 (2006): 288. Also see the final footnote in Hauerwas's response to Stout. Hauerwas, *Performing the Faith*, 241 n. 56.

14. *Journal of Religious Ethics* 33, no. 4 (2005).

15. Stout, *Democracy and Tradition*, 101.

16. Ibid., 2.

17. To be sure, Emerson, Whitman, and Dewey do share a prima facie claim to greater American relevance than Locke: unlike Locke, they are Americans—and influential ones at that. But in contemporary church–state conflicts (and in the secondary literature on those conflicts), their vision is largely absent. Stout hopes to change the terms of the debate by replacing Rawls's secular political vision with Emerson's democratic vision. Were we to do this, he believes, the Traditionalist's antiliberal backlash would be unnecessary. Stout may not be far from the mark, but what he leaves out is an engagement with other influential forms of liberalism (especially Locke's). If Locke is close to Rawls, then it will not be so easy to extricate Rawls's position from the debate. But if Locke is close to Emerson, even Stout's alternatives may not sufficiently change the terms of the debate.

18. For a more sustained defense of the above claims, see Perry, "Subverting the Republic," chap. 4. There is of course much dispute over the manner and degree to which Locke influenced the American founders, but much of this dispute can be dismissed if I am clear about the scope of the claim that I am making: On the specific issue of relating church and state harmoniously, Locke was a definitive source for those founders who most shaped the documents most important at that time and most cited in today's disputes (including the Declaration of Independence, the Constitution, the Memorial and Remonstrance, the Federalist, and others). Most of the arguments against Lockean influence either focus on a different founder, or focus on an issue besides the one I have identified. For Locke's influence on the documents listed, see Vincent Phillip Muñoz, "James Madison's Principle of Religious Liberty," *American Political Science Review* 97, no. 1 (2003): 17–32; Vincent Phillip Muñoz, "Religious Liberty and the American Founding," *Intercollegiate Review* 38, no. 2 (2003): 33–34; S. Gerald Sandler, "Lockean Ideas in Thomas Jefferson's Bill for Establishing Religious Freedom," *Journal of the History of Ideas* 21 (1960): 110–16; C. Bradley Thompson, *John Adams and the Spirit of Liberty* (Lawrence: University Press of Kansas, 1998); and

Michael Zuckert, *The Natural Rights Republic* (Notre Dame, Ind.: University of Notre Dame Press, 1996). For a study of his influence more broadly (such as on American clergy), see Steven Dworetz, *The Unvarnished Doctrine: Locke, Liberalism, and the American Revolution* (Durham, N.C.: Duke University Press, 1990).

19. Locke, *Letter Concerning Toleration*, 15.

20. Stout, *Democracy and Tradition*, 11.

21. E.g., see various essays in Nicholas Wolterstorff, *Educating for Life: Reflections on Christian Teaching and Learning* (Grand Rapids: Baker, 2002); and Nicholas Wolterstorff, *Educating for Shalom: Essays on Christian Higher Education* (Grand Rapids: William B. Eerdmans, 2004). The best summary of Kuyper's politics is Nicholas Wolterstorff, "Abraham Kuyper," in *The Teachings of Modern Christianity on Law, Politics, and Human Nature*, ed. John Witte and Frank S. Alexander (New York: Columbia University Press, 2006), 307.

22. Wolterstorff, "Abraham Kuyper," 307.

23. E.g., John Bolt, *A Free Church, a Holy Nation: Abraham Kuyper's American Public Theology* (Grand Rapids: William B. Eerdmans, 2001); and Nancy Pearcey, *Total Truth: Liberating Christianity from Its Cultural Captivity* (Wheaton, Ill.: Crossway Books, 2005).

24. Written primarily by Karl Barth in 1934, the Barmen Declaration was the Confessing Church's definitive rejection of Nazism. It is relevant to the present debate because it bases political conclusions on a thoroughly theological foundation. It therefore embodies the sort of politics that the Traditionalists should seemingly be able to affirm.

25. Stout, *Democracy and Tradition*, 108.

26. Institute on Religion and Democracy, "Christianity and Democracy," *First Things*, no. 66 (October 1996): 30–36.

27. George Hunsinger, *Disruptive Grace: Studies in the Theology of Karl Barth* (Grand Rapids: William B. Eerdmans, 2000), 75.

28. One might make a similar case regarding Richard John Neuhaus's support for the second Iraq war. From the Traditionalist perspective, certain strands of Catholic theology, as with Wolterstorff's Calvinism, could be a valuable resource for Christian political thought. Yet again their fears are confirmed: when Neuhaus and George Weigel bring Catholic political thought together with a confidence in American democracy, they conclude that the president and not the pope possesses the authority and charism for deciding when Catholic citizens go to war. See Richard John Neuhaus, "The Public Square," *First Things*, no. 133 (May 2003): 76–92; and Rowan Williams and George Weigel, "War & Statecraft: An Exchange," *First Things*, no. 141 (March 2004): 14–21.

29. Jeffrey Stout, "Comments on Six Responses to Democracy and Tradition," *Journal of Religious Ethics* 33, no. 4 (2005): 716–18.

30. At points, Stout seems aware that Neuhaus does not quite fit his typology. He writes, "Neuhaus is more favorably disposed toward modern democracy than Milbank is, he nonetheless bemoans 'a religious evacuation of the public square.'" Stout, *Democracy and Tradition*, 92.

31. Jeffrey Stout, letter to author, March 6, 2004. For an interesting study, see Jan Feldman, *Lubavitchers as Citizens: A Paradox of Liberal Democracy* (Ithaca, N.Y.: Cornell University Press, 2003).

32. There are many other voices of importance: Mill, Rousseau, Kant in his way plays a role, not to mention Rawls. But these often operate in the shadow cast by Locke, at least in the American political context.

33. For the past half century, most historiographical studies of the founding era have argued either for a thoroughly Lockean or thoroughly un-Lockean founding. Recent work shows

that it was definitively, but not thereby exclusively, influenced by Locke. The literature on the topic is massive, but two introductory studies that effectively summarize the terms of the debate are Alan Gibson, *Understanding the Founding: The Crucial Questions* (Lawrence: University Press of Kansas, 2007); Zuckert, *Natural Rights Republic.*

34. E.g., Garry Wills argues that Hutcheson and not Locke influenced the founders (via Jefferson), but even he concedes that this is not the case in the area of religious toleration. Garry Wills, *Inventing America: Jefferson's Declaration of Independence* (Garden City, N.Y.: Doubleday, 1978), 361. Similarly, the debate between writers such as Joyce Appleby and Lance Banning about Locke's influence on the founders is primarily about economic issues, not religion. Joyce Appleby, *Liberalism and Republicanism in the Historical Imagination* (Cambridge, Mass.: Harvard University Press, 1992).

35. Zuckert, *Natural Rights Republic,* 123.

36. Locke, *Letter Concerning Toleration,* 15.

37. See Sandel, *Democracy's Discontent,* 5; emphasis added.

38. Michael Quirk, "Stanley Hauerwas: An Interview," *Cross Currents* 52, no. 1 (2002): 10.

39. C. B. Macpherson, *The Political Theory of Possessive Individualism: Hobbes to Locke* (Oxford: Clarendon, 1962). Contemporary Locke scholars typically examine Macpherson's reading of Locke alongside the interpretation of controversial political philosopher Leo Strauss. See Leo Strauss, *Natural Right and History* (Chicago: University of Chicago Press, 1953).

40. See John Locke, *Two Treatises of Government,* ed. Peter Laslett (Cambridge: Cambridge University Press, 1960).

41. Perez Zagorin, *How the Idea of Religious Toleration Came to the West* (Princeton, N.J.: Princeton University Press, 2003), 245.

42. If Locke began composition in November 1685, as many believe, this was within two weeks of the revocation of the Edict of Nantes. This event unleashed a way of Catholic persecution against French Protestants, some 200,000 of whom escaped to the Dutch Republic and elsewhere. Many of those who remained were subjected to enslavement on galleys, torture, and murder. Locke, *Letter Concerning Toleration,* xv. Also see the introduction to John Locke, *The Reasonableness of Christianity as Delivered in the Scriptures,* ed. John Higgins-Biddle (Oxford: Clarendon Press, 1998).

43. Charles Taylor, "Religion in a Free Society," in *Articles of Faith, Articles of Peace,* ed. James Davison Hunter and Os Guinness (Washington, D.C.: Brookings Institution Press, 1990), 100.

44. Ibid., 100.

45. Ibid.

46. Ibid., 101.

47. Niccolò Machiavelli, *The Letters of Machiavelli,* trans. Allan Gilbert (Chicago: University of Chicago Press, 1988), 248.

48. Locke of course realizes that a given ruler may violate the just bounds if he is corrupt or foolish, but this does not undermine the system.

49. Locke, *Letter Concerning Toleration,* 17.

50. Ibid., 18.

51. Ibid., 17.

52. Ibid., 19.

53. Ibid., 21.

54. Ibid., 23.

55. E.g., "The end of a religious society (as has already been said) is . . . the acquisition of eternal life. . . . Nothing ought nor can be transacted in [the church] to the possession of civil and worldly goods." Locke is clear throughout that "care of souls" refers to the alternatives between "eternal happiness or misery." Locke, *Letter Concerning Toleration*, 31.

56. Ibid., 31.

57. Ibid., 18.

58. I do not mean to unfairly "pick on" Falwell or Robertson; however, their public visibility make them useful representatives of politically conservative Christianity in the United States.

59. Much more could be said about Budziszewski's comments, including asking whether his article quite delivers the "grace" and "wit" promised by its title—especially as he advises that when a homosexual believes a Christian hates him for being gay, the Christian should respond, "Of course I don't hate you, but a pretty good case could be made that you hate yourself." However my goal here is not to provide an analysis of his arguments, but simply to offer an example of a Christian argument against homosexuality. Budziszewski is by no means an extreme member of the so-called Religious Right; he is an intelligent, well-published, tenured professor at the University of Texas. His main field of study is natural law.

60. This treatment of Budziszewski's position is extremely brief. For more detail, see Perry, "Subverting the Republic," 52–66.

61. Conveniently for my purposes, Budziszewski elsewhere provides an interpretation of Locke's work, allowing the reader to see how it relates to the views stated here regarding homosexuality. See J. Budziszewski, *Written on the Heart: The Case for Natural Law* (Downers Grove, Ill.: InterVarsity Press, 1997), 116.

62. *Lawrence v. Texas*, 539 U.S. 558 (2003), quoting *Planned Parenthood v. Casey*, 505 U.S. 833 (1992).

63. Locke, *Letter Concerning Toleration*, 43; emphasis added. In the immediate context of the quotation, Locke is not actually making a normative claim, but it is clear from the whole of the *Letter Concerning Toleration* that it does represent his own position.

64. These sequels were written primarily against Jonas Proast's three critiques, collected in Jonas Proast, *The Argument of the Letter Concerning Toleration* (New York: Garland, 1984).

65. Marshall, *John Locke, Toleration*, 541.

66. Locke, "98 Errors," in *Writings*, 82.

67. We can of course imagine ways Locke could make his principle more nuanced: Lying about the existence of a fire in a crowded building certainly poses a direct enough harm to be criminal, even if it is not actually perjury.

68. John Courtney Murray, *We Hold These Truths: Catholic Reflections on the American Proposition* (Garden City, N.Y.: Image Books, 1964).

69. Though Hollenbach's work is (self-consciously) theoretical rather than historical, it does depend on implicit historical premises, and the occasional places he mentions the historical figures are clues to this. What he says in those places is wonderfully characteristic of the interpretation of Locke described above. E.g., "This is not to make a revisionist historical claim that Locke or Jefferson held the view of rights proposed [by the U.S. bishops. But they ought to have]." David Hollenbach, "A Communitarian Reconstruction of Human Rights: Contributions from Catholic Tradition," in *Catholicism and Liberalism: Contributions to American Public Philosophy*, ed. David Hollenbach and R. Bruce Douglass (Cambridge: Cambridge University Press, 1994).

70. Brian Stiltner, *Religion and the Common Good: Catholic Contributions to Building Community in a Liberal Society* (Lanham, Md.: Rowman & Littlefield, 1999).

71. Nicholas Wolterstorff, "Why We Should Reject What Liberalism Tells Us about Speaking and Acting in Public for Religious Reasons," in *Religion and Contemporary Liberalism*, ed. Paul Weithman (Notre Dame, Ind.: University of Notre Dame Press, 1997). Nicholas Wolterstorff, "An Engagement with Rorty," *Journal of Religious Ethics* 31, no. 1 (2003): 129–39; Wolterstorff, *John Locke and Ethics of Belief*. Nicholas Wolterstorff, "Do Christians Have Good Reasons for Supporting Liberal Democracy?" *The Modern Schoolman* 78 (2001): 229–48; Wolterstorff, "Abraham Kuyper," 299.

72. See John Witte, "The Biology and Biography of Liberty: Abraham Kuyper and the American Experiment," in *Religion, Pluralism, and Public Life: Abraham Kuyper's Legacy for the Twenty-First Century*, ed. Luis Lugo (Grand Rapids: William B. Eerdmans, 2000); John Witte, "Facts and Fictions about the History of the Separation of Church and State," *Journal of Church and State* 48, no. 1 (2006): 15–46; John Witte, *God's Joust, God's Justice: Law and Religion in the Western Tradition* (Grand Rapids: William B. Eerdmans, 2006); John Witte, "How to Govern a City on a Hill: The Early Puritan Contribution to American Constitutionalism," *Emory Law Journal* 39 (1990): 41–64; and John Witte, "A Most Mild and Equitable Establishment of Religion: John Adams and the Massachusetts Experiment," *Journal of Church and State* 41, no. 2 (1999): 213–52.

73. Richard John Neuhaus, *The Catholic Moment: The Paradox of the Church in the Postmodern World* (San Francisco: Harper & Row, 1987); Richard John Neuhaus, *The Naked Public Square: Religion and Democracy in America*, 2nd ed. (Grand Rapids: William B. Eerdmans, 1984).

74. Michael Novak, "The Achievement of Jacques Maritain," *First Things*, no. 8 (December 1990): 39–44; Michael Novak, "The Faith of the Founding," *First Things*, no. 132 (April 2003): 27–32; Michael Novak, *Free Persons and the Common Good* (Lanham: Madison Books, 1989); Michael Novak, *On Two Wings: Humble Faith and Common Sense at the American Founding* (San Francisco: Encounter Books, 2002); Michael Novak, *The Spirit of Democratic Capitalism* (New York: Simon & Schuster, 1982); Michael Novak, "War to Topple Saddam Is a Moral Obligation," *The Times*, February 12, 2003.

75. Stout, *Democracy and Tradition*, chap. 3.

76. Perhaps unsurprisingly, we again encounter religious arguments about homosexuality, for that is the issue foremost in Rorty's mind. He writes that biblically based arguments against homosexuality ought to be excluded because they are "bad taste," "reckless persecution," and "an incitement to violence." Those who employ such arguments "should be made to feel ashamed" and "should be shunned and despised." Rorty continues, "The occasional Gustavo Guttierez or Martin Luther King does not compensate for the ubiquitous Joseph Ratzingers and Jerry Falwells." Richard Rorty, "Religion in the Public Square: A Reconsideration," *Journal of Religious Ethics* 31, no. 1 (2003): 142–43. This directly contradicts Stout's argument that religious arguments ought to be valued precisely because of figures like King. It would be interesting to compare at length how Rorty's and Stout's positions on religion and politics are determined by their prior prudential judgment of whether the "Kings" outweigh the "Falwells."

77. It is no coincidence that Rorty describes his vision as "Jeffersonian," Jefferson being among the most Lockean of the founders.

78. See especially Mark A. Noll, *America's God: From Jonathan Edwards to Abraham Lincoln* (Oxford: Oxford University Press, 2002); and John Witte, *Religion and the American Constitutional Experiment*, 2nd ed. (Boulder, Colo.: Westview Press, 2005).

79. Wolterstorff, *Educating for Life*, 187.

On the Importance of a Drawn Sword: Christian Thinking about Preemptive War—and Its Modern Outworking

David Clough and Brian Stiltner

JUST WAR THINKERS, SUCH AS HUGO GROTIUS, RESISTED USING FEARS about the enemy's intentions as grounds for preemptive military action. This conservative rendering of what was permissible came under pressure in debates about the military responses to Iraq, Iran, and other nations seeking weapons. Those arguing for a more permissive category of preventive war maintain that a prudent leader must anticipate developing military threats and respond before an act of aggression is imminent. Though the just war tradition must respond to the changing nature of military threats, if the tradition is to remain viable as a moral framework, it is vital that it not be made more malleable in this area.

The just war tradition has long allowed preemptive attacks on the basis of self-defense but not preventive wars to preclude a future threat from emerging. In their discussion of when it is appropriate to pursue justice through going to war, the classic architects of the just war tradition were cautious in using fears about the enemy's intentions as grounds for preemptive military action. For Hugo Grotius (1583–1645), such action required "moral certainty" about both the enemy's power and intentions; he followed the Roman historian Livy (c. 59 BC–17 AD) in condemning preemptive killing "before a sword had been drawn." However, this conservative rendering of preemption has been put under intense pressure by advocates of an expanded approach to preemption as part of the so-called war on terror. The pressure toward expanded preemption was seen most clearly in the 2003 invasion of Iraq, but it had precursors before 2001, such as the Israeli missile attack on Iraq's Osirak nuclear reactor in 1981 and the U.S. bombings of Libya in 1986 and of Sudan in 1998. This pressure will continue for some time to come, because the problems of nuclear weapons proliferation and international terrorism are not going away any time soon. Those arguing for a more permissive category of preemption maintain that, under current conditions, a prudent leader must anticipate developing military threats and respond before an act of aggression is imminent. On the other side are those who argue that loosening the standards for preemption would be illegal under international law, unjust to foreign citizens, and dangerous to global stability.

Specifying criteria for legitimate preemptive attack has been a perennial challenge for just war theories and international lawyers. Yet both the just war tradition and international law have in place a workable understanding of preemption. Historically, that understanding has served reasonably well, but it was already being challenged by weapons proliferation and the rise of international terrorism in the decades before the 2000s, and recent developments have increased the urgency of taking a fresh look at the ethics of preemption. Most academics specializing in the ethics of war have raised very critical questions about expanding preemption, especially in the case of the Iraq War. A large majority of Christian leaders and ethicists likewise resist the move from preemptive to preventive war, especially in the case of Iraq.[1]

Nonetheless, a convincing ethical case against the Iraq War does not provide a satisfactory conclusion to debates over preemption from the perspective of theological ethics, for two reasons. First, it is a fair and important question as to whether new forms of military threat do necessitate a reworking or redevelopment of the ethics of preemption. It may be that Iraq was a bad case for applying new ideas about preemption, but that other cases—such as Iran or North Korea—will be more compelling. This case will be claimed by some partisans of the so-called Bush Doctrine of preemption, so ethicists will need to clarify the criteria that would handle foreseeable threats and provocations. Second, we believe that there are key theological insights related to the discussion about expanding preemption that deserve a wider hearing.

In the face of widespread calls for making the just war tradition more permissive of anticipatory military action, we argue that it is crucial to maintain a *restrictive* definition of imminent threat as grounds for preemptive wars. In dialogue with the tradition, we take up Grotius's challenge and ponder what constitutes a "drawn sword" today. Although it is certainly necessary for the just war tradition to respond to the changing nature of military threats, we maintain that if the tradition is to have moral standing as a framework of judgment standing over the interests even of the world's most powerful nations, it is vital that it not be made more malleable in this area.

We begin by noting the confusion that characterizes the current understanding of preemptive attack. The first challenge is definitional. Since the terrorist attacks of September 11, 2001, it has become increasingly common in ethical and theological discussions to distinguish the term *preemptive war* from *preventive war*, although the use is not universal. An example is when the Catholic bishops of Germany stated in January 2003, using a variant rendering of the word: "A security strategy, which professes to be based on the idea of a preventative war, contravenes Catholic teachings and international law." They said that a preventative war was an aggressive act and so could not be defined as an act of self-defense.[2] The differentiation of these terms is also found in Michael Walzer's modern classic *Just and Unjust Wars*, first published in 1977. The concept toward which the terminologies reach is actually centuries old, as we will see when we turn to Grotius. It seems best, in this context, simply to stipulate the following definitions of the broad category with two subcategories, which we base largely on Walzer's discussion.

Anticipatory attack or war is the overarching category; these are military actions justified largely on the basis of the other party's expected and probable behavior, and they therefore inevitably depend on speculative judgments about the other party's intentions that could be accurate or inaccurate. *Preemption* is a military attack or war launched in anticipation of a serious military threat that can be reasonably construed as an imminent attack. It is a form of self-defense, or in some cases, defense of a third party, but it is illegitimate if it does not satisfy the other just war criteria. Preemption need not mean merely a reflex response with no opportunity for planning.[3] *Preventive* attack or war, in Walzer's words, "responds to a distant danger; [it is] a matter of foresight and free choice."[4] This is forward-looking military action that aims to forestall a threat from developing to the point that it will become imminent and intolerable. As Walzer indicates in his classic discussion, we can imagine a spectrum running from reflex action (hitting just as you notice someone is about to hit you in a context when virtually no deliberation is possible, which is imaginable only on the interpersonal—"domestic"—level) to the most speculative of preventive wars. Preventive war is assumed to be unethical because the threat is, as stipulated, speculative; thus many alternative options for pursuing justice are available. The question for Walzer is: If we move in our minds from the extreme of speculative war toward the extreme of reflexive self-defense, at what point do we reach the realm of justified preemption?

The concern that motivates us to write is that the current geopolitical context makes it appear advantageous for the United States and its allies to stretch the definition of preemption in the tradition to allow attacks that would previously have been judged illegitimate. In his June 1, 2002, speech at the U.S. Military Academy at West Point, President George W. Bush laid out principles that have become known as the "Bush Doctrine." One of the three prongs of this doctrine—alongside regime change and assertive American leadership—is the intention to engage in preemptive attacks. As Bush put it, the United States will "take the battle to the enemy, disrupt his plans, and confront the worst threats before they emerge."[5] Following this speech, the Bush administration was at pains to claim that this doctrine of preemption fell within the parameters set out by traditional laws of war. According to the National Security Strategy of 2002:

> For centuries, international law recognized that nations need not suffer an attack before they can lawfully take action to defend themselves against forces

that present an imminent danger of attack. Legal scholars and international jurists often conditioned the legitimacy of preemption on the existence of an imminent threat—most often a visible mobilization of armies, navies, and air forces preparing to attack. We must adapt the concept of imminent threat to the capabilities and objectives of today's adversaries. Rogue states and terrorists do not seek to attack us using conventional means. They know such attacks would fail. Instead, they rely on acts of terror and, potentially, the use of weapons of mass destruction—weapons that can be easily concealed, delivered covertly, and used without warning.[6]

Yet Bush himself emphasized the novelty of his position, stating in his 2003 State of the Union Address, "Some have said we must not act until the threat is imminent. Since when have terrorists and tyrants announced their intentions, politely putting us on notice before they strike? If this threat is permitted to fully and suddenly emerge, all actions, all words, and all recriminations would come too late."[7] Former U.S. secretary of state George P. Schultz gave his support to this innovation, blurring the categories of preemption and prevention: "President Bush has given us the concepts we need. This is a war, not a matter of law enforcement. States that support terror are as guilty as the terrorists. . . . Our goal is not primarily to punish and retaliate but to prevent acts of terror through intelligence that enables us to preempt and ultimately to eliminate the source. . . . We reserve, within the framework of our right to self-defense, the right to preempt terrorist threats within a state's borders. Not just hot pursuit: hot preemption."[8]

Having so far cited politicians, we could be tempted to regard these developments as the ways of realpolitik but not as a theoretical challenge. Yet, of course, some political theorists, theologians, and ethicists have been making arguments for expanded preemption in general or for engagement in Iraq or other countries that bear the marks of preventive war. Within Christian discourse, it is hard to locate ethicists or theologians who openly affirm preventive war, but many have argued for more permissive accounts of preemption. Jean Bethke Elshtain, who supported the invasion of Iraq and has not changed her mind since the failure to discover weapons of mass destruction (WMD), believes that there was enough evidence of imminent threat combined with a need to punish Saddam Hussein for human rights abuses. She notes that the nature of the regime matters: "Any state in breach of peace terms and believed to possess WMD will trigger a more negative assessment than a relatively transparent democratic state not similarly in breach and in defiance. Or, for that matter, a very nasty regime that has, up to this point, stood down from terrorizing its own population systematically or actually using WMD. Regime change in Iraq cannot be severed from these, and other, considerations."[9] George Weigel argued in an interview that "the nature of certain regimes makes their mere possession of weapons of mass destruction (or their attempt to acquire such weapons and the means to launch them) an imminent danger toward which a military response is not only possible but morally imperative."[10]

Even bolder is the theologian Stephen Strehle, who supported what he called a preemptive attack on Iraq on the combined basis of the WMD threat, Saddam's tyranny, and the risk of Saddam cooperating with terrorists: "It is more than likely that Saddam possesses and produces at present biological and chemical agents. It is more than obvious that Osama bin Laden would like to obtain these weapons, judging from his sudden change of heart about the Iraqi regime and his condemnation of America's invasion of that nation. No one should have an imminent threat like this hanging over them. Just the mere possibility represents a clear and present danger that needs to be eliminated and eliminated now."[11]

What is notable in all these quotations are assertions that "mere" threats, possible risks, and attempts by a regime to acquire weapons suddenly become a causus belli. This is novel in the just war tradition, despite the claims of these writers to stand within that tradition. Whether this is the way that the just war tradition should be "stretched or developed to meet new realities," as Weigel puts it,[12] is at issue in this essay.

We therefore stand at a moment when the United States is conducting foreign policy in a way that questions the classic concept of preemption and pushes it in the direction of preventive war. Is this shift necessary in light of new realities, or is it a dangerous blurring of principle? To orient ourselves in this strange new world, we now turn back to one of the cornerstones of the just war tradition, Grotius. Our hope is that attending to his reflections will be fruitful in reminding ourselves why the tradition has considered it important to make preemption a narrow category that cannot be exploited to justify any war aimed at reducing the threat of a neighboring nation. Once we have revisited his thought in this area, we will discuss its significance for the current debate.

Grotius

Hugo Grotius's 1625 work *De Jure Belli ac Pacis* (On the Right of War and Peace) is often seen both as the beginning of international law and as the moment at which the law of nations could be thought about apart from theology for the first time. If the latter is true, it was no part of Grotius's intention; for him, God's ordering of the universe meant that whatever right reason dictates should be understood as commanded or forbidden by God (1.1.10.1[13]). Grotius was known as an apologist for Christianity, and in this work he is concerned to give a properly theological basis for judgments Christian leaders had to make.[14] His work was motivated by concern about the warring habits of Christians:

"Throughout the Christian world I observed a lack of restraint in relation to war, such as even barbarous races should be ashamed of; I observed that men rush to arms for slight causes, or no cause at all, and that when arms have once been taken up there is no longer any respect for law, divine or human; it is as if, in accordance with a general decree, frenzy had openly been let loose for the committing of all crimes."[15] To the disorder of seventeenth-century Europe, with religious wars largely fought by undisciplined mercenaries on behalf of similarly matched nations, he sought to bring order based on right reason.[16]

Despite this concern for order, Grotius was no dove. He came to the conclusion that the only way to avoid a Dutch civil war was to support an effective military coup, and he was imprisoned when this effort failed.[17] While writing *De Jure Belli ac Pacis*, he was still an adviser to his former employer, the East India Company, and he argued that private parties such as the company could make war as if it were a state.[18] Against many contemporaries, he insisted that wars could be fought not just to redress an injury done but also to punish nations that breached the law of nature (2.20.40.4). He believed that European settlers in America had the right to make war against the indigenous populations if this was the only way they could avoid the disruption of their agriculture (2.2.17). As we shall see, he also believes that preemptive war can be justified in some circumstances. He writes, therefore, as one who believes war to be on occasion morally legitimate or even morally demanded but who seeks to restrict both the incidence and destructiveness of war through the codification of norms on which Christian nations can agree.

Grotius begins his consideration of the right of war with definitions. He follows Cicero in defining war as any dispute involving the use of force (1.1.2.1) and intends his discussion to apply to violent disputes between individuals as well as to conflicts between nations. By the right of war, he means those things that can be done without injustice to one's enemy (1.1.3.1). He follows Aristotle in distinguishing between natural and voluntary justice, and he identifies natural law with the dictate of right reason (1.1.10.1), which is unalterable, even for God (1.1.10.5). Voluntary law can be human or divine; divine voluntary law was given to humankind after creation, after the flood, and in the Gospel of Christ, and it is binding on everyone as soon as they are sufficiently made known to them (1.1.15). In relation to the law of nature, Grotius considers that war is justified from the instinct of self-preservation (1.2.1.1). This instinct can be seen in all animals; right reason does not therefore prohibit all violence but only that violence that "is in conflict with society," which he explains as violence that "attempts to take away the rights of another" (1.2.1.5). He cites evidence in support of the legitimacy of war from the Old Testament and from "wise" nations in history (1.2.3.1). He recognizes that arguments against war on the basis of the New Testament are more plausible, but he offers twelve arguments in favor of war from the New Testament (1.2.7) before turning to a critique of biblical arguments against war (1.2.8). He then defends the legitimacy of private wars even in the context of public authorities (1.3) and, while arguing against a general right of subjects to make war on superiors, specifies a range of exceptions to this rule, including when a king shows himself to be an enemy of the whole people (1.4.11).

In considering justifiable causes for war, Grotius begins with a clear statement that initially seems to rule out any kind of preemptive war: "No other just cause for undertaking war can there be excepting injury received" (2.1.1.4). In elucidating his position with reference to Greek, Roman, and church authorities, however, it soon becomes clear that he considers that war could be justified before an injury has been committed, because actions provoking war may be of two kinds: "An action lies for a wrong not yet committed in cases where a guarantee is sought against a threatened wrong, or security against an anticipated injury, or an interdict of a different sort against the use of violence. An action for a wrong committed lies where a reparation for injury, or the punishment of a wrong-doer, is sought" (2.1.2.1). He therefore concludes that the first justifiable cause of war "is an injury not yet inflicted, which menaces either person or property" (2.1.2.3).

Once Grotius has acknowledged the legitimacy of preemptive action, he is concerned to ensure that this permission is not interpreted too broadly. In reflecting on the legitimacy of defending against attacks on life, he cites with approval Thomas Aquinas's judgment that lethal self-defense is permissible if the killing is not intentional and there is no nonlethal alternative (2.1.4.2).[19] But this defense is only permissible when the danger is immediate and cannot justify killing on the basis of fear: "The danger, again, must be immediate and imminent in point of time. I admit, to be sure, that if the assailant seizes weapons in such a way that his intent to kill is manifest the crime can be forestalled; for in morals as in material things a point is not to be found which does not have a certain breadth. But those who accept fear of any sort as justifying anticipatory slaying are themselves greatly deceived, and deceive others" (2.1.5.1).

In support of this point, Grotius cites a string of authorities in the remainder of this section. He notes Cicero's observation that "most wrongs have their origin in fear, since he who plans to do wrong to another fears that, if he does not accomplish his purpose, he may himself suffer harm" (2.1.5.1) and his question: "Who has ever established this principle, or to whom without the gravest danger to all men can it be granted, that he shall have the right to kill a man by whom he say he fears that he himself later may be killed?" (2.1.5.1). From Xenophon, he cites Clearchus's speech: "I have known men who, becoming afraid of one another, in consequence of calumny or suspicion, and purposing to inflict injury before receiving injury, have done the most dreadful wrongs to those who had had no such intention, and had not even thought of doing such a thing" (2.1.5.1). He notes the rhetorical question in Cato's speech to the

Rhodians: "Shall we be first to do what we say they wished to do?" (2.1.5.1). From Gellius, he notes the disanalogy with the situation of the gladiator: "When a gladiator is equipped for fighting, the alternatives offered by combat are these, either to kill, if he shall have made the first decisive stroke, or to fall, if he shall have failed. But the life of men generally is not hedged about by necessity so unfair and unrelenting that you are obliged to strike the first blow, and may suffer if you have failed to be first to strike" (2.1.5.1).

In Thucydides, Grotius finds further support for concern about anticipatory action: "The future is still uncertain, and no one, influenced by that thought, should arouse enmities which are not future but certain" (2.1.5.1). Finally, from Livy, he notes the worry that "in the effort to guard against fear men cause themselves to be feared, and we inflict upon others the injury which has been warded off from ourselves, as if it were necessary either to do or to suffer wrong" (2.1.5.1).

Grotius next considers the appropriate response to a person who is planning a plot or to corrupt judicial procedure: "I maintain that he cannot lawfully be killed, either if the danger can in any other way be avoided, or if it is not altogether certain that the danger cannot be otherwise avoided. Generally, in fact, the delay that will intervene affords opportunity to apply many remedies, to take advantage of many accidental occurrences; as the proverb runs, 'There's many a slip 'twixt cup and lip'" (2.1.5.2). He recognizes that other theologians and jurists are more permissive, but he calls his opinion "better and safer," as well as being supported by the authorities he has cited.

Grotius then argues that killing is justifiable where it is the only option to prevent the loss of a limb or one's chastity, and that killing in defense of property is justifiable under the law of nature but not according to the Gospel. He then turns to larger questions of public war, and he quickly rejects the position that wars may be fought to weaken a neighboring power: "Quite untenable is the position, which has been maintained by some, that according to the law of nations it is right to take up arms in order to weaken a growing power which, if it become too great, may be a source of danger" (2.1.17). In this context, he does concede that this consideration may enter into judgments on the basis of expediency, if a war is justifiable for other reasons. He sees it as crucial, however, to recognize that preventing threats cannot become a justification for resorting to war: "But that the possibility of being attacked confers the right to attack is abhorrent to every principle of equity. Human life exists under such conditions that complete security is never guaranteed to us. For protection against uncertain fears we must rely on Divine Providence, and on a wariness free from reproach, not on force" (2.1.17).

Grotius returns to the theme in a later chapter when addressing possible unjust causes of war. The first unjust cause of war he treats is the fear of something uncertain: "We have said above that fear with respect to a neighbouring power is not a sufficient cause. For in order that a self-defence may be lawful it must be necessary; and it is not necessary unless we are certain, not only regarding the power of our neighbour, but also regarding his intention; the degree of certainty required is that which is accepted in morals" (2.22.5.1).

Obviously, this leaves us with the question of what degree of uncertainty is required in "morals," but in the following paragraph Grotius provides examples of unjust causes: "We can in no wise approve the view of those who declare that it is a just cause of war when a neighbour who is restrained by no agreement builds a fortress on his own soil, or some other fortification which may some day cause us harm. Against the fears which arise from such actions we must resort to counter-fortifications on our own land and other similar remedies, but not to force of arms" (2.22.5.2). He is also keen to state clearly that military advantage apart from necessity cannot substitute for necessary self-defense as a justifiable motive: "Advantage does not confer the same right as necessity" (2.22.6).

One final relevant text from Grotius is the passage in book 3 of *De Jure Belli ac Pacis*, where he discusses the importance of declarations of war. He cites Livy's critique of Menippus, who killed some Romans when war had not been declared and hostilities had not begun. Livy argues that the drawing of swords or the shedding of blood would have justified the attack, but that as neither had taken place, the killings were unjustified (3.3.6).

For Grotius, therefore, war may be justified on the basis of "an injury not yet inflicted, which menaces either person or property." Once he has allowed this, however, his entire concern is to avoid the permission being interpreted too widely. The danger must be "immediate and imminent in point of time." The example he gives is of an assailant who "seizes a weapon in such a way that his intent to kill is manifest" (2.1.5.1). Lawful self-defense must be necessary, which means that one is morally certain that the enemy has both the power and intention to attack. Any wider permission risks chaos; allowing persons or nations to kill on the basis of fear of being killed would be dangerous in the extreme and would result in attacking those who had no aggressive intention. We are generally not in the situation of the gladiator where we have to choose between killing or being killed, and we should not cause certain enmity in response to an uncertain future event. Otherwise, we guard ourselves against fear only by causing ourselves to be feared. It is therefore unjustifiable to wage war in order to prevent a neighbor becoming a threat; if a neighbor builds a fortification, we may want to build our own, but we are not justified in going to war. We should recognize that delaying an attack "affords opportunity to apply many remedies, to take advantage of many accidental occurrences" that would otherwise be closed to us. At all costs, we must guard against allowing that "the possibility of being attacked confers the right to attack." The human situation means that complete security is never guaranteed, and we must rely on God's providence and wariness, rather than the use of force.[20]

Appraisal

Although Grotius's text is four centuries old, and frequently relies on sources considerably older, it is hard to dispute the pertinence of his observations and conclusions for today's debates. He saw the need both to justify preemptive war and to emphasize the need to place strict limits on when war could be legitimately employed. Given its significance in the tradition, it is unsurprising that key aspects of his thought in this area are obviously present in modern accounts that determine when preemptive war could be justified. William Galston summarizes a brief discussion of preemption as applied to the Iraq war under four criteria: the severity of the threat, the degree of probability of the threat, the imminence of the threat, and the cost of delay.[21] Galston does not hold out WMD as a special type of imminent threat; rather, the nature of a threat from other nations' weapons programs can be judged by each of the four criteria. Iraq's possible possession of transferable nuclear weapons would pose an especially high risk, but Galston claims that in 2002–3, the United States was able to judge that the probability of this possession was unlikely, that the threat of Iraq's use of any WMD was "not imminent by any definition of imminence," and, therefore, that there was no severe cost in pursuing other methods of responding to the risk.[22]

We can see Galston's first three factors as attempts to specify Grotius's insistence on "moral certainty" about the power and intention of the aggressor, though they suggest scales rather than following Grotius in trying to establish a clear threshold for preemptive war. The fourth factor looks more dubious according to Grotius's categories, given that he rejects protecting military advantage and weakening a neighbor as just causes of war. From Grotius's perspective, such a consideration could open the way to preemptive war to address threats that are neither severe nor imminent, if only the perceived cost of delay is sufficient.

Walzer concludes that preemptive war is justified when a nation faces a "sufficient threat" of an offensive attack that is "imminent," which he glosses as meaning a manifest intent to injure, a degree of active preparation that makes intent a positive danger, and a general situation in which doing anything other than fighting greatly magnifies the risk.[23] Similarly to Galston, Walzer thinks that all types of risk, including the risk of being attacked with WMD, could be assessed by the same calculus.[24] Likewise, in a similar way to Galston, Walzer's first two categories could be interpreted as explications of Grotius's criterion of moral certainty about power and intention, but the third criterion of acting to avoid the growth of a risk that is not imminent or sufficient seems similar to the case Grotius rejects of a war in response to an enemy's erection of fortifications.

A third example of a modern attempt to set out criteria for preemptive war is that outlined by Neta Crawford. She identifies four criteria: the threat must be to the party itself, rather than its interests; there must be strong evidence that war was inevitable and likely in the near future; preemption should be likely to succeed in reducing the threat; and military action must be necessary, with no alternative course of action likely to work.[25] Somewhat more than Galston and Walzer, she suggests that the possibility of WMD possessed by a rogue state or a terrorist group presents a new risk that may change the urgency with which other nations must respond. But she also argues that it can be dangerous and counterproductive to lower the threshold for preemptive action.[26] Her first criterion limits what can be appropriately viewed as national self-defense and echoes Grotius's concern that preemptive wars must be confined to those confronting an urgent imminent threat to a nation. She cites the definition of national interests in the U. S. Quadrennial Defense Review of 2001, which include the "vitality and productivity of the global economy," "access to key markets and strategic resources," and maintaining the "pre-eminence" of the U.S. military. Though Grotius would not be surprised that a nation desired these ends, he clearly judged that such motivations were not legitimate justifications for war. Crawford quotes Richard Betts, who makes a point very similar to Grotius's concern that complete security is not part of the human condition: "When security is defined in terms broader than protecting the near-term integrity of national sovereignty and borders, the distinction between offense and defense blurs hopelessly. . . . Security can be as insatiable an appetite as acquisitiveness—there may never be enough buffers."[27]

These modern distillations of criteria for preemptive war have substantial common ground with Grotius, but they also move beyond him in a permissive direction in the cases of Galston and Walzer. This commonality masks a very significant contrast between the positions of European nations in the early seventeenth century and the position of the United States and its allies at the beginning of the twenty-first. In Grotius's day, nations with similar resources were vying with one another for military advantage. In this context, he could make the case that restricting the legitimate grounds for preemptive war would be to the mutual advantage of all nations, in avoiding continual warring between parties that was destructive and ultimately futile. Four hundred years later, the relevant context is global and very different. The United States currently has a substantial military advantage over its closest rivals, and it maintains this position through spending as much on its military as the rest of the world put together.[28] Though the September 11, 2001, terrorist attacks and the lack of success in military responses to them have weakened the sense that the United States can merely do as it chooses around the world, it is less clear than it would have been to Grotius's interlocutors why it would not be to the advantage of the United States to go to war to prevent the emergence of threats to its interests wherever they arise. It is therefore not surprising that there is pressure to modify the judgments of Grotius and the Christian just war tradition that followed him so as to make it more permissive of preempting threats where there is not moral certainty about the intention of an enemy to launch an imminent attack.

A second key difference between the context in which Grotius was writing and our own is the astonishing scale of threat presented by nuclear weaponry, and the potential for chemical, biological, and conventional weapons to be deployed on a scale unthinkable for Grotius and his contemporaries. One response to this change would be to argue that the just war tradition needs to be revised in relation to preemption to deal with these large-scale and rapidly deployable threats, as Weigel proposed in the interview cited above but has not yet outlined systematically. It is our view that the framework Grotius sets out can accommodate these new and much more destructive weapons without making it more permissive of preemptive war. The appropriate criteria for assessing threats should remain unchanged: Preemptive attack in self-defense is justified when there is solid reason to believe than an enemy is capable of and intends to make an imminent attack. The scale of destructive power potentially wielded by an enemy will change many factors in deciding on an appropriate policy; it will have an impact on the arms nations consider adequate for their defense, it will increase the motivation to establish and maintain good relations with neighboring nations, it should encourage states to engage in discussions about arms limitation, and it will have implications for the planning of military strategies. However, in a situation where international law is applied equally to all, it does not alter Grotius's judgment that war should not be used to prevent other nations from becoming a threat. In the context of nuclear, biological, chemical, and large-scale conventional weapons, it remains the case that making war permissible in the absence of a viable and imminent threat would make all nation-states much more vulnerable to attack based on the fears of their enemies.

It is worth noting two contexts in which this judgment that the magnitude of weapons threat is irrelevant to the norms governing preemptive war would need modification. The first is if an authoritative and credible international institution were tasked to enforce agreements on arms limitation. Provided that international agreements were policed equitably, the question of when to intervene to prevent the development of new weapons systems would then be a matter of decision for the international community, which could decide it was appropriate to intervene before threats became imminent. The key difference between this case and that in which there is no international authority is that where there is a properly functioning international body authorizing intervention, the risk of individual nations engaging in war merely to improve their strategic position in relation to other states is avoided.

Considering this case provokes the obvious empirical question of whether the existing United Nations, and the Security Council in particular, satisfies the criterion of an authoritative and credible international institution. Here we must recognize that the permanent members of the Security Council anachronistically represent a post–World War II settlement that has little relevance to international relationships at the beginning of the twenty-first century. For it to become the credible international authority necessary to function in this judicial mode, the Security Council is in urgent need of reform to make it globally representative, and its permanent members must enable this transition without regard for their narrow short-term interests.

So great is the need for this international authority, however, that we suggest that, given the lack of alternatives, even in its current unreformed state the UN Security Council is the appropriate locus for decisions about when it is appropriate to counter weapons threats. To perform this role credibly, its members must act with restraint and a commitment to the good of the community of nations. The veto power of individual permanent members means that some interventions will be rejected for bad reasons. But for nations to pursue preventive wars without Security Council approval, such as was done in Iraq in 2003, is a grave threat to world peace and at odds with the just war tradition as informed by the thought of Grotius.

The second context in which our judgment would need revision—that the power of weapons systems is irrelevant for the framework of decisions about preemptive war—is very different. We have noted the overwhelming military dominance of the United States at the beginning of the twenty-first century. If a nation-state in this dominant position decided that the defense of its interests was more important than the maintenance of norms applicable equitably to all nations, the development of new highly destructive and rapidly deployable weapons systems would obviously be of relevance in deciding when preemptive action is necessary. The greater the size of the developing threat, the greater the imperative to act to contain and eliminate it. In such a case, action might even be justified to maintain military dominance globally or regionally. It should be clear from all that we have said that such unilateral action in the absence of serious and imminent attacks on a nation is at odds with the Grotian tradition of just war thinking. We refer to it here because we see this as the clearest point of moral choice for the world's current military hyperpower; the United States can decide to pursue its interests in this mode, but it cannot do so without departing wholly from the limitations on preemptive war that Grotius set out and the just war tradition took up.

Proposal

Having examined debates concerning preemptive war in dialogue with Grotius, we close with five interlocking conclusions about the propriety and limits of preemptive war. First, Grotius appropriately reminds us that complete security is impossible for both individuals and nations. The point is one that Christians should have no problem recognizing as a true statement of the human condition. Our creaturely status means that we live with limitation, uncertainty, and dependence. The course of our lives is not fully in our hands. Some basic ways we sin are by trying to deny this reality of insecurity, by trying to take security fully into our hands, or by transgressing what is morally permissible for reasonable safety. To fear the world around us inappropriately can disclose weakness of faith and lack of trust in God. To that extent, fear may be sinful.[29] Although fear is a neutral passion that is not wrong in itself, as Scott Bader-Saye cogently presents, Aquinas sees two ways of going wrong in our fear: We may fear *what* we should not or *as* we should not.[30]

Under the first heading, we might misinterpret either the imminence or magnitude of a threat. Grotius's and Aquinas's warnings line up nicely here. Aquinas also says that we may fear a wrong object if we are inordinately attached to a worldly good. In this regard, it is proper to question whether the motives that drive a foreign policy of preventive war include fears of a loss of global military dominance, of admitting past mistakes, and of relinquishing the ability to act unilaterally. We think such improper fears have guided the Bush Doctrine and its supporters.

Under the second heading, Bader-Saye describes the negative consequence of fearing in a way that is improper: "We cannot allow our fear of evil to overwhelm our ability to seek the goods we should be seeking."[31] As applied to the "war on terror," it is illuminating how the United States and allied nations have spent tremendous resources to prevent terrorist attacks with comparatively little attention to long-term investments that would erode the sources of anger and despair that fuel terrorism. As is well known about the Iraq war, the coalition nations responded massively to the purported immediate threat and planned very poorly for the aftermath. Such could be the results of acting on the basis of fear.

Bader-Saye's theological analysis leads us to conclude that it is an improper aim of foreign policy to try to make one's nation completely secure from all threats and that fears based on insecurity are inadequate grounds for war. To rely on fear as a justification for military attack before a threat has matured to a state of objective and imminent threat is unjust and destabilizing; few nations could not find justification to attack a neighbor on this basis. This is not to say, of course, that a developing risk should be ignored; rather, it is to say, with Grotius, that the more restrictive tradition is the "better and safer" course (2.1.5.2). We also note that this caution against improper reliance on fear has deep roots in the just war tradition. J. Warren Smith interprets Augustine on this point: "'Freedom from fear' cannot for Augustine be the goal of foreign policy. Instead, he reminds us that in this age we must live with the uneasy knowledge of the fragile and transitory nature of our existence. For only by living in the fearful reality of our vulnerability and our ultimate impotence to ensure the security of our lives can we be free from the self-complacency or will to power that themselves are the very cause of our mortality and fear."[32]

This theological understanding of fear will not have as obvious a place in foreign policy deliberation, but it is crucial for religiously minded citizens and leaders to challenge policymakers who seek to create a culture of fear to win support for their proposals. As Christian citizens deliberate among themselves and speak in the public square, they could serve a valuable role by challenging false hopes for perfect security, criticizing the misguided actions that can emerge from a posture of fear, and witnessing to a more hopeful avenues of engaging one's adversaries.

Second, we argued that the massive increase in the destructive power of weapons between the seventeenth and twenty-first centuries does not necessitate or justify revising the just war tradition to make it permissive of wars fought to prevent threats from developing. The existence of nuclear weapons—often unhelpfully grouped with chemical and biological weapons presenting a much lower degree of threat under the heading "weapons of mass destruction"—is a serious threat to the security of all nations, but unilateral action by one nuclear weapons state to prevent another nation from developing nuclear weapons also presents a serious threat to world peace. The unacceptability of unilateral preventative war in these circumstances should focus attention on seeking reforms so that the UN Security Council can become the credible international judicial authority capable of making wise decisions about how to counter such threats.

Third, we have questioned the attempt to specify the conditions for legitimate preemption in the just war tradition with a criterion of costly delay. Though the reasoning behind the criterion that is explicated by Galston and Walzer can be appreciated as their attempt to combine the concepts of imminence, last resort, and proportionality, the danger of this approach is that we can imagine developments that lie far ahead of an imminent attack that a nation might identify as a costly acceleration of risk. We have seen that Grotius provides the example of an enemy building a fortress on its own soil to illustrate illegitimate preemption. Yet such an action could be interpreted as too costly to tolerate under the criteria of Galston and Walzer. This was Israel's thinking regarding Iraq's Osirak nuclear reactor in 1981. Although its worry about Iraq developing a nuclear weapon was understandable and certainly demanded a many-faceted international response, it is instructive that the UN Security Council and the United States condemned the attack as a breach of international law.

Another telling example of when a criterion of costly delay could have been misused was just after World War II, when the United States possessed atomic bombs and the Soviet Union did not. It was clear the Soviet Union had an atomic weapons program and would soon develop the bomb, which was a very costly development for the United States and the global community. Plans were drawn up in the United States for an "atomic blitz" to preempt this danger.[33]

Clearly, Galston and Walzer would not support such an action, but the introduction of cost of delay threatens to overwhelm other criteria pointing to restraint in this and other cases. Taking account of Grotius on this point would mean not admitting the cost of delay criterion except where an enemy attack is already established as viable and imminent; the cost of delay should not be used to avoid satisfying the criterion of imminence.

Our fourth conclusion is that comparison of this early twenty-first-century moment with Grotius's early-modern context helpfully reminds us that we should not adapt the just war tradition to suit our own national interests. Pragmatic self-interest, as well as concern for international peace, encourages us to recognize that we might find ourselves before too long in a situation more like Grotius's, in which nations are rivals for military and economic preeminence. Indeed, recent events show that even a hyperpower cannot afford to act in ways that disaffect significant groups of nations. As Galston nicely puts it: "It cannot be in either America's national interest or in the world's interest to develop principles that grant every nation an unfettered right of preemption against its own definition of threats to its security. . . . How can we announce a new doctrine of preemption as the centerpiece of our foreign policy while insisting that it applies to us alone and insisting that it should not become, and must not become, the centerpiece of foreign policy systems and practices everywhere else on Earth?"[34]

A world in which the possibility of being attacked confers the right to attack is a world where chaos has overtaken international order, and where the only limitations on the outbreak of war are estimations of relative military strength. Grotius's delimitation of preemption was intended to forestall just such a reality and therefore should not be lightly set aside.

Fifth and finally, we should recognize that there is much that can be done when we embrace the space that Grotius opens for diplomacy and other options. As he notes, we are rarely if ever placed in the situation of the gladiator in which our options are either to kill or be killed. In any but these exceptional circumstances, we can exercise a choice to take advantage of every opportunity to resolve a conflict short of war. It is therefore insufficient merely to argue against being more permissive of war to preempt external threats, as if the choice were to go to war or do nothing. Once we have recognized that war is an illegitimate option to respond to most threats to a nation's security, we need to attend to the wide range of peacemaking and conflict resolution practices that receive inadequate attention in reflection on the ethics of war. One valuable contribution in this context is Glen Stassen's "Just Peacemaking" project, in which he and his colleagues propose practices with the potential to contribute to peace in local, national, and global contexts, including supporting nonviolent direct action, cooperative conflict resolution, seeking to advance democracy and human rights, fostering just and sustainable development, strengthening international institutions, and reducing weapons stockpiles and trade in arms.[35] Such efforts are often successful in resolving acute crises without resort to arms. More significantly, such efforts are effective "deep prevention" strategies: avoiding the need to preempt many threats to national security by avoiding the conditions that cause and exacerbate them. Therefore, to follow the counsel of Grotius is to affirm the permissibility of preemptive self-defense under narrow criteria and to redirect the energies of nations toward the tasks of just peacemaking. Arguments for preventive war, whether in name or in any of its deceptive guises, should be rejected as incompatible with the just war tradition.

Notes

1. Examples of the broad agreement among Christian leaders are the Catholic bishops of Germany, discussed below in this essay; Bishop Wilton D. Gregory, "Statement on Iraq," February 23, 2003, www.usccb.org/sdwp/international/iraqstatement0203.htm; and "Disarm Iraq without War: A Statement from Religious Leaders in the US and UK," October 11, 2002, www.unitedforpeace.org/article.php?id=2837. Examples of theologians and Christian ethicists challenging preventive war are George Hunsinger, "Iraq: Don't Go There," *Christian Century*, August 14–27, 2002, 10; and Thomas J. Massaro and Thomas A. Shannon, *Catholic Perspectives on Peace and War* (Lanham, Md.: Rowman & Littlefield, 2003), 94. Also telling is that Christian thinkers and just war theorists who supported the Iraq War, at first and/or subsequently, felt obliged to make the case that the war could fit within the traditional just war category of legitimate preemption. It is quite difficult to find a Christian just war thinker who openly supports "preventive war" in contrast to preemptive war. We will discuss a few near-examples below.

2. "German Bishops Warn Iraq War Would Violate International Law," Agence France-Presse, January 21, 2003.

3. "There is often plenty of time for deliberation, agonizing hours, days, even weeks of deliberation, when one doubts that war can be avoided and wonders whether to strike first." Michael Walzer, *Just and Unjust Wars*, 3rd ed. (New York: Basic Books, 2000), 75.

4. Walzer, *Just and Unjust Wars*, 75.

5. George W. Bush, "President Bush Delivers Graduation Speech at West Point," White House, June 1, 2000, www.whitehouse.gov/news/releases/2002/06/20020601-3.html.

6. White House, *The National Security Strategy of the United States of America*, September 17, 2002, www.whitehouse.gov/nsc/nss.pdf.

7. George W. Bush, "President Delivers 'State of the Union,'" White House, January 28, 2003, www.whitehouse.gov/news/releases/2003/01/print/20030128-19.html.

8. George P. Schultz, "Terrorism: Hot Preemption," *Hoover Digest*, 2002, no. 3, www.hoover.org/publications/digest/4484486.html.

9. Jean Bethke Elshtain, "Jean Bethke Elshtain Responds," *Dissent*, Summer 2006, 110.

10. George Weigel, "George Weigel on Just-War Principles: Pre-Emptive Military Action against Terrorists Is Morally Legitimate," interview, ZENIT News Service, October 13, 2001, www.zenit.org/english/war/visualizza.phtml?sid=11136.

11. Stephen Strehle, "Saddam Hussein, Islam, and Just War Theory: The Case For a Pre-Emptive Strike," *Political Theology* 5, no. 1 (January 2004): 95.

12. Weigel, ZENIT interview.

13. Citations from *De Jure Belli Ac Pacis* are from Hugo Grotius, *De Jure Belli Ac Pacis*, Classics of International Law No. 3, trans. John Damen Maguire (Washington, D.C.: Carnegie Institute, 1913) and given numerically in the form: book number, chapter number, section number, paragraph number (where applicable). For example, "1.1.10.1" refers to book 1, chap. 1, sec. 10, para. 1.

14. On this point, see Oliver and Joan Lockwood O'Donovan, "Hugo Grotius," in *From Irenaeus to Grotius: A Sourcebook in Christian Political Thought 100–1625* (Grand Rapids: William B. Eerdmans, 1999), 787–92.

15. Grotius, *De Jure Belli ac Pacis*, book 1, Prolegomena, sec. 28.

16. For more details on the historical context of Grotius's writings, see Onuma Yasuaki, ed., *A Normative Approach to War: Peace, War and Justice in Hugo Grotius* (Oxford: Clarendon Press, 1993), 113 ff.

17. See Richard Tuck, "Introduction," in *The Rights of War and Peace* by Hugo Grotius (Indianapolis: Liberty Fund, 2005), xiv–xv.

18. See Tuck, "Introduction," xxvii; and R. W. Lee, *Hugo Grotius* (London: Humphrey Milford Amen House, 1930), 9.

19. Citing Thomas Aquinas, *Summa theologiae* II-II, 64, 1.

20. In a fuller study, it would be helpful to situate this discussion of Grotius alongside other key figures in the development of the just war tradition in this period, such as Francisco de Vitoria (c. 1486–1546), Francisco Suarez (1548–1617), and Alberigo Gentili (1552–1608). Gentili, for example, is much more permissive than Grotius, suggesting that one should "strike at the root of a growing plant and check the attempts of an adversary who is meditating evil" (Gentili, "The Advantages of Preventive War" in *The Ethics of War: Classic and Contemporary Readings*, ed. Gregory M. Reichberg, Henrik Syse, and Endre Begby [Oxford: Blackwell, 2006], 376). It is instructive that Grotius's more conservative view was the one preferred in the later just war tradition.

21. William A. Galston, with David Blankenhorn, Gerard Bradley, John Kelsay, and Michael Walzer, "Iraq and Just War: A Symposium," Pew Forum on Religion and Public Life, September 30, 2002, http://pewforum.org/events/index.php?EventID=36.

22. Galston, "Iraq and Just War."

23. Walzer, *Just and Unjust Wars*, 81.

24. For Walzer's approach to WMD and imminence in the case of Iraq, see *Arguing about War* (New Haven, Conn.: Yale University Press, 2004), 143–57.

25. Neta C. Crawford, "The Slippery Slope to Preventive War," *Ethics and International Affairs* 17, no. 1 (2003): 31.

26. Crawford, "Slippery Slope," 33.

27. Richard Betts, *Surprise Attack: Lessons for Defense Planning* (Washington, D.C.: Brookings Institution Press, 1982), 14–43, cited in Crawford, "Slippery Slope," 32.

28. According to the *SIPRI 2006 Yearbook* (Oxford: Oxford University Press, 2006), the United States accounted for 48 percent of global military expenditures in 2005.

29. See Thomas Aquinas, *Summa theologica*, 5 vols., trans. Fathers of the English Dominican Province (Notre Dame, Ind.: Ave Maria Press, 1981), II-II, ques. 125.

30. Scott Bader-Saye, "Thomas Aquinas and the Culture of Fear," *Journal of the Society of Christian Ethics* 25, no. 2 (2005): 95–108.

31. Bader-Saye, "Thomas Aquinas," 105.

32. J. Warren Smith, "Augustine and the Limits of Pre-emptive War," *Journal of Religious Ethics* 35, no. 1 (2007): 160.

33. See Lawrence Freedman, *The Evolution of Nuclear Strategy* (Basingstoke, U.K.: Macmillan: 1989), chap. 4.

34. Galston, "Iraq and Just War."

35. Glen H. Stassen, ed. *Just Peacemaking: Ten Practices for Abolishing War*, 2nd ed. (Cleveland: Pilgrim Press, 2004).

Crossing the Road: The Case for Ethnographic Fieldwork in Christian Ethics

Todd David Whitmore

CHRISTIAN ETHICS IS VIRTUALLY DEVOID OF ETHNOGRAPHIC FIELDWORK.
Many Christian ethicists practice "veranda ethics": They write from a vast social remove from the issues they address, like poverty and war, as observers.
Fieldwork, as illustrated by casework in Northern Uganda, provides a way to
overcome this remove.

A quarter-mile-long plume of dust rises from the main road leading into the
Komakec Internally Displaced Persons camp in Northern Uganda.[1] The wet
season is supposed to have started already, but the rains have not come. The
vendors and their storefronts will soon be covered in dirt powder, making
them look like orange-red ghosts. *Aya*. Most of the stores have been long
closed anyway because of the danger of transporting goods and money to
Kitgum, the trading center fifty kilometers to the south. The rebel Lord's Resistance Army (LRA) has been at war with the Ugandan government for
twenty years now, and it regularly raids supply trucks. Komakec is remote,
ten miles by mountain from the Sudan border to the north. Lilly, my hostess,
is peeling cassava, and she raises her head from her task only when loudspeak-
ers blare what to me is an unintelligible screech. Lilly puts her peeling tub
aside and gets up quickly.

"The UN trucks. They are announcing food distribution day."

"When is it?"

"Now."

For security reasons, the United Nations World Food Program (WFP)
does not announce in advance when it is coming; as a result, the people in the
camps do not know how to ration the little food that they have. It may be
three weeks before the next distribution, it may be six. All the more important
will it be, then, that you put aside whatever you are doing when the food
trucks do come. There is a funeral today for a twenty-six-year-old teacher
who has died of AIDS. Her ritual sending-off will have to wait.

Children pour out of the primary school, and two boys rush past my quarters wearing women's pink sleeveless tops backward. The school's colors are pink and blue, and if the family cannot afford the uniforms, they try to match colors from whatever donated clothes arrive. In an irony Reinhold Niebuhr would appreciate, Western largess has suppressed clothing production in East Africa. In this case, there are few pink men's shirts, so the boys must wear women's clothes. They figure that the buttons must go in front to more closely match the standard-issue school shirts, even if this makes the fit even worse than it already is.

Lilly asks me to put the sifting basket of *sim-sim* grain inside. This is the first growing season safe enough for planting the crop since the camp formed nine years ago. Last year, eight women went a kilometer beyond camp boundaries in dry season to get water, and the rebels cut off the ears, noses, and lips of three of them as a warning to others in the camp not to venture out. That they did not do the same to the other five women only underscores the absurdity that marks this fever dream of a war. Even now, fifteen rebels have been spotted not far northwest of the camp, and fifteen more about ten kilometers south. The people of Komakec are even more heavily dependent on the WFP food than they are on donated clothing.

"Come with me," Lilly says. "I may need your help in carrying the bags."

I go with Lilly to the main road. The UN SUVs are still there, still blaring. One almost clips a *mego*, an older woman, as she scurries across the street in flip-flops while balancing an empty red plastic washtub on her head. Augustine, the seminarian who sometimes visits, passes us on his bicycle with his Hello Kitty book bag slung over his shoulder. Lilly and I follow the stream of people and turn off the main road toward a field where workers are unloading four semi trucks of food. On the way, we meet up with Okec Joseph.

"Come. See for yourself," he says, gesturing toward his feet, where sit two small bags of grain. "One is for me and one for my friend who cannot make it. One bag each. You see that it is not enough."

Okec is about six foot two and perhaps a hundred and thirty pounds. He is nattily dressed for someone in an Internally Displaced Persons camp, a sign that he has not given in to *arege*, the local cassava-based drink brewed in makeshift stills outside the mud and thatch homes to fend off the psychologically crippling mix of jobless boredom and wartime anxiety. His dark blue driver's cap tops off his well-pressed if threadbare polyester shirt and pants worn down to a shine. The food bags appear to be about two kilograms each. A bag is supposed to last a person a month. The people in the camp tell me that they last a week, maybe a week and a half if they eat just one meal a day. My mind flicks back to my kitchen table in South Bend, where I read an article by an official of the WFP who makes a deus ex machina afternoon visit to Pabbo Internally Displaced Persons camp and, after noting the security and health hardships of the people there, announces, "The one thing the people of Pabbo have going for them is that they are not hungry."[2]

Okec holds his hands out plaintively.

"You go home and tell them it is not enough."

Very few Christian ethicists do ethnographic fieldwork as part of their research.[3] If we follow the classic definition of ethnography as set out by W.H. R. Rivers and embodied in a pioneering way by Bronislaw Malinowski, then the numbers are even fewer. Rivers writes that the anthropologist should live for "a year or more" among the people in question, learning the language and developing a personal relationship with them, and in the process witnessing "every feature of life and custom in concrete detail."[4] Here is where the practice of ethnography, with its emphasis on *participant* observation, goes well beyond doing field interviews. We write about poverty, though few of us have ever lived in such conditions. We apply the just war tradition to make judgments about the morality of this or that conflict, but few of us have been in a war zone for any length of time, and those who have have yet to integrate that experience into the presentation of their research. Health care ethics appears to be one of the few areas where some Christian ethicists do sustained fieldwork, but even here such efforts are in the minority. What is more, almost no works in Christian meta-ethics involve cross-cultural comparison. Where such comparison does take place, it is intertextual.[5] We are a discipline of texts. To make our judgments, we read and think about what others have written. This methodology is problematic when the point of comparison, if comparisons are sought at all, is a part of the world like sub-Saharan Africa, where large portions of the population, and even the majority, do not read or write, and the cultures in question pass on their traditions orally. For the Christian ethicist to only read texts is for him to access only the most powerful of people.

I suggest strongly that the lack of ethnographic fieldwork is a failure in the broader discipline of Christian ethics both as regards its being a discipline pertaining to the moral life and as a form of ethics that claims the modifier "Christian." With respect to the former, most theological ethicists in the United States accept, at least in principle, some form of epistemological theory indebted to the sociology of knowledge, the claim that where we are socially located shapes what we know. For those who do hold to some form of this epistemological theory, the question is this: Why has there not been a concurrent shift in method that takes into account peoples' particularity? To be performatively consistent, particularist moral theory requires particularist methodology, and that means the practice of fieldwork if Christian ethicists are to make claims about people and institutions beyond their own local communities.

The lack of fieldwork is also a failure of an ethics that claims to be in some way Christian. Though there is nowhere near a consensus on how the Christian moral life is to influence the discipline of ethics, the turn to virtue ethics by scholars as different as Stanley Hauerwas, William Spohn, and James Keenan suggests that the question of who Christian ethicists are as people is related to how we are to go about doing our research. These three, along with others, make explicit the links between scripture, the person of Jesus, and the doing of virtue ethics. There is a strong consensus in biblical interpretation that Jesus has a specific concern for those people who are marginalized and even goes out of his way to attend to them. There is also a consensus that this activity, coupled with his claims of an impending new order that recognizes God's care for the poor, gets him killed. Christian virtue ethics that focuses on Jesus as exemplar must itself display that activity of going out to the stranger at some risk to the ethicists themselves. It is not enough to say that Christians in general ought to do such; if Christian virtue ethics as method is to follow Christian virtue ethics as theory, with its emphasis on exemplification, then the research and writing of Christian ethics must itself be a display of what it means to follow Jesus. Ethnographic research and writing methods can aid in this process.

The Displacement of Particularity in Christian Ethics

"No photos." I turn and see a man bisecting the lines of people waiting for their food as he makes his way toward me. The Acholi know not to stand in the midday sun, but this field is the only open space large enough for the semi trucks, and if one waits until late afternoon, others will have taken the food. It seems like there should be enough. Rows of white fifty-kilogram plastic-weave bags emblazoned with "USA—Whole Dry Yellow Peas—Not to be Sold or Exchanged" run forty long and stack four high. But twenty-two thousand people live in Komakec camp, some of whom have already whispered to me that there were supposed to be four foodstuffs delivered today and only two arrived. It appears that somewhere between WFP central planning in Rome and the ground of Komakec, half the food has gone the way of corruption. "He is not a journalist. He is a professor."

Otum, Lilly's husband and my host, intercedes for me. The official now is before us. He is short, perhaps five-two. His clipboard serves to communicate his authority. Unlike Okec, he has new clothes. His shoes are remarkably free of dust.

"You are a professor?"

"Yes."

"Not a journalist?"

"No."

"For what are you using the photos?"

"My research and teaching."

"A professor."

"Yes."

"Okay then."

"I'm sorry?"

"You may take photos."

At first, I am simply glad to continue taking photographs. After a half-hour more of shooting, I take a break, find space in the crowd under a mango tree, the only shade, and begin writing up my notes. The act of writing prompts previous conversations I have had to come to mind. When I first arrive in Uganda, Lieutenant Colonel Shaban Bantarisa, the spokesperson for the government army and the gatekeeper for all persons heading to the North, is at first reluctant to let me go. But then he smiles, wishes me well, and even permits me to take my camera when I tell him I am a professor, and in particular a professor of theology. The security officer for Komakec camp, after hearing that I am a professor, says, "So, we work together. We do not like bad things said about this camp. Some people say bad things. We work together."

Later this week, the government will send two "spies" posing as curious camp residents to visit me while I write outside my quarters. I know that they are spies because they ask me how long I am staying, which is a grave offense against the Acholi practice of hospitality. When they ask what I am doing here, I—now knowing the rhetorical valences—tell them, "I am a professor, not a journalist. I am doing research." They leave and do not return, and I am left alone for the rest of my stay. In their experience, professors do not have anything to say that the rest of the world is interested in hearing. We are taken to be harmless, even when we have photographic evidence of criminal activity.

In his 1985 address to the Catholic Theological Society of America, James Gustafson fired a salvo titled "The Sectarian Temptation." His primary target in Christian ethics was the work of Stanley Hauerwas, and the latter's efforts to sustain a form of Christian uniqueness. Gustafson's argument is that Hauerwas's views do not hold up theologically or sociologically and that the result is pernicious. Theologically, Hauerwas's understanding of God is too narrow and exclusive. "In Christian sectarian form God becomes a Christian God for Christian people; to put it most pejoratively, God is assumed to be the tribal God of a minority of the earth's population." It is a sociology that fails, Gustafson argues, because the material conditions for the kind of community that Hauerwas describes, one where its members are informed predominantly by a singularly Christian interpretation of the world, do not pertain in a pluralistic world where multiple perspectives vie for our attention and allegiance. The effects of the "sectarian" option are pernicious because Christians fail to take responsibility for the world.[6]

Hauerwas responded in "Why the 'Sectarian Temptation' is a Misrepresentation": "Show me where I am wrong about God, Jesus, the limits of liberalism, the nature of the virtues or the doctrine of the church—but do not shortcut that task by calling me a sectarian."[7] However, Gustafson renewed his criticisms in his 2004 book *An Examined Faith: The Grace of Self-Doubt*, this time aiming at a wider range of scholars, including Hauerwas, who write under the rubrics of "post-liberalism," "narrative theology," and "radical orthodoxy."[8]

I suggest that the exchanges between Gustafson and Hauerwas can gain greater clarity if we distinguish between kinds of particularity. There are, it seems, at least three kinds: epistemological, empirical, and socio-Christological. Gustafson and Hauerwas agree on the first kind and diverge on the importance of the second and third. Epistemological particularity is the claim that what we know is profoundly shaped by our social location. Gustafson sites his indebtedness to the sociology of knowledge in his stress on epistemological particularity. It is noteworthy that he also recognizes Hauerwas's epistemological particularity.[9] Hauerwas grounds his account of epistemological particularity in the narrative theories of Alasdair MacIntyre, Hans Frei, and George Lindbeck. Without narratives rooted in lived traditions that provide the interpretive context for moral statements, such statements are unintelligible. All social ethics is, in Hauerwas's words, "qualified ethics," that is, ethics qualified by what we know as framed by the narrative of a particular tradition.[10]

True to his roots in the sociology of knowledge, Gustafson insists that epistemological particularity ought to entail empirical particularity—that is, the specifics of life lived, especially as known through the social and natural sciences. Gustafson grounds his empiricism theologically: The God who creates and sustains us creates and sustains the entire universe, including the social and natural sciences and sources of knowledge that come from the general culture. Not to engage with these sources is to deny God as their source.[11] Though Hauerwas insists that the church is "an empirical reality," he does not make much overt use of the social and natural sciences. Moreover, despite his emphasis on the necessity of the narrative display of Jesus and Christlike people for readers and listeners to learn to "imitate a master," there is little descriptive detail in his work. He sometimes tells of an incident to launch an article, or, in homiletic style, to illustrate a point, but there is no sustained description. The article most like an ethnography in its analysis of lived detail is his account of a novel, *Watership Down*.[12]

It is the particularity of Jesus' life and the desire for particularity in Christian life that focuses Hauerwas's work. His stress on Jesus' life is an effort to counter those Christologies that emphasize only his death and resurrection. Therefore he gives priority to Jesus' life as an exemplification of what it means to live in accordance with the Kingdom. When Christians seek to imitate Jesus, they find themselves "distinctive," "apart," "peculiar," "interesting," and even "entertaining" in relation to the world. The result is "a polity unlike any other."[13] Thus Christology is socio-Christology.

If Hauerwas trades off empirical particularity as part of an effort to reinvigorate a Christian particularity, Gustafson appears to do the reverse. *Nowhere* in either "The Sectarian Temptation" or *An Examined Faith* does Gustafson even consider the possibility that science may need to make adjustments, even small ones, in light of theology. It is always theology and ethics that needs "to reconsider their subjects and methods in response to other disciplines that intersect them." In his own constructive work, this leads him to reject the ideas of providence, a personal God, and Jesus as the Christ. In "The Sectarian Temptation," he is most direct: "Jesus is not God." In *An Examined Faith*, he lists the idea that God became human as an example of "exaggerated religious rhetoric."[14]

It appears to this reader that Gustafson's theology is no longer Christian except perhaps in a vestigial cultural sense. I say this not as a criticism but as a description of his project, and Gustafson himself admits as much. In his words, his "stoical piety may be more Swedish, or even northern Swedish, than Christian." Though Gustafson's move is not Christian, it is theological. In his effort to preserve God as the sovereign God in the face of the history of Christian anthropocentrism and contemporary science, he finds it imperative to reject a God who reveals himself in a unique way in Jesus Christ. "God will be God!" Gustafson exclaims in conclusion, and for him that means that God could not have become Jesus.[15]

The trade-off between empirical and socio-Christological particularities, which both Gustafson and Hauerwas appear to accept, is a false one. It is possible to chart a theological approach that draws upon the sciences as an integral part of an ethic that views the task of the Christian as one of imitating Jesus. Indeed, a Christian ethic that rejects the trade-off is necessary if the discipline is to move away from a philosophically driven liberalism-versus-communitarianism debate that is neither empirically particular nor particularly Christian. Moreover, if my fieldwork in Northern Uganda is any indication, such an ethic is far more likely to be as relevant to other public discourses as Gustafson requires it to be and as much of a threat to the status quo as Hauerwas wants it to be, such that when I tell security personnel that I am a professor of theology, they confiscate my notes, camera, and passport.

On Making a Sharper Cultural Turn

"We are a cursed people." It has been a long day, and dusk is beginning to settle. Otum stands up from his wood-slat folding chair and turns off the radio in the middle of an announcement for the next meeting of a land mine survivor group. This is the most dangerous time of day—light enough for the rebels to see but dark enough so that their faces might not be identified.

"Komakec camp started in 1997 when the LRA killed five hundred fifty Acholi," Otum continues. "Then the government bombed the camp to get the rebels and killed four hundred seventeen more. It is a curse. At first the rebels did not have guns. They beat people and used machetes. They cut people up. Lips, the penises of men, breasts of women. It is only through the Sacred Heart of Jesus that this will end. All human efforts have failed. The peace talks have failed. It is only through prayer to the Sacred Heart of Jesus. People go to the *ajwagi*, the spirit medium and herbal healer, even Christians, but the *ajwaka*'s power is evil."

Almost three-quarters of Acholi are at least nominally Roman Catholic. The rest are either Anglican or Evangelical. Almost all continue to practice traditional Acholi religion and go to the *ajwaka* when they have particular problems, like infertility or *cen*, a vengeful spirit, haunting them. Thus far, I have interviewed four *ajwagi* at length, and they have called upon their *jogi*, their spirits, who come to them in dreams, for me. True to the demographic, three of the *ajwagi* are Roman Catholic. One was married in the Church. Another's primary *jok* took her in a dream to Bethlehem to show her what is now one of her most powerful herbs.

Olara, Otum's brother-in-law, unfolds a chair and enters a counteropinion.

"I have seen the good that the *ajwaka* can do. Some are evil, but others are good. The man you see before you today—I am here only because of the *ajwaka*."

Olara has had his share of misfortune. He once was a star defender for the local soccer club, but the rebels attacked their lorry when the team was on its way to a match in Kitgum. Komakec jumped off the truck to escape into the bush and blew a ligament in his knee. Adrenaline carried him into a ravine where the rebels somehow did not notice him. Later, he would have to give up his business because of the danger of transporting goods to and from Kitgum. He lives off of WFP food and what he can grow in a small garden. An *ajwaka* treated his depression. A champion debater when in school, he is again inquisitive and articulate.

"I am a man of science," he continues. "I look at what works. I would not be here if not for Aya Matina."

Richard Miller argues that ethnography can enrich religious ethics by directing the latter's attention to the fine grain of persons' ordinary lives and how those lives are mediated culturally. Ethnography holds out the alternative of an ethics that proceeds, as he says, "from the bottom up," and builds theory in light of close observation of the day-to-day lives of persons.[16] What gives Miller's agenda further credence is the fact that he has attempted to carry it out in his own monograph-length work, *Children, Ethics, and Modern Medicine*, for which, among other things, he served as a participant observer in a pediatric intensive care unit for six months.[17] To ground and illustrate what work from the bottom up looks like, Miller draws upon Clifford Geertz's concepts of "experience-near" and "experience-distant" to develop the ideas of "ethics-near" and "ethics-distant." Religious ethics that is attentive to culture, in his words, "tacks back and forth" between fieldwork (ethics-near) and the work of theorizing (ethics-distant). Miller is clear that such a methodology will require new genres of writing in Christian ethics, approaches that are less fastidiously closed and more open-ended.[18]

The chief problem with Miller's work is that it does little if any of the tacking back and forth that he calls for. In the process, he rules out certain kinds of religious claims even before they can enter the conversation. The overall argument of *Children, Ethics, and Modern Medicine* is that pediatrics ought to reverse the general ordering of autonomy over beneficence that holds for adult medicine. The book draws on Immanuel Kant's principle of universalizability to argue for beneficence and against indifference. Miller then turns to John Rawls's argument from the "original position" as set out in *A Theory of Justice* for "principles of paternalism." The turn to Kant and Rawls is fueled by Miller's conviction that only philosophical, as opposed to religious, ethics can yield universal principles: "Various religious traditions have approached such issues with reference to the command to love others. . . .Venerable though these traditions are, they fail to indicate why persons who are not religious . . . should care for others. That is, they do not provide a general basis for the duty to care."[19] These aspects of Kant and Rawls provide the given framework for the rest of the book.

For an ethics interested in ethnography, Miller's choice of this particular genre of liberal political philosophy to frame the presentation of his research is an odd one. This is because both Kant and Rawls develop their moral systems precisely by prescinding from empirical particulars. In their view, lived reality is an obstacle to the construction of ethics, not a source of insight. Rawls constructs a "veil of ignorance" around the fictive actors who develop moral principles in the original position precisely so that they do not know any situational particulars. These actors are presumably "objective" observers as opposed to participant observers. Within such a genre, ethnography can do no more than provide illustration or fill in the details of a moral framework already constructed from nowhere in particular. It cannot challenge the theoretical moral constructs.

Moreover, Miller shares the bias of this genre of political liberalism that religiously based reasoning is particularistic and parochial in a way that secular moral philosophy is not. The assumption is that certain secular accounts of the right and the good, because they are from nowhere in particular, are the only ones that are universal and thus fair. Miller cites with approval this aspect of

Rawls.[20] The universalistic presumption as developed strips religious reasoning of having any moral force at all. The key question is whether the religious reasoning fits the liberal political framework. Even where it does so, it lacks the wherewithal to move rational argument; what we have in the liberal view is not so much religious argumentation, when it occurs, but argumentation that happens also to be religious. Such a view cuts against the effort in anthropology to interpret cultures as much as is possible in their own terms.

All the above difficulties manifest themselves when Miller turns to specific cases. For instance, "Billy Richardson" is a four-year-old with Hurler syndrome, a degenerative metabolic disorder. It is common for children with the syndrome not to live past two years. Aggressive treatment, which might have improved Billy's condition but not cured it, fails. Multiple organs break down. In light of interviews with Billy's parents, Miller interprets their interest in keeping their son alive in terms of his ability to be an occasion of neighbor love for them and others. God is acting through Billy, they reason, so that they and others can display their love for him and each other. God will act through Billy again when God wants Billy's life to end. Miller counters, "We cannot let religion trump a child's basic medical interests. At times religion must bow to common morality and in pediatric medical contexts, that means honoring a patient's basic interests."[21]

My concern is not with Miller's conclusion but with the role of ethnography in his moral method. Here, ethnography simply serves to illustrate the priority of beneficence over autonomy in pediatric practice. By design, however, the reasoning from the Richardsons' own subculture cannot challenge the grand theory. Though Miller uses an interpretation of Calvin to show traditional backing for the Richardsons' views, he rules out those views as "supernatural piety" and "religious fanaticism."[22] Perhaps even more telling, he then uses different interpretations of Calvin and Aquinas to counter the Richardsons. He brings in these latter interpretations only after the conclusion that religion "must bow" to political liberalism; the force of the theological arguments, then, is simply to show that there are forms of religion that stay within the bounds of political liberalism as previously constructed; ethnographically elucidated religion not only cannot challenge the grand theory but cannot really support it either. From the standpoint of moral argumentation, culture, in this case culturally mediated religion, does not matter. Ethnography has little substantive to add to religious ethics at this point.

It is important to note Miller's rhetoric in his discussion of the Billy Richardson case: Religion that is outside the bounds of political liberalism is "fanatic," that is to say, without coherent and intelligible reasoning. Any religion that ethnography brings forward that does not fit the liberal grand theory is ruled out of court. It is interesting that Miller also calls this kind of religion "supernatural" as opposed to "natural" and that his own rhetoric has moved from specific references to Rawls to reference to "common morality." That is to say, he has taken a particular tradition, an intellectual culture, of moral philosophy and, without building a case for it through what anthropologists George Marcus and Michael Fischer call "critical juxtaposition" with other cultures (in fact by abstracting from questions of particular cultures) has identified the tradition of liberal political philosophy as "natural" and "common."[23] It is at this point that Miller clearly moves beyond liberalism as a political theory as Rawls intends to liberalism as a comprehensive theory of the good. This is precisely the kind of move that many anthropologists worry about in their anxiety about the hegemony of certain modes of Western thought.

If Miller's approach is indicative, then the problem is not, as Gustafson would have it, that of sectarian *withdrawal from* participation in society but that of society's a priori *exclusion of* a wide range of Christian conviction from public discourse. The Richardsons clearly want to participate in the decision making regarding Billy's life; Miller's Rawlsian framework will not let them. If this method were applied to Northern Uganda, where much of the interpretation of the war turns on the relative power of Christ versus that the *ajwagi*, as a matter of principle few if any of the people of Komakec could speak on the issues that pertain to their lives.

Although Gustafson does not rely on Rawls, he shows a similar pattern of a priori exclusion. He repeatedly makes the claim that few people use theology as a first mode of discourse. However, if the Richardsons are at all indicative, this is not the case. At one point, Gustafson concedes that there has been "significant growth" in the "numbers and influence" of such people. The matter seems to be more accurately that he does not know these people. "Bible-speak or theological terminology is not the first language of anyone, including biblical theologians, with whom I have ever conversed." Such an admission on Gustafson's part testifies to the limits of his own experience of cultural juxtaposition. Though his theological account of interdependence mandates social participation, it seems that Gustafson himself "withdraws," to use his term, much more rapidly from participation with evangelical Christians than he does, say, from economists who depict humans as purely rational actors. In other words, he is selective about his own participation. He objects to evangelicals as having "virtually magical expectations of divine intervention," but the same could be said of those economists who hold that each of us pursuing our own self-interest inexorably benefits all people.[24] Again, my point here is not that Christian ethicists ought not make assessments about such claims, but that they ought not to make those assessments until serious cultural juxtaposition has taken place.

Miller's contributions are twofold. The first is his initiative to engage in ethnography. Fieldwork is time consuming, with no promise of any intellectual payoff. The second is the insight that the open-ended nature of life itself as testified to in fieldwork will require new genres of writing Christian ethics, modes of writing that, in tacking back and forth between ethics-near and ethics-distant, will of necessity be less formalistic than the forms of Christian ethics dependent on Anglo-American moral and political philosophy. My attempt in this essay is to exemplify this dialectical form of writing. Here, the breaks between sections are sharper, because one does not "transition" in dialectical reasoning as one does in linear reasoning, with sentences functioning like intellectual global positioning system units to tell the reader where he or she is heading. The thick description of ethics-near and the critical analysis of ethics-distant do not so much entail as push each other, and the breaks between them reflect the abrupt movement between life in the field and that in the academy much more accurately than the modes of writing currently most prevalent in theological and philosophical ethics. Miller is correct: The full integration of ethnography into Christian ethics will require us to change the way we write.

The anthropological literature carries forward Miller's agenda in two ways. First, its rejection of objective observer epistemologies in favor of "cultural juxtaposition" means that ethnography must be reflexive. Anthropologists do not simply report on the other but rather engage in a process of interpretation that sheds light back on the researcher and his or her own culture. At times that light will illuminate aspects of Western culture in general; at other times the beam will focus more narrowly on the practice of ethnography itself. What this means for Christian ethics is that analysis of the production and consumption of the discipline is a constitutive part of the discipline itself, including the fact that the series of all-or-nothing gauntlets that structure entry into the discipline—getting into graduate school, passing exams, finishing the dissertation, getting a job, getting renewed, and getting tenure—all in a context that emphasizes more and more production of writing militates against the kind of unwieldy, time-consuming, and expensive research that Miller's agenda calls for.[25]

The second practice in anthropological literature also follows from the rejection of naïve, God's-eye-view realism: An increasing number of ethnographers are placing themselves in the text as a means of displaying that they are encumbered in what they do and see. Their writings are still not first and foremost about these ethnographers themselves, and so do not constitute autobiography; rather, the effort is to take epistemological particularity seriously and come clean on the fact that any account of the other necessarily is told through the writer.[26] In the theological literature, this is the genre of the confession. Traditionally, the confession is a form of self-writing meant to convey less the self than God and the world. Confession is writing that uses the self to testify to God and the world God has made. Found in writings from Augustine's *Confessions* to Dorothy Day's *The Long Loneliness*, it is a mode of representation marked by a double movement; it both allows the self to be present in the text and ultimately, if it works as confession, de-centers the self in that writing.[27]

Risking Imitation

The man lies in the dirt on his side outside what appears to be his bamboo and mud home. He is covered everywhere with the red-brown dust, even his teeth and—I am not sure why I notice—inside his ear. His voice is barely audible.

"I am just waiting for my time."

That is enough for Sister Cecilia. She orders me to lift him from under his arms while she takes his legs. We carry him inside. It takes a moment for our eyes to adjust to the darkness. The hardened dirt floor is perhaps eight feet in diameter. Two old and tearing UN food bags stuffed with his belongings hang from the bamboo roof beams. The roof covering is flame-retardant blue plastic, distributed by the UN because of the prevalence of multiple-structure fires in the crowded camp compounds. The plastic is not as breathable as thatch, however, making the inside of the homes hotter and more stifling. My nostrils burn, and again I cannot see. The man has not been able to make it to the shitting trench.

He tells us his name is Santo and that he is paralyzed from a fall he had some years ago while doing construction. His wife is dead, and his son is drunk too much of the time to take care of him. He tells us that he does not have "the sickness," AIDS, but the men tend not to admit to it in any case, so at this point we cannot trust his answer. Incidence is higher than 30 percent in some camps. I notice a bicycle leaning against the wall, and wonder whether this is from before his fall or whether someone else is already using his home as a storage hut, as if it were vacant.

Sister Cecilia orders a woman outside to bring two washbasins, two washcloths, some soap, and a jerrycan of water. She gives a boy some coins and sends him to the market to get boiled chicken, rice, and *boo*, a dark spinach-like green. She turns to me.

"Can you do this?"

I nod. I have been joining her on her rounds of visiting those who are too sick to make it to the infirmary, which itself has no drugs except quinine for malaria, but so far we have just been checking in on people. Most have others to do the care. She clarifies so as to double-check.

"We are going to bathe him."

"Yes."

A girl arrives with the washtubs, soap, and washcloths. Another brings the water. Cecilia pulls two sets of latex gloves from the pocket of her habit and hands one to me. She has known that she would be doing this.

A finger of one of my gloves rips as I am putting it on. Cecilia insists that I take one of hers. I refuse. She insists again.

"I can work with just one. I do not want you to get sick," she says.

We strike a compromise. I take her glove, and she takes my ripped one, which will protect her better than none at all, and puts it on her left hand.

Cecilia carefully pours water from the yellow plastic jerrycan into each of the wash basins. It is twenty-liters-of-pump-water heavy, and she sweats from under the band of her habit headpiece. She is powerfully built, and her body does not bend with the ease that seems to come preternaturally to so many Ugandan women.

For the next hour and a half, I follow the pattern of her actions, she with one basin to wash, me with the other to rinse. We wash his head and neck first, including inside his ears. Then we wash his chest, shoulders, and arms. He looks like an emaciated Bill Russell. His skin now glistens like polished black onyx.

"You can tell by how his skin shines now that he does not have the sickness," Cecilia observes. "He is only starving."

Santo's paralysis keeps him from even registering to receive WFP food, let alone pick it up, and he has no one to do it for him. With all due respect to the UN official who took the unusual step of actually visiting here, this is one person in Pabbo who is in fact hungry.

We wash his legs, genitals, buttocks—yes, deep into the crack; if there are parasites nesting there, we want them out. We change the water, then wash his feet. His clothes are putrid and infested with lice; we cannot redress him in these. I run to the parish and get a set of mine. When I return, the food is just arriving. We dress him, stay with him while he eats, and tell him that we will return to bathe and feed him again.

I follow Cecilia outside, where she asks a woman to coat the interior of Santo's home with a dirt-and-cow-dung mixture. It smells for half a day but gets rid of the lice.

"How much will you pay me?" the woman responds.

I think of Father Olweny's comments about what he calls "the NGO [nongovernmental organization] effect" on residents of the camp. "The NGOs, they do not know the people, so when they ask them to do something—even just an interview—they pay them. Now I cannot even call a parish meeting without people expecting to be paid."

Sister Cecilia asks another woman if she will watch over Santo and perhaps share some food with him. She declines, but for a different reason. Santo may be worse off, but he is not the only one who is hungry.

"We do not have enough. We eat only once a day. If we try to feed him, we will starve too."

During the rest of my stay at Pabbo, Cecilia and I return several times to bathe and feed Santo, leaving him with enough food until we can come again. When I leave Pabbo, I give Cecilia enough money for another month of her visits.

"God will intercede," she replies. "You will see. He will bring an end to this war, this suffering. He is patient, but his patience is coming to an end. God will intercede."

In tacking back and forth between ethics-near and ethics-distant, the Christian ethicist relies not just on abstract theory to inform and be informed by ethnographic practice. He or she also brings the Gospel to bear on fieldwork. The weight that Christian ethicists give scripture in their deliberation varies from practitioner to practitioner, and it is not necessary to adjudicate that debate now. I follow the view of William Spohn, who takes not only scripture but also the life of Jesus related in scripture as the primary but not sole resource in the moral life of the Christian. Spohn, like Hauerwas, emphasizes how the narrative of the life of Jesus presents the paradigm for the Christian life and that virtue theory helps explicate the dynamic of Christian imitation or reenactment of the story much more adequately than other ethical theories.[28] At the same time, Spohn acknowledges an ample role for the social sciences, and even, like Gustafson, holds that empirical science can set limits on theology.[29] Spohn's ethics is one that attempts to be empirically particular while remaining particularly Christian.

The question then arises as to which text or texts to juxtapose with the ethnographically based story of Cecilia and Santo. Spohn takes the title of his book, *Go and Do Likewise*, from Jesus' concluding admonishment to the story of the Good Samaritan. This parable is apt because the patterns of this biblical narrative find reenactment in the story of Cecilia and Santo. Cecilia comes upon a prone stranger whom others have passed by. She attends to Santo's immediate needs, and then she seeks out others to contribute to his care while assuring him and them that she will be back to check on his progress. Though at the time I am not consciously reliving the parable, I try to model Cecilia (rinsing after her washing, leaving money for Santo's care before I leave Pabbo) as she reenacts the story of the Samaritan, who in turn embodies Christ's love commandment.

However, if the parable is to serve its full purpose so that the juxtaposition illumines not only analogical similarity but also dialectical dissimilarity, more extrapolation is necessary. Most Western readings of the story draw upon the goodness of the Samaritan to focus on the social risk and scandal of his crossing the road. Spohn follows suit: "A Jewish audience would have been shocked by holding up a Samaritan as an exemplar, while discrediting the respected priest and Levite."[30] To be sure, this reversal is an integral element of the story. However, Spohn and many other commentators leave a crucial component out.

If we recast the story in Northern Uganda, the person who sees someone lying on the other side of the road wonders, "Is he LRA? Is he government? Is he someone, an outspoken critic, whom the government soldiers killed last night, left by the side of the road, and are now claiming is LRA or was killed by the LRA, in order to divert attention from their own actions? Are those who beat, mutilated, or killed him still around? Is the man lying in the road someone gone mad with *cen*, an angry spirit cast upon him by a vengeful *ajwaka*?" In other words, the danger of being a Samaritan in Acholiland is not just social, though it is that too, but quite literally physical. Crossing the road puts one's life at risk. When Cecilia first decides to care for Santo, she does not know if he has AIDS or any of a number of other diseases. At the time we visit Santo, cholera is cutting a wide swath through vast sections of Northern Uganda and is moving toward Pabbo. Has it arrived in the person of Santo? She does not know. Her offer of her latex glove, when mine rips, is not simply a symbolic gesture.

Though both Hauerwas and Spohn discuss the cross, their account of *imitatio*-based ethics infrequently mentions and rarely if at all discusses the physical risk and risk of life that is attendant upon the effort to follow Jesus. This is the case even though Jesus himself is clear that his disciples must suffer the same fate that he will: "If any want to become my followers, let them deny themselves, take up their cross and follow me. For those who want to save their life will lose it, and those who lose their life for my sake, and for the sake of the gospel, will save it" (Mark 8:34–35). To be sure, Jesus is speaking metaphorically, but he is not speaking only so.

The question arises as to why Spohn, Hauerwas, and other ethicists who emphasize Jesus as exemplar fail to highlight sufficiently where this path might well lead for the disciple. It cannot be that society is any more Christian and less violent than before, at least in Hauerwas's judgment.[31] One possibility follows from the epistemological affirmation with which we started: What we know is shaped by our social location. Not only Spohn and Hauerwas but also most members of the Society of Christian Ethics—as the criteria for professional membership virtually assure—are not in a situation where their life is at ongoing risk. The social production and consumption of what is called Christian ethics, particularly in the United States, virtually rules it out. It is instructive, then, to consider Martin Luther King Jr.'s reading of the Good Samaritan. His call to his listeners to use their imaginations fits with Spohn and Hauerwas' ethical theories:

> Now you know, we use our imagination a great deal to try to determine why the priest and the Levite didn't stop. . . . I'm going to tell you what my imagination tells me. It's possible that these men were afraid. You see, the Jericho road is a dangerous road. . . . In the days of Jesus it came to be known as "Bloody Pass." And you know, it's possible that the priest and the Levite looked over that man on the ground and wondered if the robbers were still around. Or it's possible that they felt that the man on the ground was merely faking. And he was acting like he was robbed and hurt, in order to seize them over there, lure them there for quick and easy seizure. And the first question

the Levite asked was, "If I stop to help this man, what will happen to me?" But then the Good Samaritan came by. And he reversed the question: "If I do not stop to help this man, what will happen to him?"[32]

In the face of the violence he is sure that he will encounter, King seeks to embody the Samaritan, and he calls his listeners to do so as well. He tells them to ask what would happen to the Memphis sanitation workers, who lack basic necessities, if he and his audience do not stop to help. That he is not ignorant of the implications is evident in the fact that he then relates the story of his being stabbed at a book signing several years earlier, and he wants to convey that there may well be similar dangers for his followers. As an outspoken, politically active black man in the 1960s, his social location makes the risks clear to him. The day after his Memphis speech, he is shot.

It is possible to enlarge the analysis from the reading of this specific parable to an interpretation of the Gospel more generally. Hauerwas reads the question of violence to be "the central issue for any Christian social ethic." The implication, as he understands it, is that Christians ought to be noncoercive and nonviolent in their being and actions as Jesus was noncoercive and nonviolent in his. Spohn follows a similar logic.[33] To be sure, the question of nonviolence is an important one, and I am inclined to agree with their conclusion. Still more fundamental than whether the Christian is willing to coerce or kill, however, is the question of whether he or she is willing to die. The Good Samaritan follows the Great Commandment, which Jesus fills out elsewhere (thus making the risks of the Good Samaritan explicit) when he says, "This is my commandment, that you love one another as I have loved you. No one has greater love than this, to lay down one's life for one's friends" (Jn. 15:12–13). As before, a legalistic listener might ask, "And who are my friends?" and the story of the Good Samaritan would naturally follow.

It may well be that someone who, under certain circumstances, is willing to kill for the state is also willing to die for Christ and that this latter willingness sets limits on the former. It suggests that a Christian soldier who sees the defense of the innocent in his country as at least not inconsistent with his faith and perhaps even an expression of it may be closer to Christ than the professed pacifist whose nonviolence never becomes personally precarious.[34] My point here is not to reenter the just war–pacifism debate. In fact, it is to suggest that the debate is misplaced if it is taken to be the fundamental question of Christian social ethics, and that such misplacement is in part the product of Christian ethics being done in a social location that is itself not precarious, especially when done by ethicists of an age such that the decision of whether to partake in killing or not does not risk the alternatives of imprisonment or death for the ethicist.

It is noteworthy that when Spohn quotes John Paul II on how, in the Christian context, solidarity "seeks to go beyond itself" to take on the qualities of "total gratuity, forgiveness and reconciliation," he chops off the end of the paragraph midsentence, indicating conscious redaction. The first part of the last sentence reads, "One's neighbor must be loved, even if an enemy, with the same love with which the Lord loves him or her." Spohn excises the second part of the sentence, which spells out the implications of that imitation in "same love": ". . . and for that person's sake one must be ready for sacrifice, even the ultimate one: to lay down one's life for the brethren."[35]

If we follow John Paul II and the person whom he tries to imitate, then we must insist that the cross involves the willingness to risk our lives in the practice of following Christ. This does not mean that we do not use prudential judgment in assessing risk. The aim is to be in solidarity with and love of the other in God, not the risk itself. Still, a life where risk, real bodily risk, on behalf of solidarity is never at stake raises questions about the commitment to love in the first place. Oppression is structural violence; if we never become exposed to the violence, this is an indication that our commitment, our response to God's gift of grace in Jesus Christ, is questionable. Willingness to risk is an indication, even if it is not the only one, of commitment to love one's neighbor.

That commitment takes on a particular edge for the Christian ethicist working out of the virtue tradition. The claim there, at least in theory, is that displaying the ethic is as important as articulating it, if not more so. Hauerwas's well-known dictum is that "the church does not have a social ethic; the church is a social ethic." Reinterpreting this claim in light of the above, then, we can say that "the Christian ethicist, if he wants to have an ethic of following the life of Jesus, must also attempt to be and to display that ethic and all of its inherent risks, not for the sake of risk but for the sake of truthfulness in following Jesus."

Lived method ought to be consistent with intellectual theory. Ethnographic fieldwork presents the opportunity for Christian ethicists to move, at least temporarily and perhaps for extended periods of time, out of a social location that blinds us (to continue Spohn and Hauerwas's ocular metaphor) to the full implications of discipleship. The anthropological literature includes writings on the physical as well as psychological dangers of fieldwork.[36] For the Christian ethicist, fieldwork is a way of remaining in the academy while we go about being Christians.

Final Confession

"It is not enough."[37] Otim James sits across from me in the dining room of the Catechist Training Center outside Gulu, the largest town in the North. It is well after mealtime, so we are alone. At sixteen years old, Otim James is the male head of a family of at least six—there may be more. He wears a white T-shirt and blue basketball warm-up pants with stars going down the sides.

They are too long for him and drag when he walks. I tell him that this is in style in the United States, and he smiles.

Otim James's father died last year, probably of AIDS. We know this because his mother is in the hospital in Kitgum town for treatment. The rebels abducted and killed Otim James's older brother when he was riding a bicycle home for school holiday. The brother was in S6, the equivalent of a senior in high school, and on the cusp of obtaining the virtually impossible in Northern Uganda: a diploma in the camps. The Training Center must seem like a resort and spa to Otim James. It has running water and, at least most of the time, electricity. He will have his own room tonight with an off-the-ground bed so that the mice and lizards will not crawl on him while he sleeps.

This is not why he has come, however. He has made the journey from Lokung to request—no, demand—his school fees for the next year. His visit seems presumptuous only to the uninitiated. When I first met Otim James, a friend of Lilly and Otum's, I gave him a soccer ball. To me, it was simply a gift. To him, it was the beginning of a relationship. He has come to ask for 160,000 Ugandan schillings, about $110, for tuition for next year, and I have given it to him. He needs more.

Gustafson's voice enters my head. It is impossible to leave his seminar.

"You cannot be God. God will be God."

"No," I insist, "be *like* God. Spohn. Tracy. Analogical imagination."

"It is still anthropocentric."

"No. No. No. The person is in the story but not the center of the story."

"Mr. Todd, it is not enough."

Otim James breaks up my reverie.

"I need to pick up my mother at the hospital and take her home."

Of course. Otim James needs to get home. He literally has spent his last schilling getting to the Training Center.

It will never be enough. Though I tell Otim James when I give him the travel money that next year when I come back I will not be able to afford his school fees and he nods, I know now that he will ask again. It is precisely in the practice of fieldwork, the particular relationships with the particular people of Acholiland, while trying in some way to follow Jesus that I am most aware that I am encumbered and that the occasion of a person also being God is a unique and exclusive event in history. Borrowing from the traditional accounts of the "uses of the law," we can call it the first use of the exemplar: However much we may try to imitate him, the attempt to follow Christ in the particularities of face-to-face encounters with others throws us back on the fact that we are not Christ. I cannot do a modern-day loaves-and-fishes miracle and ensure that all the people in Komakec will have enough food. I cannot make Santo get up and walk. I cannot make the war end. Whatever we do, being in the field forces upon us the fact that it is not enough. God will remain God.

Notes

1. I have changed the name of the camp and of some of the persons in order to protect the latter.

2. Michael Stayton, "A People Held Hostage," *Wabash Magazine*, Spring 2006, 41.

3. Examples of members of the Society of Christian Ethics who do some form of fieldwork as a direct part of their research include Melissa Browning, Peter Gathje, Richard B. Miller, Christine Pohl, Melissa Proctor, Christian Scharen, and Ana Marie Vigen. In my own case, at the time of the publication of this essay, I have done five months of fieldwork in Kenya, Uganda, and Sudan. In the next three years, my research plan is to do between twelve and twenty-two additional months, depending on institutional resources. At present, I have an intermediate facility with the Acholi language and will be working with an Acholi tutor to bring it up to full proficiency by the summer of 2008. I spend most of my time in the field living in Internally Displaced Persons camps under the welcoming hospitality of the people who live there. In addition to living and working with the people, I conduct video field recordings of Acholi stories, songs, dances, and ceremonies. In the summer of 2007, I initiated a pilot project to reintroduce working oxen into northern Ugandan villages. The war has devastated this base of the Acholi economy.

4. W. H. R. Rivers, as quoted in *Notes and Queries on Anthropology*, by B. Freire-Marreco and J. L. Myers (London: Royal Anthropological Institute, 1912), 143.

5. See, e.g., Lee H. Yearley, *Mencius and Aquinas: Theories of Virtue and Conceptions of Courage* (Albany: State University of New York Press, 1990).

6. James M. Gustafson, "The Sectarian Temptation: Reflections on Theology, the Church, and the University," *Proceedings of the Fortieth Annual Convention: The Catholic Theological Society of America* 40 (1985): 92, 86, 84.

7. Stanley Hauerwas, "Why the 'Sectarian Temptation' Is a Misrepresentation: A Response to James Gustafson," in *The Hauerwas Reader*, by Stanley Hauerwas, ed. John Berkman and Michael Cartwright (Durham, N.C.: Duke University Press, 2001), 95, 97.

8. James M. Gustafson, *An Examined Faith: The Grace of Self-Doubt* (Minneapolis: Fortress Press, 2004): 40, 85.

9. Gustafson, *Examined Faith*, 37, 113 n. 3.

10. Hauerwas, *Hauerwas Reader*, 251, 371–72; and also 71, 112, 152, 169, 274, 381–82.

11. Gustafson, *Examined Faith*, 88, and see also 44; Gustafson, "Sectarian Temptation," 83, 84, 91.

12. On the claim that the church is an empirical reality, see Hauerwas, *Hauerwas Reader*, 382; For examples of short descriptions of incidents used to launch stories or illustrate points, see 75, 246–47, 255, 265, 540, 556–57. For Hauerwas's treatment of *Watership Down*, see 171 ff.

13. Hauerwas, *Hauerwas Reader*, 117, 119; also see 72–73, 77, 378.

14. Gustafson, *Examined Faith*, 10; see also 11, 12, 14, 17, 33, 47–48, 51, 77, 83, 85, 107. Also see Gustafson, "Sectarian Temptation," 93 (Jesus is not God).

15. Gustafson, "Sectarian Temptation," 93; Gustafson, *Examined Faith*, 106–7, 110. For a reading of Gustafson that also interprets him as a stoic, see Gilbert Meilaender, "Review, *Ethics from a Theocentric Perspective*," *Religious Studies Review* 12, no. 1 (January 1986): 11–16. For where Gustafson rejects providence, see *Examined Faith*, 97–98, 103, 107; for his claim that a personal God is incompatible with science, see *Examined Faith*, 27, 91–92.

16. Richard B. Miller, "On Making a Cultural Turn in Religious Ethics," *Journal of Religious Ethics* 33 (September 2005): 410.

17. Richard B. Miller, *Children, Ethics, and Modern Medicine* (Bloomington: Indiana University Press, 2003), 9.

18. Miller, "On Making a Cultural Turn," 415–17, 439.

19. Miller, *Children, Ethics, and Modern Medicine*, 26.

20. Ibid., 32.

21. Ibid., 157, 160.

22. Ibid., 162.

23. George E. Marcus and Michael M. J. Fischer, *Anthropology as Cultural Critique: An Experimental Moment in the Human Sciences* (Chicago: University of Chicago Press, 1986). Miller draws upon Marcus and Fischer and even cites the concept of "cultural juxtaposition."

24. Gustafson, *Examined Faith*, 65; see also 8, 9, 84. On the theology of economics, see Duncan K. Foley, *Adam's Fallacy: A Guide to Economic Theology* (Cambridge, Mass.: Belknap Press, 2006).

25. For an example of anthropological literature that turns ethnographic method on the discipline of anthropology itself, see Marilyn Strathern, *Commons and Borderlands: Working Papers on Interdisciplinarity, Accountability, and the Flow of Knowledge* (Oxford: Sean Kingston Publishing, 2004).

26. For an excellent example of this kind of writing, see Michael Jackson, *At Home in the World* (Durham, N.C.: Duke University Press, 1995).

27. The genre of autobiography, which aims to portray primarily the self, is a more recent development. Most accounts date the start of the genre of autobiography with Rousseau's *Confessions*. Despite the traditional title, Rousseau's effort was to write about his self: "I have resolved on an enterprise which has no precedent, and which, once complete, will have no imitator. My purpose is to display to my kind a portrait in every way true to nature, and the man I shall portray is myself. Simply myself." Jean-Jacques Rousseau, *The Confessions* (New York: Penguin Books, 1954), 17.

28. It is testimony to Gustafson as a teacher that he has students with such a wide range of approaches. This article is dedicated to William Spohn. *Kyre Eleison*. For emphasis on the life of Jesus, see William C. Spohn, *Go and Do Likewise: Jesus and Ethics* (New York: Continuum, 2000) 10, 22, 29, 32, 64, and throughout. On imitation or discipleship that seeks to follow the person of Jesus, see 1, 2, 9, 10, 25, 31–33, 56, 60–61, 64–65, and throughout; and Hauerwas, *Hauerwas Reader*, 225, 254, 280. For the role of narrative, see Spohn, *Go and Do Likewise*, 61, 173–74. On vision, see ibid., 75–119. On virtue theory, see ibid., 27–32. Spohn makes a much stronger statement than Gustafson does when he says that Jesus, "incarnates theocentric piety and fidelity." Gustafson, *Ethics from a Theocentric Perspective, Volume One: Theology and Ethics* (Chicago: University of Chicago Press, 1981), 276.

29. Spohn, *Go and Do Likewise*, 21–22, 58–59, 63, 70; and see 3.

30. Ibid., 91; on the difference between analogy and dialectic, see 59–60, 87, 108.

31. Hauerwas, *Hauerwas Reader*, 201.

32. Martin Luther King Jr., "I See the Promised Land," in *A Testament of Hope: The Essential Writings and Speeches of Martin Luther King, Jr.*, by Martin Luther King Jr., ed. James M. Washington (San Francisco: HarperSanFrancisco, 1990), 279–82.

33. Hauerwas, *Hauerwas Reader*, 390–91, and also see 126, 133, 144, 195–98, 255; and Spohn, *Go and Do Likewise*, 78–79, 81.

34. It is odd that while we consider it normal for a soldier to risk life on behalf of the state—presumably not as high a good—we do not think of it as normal for Christians to risk their lives on behalf of the Kingdom.

35. Spohn, *Go and Do Likewise*, 181; the quotation is from John Paul II, *Sollicitudo Rei Socialis*, 40.

36. Raymond M. Lee, *Dangerous Fieldwork* (Thousand Oaks, Calif.: Sage Publications, 1995); Carolyn Nordstron and Antonius C. G. M. Robben, *Fieldwork under Fire: Contemporary Studies of Violence and Survival* (Berkeley: University of California Press, 1995).

37. The dialectical method that I am drawing upon in this essay does not permit of tidy "conclusions" that summarize and so compress and reduce the descriptions and analysis that precede it. At best, I can present a final movement, in this case a final confession that is only final for now and cannot be taken as conclusive.

Book Reviews

Review of

An Ecological Christian Anthropology: At Home on Earth?

ERNST M. CONRADIE

Burlington, Vt.: Ashgate, 2005. 264 pp. $99.95.

Christian Environmental Ethics: A Case Method Approach

JAMES B. MARTIN-SCHRAMM AND ROBERT L. STIVERS

Maryknoll, N.Y.: Orbis Books, 2003. 325 pp. $20.00.

Discussions of the natural environment and its relevance for faith and morality are not new to Christian thought, but our contemporary circumstance is. In the last few decades, human beings have grown increasingly aware of our position as the dominant species on the planet. In the last few years, our society has begun to develop tools to talk about this reality in new ways, most particularly as global warming becomes an accepted, mainstream topic in political discourse. In this time, it is crucial that Christian ethicists understand how our traditions and our discipline can nurture clear, careful, and constructive discussion about the relationships between human beings and our nonhuman environments. The two texts reviewed here contribute in very different ways to that project.

Robert Stivers and James Martin-Schramm have produced a resource for teaching, appropriate for undergraduate classes and for church groups, but they also make a methodological argument to ethics teachers. Their book provides nine case studies in order to "ground Christian ethical reflection in reality," raising difficult questions of environmental ethics in concrete ways and inviting readers to "bring ethical resources from diverse Christian traditions to bear on specific situations with all their differences" (p. 47).

The cases are all based on real environmental problems and debates in the United States, and many were clearly researched in discussion with the activists, leaders, and citizens involved—although the names of individuals and some locations are changed. In each case, complicated issues are discussed, but a concrete, debatable question clearly emerges. Thus, a case about the George W. Bush administration's energy policy, global warming, and proposals to drill in

Journal of the Society of Christian Ethics, 27, 2 (2007): 297–322

the Arctic National Wildlife Refuge is made personal when it is framed through the eyes of a high school civics teacher deciding how to offer an "evenhanded" but honest perspective to his students. Other cases introduce nuclear waste storage, property rights, urban development, genetic engineering, and deforestation in such a way that readers can understand how individual decisions make a difference and classes can have informed and engaging discussions about how such decisions should be made. This not only makes the cases relatable but also demonstrates that questions of environmental ethics occur and must be understood on international, national, state, and local levels.

What is most admirable and useful about this book is that the authors do not allow their emphasis on concrete problems and individual decisions to oversimplify the cases they present or the tools they offer to engage them. Each case is followed by a lengthy commentary in which theological, political, and environmental background expands on what is at stake, and resources throughout the text establish ethical terminology in order to inspire and equip sophisticated moral discussions. Thus, a case about water rights in northern Washington State includes not only an account of landowners conflicted by the cost of compliance with the Endangered Species Act but also a commentary that explores different theories of justice, the theological significance of water, and a history of legal property rights.

The first two chapters of the book lay a foundation for the cases, providing brief synopses of the phenomenon of environmental degradation and the role of Christian faith in responding to it. Martin-Schramm and Stivers argue that environmental degradation is caused in large part by the "attitudes toward nature" that make it conceivable, and so the Christian tradition has important and unique contributions to make in response to such attitudes. They develop an "ethic of ecological justice" based on biblical, theological, and traditional sources, emphasizing "four norms: sustainability, sufficiency, participation, and solidarity" (p. 37). It is not altogether clear how much this perspective influenced the writing of the cases themselves or how much influence it should have on the ways readers think about them. Indeed, most of the cases would have a great deal to teach both non-Christians and Christians who do not share this commitment to ecological justice.

So, the role of the theological foundation for this text remains unclear. But that is perhaps appropriate; this is a book about applying ideas to concrete cases, designed for students and their teachers. Indeed, as helpful as the cases themselves is a brief appendix of resources for teaching, which explains various assignments that could be developed from the text as well as classroom exercises to explore the range of opinions about environmental issues and the importance of autobiography in understanding our own positions. The book is well written and clear enough that virtually all students and church groups can use and learn from it. I have used it in my own undergraduate environmental studies class and found it a useful resource for the whole class. Its realistic and case-based approach helped me to reach and relate to students who were uninspired by more traditional academic articles and books, which is perhaps the best feature of *Christian Environmental Ethics: A Case Method Approach*.

Ernst Conradie has written a different kind of book. Whereas Stivers and Martin-Schramm offer a tool for teaching environmental ethics that emphasizes the intersection of personal, political, economic, and historical concerns with theological ethics, *An Ecological Christian Anthropology* is a specialized academic text that attempts to articulate a particularly Christian perspective on the nature of human beings in the world. Conradie's primary methodological concern is that any theological perspective on ecological concerns must be based in "the Trinitarian and soteriological heart of Christian theology" (p. vi), and so this work is one part of a broader project: a comprehensive, systematic ecological theology that remains faithfully and authentically Christian.

The book's central argument is that human beings are not at home on Earth. Though Conradie agrees that the Earth can be understood metaphorically as the "house" of humanity, any claim that we are currently at home here is a "romantic fantasy" that ignores both the unavoidable predation and suffering on this planet and the undeniable sinfulness of human life here (p. 48). This argument explicitly challenges most of the environmental theology that has come before it, which has frequently appealed to a sense of belonging on Earth and a dismissal of otherworldly theology as inherently harmful to environmentalist causes.

Conradie suggests that a faithful and effective justification for environmental ethics can be established by articulating human responsibility not primarily through our relationship to the Earth but rather our relationship to the Creator. It is in obedience to God that we should live on Earth, and our work should be to prepare this house to become God's home. "*Home is an eschatological concept*" (p. 228; emphasis added), he writes, meaning that we treat other species and future generations with care and respect not because we are currently at home with them but rather because of a faithful hope that our work to do so will be recalled by God in a better future.

Developing this argument, Conradie suggests that "stewardship" is not the best way to characterize human responsibility toward the rest of the world, particularly because he finds most theological discussions of the concept point to the pervasive reality of human sin. He suggests instead an ethic of "preparation," which sees our responsibility to the Earth as one of "preparing for the way of the Lord" (p. 229). This capacity to look toward the future and develop our lives in light of it is, he suggests, what makes human beings distinctive. The theological anthropology developed in this book, then, sees human life "as a journey of discovery of our finitude and therefore of that which transcends it" (p. 81).

An Ecological Christian Anthropology makes an important contribution to environmental theology and ethics, demonstrating a far more orthodox and uniquely

Christian theology than most in this field. Perhaps the greatest strength is the care Conradie takes to respond to the discourse of environmental theology; well over a thousand footnotes attest to the care with which he approaches this field and make this book a valuable scholarly resource from a purely bibliographic standpoint.

A weakness is that it is not always clear how comprehensive this approach can be in understanding environmental issues. Conradie strives toward an "ecological" theology, but he does not satisfactorily define what that adjective means for him, and it is clear from the text that it does not require any extensive attention to the science of ecology. Along similar lines, he assumes that "earthkeeping" is an important goal for all theology, but he does not define this or justify it as a motivating factor. Missing from this text is any careful discussion of environmental degradation as a multivalent phenomenon like that provided by Martin-Schramm and Stivers. Conradie is clearly motivated by the contemporary degradation of the Earth's ecosystems, but his methodological focus on speaking in almost exclusively theological terms seems to prevent him from discussing these events at length. This leads him to miss some aspects of the literature he critiques. I would argue, for instance, that the theologians and ethicists Conradie accuses of ignoring sin do not do so at all but rather redefine the concept in a manner that incorporates environmental degradation, precluding it from his narrow categories of acceptable theological discourse.

Conradie does not convince me that environmental theology and ethics should be overly concerned with remaining "authentically Christian." He argues that this is necessary to avoid falling into "an all too shallow form of natural theology" (p. 41), a concern I can respect but do not share. I am particularly concerned that the theology described in this book neglects the absolute necessity of interdisciplinary dialogue about the nature of creation and human existence—dialogue which, Conradie seems to suggest, theology can at most "overhear" while remaining faithful to the theological truths of God's Word.

Despite the fact that he has not convinced me, I am very impressed by Conradie's argument and learned a great deal from it about the variety of theological approaches possible in contemplating and responding to environmental degradation. His deeply scholarly, "authentically" theological text calls attention to what is not accomplished in Stivers and Martin-Schramm's. Though their book is designed to teach a broad spectrum of ideas about environmental ethics as an interdisciplinary pursuit, it does not contribute as directly and explicitly to the scholarly conversation of environmental theology and ethics, and the authors do not carefully explain what is "Christian" about their perspective or reflect on how that identity matters.

Although these two books are vastly different, they suggest the sophisticated dialogues that Christian ethicists and theologians are beginning to have about environmental degradation. In *Christian Environmental Ethics: A Case Method Approach*, two ethicists offer a tool to help teach this field to nonprofessional audiences. In *An Ecological Christian Anthropology*, a theologian offers a critique of the many ethicists he sees as willing to sacrifice theological traditions in order to claim that human beings are at home on Earth. In both these texts, it is clear that a vibrant and vital conversation is taking place about how Christian thought and Christian morality will interact with environmental crises in the contemporary world.

Kevin J. O'Brien
Pacific Lutheran University

Review of
Sharing Food: Christian Practices for Enjoyment

L. SHANNON JUNG
Minneapolis: Fortress Press, 2006. 176 pp. $15.00.

We Westerners know that we have problems with food; we are just not certain where the root of our problems lies. Does it lie with *what* we eat—that our carbohydrate levels and protein levels need to be altered, as many popular diet plans suggest? Or does it lie with *how* and *where* we eat—that, as the Slow Food movement suggests, the Western diet is just too focused on eating quickly? Or is the chief issue what *kind* of diet to have: Mediterranean, French, or Chinese?

The best trait of L. Shannon Jung's work is that he focuses on none of these questions in isolation. He proposes instead that the heart of Western issues with eating involves a lack of joy (and a related inability to share food), which shows itself in our myriad difficulties with food from anorexic bodies to giving and receiving hospitality to the food Christians eat in the Eucharist. This focus on sharing and joy gives his book a different slant than the numerous recent books about honoring our bodies, or hospitality, or Christian feasting.

This book is clearly intended for a lay audience; each chapter includes a range of personal stories and discussion questions. Though Jung raises some questions that may be of interest to scholars, the book will be best used in an undergraduate course or a local church adult study group. Each chapter features questions to help people consider specific food practices that might help them live more joyfully. *Sharing Food* is a companion piece to Jung's earlier work, *Food for Life:*

The Spirituality and Ethics of Eating, which he says provides scriptural and theological underpinnings for the work he does in *Sharing Food*.

Although *Sharing Food* helpfully considers our contemporary difficulties with food, its readers would have been better served if it had incorporated the theological and scriptural elements from *Food for Life*. Jung's reasons behind the practices he suggests in *Sharing Food* would make a far stronger statement if the practices themselves were seen as theological. For example, fasting and feasting are theological statements *as practices*. The person who fasts is, by the very practice, saying something about God. The assumed distinction between theology and practice is especially a concern, given Jung's audience. There are numerous points in *Sharing Food* where there are latent (or obvious) allusions to theological concepts but where people would need the scripture and theology from *Food for Life* in order to recognize them.

Thus, in the chapter "Feasting in Community," Jung considers what it might mean for North Americans to celebrate by feasting. He rightly suggests that we do not know how to feast because we do not know or experience what it means to fast, but he might also have brought in important points from his earlier book about the theological meaning of desire. Our inability to savor food also stems from a desire to avoid pain and a suspicion that happiness cannot truly happen unless we are in control of producing it (p. 58). Jung does not develop these ideas fully in either of his books, but they are worth further consideration, especially because the point is not immediately obvious in our consumer culture. To take joy and delight in food and in the sharing of it means relying on God's grace. Dependence on God as opposed to personal control is an important theological topic that deserves far more discussion in this book.

The chapter on the Eucharist, titled "The Master Practice of the Lord's Supper," demonstrates the false distinction between the "practices" contained in this book and the "theology" contained in *Food for Life*. Jung suggests that in this chapter he is "draw[ing] on all the everyday elements that form the basis of these practices and indicates how they are incorporated into the master practice or sacrament of the Lord's Supper" (p. 7). Yet, in this chapter particularly, it makes little sense to say that there is a specific focus on practice distinct from theology, because Jung himself brings up a range of theological questions, including incarnation, ecclesiology, and the paschal mystery. His audience needs more in-depth theological reflection to consider fully what he discusses in this chapter.

In the final chapter, "Living with Jouissance," Jung discusses the necessity of receiving hospitality as well as giving it. He recounts a story in which five people stayed at a house overnight. The hostess asked the five what they wanted for breakfast; but four, desiring not to impose on the hostess, requested only cornflakes. The fifth responded to her request by ordering a full breakfast. In the story, the hostess clearly enjoyed making his breakfast and watching him enjoy it far more than she enjoyed fixing the bowls of cornflakes. Being able to share with others requires rejoicing in others' desires to share with us. One part of receiving hospitality, though only hinted at in this chapter, is the development of virtues like humility; we cannot suppose ourselves to be better than others because *we* share and others do not.

On the whole, Jung makes good use of personal anecdotes to engage his audience, and he considers very timely questions about food. Students will find his discussion of food and food practices useful for considering ways to live the Christian life joyfully.

Jana Bennett
Hampden-Sydney College

Review of
God and the Evil of Scarcity: Moral Foundations of Economic Agency

ALBINO BARRERA, OP
Notre Dame, Ind.: University of Notre Dame Press, 2005. 287 pp. $22.00.

The Reverend Thomas Malthus (1766–1834), an Anglican churchman and early economist, casts a long shadow in the industrial world. His famous *Essay on the Principle of Population* argued that food supplies and population were inextricably linked; food scarcity provides the only check on human population growth, thus condemning the majority of humans to lives of misery and vice in the pursuit of survival. Two centuries later, the idea that human misery is due to poor family planning on the part of individuals, rather than communal or systemic failures in economic distribution, has proven highly attractive to those who would absolve themselves of their neighbors' suffering.

Albino Barrera, an economist and theologian at Providence College, skillfully and lucidly revisits scarcity with an eye toward encouraging a mindset of economic agency in place of Malthusian resignation. Barrera argues that scarcity—in the sense of material limitations—is indeed a part of God's created order but that God specifically intends these limitations to be occasions for human beings to participate actively in God's provision for God's creatures. The earth can provide more than enough goods for human flourishing, if only human beings will do their part to make it happen for one another. In many ways, this book can be seen as an in-depth theological companion for his other, more economically focused 2005 work, the excellent *Economic Compulsion and Christian Ethics* (Cambridge University Press).

Barrera makes his argument in two broad strokes—one speculative, and one scriptural. Part I seeks wisdom in Thomist metaphysics. God is perfect, and God's creation is therefore also perfect. Creation would not be perfect if its creatures were doomed to a life of inevitable scrounging for survival; thus, we can infer that God provided a world of material sufficiency to sustain human life. However, this plenitude is *conditional* upon the activity of human beings who, as second causes, must use their rationality to participate in providing for one another. This means that sacrifice on the part of some humans for the sake of others is required; but through this process of participation and sacrifice humans are perfected, both individually and collectively. Scarcity is a fact of earthly life, but it is well within humans' control to ameliorate its effects. Furthermore, God expressly intends us to do so.

Part II is an exegesis of both Old Testament and New Testament teachings on matters of material provision. Barrera argues that God's intervention in Israel's life—particularly the promise of land and solicitude for the poor—shows concern for the economic life of God's people. Israel's economic law is a specific invitation to participate in God's righteousness by providing for and sustaining one another; its economic actions are an important means by which Israel grows closer to God in likeness, much as a child grows more like its parents. This participatory theme is continued in Pauline theology, in which concrete good works and embodied righteousness are seen as a taking part in the life of Christ; in the economic realm, this involves hard work, self-sufficiency (to the extent possible), and sharing with one's neighbors. Barrera convincingly concludes that both Israel and the early churches understood that their collective economic lives, insofar as they embodied God's righteousness, would not only be beneficial to themselves but would also be instrumental in drawing others to God's goodness.

In part III, Barrera addresses the nature of scarcity and then, wisely, takes pains to distinguish his vision from Malthus's. It is unclear, however, whether he is ultimately successful in distinguishing himself from Malthus as much as he would like. For example, Barrera critiques Malthus's argument that economic scarcity is necessary for goading humans out of their natural torpor (p. 4); but then he later argues that, without "existential scarcity," humans would have no reason to strive for anything or share with their neighbors (p. 170). In other words, conditions of material superfluity would do away with the need for "being by doing." Both arguments seem to fall flat in the face of Barrera's own Thomist claim that the good is more than powerful enough to attract people to itself without any help from evil. One wonders, then, whether the preservation of the scarcity paradigm (though perhaps useful among economists) is particularly helpful to Barrera's theological argument. Likewise, his choice to speak of created human finitude in terms of "metaphysical evil" seems to betray a Malthusian ambivalence about the goodness of embodied human existence; to wit: "Would that human beings were not corporeal" or at least not "too dependent on material inputs" (p. 159). A resounding affirmation of human bodily limitations as inherent (rather than a hindrance) to human perfection would help rather than hurt Barrera's argument about our particular participation in God's righteousness. Moreover, it would guard against the twin Malthusian impulses to devalue those with ostensibly greater bodily limitations (historically, women, the elderly, the poor, or the disabled) and to lament the creation of any more corporeal, dependent humans (historically, those born into situations of real economic scarcity).

Nevertheless, Barrera may not feel the need to depart from Malthus as much as some theologians might like. He argues that Israel's economics was not so different from its neighbors' except in its theocentrism; perhaps likewise, he feels he can embrace Malthusian scarcity with some theological adjustments. In any case, he makes a generally persuasive ethical argument in favor of the need for justice and restorative economic activity on the part of human actors. The book is masterfully crafted and beautifully written, and it is important reading not only for scholars of economic ethics but also for students in need of an introduction to questions of scarcity and theodicy. Barrera also has a gift for demonstrating the significance of methodology in theological ethics, which can be an inspiration to those seeking to make sense of the larger conversation and to locate their own thinking within it.

Kathryn D. Blanchard
Alma College

Review of
Just Love: A Framework for Christian Sexual Ethics

MARGARET A. FARLEY
New York: Continuum, 2006. 323 + xiii pp. $29.95.

Margaret Farley's *Just Love* has been long awaited by many in the field of Christian ethics, and the majority will not be disappointed. Some will quibble that there is not enough Christian theology, others, that it does not sufficiently focus on the particular experience of women, but most will agree that her approach is both appropriate and original, and a major contribution to the field.

The most noticeable difference between *Just Love* and other books in Christian sexual ethics is that it does not begin with the sexual teachings of the Christian tradition but instead consults Christian tradition as one of, and not the principal one among, a number of sources. For over forty years, most sexual ethics texts have been structured around Christian sexual teachings by scholars attempting to explain how one or another of these teachings, or even all, had become problematic and should be reformed or jettisoned altogether. Though much of the Christian sexual tradition is marred by blatant misogyny and a body/soul dualism that disdains all things physical, Farley moves beyond refuting and dismissing this tradition and engages the strengths of the Christian moral tradition: its teachings on holiness, justice, and love in relationships with God and with others.

Farley begins her book with surveys of the theories of Foucault and Mac-Kinnon; of sexuality in Greece, Rome, Judaism, and early Christian thinkers; and of philosophy and medicine. She further complicates and enriches the quest for useful sources for theories of sexuality and sexual ethics by turning to a variety of cross-cultural and interreligious perspectives on sexuality. Perhaps the most traditional section of the book surveys particular sources for Christian sexual ethics—the familiar quadrilateral of scripture, tradition, secular disciplines of knowledge, and contemporary experience. By the time one arrives at this section, the opening chapters have already demonstrated that Farley's surveys of contemporary experience and secular disciplines of knowledge are significantly broader than previous treatments they have received. My one quibble is that she dismisses too quickly the contributions of biological research, but many others will not agree.

Farley follows this survey of sources with a discussion of the body and gender, delineating love, desire, and sexuality as the primary elements in sexual experience. Then she shifts to the relationship of sexuality and justice, surveying a number of alternative ethical emphases by contemporary ethicists working on sexuality. Many will undoubtedly consider chapter 6 to be the meat of the book, due to the lingering association of sex with norms and laws. Farley's norms are grounded in an understanding of the human person that demands respect for the autonomy of persons, respect for the relationality of persons, and respect for persons as sexual beings in society. Persons are ends in themselves by virtue of both their freedom, which is their ability to choose their actions and to self-create, and their ability to love, which also involves choice. It is this quality of being ends-in-ourselves that grounds Farley's seven norms for just sex: (1) Do no unjust harm, (2) free consent of partners, (3) mutuality, (4) equality, (5) commitment, (6) fruitfulness, and (7) social justice. These are all very well developed. The first six norms treat the sexual relationship itself, and the seventh pertains to the way society should treat all sexual beings, for example, in issues of sexual and domestic violence, gender justice, and discrimination against gays, lesbians, and transgendered persons.

The final chapter and a half apply this framework to specific controversial issues in Christian sexual ethics, including short treatments of prostitution, masturbation, and pornography, as well as more developed treatments of marriage and family, same-sex relationships, and divorce and remarriage. There is also a gem of a discussion about sexual practice among the young, whose immaturity makes them not only both abnormally vulnerable in sex but also frequently incapable of applying norms. University audiences will appreciate Farley's frankness and up-to-date knowledge of current sexual trends among the young.

The extended treatment of marriage and family, same-sex relationships, and divorce and remarriage includes a long historical-sociological section on marriage that includes Christian trends and influences, and argues for both a flexible, functionally based understanding of family and for the importance of fidelity. Throughout the book, Farley argues that the goal of Christian life is close relationship with God and that the role of sexual ethics is to guide us to choices and lifestyles that support us in deepening this relationship with the divine. Her treatment of commitment realizes that, though there may be minimal levels of commitment that do not violate any of the norms developed above, only the promise of lifelong commitment allows partners to fully support each other's deep relationship with the divine that religious persons are called to create.

Throughout, *Just Love* exemplifies the realism and caution that it calls for, giving examples of both actions and situations that meet minimal ethical demands and those that support personal moral and spiritual growth—all out of a realization that we engage in ethical reflection and moral choice not only from different situations but also from different stages of self-knowledge, maturity, and spiritual growth. Just as the major thinkers who created our inherited framework for Christian sexual ethics had few sources in scripture or tradition upon which to found their teaching, and therefore turned to natural law, so Farley has in some sense returned to their starting point. She does not invoke the term natural law for her approach—perhaps because the natural law tradition in sexuality is so contaminated both with physicalism and essentialism—but in a very analogous way, she brings together what we know about embodied, sexual human beings from our experiences of sexuality with what we can learn about them from the secular disciplines, examining it all in the light of what scripture and the theological tradition tell us about the kinds of persons we should be and the kind of relationship with the divine that we should cultivate. This approach makes this book accessible and relevant not only to Christians but also to religious persons in general, as well as to many nonreligious persons who share similar visions of human persons.

Christine E. Gudorf
Florida International University

Review of
By Knowledge and by Love: Charity and Knowledge in the Moral Theology of St. Thomas Aquinas

MICHAEL S. SHERWIN, OP
Washington, D.C.: Catholic University of America Press, 2005.
270 pp. $54.95.

Michael Sherwin's *By Knowledge and by Love* represents a very important contribution to contemporary scholarship concerning the moral theology of Thomas Aquinas, and it will be of special interest not only to those working in the area of Thomistic ethics but also to those working in the areas of moral psychology and virtue ethics more broadly considered. Demonstrating an adept synthesis of contemporary scholarship, Sherwin offers a carefully nuanced rereading of Aquinas's moral psychology and treatment of the theological virtues in order to clarify Aquinas's perspective on the relationships between the virtue of charity and our knowledge of God and between the will and intellect in human action.

In so doing, Sherwin is especially concerned to respond to the recent interpretation of Aquinas's moral theology by James Keenan (in his *Goodness and Rightness in Thomas Aquinas' Summa theologiae*), who attempts to position Aquinas within the broad framework assumed by contemporary proponents of the idea of fundamental option (in addition to Keenan, Sherwin identifies Karl Rahner and Josef Fuchs). To theologically counterbalance the generally act-centered character of the manualist tradition in Roman Catholic moral theology—and, in particular, the traditional affirmation that one's relationship with God could be absolutely compromised with the commission of a single mortally sinful act—advocates of the idea of fundamental option have typically sought to reinterpret traditional categories of sin and grace so as to arrive at what might be considered to be more pastorally flexible conclusions in dealing with cases of chronic moral weakness or moral failure. To this end, these "theologians of moral motivation" (as Sherwin describes them) have maintained that one is able to remain in right relationship with God in spite of the presence of habitual patterns of serious sin or moral wrongdoing. By appropriating Rahner's distinction between the transcendental and categorical aspects of human freedom, they have argued that the core of the divine–human relationship is situated at a level of human personhood corresponding to the human will's fundamental receptivity and orientation to God, which remains both distinct from and independent of human cognition and the plane of concrete human action. Accordingly, the moral goodness of the human person is conceived in isolation from the morality of particular acts.

This more general theological claim concerning the autonomy of human goodness is worked out in a particular way in *Goodness and Rightness*, where Keenan argues that in an attempt to preserve human freedom (in his mature thought), Aquinas comes to affirm the priority and autonomy of the will over the intellect, insofar as he distinguishes between the activity of the will on the level of specification and the first exercise of the will in acting, the latter of which—in a manner that is strikingly similar to the idea of the will's exercise of fundamental freedom—is said to occur antecedently to the exercise of practical rationality. By affirming the primacy of the will in this way, Keenan maintains, Aquinas thereby implicitly endorses the relative "compartmentalization" of goodness and rightness that characterizes the theology of moral motivation.

In response to Keenan, Sherwin persuasively argues that the theory of love underlying the theology of moral motivation cannot be considered a faithful rendering of Aquinas's thought, because, on the one hand, for Aquinas, will and intellect work cooperatively and in tandem with one another in every human act, and on the other, love and knowledge, both natural and supernatural, are necessarily interconnected in a way that is structurally analogous to the relation between intellect and will. Sherwin suggests that in separating goodness from rightness, the theologians of moral motivation have erroneously driven a wedge between intellect and will, and between knowledge of God and love, by making charity something that exists independent of explicit knowledge of God and by making the movement of charity independent of practical reasoning and of concrete moral action.

Through a careful and well-balanced interpretation of the development of Aquinas's views concerning the respective roles of intellect and will in the psychology of human action, Sherwin illustrates how the shift in Aquinas's later writings concerning the will's causality actually displays his commitment to a much tighter integration of intellect and will, and of knowledge and love, and reveals more clearly their mutual influence and interdependence. Drawing on the Augustinian principle that what is loved must first be known, Sherwin argues for a reciprocal relation between both intellect and will, and between knowledge and love. In the former case, without the will's appetite for the good, reason would remain inert, whereas without reason's direction and specification, the will would lack its appropriate directiveness. Together, they form a unified twofold principle of human action; and yet, because the anterior motions of both intellect and will have their source in the first principles of our created nature, and are mutually informing (insofar as reason directs will and will shapes reason), the extremes of voluntarism and intellectual determinism can be successfully avoided. Similarly, in the case of knowledge and love, the theological virtues as the graced elevation of the natural principles of the human person display an interconnection and interpenetration, such that charity's act presupposes the conceptual knowledge that is faith and provides the will with its object (thereby affording faith a structural priority), whereas charity animates faith by directing it toward its end in union with God. As in the case of intellect and will, the theological virtues always operate in tandem to move the human will toward its proper end.

Aside from his convincing analysis of the intrinsic relationship between intellect and will and charity and knowledge in Aquinas's moral theology, Sherwin's treatment of charity's status as a virtue is equally compelling. He is certainly correct to argue that if charity is to be considered a virtue, it must spring forth into a more or less recognizable shape or form of life—even if there is an aspect of the virtue of charity pertaining to its proper act that is beyond human measure. To strive to be charitable, we must have some idea of what a life informed by charity would look like—a claim that, as Sherwin points out, fits closely with Aquinas's affirmation in the Tertia Pars of the need for the moral exemplarity of the Incarnation. One suspects that the neuralgic point about which Sherwin and the theologians of moral motivation ultimately disagree is as much that of the particular concrete shape that the life infused with charity might assume as it is the "technical" issue concerning the formality of goodness. This point aside, Sherwin's excellent book should be considered essential reading for all students of Aquinas's moral theology.

James E. Helmer
University of Notre Dame

Review of

John Howard Yoder: Mennonite Patience, Evangelical Witness, Catholic Convictions

MARK THIESSEN NATION
Grand Rapids: William B. Eerdmans, 2006. 235 pp. $20.00.

Mark Thiessen Nation reminds us in *John Howard Yoder: Mennonite Patience, Evangelical Witness, Catholic Convictions* of the enduring importance and relevance of Yoder's work for Christian social ethics. The subtitle of Nation's book informs the reader of the location of Yoder's work in the Mennonite tradition;

of Yoder's essential evangelical commitments to the Gospel of Christ as the shape of Christian ethics; and of the necessity of ecumenical conversations and commitments around unifying convictions of Christian faith. Nation skillfully and insightfully elaborates on the ways and contexts in which Yoder's Mennonite patience, evangelical witness, and catholic convictions were shaped, and on the contributions they made and continue to make. He allows Yoder to speak for himself by introducing us to his well-known works, as well as unpublished material, lectures, works in process at the time of his death, personal conversations, and popular publications. Nation provides rich analyses of Yoder's material, adding his own interpretations and explanations based on his broad knowledge of and familiarity with Yoder's work, as well as insights from his friendship with Yoder. At a minimum, Nation offers us a solid overview and extensive bibliography of Yoder's work, which will be exciting to those familiar with Yoder and helpful for those being introduced to him through this book.

Although Nation reminds us of Yoder's contribution to Christian ethics, he also makes important contributions to the field through his analyses and interpretation of Yoder's work, including two important areas: correcting the misrepresentation and caricaturing of Anabaptist ethics as sectarian withdrawal, and of pacifism as passivity in the face of wrongdoing and injustice. In chapter 4, "The Politics of Jesus, the Politics of John Howard Yoder: An Evangelical and Catholic Peace Theology," Nation explores Yoder's influence in placing Christian pacifism in mainstream theological conversations. He notes that pacifism for Yoder was not a social program or response but instead a central conviction of "evangelical witness" that was rooted in his understanding of the Gospel. Nation notes with a bit of irony how superficial are the charges against Yoder's pacifism—as naive, utopian, and unrealistic—given the extent to which Yoder himself engaged with alternative perspectives. Nation writes: "Yoder's substantial engagements with the major challenges and alternatives to Christian pacifism are significant. They indicate he was quite conversant with these positions and therefore knew the alternatives to his own position and took them into account as he formulated his own views" (p. 134). Nation observes that Yoder's commitment to pacifism also contributes to greater clarity among just war adherents by challenging them to take more seriously the need to minimize violence through restraint and to address the conditions necessary for securing a just peace (p. 141).

In chapter 5, "'Social Responsibility' or the Offense of the Cross?: Yoder on Christian Responsibility," Nation addresses the allegation that Anabaptist ethics, vis-à-vis Yoder, legitimates sectarian withdrawal and abdicates Christian responsibility. Nation sets forth Yoder's own ecumenical involvement, his "catholic convictions," and his "intellectual engagement with Christians from other traditions" (p. 145)—all grounded by his "Mennonite patience" and practice—as evidence that Yoder himself was not sectarian. Nation comments, however, that Yoder's earlier work could be construed as advocating the renunciation of social responsibility, especially when viewed polemically against the dominant view of Niebuhrian social ethics that understood responsibility as a "commitment to consider the survival, the interest, or the power of one's own nation, state, or class as taking priority over the survival, interest or power of other persons or groups, of all humanity, of the 'enemy,' or of the church" (p. 149). Yoder's conception of responsibility could not be severed from his theological claims about the "proper dichotomy . . . between church and world, orders of redemption and orders of conservation" (p. 155). Within this framework, Nation tells us that Yoder actually "encouraged Mennonites in active engagement with the larger world, thinking them too separate" (p. 169). Yoder's work calls Christians to take more seriously their service to the world as Christian disciples and to consider peacemaking the most responsible response to violence, injustice, and evil in the world.

Through his exploration and analyses of Yoder's "Mennonite patience, evangelical witness, and catholic convictions," Nation has made two other contributions. One is raising our awareness of the relationship between scholarship and service to the church that is exemplified by Yoder's work. Nation writes that "Yoder saw all of his academic work as converging in a single task: to help us hear the voice of Jesus as he calls us to discipleship" (p. 143). Yoder's scholarly endeavors cannot be understood outside the context of the church, which is perhaps why his work is often misunderstood. However, Nation serves us by reminding us that the scholarship of Christian ethicists is a form of service to the church and world. He also aptly illustrates the interdisciplinary impetus and necessity of Christian social ethics by presenting Yoder as a model. Even though Yoder's doctoral thesis was in historical theology (p. 125), his work built bridges between biblical studies, theology, and ethics, addressing what Bruce Birch and Larry Rasmussen identified as a "failure [of communication between those working in biblical studies and those in ethics]" (p. 112).

Although I was hoping for more biographical information on Yoder, Nation affirmed again the importance of Yoder's contribution to Christian social ethics. This is an important book for those who think we know Yoder and for those needing an introduction to him. Nation reintroduces us to the enduring relevance and significance of Yoder's "Mennonite witness, evangelical witness and catholic convictions." He also makes possible meeting Yoder for the first time.

Wyndy Corbin Reuschling
Ashland Theological Seminary

Review of
Christians and a Land Called Holy: How We Can Foster Justice, Peace and Hope

CHARLES P. LUTZ AND ROBERT O. SMITH
Minneapolis: Fortress Press, 2006. 168 pp. $15.00.

North American Christians experience an understandable reluctance to offer a political critique of the Israeli and Palestinian conflict, to say nothing of suggesting peace-building practices in the "land called holy." Both Muslims and Jews carry in their historical memories the massacres of their unarmed populations during the Crusades as well as the many injustices committed during the years of the British mandate over Palestine. As a Lutheran author, Charles P. Lutz acknowledges the residual cultural effects on twentieth-century Germany of Martin Luther's writings against Jews who refused conversion. Yet Lutz and his coauthor, Robert O. Smith, suggest a role for Christian peacemakers which might be exercised in dialogue with that remnant of indigenous Palestinian Christians whose presence forms a buffer in the region. They argue that the shrinking Christian population in Palestine—due to a desperate flight from violence and impoverishment, along with the loss of moderate Jewish citizens of Israel—injures prospects for peacemaking in the Holy Land. Both Arabs who reject militant fundamentalism and Israelis opposed to illegal settlements in Gaza, the West Bank, and East Jerusalem are weakened by the exodus.

Smith applies a hermeneutic of suspicion to the claims of fundamentalist movements that employ selective biblical interpretations of the land as holy for us. Not only does the bible offer a more limited promise, but scriptural scholars such as Walter Brueggemann argue that "biblical land traditions must insist that land possession is held, according to that tradition, only as land practices are under the discipline of neighbor practices grounded in the Torah." Smith's historical synthesis of the three Abrahamic religions' relationships with Jerusalem's holy places sets the framework for his critique of both Christian and Jewish Zionists. Christians might be startled to read that until Constantine's establishment of Jerusalem as the center of Christian concern, little attention was paid to the city. Yet afterward, Jews were forbidden entry to the Holy City for centuries.

Historical memory must be acknowledged if Christians wish to contribute anything to peace in the Holy Land. The awareness that Palestinians have limited access to water from the Jordan, while their population pushes against an overburdened ecosystem, challenges all of us to seek greater equity. Moreover, the authors' intermittent theological reflections on the land as sacred to Jews, Christians, and Muslims alike might offer one foundation for their religious ethic. Given the desire to place a short text in the hands of general readers, they do not develop their insights into a theology of the land. Yet further work might provide common ground for interreligious peacemakers, as well as a spirituality that could deepen their prayer as they seek justice in the land. This short book offers much practical advice for Christians who desire to act in solidarity with peace builders from Israel and Palestine. By amplifying the voices of those seldom heard in the United States media, American groups contribute to a hoped-for resolution.

Christians might engage in pilgrimages, peace witnesses near the separation wall or occupied areas, boycotts of goods produced in illegal settlements, or a variety of nonviolent actions meant to amplify the voices of unarmed victims. Prayer empowers the peacemaker whether alone or with others. Peace-building practices of solidarity that are undertaken in conjunction with both Jewish and Palestinian groups promise greater success. Jewish organizations (e.g., Brit Tzedek v'Shalom, Not in My Name, the Tikkun Community, Rabbis for Human Rights, and the Joint Coalition of Women for a Just Peace) offer practical insight as well as greater hope for nonviolent changes. Palestinian nongovernmental efforts (including the Bethlehem Media Center, International Solidarity Movement, Palestinian Center for Rapprochement between People at Beit Sahour, and Palestinian environmental organizations) address issues and engage in normative peacemaking practices.

Christians and the Land Called Holy will appeal to those who realize that no military solution exists in the region yet see that diplomatic efforts have repeatedly floundered as extremists on both sides mobilize counteraction in response to the "others' violence." It argues that normative peace-building practices can make possible future movement toward reconciliation. Though high-level meetings among governmental actors remain a key element, the authors demonstrate the trail of successes followed by sabotage through assassination or provocation. The movement of 8,500 settlers from Gaza in 2005 promised new hope, albeit short-lived. With each failure or delay, hope is diminished and the resort to violence is encouraged. Still, the political will for transformation takes root in communities of people who do small things. When Christian Peacemaker Teams accompany people who seek safe passage to harvest their olive trees, or the Women in Black embody a nonviolent presence for justice, another vision takes root. Cultural imagination stimulates hope as well as violence. Without grassroots hope for peace, diplomacy is doomed to fail.

Christians and a Land Called Holy should be read as a general introduction for U.S. Christian communities to a complicated international problem. Students and nonspecialists will find in the text a succinct history of the struggle for control of the Holy Land. Because the American media often fails to communicate the perspectives of average people in Palestine, the authors urge Christians on pilgrimage to talk with indigenous Christians there and to support grassroots efforts. They do not intend to address those who are not Christian, but many Jewish communities and university departments have also invited speakers from their own peacemaking organizations. This is a fine contribution to an effort to "foster justice, peace, and hope."

Rosemarie E. Gorman
Fairfield University

Review of
God's Companions: Reimagining Christian Ethics

SAMUEL WELLS
Oxford: Blackwell, 2006. 232 pp. $27.95.

Samuel Wells's latest offering is perhaps best conceived as an extension of the body of work he is quickly amassing. In fact, apart from this consideration, *God's Companions* falls short of doing what its subtitle suggests, namely, re-imagining the field of Christian ethics. It would be more helpful to think of Wells's entire project as an effort at reimagining Christian ethics and of *God's Companions* as one facet of this endeavor. Wells in a way admits the point, stating that the work is an expression of a dissertation chapter he decided not to write, as well as a complement to what he has done in *Improvisation* and especially the pieces coauthored with Stanley Hauerwas in the *Blackwell Companion to Christian Ethics*. One must emphasize this codependence at the outset because *God's Companions* is the kind of book that can easily be dismissed by the academy as an "excessively pious" work. When one ventures to consider a field such as Christian ethics in terms of the Christian liturgy, employing on occasion experiences from parish ministry as well as citing extensive passages of scripture and commenting on them in an allegorical fashion, one runs the risk of alienating those wishing to find a "more serious engagement" of the subject matter.

Of course, the issue rests on what one considers to be "serious" theological work, and for Wells, as for a number of thinkers in the field (probably a small, yet detectable constituency), the theological and ethical tasks are joined under the broader rubric of worship, which would be for these authors the most serious ethical activity one could undertake. Essentially, Wells's corpus calls for a re-consideration of Christian ethics in which God, the church, and the church's practices are definitive for determining the shape of the ethical task. In this sense, Wells is outlining a program of ecclesial ethics that is perhaps better summarized by the category of "moral theology" than "Christian ethics" per se, especially because he speaks of how Christian ethics is an accommodating discipline that was conceived within the zeitgeist of modernity—or, to echo his own words, a field that fills a gap between what God gave the people and what people have come to feel they still need.

This clarification and a number of others that characterize Wells's approach do not make a sustained appearance in *God's Companions*. On the contrary, one finds in this work an effort at *displaying* a number of basic claims within this general argument. These displays suggest that, in being God's companions, Christians are called to worship God, be God's friends, and eat with God—a tripartite schema that informs the three sections of the work: God's offering of Christ's body in Jesus, the church, and the Eucharist. In substantiating these claims, Wells is led to consider a number of practices that he believes are indispensable for the moral life of the church. Obvious examples like the sacraments are included, but he also considers oft-neglected practices, including the recitation of the creed, the sharing of the peace, thanksgiving, and so on. Essentially, he is calling on the church to consider what it does in the liturgy as being morally significant.

At one point, Wells summarizes his general argument as a plea for the church to recognize God's plenteous gifts in the activities of answering God's call and living a reconciled life (p. 112). This move is a pivotal one, for at various times he emphasizes God's revelation to the people as both abundant and sufficient. These two themes contradict much of what is taken for granted in Christian ethics as a whole, because themes of scarcity are standard fare in the discipline. Wells wishes to reverse the argument, stating in effect that what the church sometimes finds as a limit or a disability can actually be a gift: an opportunity for the Christian community to draw together in imaginative creativity. For those sympathetic to Wells's project, reversals of this kind propel the work in a number of suggestive ways.

Those who find Wells's general approach disagreeable from the outset are likely to remain unconvinced by *God's Companions*, an outcome largely due to his methodology. In introducing the piece, Wells all too briefly proposes that the ethical task can be envisioned as descriptive, comparative, or persuasive. The method of choice in *God's Companions* is unequivocally descriptive, and this feature is perhaps the book's greatest weakness. Wells states that he hopes not to engage in a "paper debate" but rather to overwhelm the reader with examples, a move that is apparently aimed at prompting further considerations beyond the contours explored in the book itself. Given the sheer unconventionality of the work, however, one wonders if Wells would have benefited from expanding its scope into the realm of comparison for the general purposes of persuasion. As such, the work does not significantly engage the vast literature within the field of Christian ethics, and it appears that Wells believes he has excused himself from this need given his assumed methodology. This feature of the work is lamentable, not because the Christian liturgy is itself insufficient for re-narrating the ethical task, but because those who are aware and predisposed to "traditional" ways of doing Christian ethics could have a number of questions along the way.

For those with strong reservations, the first four chapters of the *Blackwell Companion* solidify and substantiate Wells's orientation. *God's Companions* is in many ways the expanded edition of the *Blackwell Companion*'s chapter 2, but this chapter has the advantage of being complemented by others that include the kind of necessary justifications for embarking on such new terrain. In other words, these other chapters in the *Blackwell Companion* demonstrate a rationale for such a significant departure from what is believed to be the way one does Christian ethics today. On its own, *God's Companions* does not provide a similar vision because it offers a response to an already-assumed predicament. But in proposing this alternative in the way that he has, perhaps Wells is doing something altogether different; perhaps he is actually calling his readers to *participate* in the life of the church's liturgy with the understanding that this activity is morally constitutive. If this is the case, then, *God's Companions* is above all an extended invitation to do so.

Daniel Castelo
Seminario Bíblico Mexicano

Review of
Talking with Christians: Musings of a Jewish Theologian

DAVID NOVAK
Grand Rapids: William B. Eerdmans, 2005. 267 pp. $25.00.

In a cover blurb for this collection of essays, Robert W. Jenson says he does not know why the author calls them "'musings,' for they are far too incisive for that." I agree, and I would add "subtly and rigorously argued." Novak, a professor of Jewish Studies at the University of Toronto, has brought together in this volume fifteen essays representing twenty-five years of commitment to Jewish–Christian dialogue. The essays discuss, among other things, the relationship of law and eschatology, the meaning for Jews of Edith Stein, and the moral crisis of the West. But Novak is engaging not just issues but also key figures: Maimonides and Aquinas, from among the elders; Buber, Heschel, Barth, and Tillich, from more recent generations; and, in a particularly illuminating essay on theology and philosophy, Jenson himself.

Although each essay stands on its own, certain themes recur. Let me focus on four. The first is captured by an essay's title, "From Supersessionism to Parallelism." Here, Novak refutes both Christian supersessionism and Jewish countersupersessionist claims that Christians in fact worship another God altogether. Christianity and Judaism are, rather, two distinct traditions growing out of the same roots, but in parallel fashion. This parallelism is so thoroughly worked out that Novak can be remarkably sympathetic even to the mutually exclusive faith claims of the two traditions. The practical import of this stance is evident as Novak defends the Vatican's 1998 statement on the Catholic Church and the Holocaust (tarnished though it is, in Novak's view, by an ill-advised attempt to vindicate Pius XII). Novak argues that the "apology" for the Holocaust that many sought was simply not the right response; the "act of repentance" the statement called for, conversely, was both appropriate and theologically profound. Novak chides his Jewish brothers and sisters for failing to grasp, precisely on parallel Jewish grounds, why the Vatican chose the proper path.

A second theme is the role of philosophy as a proper locus of and vehicle for dialogue. That is, certain theological claims of the two traditions may be in conflict and thus provide no common ground for dialogue. But the parallel theologies, especially of creation, open ample space for philosophical inquiry as the "*ancilla* [handmaid] *theologiae*." So, in the case of Tillich and Buber, commitment to philosophy (more explicit in the case of Tillich) enhanced their respective understandings of Exodus 3:14 and thus deepened their dialogical exchange. Novak especially appreciates the importance of Kant as a mediator, though he rejects certain aspects of his thought, notably his claims about moral autonomy. Given the role that Kant has played, in Protestant theology especially, Novak's engagement of Kant enriches his engagement of Christianity. More attention to Catholic use and critique of Kant, á la transcendental Thomism, might have enriched the dialogue further still.

A third theme is religion's proper relationship to the public realm. Though the two traditions, which hold in common a commitment to the Kingdom of God, can live with "secularity," "secularism" as a social ideology and agenda must be resisted. Individual Jews and Christians may be "participants" in other societies, but they may not, in a radical sense, be a "part" of them in the way they are a part of their respective religious communities. Of particular importance, the two traditions can learn from each other how to negotiate authentically their respective relationships with civil society.

When it comes to dialogue, Novak is clear about what is required: Seek to put the other tradition in the best light possible; avoid disputatious attitudes and behavior, proselytization, syncretism, relativism, and triumphalism. This fourth theme is fully discussed in the first essay, but I place it last to emphasize that Novak has admirably followed his own principles from beginning to end. But the principles are more than simple ground rules for discussion. They clearly jibe with Novak's theology, such that one could surmise that different theological commitments might yield different rules for dialogue. Put otherwise, theological commitments and claims, and not just procedural norms, are once again at the fore in this volume.

Novak calls himself a "traditional Jew," and as such he unambiguously affirms revelation and a revealing God. Even his forays into philosophy include intriguing claims about the inevitably "theological" character of philosophy engaged in by Aristotle and others, and his readings of the traditional "proofs" for God's existence are "statements of the ontological conditions and postulates of revelation." But even those—perhaps especially those, Jewish or Christian—who consider themselves less traditional, or in some fashion dissenters, would do well to count Novak as a dialogue partner. His unusual capacity to illuminate one's own faith tradition through engagement with another tradition can bring fresh understandings of, and deepened commitment to, traditional tenets of faith.

At the same time, the dialogue reflected in this volume might be furthered by attention to issues less settled than Novak seems to allow. From the Christian side, let me suggest two, one "ecclesiological" and one ethical. In his defense of the Vatican's Holocaust statement, Novak accepts a virtual equation, albeit nuanced, of the "church as such" with the "magisterium." But this equation has for some time been problematic in respectable quarters of Catholic theology. As for ethics, Novak repeats in several essays the conviction that certain norms, contained in Noahite law, are basic in the two traditions. These include "the prohibition of killing innocent life" and "the prohibition of the sexual practices of incest, adultery, homosexuality, and bestiality." Clearly, proscriptions against homosexuality and possibly the killing of the innocent will be debatable for some, especially at the level of material norms.

However, as many detailed discussions in this volume already suggest, Novak is quite aware that the challenge both Jews and Christians face is not only to find parallels between the traditions but also to negotiate the sometimes very sharp divisions within each. The wisdom in these "musings" strongly suggests that the intratraditional fissures that beset both Christians and Jews will be better addressed if the two traditions, following Novak's example, continue to learn from each other.

William George
Dominican University

Review of

Apocalypse Now? Reflections on Faith in a Time of Terror

DUNCAN B. FORRESTER
Aldershot, U.K.: Ashgate, 2005. 152 pp. $29.95.

Against the backdrop of a decidedly desecularized world, Duncan Forrester identifies a threefold responsibility incumbent upon theologians and religious persons of the West: (1) "To interpret to our secular societies the continuing power, significance, and meaning of religious discourse about, and in, the public sphere"; (2) "to engage in direct, and sometimes hard-hitting dialogues within and between religions"; and (3) "to avoid the idealism which does not take interest, sin, and brokenness seriously in the efforts to produce good out of the political process" (p. 10).

Forrester is well positioned to articulate such a responsibility. A veteran of the long-running debates loosely grouped under the heading "public theology," his recent collection is an effort to interpret the post–September 11, 2001, "signs of the times" and in the process provide evidence of specific ways religious discourse contributes to understanding and confronting the changing nature of conflict in the twenty-first century. His reflections move briskly between various times of terror and the theological responses each generates. In remarkably few pages, he covers a wide range of historical as well as disciplinary debates. The result is a stimulating, though at times insufficiently nuanced, discussion of ongoing conversations within and between the social sciences and theological studies.

Two related moves hold the chapters together. The first appropriates the apocalyptic framework of early Christianity as an analytical tool for coming to terms with what might best be characterized as contemporary iterations of the theodicy problem. "Two 'Terrible Manifestos,'" (his prologue) and "Tsunami Now?" (his postscript) suggest that the ambiguously defined war on terror and the 2005 tsunami are proxies for the persistent question of moral and natural evil that has kept theologians busy for centuries. For Forrester, the war on terror and the tsunami recall dimensions of previous historical periods identified within religious traditions as apocalyptic. He reclaims apocalypse as a necessary correction to reductionistic accounts of the diverse religious responses that animate the post–September 11 period.

Forrester's second move locates the apocalyptic framework within a broader conversation about the continuing relevance of neoorthodox theology. The

"Two 'Terrible Manifestos'" refer to the "Manifesto of the Ninety-Three German Intellectuals to the Civilized World" (1914)—the document Karl Barth described as the unmasking of liberal theology—and the "Letter from America: What We Are Fighting For" (2002). The "Letter," signed by prominent American intellectuals, highlights America's status as the lone superpower in its just war defense of the war on terror. With regard to both these documents, Forrester expresses worry about the role of theology, arguing that theology, when present, serves at the pleasure of "the Powers" and in the process loses its critical edge—conforming to, rather than transforming, the world.

Students of Reinhold Niebuhr will appreciate Forrester's attempt to retain an appropriate distance between God and humans. The litany of past and present terrors he recites throughout the chapters (e.g., Roman imperialism, the Holocaust, apartheid) serves as a constant reminder of human finitude and the persistence of sin. Public theology in a Niebuhrian key always takes place within the long shadow cast by finitude and sin. And like Niebuhr, Forrester believes that humility—both epistemic and political—must be cultivated as the first virtue of the *public* sphere, to "temper, not sever, nerve of action," as Arthur Schlesinger suggests (p. 75). For Forrester, it is these dimensions of Niebuhr's thought, often lost in translation when picked up by political realists, that constrain political action and subordinate political means to the theologically informed ends of reconciliation and restored peace. Modern iterations of Christian political realism "must be able to cope with the ambiguities of the 'real world,' and respond not only to decisions and crises but also to their aftermath. It needs a theological framework which recognizes that sometimes we have to do things that are sinful but necessary" (p. 94).

Apocalypse Now? makes no claims to be a *systematic* twenty-first-century revision of neoorthodox theology or the versions of political realism that emerge from it. Yet his kerygmatic focus on forgiveness and reconciliation, his critical engagement with virtue theory as a framework for analyzing the religious dimensions of suicide bombing, and his appropriation of apocalyptic as a source for sustaining hope all witness to ways in which religious discourse continues to possess "power, significance, and meaning" in the public sphere (p. 10).

The cast of theoretical interlocutors that populate Forrester's reflections indicate something of the broad, interdisciplinary nature of public theology. This may be reason enough to forgive him for his cursory critique and appreciation of various public intellectual icons such as MacIntyre, Fukuyama, and Rawls. The critiques he rehearses have already been well established—for example, the conflict between religious and political virtues is not a function of the fragmentation of the modern world (a story of decline)—but of human history more generally, and so on. For those well versed in these debates, less may be more. For those less well versed, however, these cameos may give a false, and at times outdated, impression of what is at stake in these debates. One clear lacuna, for example, is the work of globalization theorists such as Roland Robertson, who has endorsed a more sophisticated inquiry (compared with Huntington, at least) into the relationship between religion and contemporary societies.

This last point raises the question of readership. For whom are these reflections offered? According to Forrester, likely readers are those "who are trying to relate faith to these awful events, who are seeking to 'discern the signs of the time,' and respond appropriately" (p. vii). With this readership in mind, many of his reflections may be best seen as providing a jumping off point for further discussion—perhaps in an adult Sunday School class—of the merits of a just peacemaking approach to conflict resolution, of the limits and possibilities of truth and reconciliation processes, and the like. And in this way, Forrester fulfills his responsibility as a *public* theologian to discern the signs of the times but leaves it to *individual* believers—those "who know they have been forgiven"—to break into the public sphere by breaking up the "log-jam of vengeance" through their "individual acts of forgiveness, healing, and reconciliation" (p. 113).

Matthew Bersagel Braley
Emory University

Contributors

David Clough is a senior lecturer in theology at the University of Chester, England. He received his doctorate from Yale University in 2000 and was previously tutor in ethics and systematic theology at Saint John's College, Durham. He is the author of *Ethics in Crisis: Interpreting Barth's Ethics* (Ashgate, 2005); his essay for this volume grew out of his collaboration with Brian Stiltner on the book *Faith and Force: A Christian Debate about War* (Georgetown University Press, 2007).

Elizabeth Agnew Cochran is an assistant professor of theology at Duquesne University. Her research focuses on issues in contemporary virtue ethics and the history of ethics. She received her PhD from the University of Notre Dame in 2007 and is pursuing ordination in the United Methodist Church.

John P. Crossley Jr. retired in the spring 2007 after thirty-seven years teaching in the School of Religion of the University of Southern California. For the past several years, his research has focused on the ethics of Friedrich Schleiermacher. His latest articles are "The Religious Ethics Implicit in Schleiermacher's Doctrine of Creation," in the *Journal of Religious Ethics* 34, no. 4 (December 2006); and "Historical Consciousness in Hegel and Schleiermacher: A Comparison," in *The State of Schleiermacher Scholarship Today: Selected Essays*, edited by Edwina Lawler, Jeffery Kinlaw, and Ruth Drucilla Richardson (Edwin Mellen Press, 2006).

Lisa Fullam is an assistant professor of moral theology at the Jesuit School of Theology at Berkeley. Her research interests include virtue ethics, medical and sexual ethics, and the interplay of ethics and spirituality. A former veterinarian, she received her ThD from Harvard Divinity School.

Christopher D. Marshall is the Saint John's Associate Professor of Christian Theology in the Religious Studies Department of Victoria University, Wellington. His research interests focus particularly on biblical ethics, criminal justice reform, and peace theology. Among his major publications are *Faith as a Theme in Mark's Narrative* (Cambridge University Press, 1989); *Kingdom Come: The Kingdom of God in the Teaching of Jesus* (Impetus Publications, 1993); *Beyond Retribution: A New Testament Vision for Justice, Crime and Punishment* (William B. Eerdmans, 2001); *Crowned with Glory and Honor: Human Rights in the Biblical Tradition* (Pandora Press, 2001); and *The Little Book of Biblical Justice* (Good Books, 2005).

William McDonough is an associate professor of theology at the College of Saint Catherine in Saint Paul. He has written essays on virtue ethics for this journal, and in 2003 he coedited the book *Revelation and the Church: Vatican Two in the 21st Century* (Orbis Books) with the Roman Catholic bishop Raymond A. Lucker.

John Perry is an Edward Sorin Postdoctoral Fellow at the University of Notre Dame. He is a graduate of the University of Minnesota, Fuller Theological Seminary, and the University of Notre Dame. He writes and teaches on political theology, scripture and ethics, historical theology, and the philosophy of religion. His publications include articles in the *Journal of Church and State, Calvin Theological Journal, Mennonite Quarterly Review*, and other journals.

Margaret R. Pfeil is an assistant professor of moral theology at the University of Notre Dame. Her articles have appeared in *Louvain Studies, Josephinum Journal of Theology*, and the *Mennonite Quarterly Review*. She is currently finishing the book *Social Sin: Social Reconciliation?* and with Margaret Eletta Guider, OSF, she is coediting a volume *White Privilege: Implications for the Church, the Catholic University, and Theology*.

Julie Hanlon Rubio is an associate professor of Christian ethics at Saint Louis University. She is the lead author of the essay "Women Scholars in Christian Ethics: The Impact and Value of Family Care" in the present volume. Her coauthors for this essay are Barbara Hilkert Andolsen, the Helen Bennett McMurray Professor of Social Ethics at Monmouth University; Rebecca Todd Peters, assistant professor of religious studies at Elon University; and the Reverend Cheryl Kirk-Duggan, professor of theology and women's studies at Shaw University Divinity School.

Gerald W. Schlabach is an associate professor of theology at the University of Saint Thomas in Saint Paul. He holds a PhD in theology and ethics from the University of Notre Dame and an MA in theological studies from the Associated Mennonite Biblical Seminary. Though his interests range widely among the issues of peacemaking, social justice, globalization, and the integrity of traditional communities, a unifying theme in his work is his concern to link Christian social ethics with ecclesiology and missiology.

Brian Stiltner is an associate professor and chair of the Department of Philosophy and Religious Studies at Sacred Heart University in Fairfield, Connecticut. He formerly directed Sacred Heart's Hersher Institute for Applied Ethics and founded its Center for Catholic Thought, Ethics, and Culture. He is the author of *Religion and the Common Good* (Rowman & Littlefield, 1999) and, with David Clough, of *Faith and Force: A Christian Debate about War* (Georgetown University Press, 2007).

William Werpehowski is a professor of Christian ethics in the Department of Theology and Religious Studies and director of the Center for Peace and Justice Education at Villanova University. He is the author of *American Protestant Ethics and the Legacy of H. Richard Niebuhr* (Georgetown University Press, 2002) and the coeditor, with Gilbert Meilaender, of *The Oxford Handbook of Theological Ethics* (Oxford University Press, 2005).

Todd David Whitmore is an associate professor in the Theology Department at the University of Notre Dame. He is also the director of the Program in Catholic Social Tradition and a Faculty Fellow with the Kroc Institute for International Peace Studies, both at Notre Dame. His essay in the present volume, "Crossing the Road: The Case for Ethnographic Fieldwork in Christian Ethics," is the first publication of his project to bring together ethnography and theology. He has delivered papers on this topic at meetings of the American Ethnological Society, the Canadian Anthropology Society, and the American Anthropological Association, as well as the American Academy of Religion.

WEIGHING IN

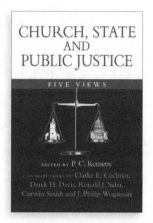

CHURCH, STATE AND PUBLIC JUSTICE: FIVE VIEWS
P. C. Kemeny, editor

Who is responsible for bringing social justice?
Five noted contributors write from
their distinct traditions:

- **Clarke E. Cochran:** Catholic Perspective
- **Derek H. Davis:** Classical Separation Perspective
- **Ronald J. Sider:** Anabaptist Perspective
- **Corwin Smidt:** Principled Pluralist Perspective
- **J. Philip Wogaman:** Social Justice Perspective

IVP Academic
Evangelically Rooted. Critically Engaged.

630.734.4000 · *ivpacademic.com*

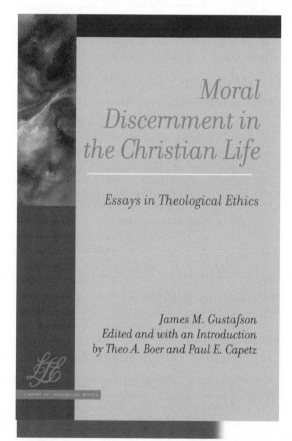

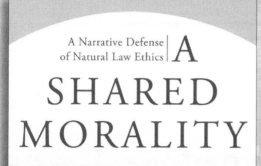

READING

From Pews to Polling Places
Faith and Politics in the American Religious Mosaic
J. Matthew Wilson, Editor
"[A] timely and enlightening volume . . . an impressive roster of leading scholars . . . brings readers up to date on the politics of religious belonging in America."
—Andrew Murphy, Valparaiso University
978-1-58901-172-4, paperback, $26.95
Religion and Politics series

The UN Secretary-General and Moral Authority
Ethics and Religion in International Leadership
Kent J. Kille, Editor
"What can be learned from the ethical principles and religious beliefs held by previous secretaries-general? How have these ideas affected the office itself and the claims of many for its moral authority? This book offers richly detailed case studies in ethics and statesmanship at the UN. It is a welcome and much-needed addition to our understanding of how the UN works."
—Joel H. Rosenthal, president,
Carnegie Council for Ethics in International Affairs
978-1-58901-180-9, paperback, $29.95

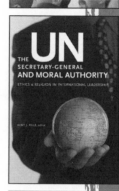

John Cuthbert Ford, SJ
Moral Theologian at the End of the Manualist Era
Eric Marcelo O. Genilo, SJ
"This study leaves no stone unturned in exploring the significance of Ford's achievements in moral theology. Even those familiar with the life, times and contribution of John Ford will discover surprises here, as Genilo documents with great acuity the richness of Ford's thought and his legacy."
— Thomas J. Massaro, SJ, Weston Jesuit School of Theology
978-1-58901-181-6, hardcover, $49.95
Moral Traditions series

The Rights of God
Islam, Human Rights, and Comparative Ethics
Irene Oh
"An important addition to the literature on comparative religious ethics and on Islam and human rights."
—Sohail Hashmi, Mount Holyoke College
978-1-58901-184-7, paperback, $24.95
Advancing Human Rights series

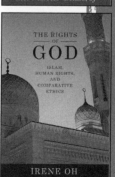

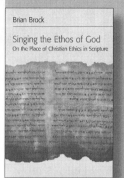
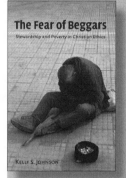
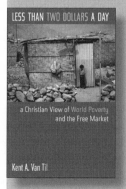